RESIST

RESIST

HOW A CENTURY OF YOUNG BLACK ACTIVISTS SHAPED AMERICA

RITA OMOKHA

ST. MARTIN'S PRESS ≋ NEW YORK

The Library of Congress Cataloging-in-Publication Data is available upon request.

ISBN 978-1-250-29098-4 (hardcover)

ISBN 978-1-250-29099-1 (ebook)

Our books may be purchased in bulk for promotional, educational, or business use. Please contact your local bookseller or the Macmillan Corporate and Premium Sales Department at 1-800-221-7945, extension 5442, or by email at MacmillanSpecialMarkets@macmillan.com.

First Edition: 2024

10 9 8 7 6 5 4 3 2 1

CONTENTS

Introduction: African, American   *vii*

▌The Scottsboro Nine Generation
▌& the Making of Black Youth Activism

1. A Revolution Awakens: The HBCU Revolts &   3
Ella Baker (1920–30)

2. A Resistance Rises: The Scottsboro Nine   27
(1930–40)

3. An Uprising Comes: The Gentlemen's   58
Agreement & the Bates Seven (1940–50)

▌▌The *Brown v. Board of Education* Generation
▌▌& the Civil Rights Era

4. The Civil Rights Movement: Barbara Johns   81
(1950–60)

5. The Revolt Cemented: SNCC & Charlie   108
Cobb (1960–70)

6. Black Power Rises: The Wilmington Ten &   131
the Students Against Apartheid Movement
(1970–90)

III The Trayvon Martin Generation & a New Wave of Young Revolutionaries

7. Tougher on Blacks: The Jena Six (1990–2010)   171

8. A Resurrection of Black Liberation: Johnetta Elzie (2010–19)   198

9. The Matter of George Floyd: Darnella Frazier & the Twenty-First-Century Freedom Fighters (2020)   238

Epilogue: It Continues, in Retrospect   273

Acknowledgments   287

Notes   289

Index   323

INTRODUCTION

AFRICAN, AMERICAN

To be African American
is to be African without any memory,
and American without any privilege.

JAMES BALDWIN

I am African. I am American.

Nigeria made me, Black America raised me.

My roots dig deep in Nigerian soil, while America has nourished my branches for more than two decades. Yet, the fruit I bear holds the essence of both lands. Like a tree nurtured by two suns, my identity defies simple categorization. It's a unique blend—a testament to the richness of embracing intertwined belonging.

I belong to the Édo people.

That's one of the hundreds of vibrant tribes that make up the rich mosaic of Nigeria. Though we share similar features, our identities are deeply infused by our ethnicity, dialects, and unique tribal customs. Our belief systems—Christianity, Islam, and other traditional religions—coexist, shaping our perspectives and enriching our communities. And while colorism permeates, the concept of *race*, as understood elsewhere, simply doesn't hold the same weight.

Yet in the United States, my identity has been defined by this uniquely American construct of *race*. Those physical characteristics of skin color, hair, facial features are prominent. My tribe holds no value. Despite this flawed framework, I've since come to wholly embody "Nigerian American." I favor that designation because it pays homage to the two distinct individualities that make me, me.

For years though, those two identities felt at odds, at once fraught yet covetous of each other. As though pledging allegiance to one meant disregard for the other. Throughout, I never understood nor appreciated my American Blackness the way I could have. A surrogate one, yes, but still, there's a belonging there I neglected.

For Black immigrants—I'd assume this is true for most immigrants—our identity in America of just being *Black*, without a sense of a cultural *home* within that identity, presents myriad confusions.

In Nigeria, I'm not a *Black* girl.

I'm not a *Black* anything.

I am my mother's last-born child and only daughter from Benin City, in the southern region of Nigeria, just 250 miles south of the country's capital city of Abuja.

I am the granddaughter of an unlettered woman who rose to run a small business as a local Guinness and Coca-Cola distributor.

I am not this color America relegated me to.

This is what I have struggled with all these years: Having one foot in and out of America's definition of who I am. Having one foot in and out of the many groups I find myself in, constantly toggling between three worlds: Black America, white America, and my Nigerian culture. Contending with this skin so problematic in America—skin that in Nigeria is synonymous with endless striving and a pursuit of excellence. I come from a history full of it.

The stories our ancestors passed down to us were of kings and queens, colonization be damned. Stories of flourishing in gold and oil and gemstones. Academically and professionally, the grind for achievement was instilled in us because everyone strives for the same caliber of accomplishment. To go from a country full of this to one stripped of it for racially *Black* people doesn't quench our thirst for success.

Many foreigners to America see what feels innate to the native.

That newness breeds prospect and appreciation. Immigrants gravitate toward the idea that America carries out a true democracy. Though a marred one, it is better than none or fascism.

Like many immigrants, Mom came to this country in 1992 wide-eyed and gazed upon its endless feast of opportunities and upward mobility, concluding that America provides for those who work hard. Fleeing from a corrupt government with lawlessness and instability, she quickly adopted this nation as a means of survival. And for some time, it all seemed so simple.

When my brothers and I joined Mom in the South Bronx in 1995, her vision of America became ours too. She charged us with representing our heritage exceptionally well. There's a Nigerian saying in our Pidgin English: "Naija no dey carry last," which means Nigerians should never come in last place. That was Mom's core message to us: persevere and succeed. Race, racism, and the like were never discussed; they were never factors in our quest of American success. Our goal was to be ambitious and unwavering in our pursuit, even if it meant inadvertently ignoring America's complex history.

By coming to America, we unknowingly became part of the Black American community. Though racially similar, there were deeply rooted differences between *them* and *us*. It's those generational and lived experiences that have long divided us. Their history of brutal oppression is one we, Black immigrants, don't have and one I didn't understand. It remains the wedge and genesis of tensions between Black Americans and Black immigrants. For the Black American, there's the endless fight to be equal to whites politically and economically, and for the Black immigrant, there's the romanticized view of America as a place of limitless opportunities. The latter was why Mom instilled in my brothers and me that America only rewards those who keep forging ahead, even when it hurts or doesn't make sense or when peace is lacking. We were taught to fight for what we knew we were capable of.

These reflections of identity and belonging swirled in my head as I grew up, but I never seriously interrogated them because since arriving in this country, my family has been in survival mode. From the South Bronx to the North Bronx, Mom working multiple jobs to keep us together, to assimilation woes and wails, there wasn't time to mine this all-important part of my life beyond split-moment introspections.

And I certainly never expected to write a book about race relations as they relate to young Black activists and their significant political and cultural impact on American democracy. But fate led me here.

It began on May 25, 2020.

That's the day George Floyd, a Black man, took his final breaths under the knee of a white Minneapolis police officer. That Memorial Day also happened to be five days after I graduated from Columbia University with my master's in journalism.

It's a day I can never forget. And no, a Black man being senselessly murdered at the hands of police wasn't new. I understood that policing is rooted in white supremacy. I know that. We all know that. But the savageness of George Floyd's murder shook me in ways I could've never imagined. Seeing his lifeless body lying there from the glow of my phone in the dark of night, I came undone. Secondhand trauma is what experts call it.

As I listened to George Floyd beg the officers to let him breathe, my head churned with so many sentiments. Mostly that he could be any one of my four brothers. The most haunting thought was: This is happening in the same America I had loved unconditionally, blindly even, since arriving as a little girl.

The same America that had pulled Mom from obscurity. America had hand-selected her because of her brilliance and excellence. She was a beneficiary of the Immigration Act of 1990. Prior iterations excluded people like her. That particular round of admission allowed her onto American shores because she was a highly skilled registered nurse.

The same America that Mom boasted with pride about when she got green cards for my family in 1995, and naturalized citizenships for most of us a few years later.

I struggled to understand how this was the same country that provided Mom with everything she needed to jump-start her version of the American dream: stable income, food, shelter, and ongoing job training. She even had good insurance, the kind for government employees. Those basic things that people who looked like her, who were born in the same country she now lived in, struggled to attain regularly so they too could enjoy the same experiences Mom came to revel in.

But it was.

That Monday in May, it became glaring that Mom's mandate to us wasn't enough for people who looked like *us* in real America. It dawned on me that her idealized version of America didn't exist.

I remember the viral video so vividly: George Floyd's limp body, hands shackled behind him, the black tank, the white foam oozing from his mouth, being wheeled into that ambulance. Watching it, I couldn't place the emotions I felt. So, I did what I could do within my reach and jolted into action. I felt I had a license to do so with my newly minted journalism degree. I thought, *Why not use my voice to process and dredge this moment?*

I wrote a reported essay titled "George Floyd Could've Been My Brother" for *ELLE*.

In 2005, my eldest brother, Manny, was unjustly stopped, frisked, and arrested while attending a predominantly white New York college in Plattsburgh—a town with a 90 percent white population. Mom didn't sleep for months, thinking about her baby boy locked in a cell. We were broke, broke. No fancy lawyers were going to come to our rescue. And soon enough, Manny, a green card holder, was deported. In the chaos of the moment, and not knowing what we didn't know, Mom was simply happy that he was free in Nigeria. She never pursued the case any further. She couldn't even if she wanted to—she had exhausted all her financial options working on his bail and attempting to find a private lawyer. In defeat, Mom kept her head down and persevered as she had always done—we all did.

Fast forward to that day in 2020, watching George Floyd gasp, struggle, and cry. I saw Manny.

Manny could have easily become another statistic. The kind that doesn't make it home. The kind that too many mothers have had to prematurely bury. That America felt new—unrecognizable—to me. The wool was finally being pulled from my eyes.

That notion pressed on me more and more as I contended with George Floyd's death. What if Manny hadn't survived his police encounter? What then? Would Mom have been forced to stand in front of flashing cameras and elongated microphones, seeking justice and accountability? How would she have carried on?

Armed with a new sense of purpose, and that new *license*, I was emboldened to excavate the truths of our world. I felt compelled, more than ever, to explore race relations in America.

So, insecure and in my feelings—conflicted, ashamed, anxious— with one backpack and an oversized MZ Wallace handbag, I took to the road on September 12, 2020.

Using one of the awards I received at graduation, the Pulitzer Prize Traveling Fellowship, I funded my travel to thirty states in thirty-two days.

I traveled by plane and car.

I used four rental cars.

Traveled 13,559 miles.

Twenty-three gas station stops.

Sixteen hotels and one bed-and-breakfast in Stuart, Nebraska.

I drove a black Buick Encore, a red Mini Cooper Countryman, a blue Hyundai Venue, and a black Kia Forte.

I met and spoke with 127 people.

My pilgrimage for understanding my Blackness began to come into complete focus. One stop, in particular, completely seized me.

In Portland, I attended my first-ever protest, completely led by Black teens. It was mesmerizing, watching them stomp, scream, and cry for the America they hoped for. George Floyd's murder had revived these youth-led galvanizations across the globe. The likes of which we hadn't seen before. The likes of yesteryear, when the longing for elemental human rights was palpable.

The young ones I met that day had a different American experience than those of prior decades. They'd grown up in the twenty-first century, when roughly ten thousand people of color have had fatal encounters with police officers. The majority of them,

Black men. And George Floyd's murder was the latest seismic one of this era.

Today's youth have become a generation forced to witness, from infancy, the perpetuation of injustice and the normalization of othering and subjugation. But in recent years, when such injustices occur, these atrocities pop up on their screens nonstop. And when such deadly moments do happen—as they often do, and we've grown numb to them—hashtags trend. Horrific posts go viral. People retweet and call for swift action. In a blink, thousands flood the streets with pumped fists. All significant markers of the modern social justice movement.

My cross-country trip was also revealing in visceral ways: A whirlwind of emotions where each gust left me both tossed and turned. At once, the world felt impossibly broken yet brimming with potential for repair.

Not only was the Black community reeling from the unjust deaths of Ahmaud Arbery, Breonna Taylor, and George Floyd—killings that compounded the next—there was a growing global uprising to contend with. The protests were multigenerational, multiracial, with a goal of pressing for justice and accountability and lasting change. The kind of galvanizing rooted in hope. The kind of hope that chips away at change. The kind I needed in this quest to understand who I was in it all.

When I hit the road, I thought most about what this moment meant for me as a Nigerian woman. There was a strong desire to learn from all those systematically neglected by this country, to seek to know more, to seek to do and be better. To understand the current state of American culture and injustice, I knew I had to go be in it to see and better understand how it is lived. Because the more we learn about each other and society, the further we move from the oblivion and hate that stems from ignorance. And the quicker we can move to the acceptance that comes from education and understanding.

As I navigated back roads and bustling cityscapes, the crucible of

2020 America was a constant companion on my journey. Each encounter, each story, felt like a chapter in a shared narrative, urging me to delve deeper, to connect the dots between personal growth and collective understanding. And that's why 2020 marks both the conception and culmination of this book's century-long examination. It was a defining year. Not only for me but for America.

Once-in-a-century pandemic aside, 2020 was also year four of Donald Trump's presidency. With his brazen, intolerant leadership style came an explicit show of xenophobia, racism, and white supremacy ideology, now commonly known as Trumpism, a reactionary dogma in response to his predecessor, Barack Obama. Even his 2016 presidential campaign slogan, "Make America Great Again," was a nod to exclusionary American exceptionalism. The idea that all Others don't belong. The constant *us* vs. *them* ideology stoked fear that America is less of a country because *those* people from *those* "shithole countries," as Donald Trump once called nations like Nigeria, decided to flood *our* land.

Donald Trump's basis of leadership was fear. When he was in office, hate crimes increased by 20 percent. White supremacists were invigorated. Conspiracy theories ran amok. Interestingly, the more he governed and the more he riled his base, the more it became clear that the fear wasn't of *us*—of all the Others in America. The fear was in the difference in who *we* were—what we represented—to *them*. It was in the lack of knowing *us* and understanding our story. Knowing, intimately, intentionally, our history.

I recognized this incognizance within myself during the trip. So, it's no wonder the compounded and tumultuous happenings of 2020 America served as a brutal awakening, jolting me face-to-face with the harsh realities simmering beneath the surface. This underbelly of America was a truth I had been shielded from by Mom's unique immigrant experience. Her vision of America—what it represented for her and the opportunities it held for her children—had filtered my perception, creating a protective layer of optimism.

So for me, witnessing George Floyd's death—how he died—became symbolic of the struggles of all those othered in American society. And for the first time, as I watched him cry out for help, it hit me: *I* am part of *them*. The *them* that didn't understand what the Others had endured. There was no distinction. That image of a white police officer kneeling on the neck of a defenseless Black man revealed the power dynamics in everyday society. The very dynamics I had come up in and knew all too well but, then again, didn't really know at all. Contemporary subjugation and exclusion became abstractions of that very knee.

Every time I remembered George Floyd's screeches in agony or saw flashes of his final moments, I thought, *What did this man do to deserve any of this?* Remembering still, the officer calmly kneeing him harder and harder, his cries growing louder and louder, my guilt inflamed. It took his death to expose my complacency in race relations in America. After all, I had benefited from my immigrant status in subtle ways—in acceptance into elite programs in high school or college or to top-paying jobs. At times, I'd even walked taller, chest out, chin up, at the idea that, yes, I was indeed different in *their* eyes. I had made it. I was the success Mom fought hard for me to become. It was in how I began intentionally accentuating my introductions, hands stretched, explaining my last name with "I am Nigerian." Translation: I am not this *Black* or African American society had come to know when they saw people who looked like me. Subconsciously, in searching for identity, I didn't want to be associated with the stereotypes I was fed by society and had unintentionally bought into.

Now, though, this America no longer felt like the one where I had been proud to declare emphatically "I am Nigerian" as a way to distinguish myself, to cement what I saw as my celebrated identity in the white gaze. This America no longer felt like the same one I had been loyal to—that had given me opportunity after opportunity to thrive.

This America, I did not know.

The more I thought about those opportunities and why I had been given them, the more I confronted the notion that the gatekeepers and decision-makers in America, at least those in my experience, had been white. So, the idea of fairness, equality, and justice slants in that same direction. The cycle of equivalency exists within the cycle of gatekeeping, and those who hold the keys continue to cycle in more of the same or those willing—like I was—to contort to whiteness. Parity, then, can never be if parity means more of *us* than all Others.

This, I think, was what those wide-eyed, young protestors in Portland had grown so keenly aware of, coming up in a system that had exposed its inadequacies, where compounded injustices are now readily available to witness on screens. What had that said of me that I had been complicit with this cycle? Reveling in being one of the select few of the Others that the *gate* was breached open for?

Thirty states in thirty-two days was quite a feat that has forever transformed me. The depths of my empathy began to run deeper. At once, I loved America and, in another blink, mourned what it could be if every day America shared the compassion needed to push forward the intentionality of unity.

Upon my return, I began deconstructing African American history, explicitly looking to find those—the celebrated and unsung figures—that came before the young voices I had encountered, who reformed and defended American democracy. Curious about the nature of their Blackness juxtaposed against their ancestors', but also mine. Because, for the first time it dawned on me, without *them*—those ancestors—America couldn't be a reality for me.

It is no question that 2020 saw the Lazarus of social justice movements led by Black young people across America. We can't forget that the viral video that catapulted the world into a monumental movement, leading to unprecedented accountability for the officer who killed George Floyd, was brazenly filmed by seventeen-year-old Darnella Frazier.

But, for me, 2020 also illuminated the underappreciated role of Black youth in sociopolitical organizing throughout history.

The mere fact that I can have my voice heard, dream beyond my zip code and circumstances, and walk down the streets of America free is because of *them*. Those who fearlessly stepped out and dared to scream for righteousness, dared to be seen, dared to covet an America that lived up to the expectations of forming a more "perfect union, establish[ing] justice, insur[ing] domestic tranquility, provid[ing] for the common defense, promot[ing] the general welfare, and secur[ing] the blessings of liberty to ourselves and our posterity"—all the promises for "We the People."

It is because of them that I am who I am in America. It is because of them that I can be who I want to be in this land of plenty.

Portland reminded me of this possibility.

Though led by Black teens, the crowd that day included people of all shades and backgrounds. All stomping for the America they wanted. Riled up and angered by this one symbolic, horrific death. As I watched them and documented their anguish, I thought again about how we got here. Then about all the ones—like the young, bold reformers I was encountering—who had fought for this present-day America. In small and mighty ways.

That's what has fascinated me in journeying into history. To think I had navigated America all those years, aloof to the facts of this nation. Blinded to the realities in front of me. But that's the trap of insulation, of walking without intentionality. That's where "you don't know what you don't know" becomes a dangerous paradox. How, then, would you know what you need to know? How, then, could you know to tap into intentionality to learn what you don't know? The default setting is to see the vastness of the world through your immediate radius. People can only live what they learn.

That's where education—history, most of all—plays the most significant role in our development. It plants a seed that blossoms with still more education and intentionality of deeper questioning. It could begin in structured settings like schools, at home, or, once you've been kick-started, individually. Like it did for me on May 25, 2020. That's what excites me about being a storyteller. That's why I call it a gift, because I get to glean from the boundless constellation of human experiences. It's a journey of endless discovery. Researching, conceptualizing, and writing this book was the greatest gift. I got to spend invaluable time delving into a history and culture that had been a formidable force in forming who I am today. Yet, because I once lacked intentionality, I didn't know its depth. And depth is the prerequisite to understanding.

The seemingly ordinary young people in the following pages decided to no longer stay quiet, and moved mightily. What appeared just and right to them, in the simplicity of taking one step after another, added up to extraordinary moments and changes in America. Through what we now know to be their experiences of ache and suffering, came purpose.

Those young ones in Portland, and the ones highlighted here, taught me the way forward is through understanding the past. That we cannot ignore racial inequality because it will only get worse if we do nothing. That, in order for progress to transcend its historical fractures in an inherently divided nation, we must intentionally probe history, mining for lessons that unite, to gain perspective.

They taught me to make history personal.

PART I

THE SCOTTSBORO NINE GENERATION & THE MAKING OF BLACK YOUTH ACTIVISM

1

A REVOLUTION AWAKENS

The HBCU Revolts & Ella Baker

I didn't break rules, but I challenged rules.
And I didn't have senses enough not to do the speaking,
even to groups that were older than I.

ELLA BAKER

As I excavated history in search of a North Star to say, "there, there is where most of what I recognize today as the framework for civil disobedience, social activism, and community organizing," where could I have possibly begun if not with an unflinching, tenacious Black woman?

A still but daring force.

A shoulder upon which I stand.

Whose warfare paved the way for the likes of me and the many generations of native and surrogate African Americans to become beneficiaries of the freedoms we walk in, day in, day out, without much thought.

Many could easily name a dozen Black men in a blink if asked about consequential leaders in the fight for righteousness.

You probably just did.

I'm sure Martin Luther King, Jr., Malcolm X, Asa Philip Randolph, John Lewis, or Marcus Garvey came to mind. Or, perhaps, Thurgood Marshall or W.E.B Du Bois or Bayard Rustin.

But bolstering those voices was a firebrand.

A woman focused on bottom-up, people-powered campaigning.

An effective in-the-background strategist and changemaker.

A woman, who, after years of steering such leaders while in the shadows, would be crowned the mother of the civil rights movement.

Before Ella Josephine Baker charged generations of stalwart warriors, always intent on strong people not needing leaders, her grassroots efforts began when she was a teenager, whetting her voice as a student at Shaw University. And before that, growing up on a farm purchased by her once-enslaved grandfather in Littleton, North Carolina.

Ella is my starting point not because Black women are regularly erased from public memory or obscured from historical portrayals of resistance.

I begin with Ella because her approach, though powerful, was simple.

She used a pen to write letters. She used her restraint to say "no" when needed. She used her mighty voice to speak for those who couldn't. She used her diplomacy to build communities. She used what was in her hands, what was available to her, within her reach.

It is this—Ella's dignity and humility—that I believe resonated so powerfully with the leaders she helped grow. As the movement for a just civilization and parity for African Americans progressed, she started, influenced, and built organizations and people whose impact remains essential.

Focused on economic justice, suffrage, and education rights, Ella challenged leaders while uplifting women and children. She had a deliberate hand in several progressive movements of the twentieth century, from the Young Negroes' Co-operative League during the 1930s Great Depression era to the National Association for the Advancement of Colored People in the 1940s to the Southern Christian Leadership Conference in the 1950s to the Student Nonviolent Coordinating Committee, Southern Conference Educational Fund, and the March on Washington in the 1960s.

To understand the woman she became, the circumstances Ella came up in is where we begin.

NOVEMBER 11, 1918. WORLD WAR I ENDS.

More than four years of war had gone by.

More than 16 million soldiers and civilians dead.

Alongside allies Russia, France, Britain, Italy, and Serbia, America found victory in the First World War over the Central Powers—Austria-Hungary, Bulgaria, Germany, and the Ottoman Empire—ushering in a new way of life across the country, later labeled as a period of prosperity.

Soldiers returned with new philosophies and skills. Sweeping changes came to electricity, science, and technology, reforming societal and economic progress in consumerism and transportation. Businesses boomed, fueling the economy, heightening a sense of security.

In effect, the modern era of capitalism had kicked off.

The notion of social and cultural independence and voting also began taking hold for women. For Black Americans too.

Still, lynchings persisted in the racially segregated South, where Jim Crow laws enforced white supremacy and systemic discrimination against Black Americans in every aspect of public life, from voting to education. Black Americans also endured violence and intimidation from white citizens who acted with impunity. However, Black Americans began thriving economically and politically more than in any other decade, largely thanks to the Great Migration, when millions fled from the rural South to industrial cities in the North to find work and fill labor shortages created by the war in the auto, meatpacking, and steel industries.

This uplift, though, threatened the social order of Jim Crow, unsettling some white Americans. So much so, towns that feared racial integration began to make it known that Black Americans weren't welcome in their neighborhoods, discouraging and threatening them with bigoted signs.

Cool Summers, Mild Winters, No Blizzards, No Negroes
Whites only after dark.
A Good Place to Live. No Negroes.
N*gg*r, don't let the sun go down on you in this town.

Areas that existed under this blatant discriminatory housing covenant—which still exists in some parts of the South—were coined "sundown towns." Death lurked if a Black person was caught in those places after dark. Black Americans were welcomed to work in these towns but could not live there. If they dared stay after sunset, they were beaten, terrorized, and arrested.

This outright threat of death, however, didn't stop Black Americans from walking deeper into their unexplored freedom. With their increasing presence in Northern states came a surge in the visibility of Black culture. The Harlem Renaissance was particularly resonant. Music, marked by jazz and blues, formed a cultural movement of African Americans reveling in the postwar bliss with expressions of artistic dances like the cakewalk, the flea hop, the black bottom, and the Charleston. All expressed freedom through bodily movement. A symbolic physical signal that was wildly, deliberately antithetic behavior of their enslaved ancestors who were used to having their bodies routinely abused, observed, and handled.

The Renaissance's popularity and its bold expressions of liberation propelled a rise in membership of the white supremacist group the Ku Klux Klan, which was already seeing a surge since the release of the 1915 film *Birth of a Nation*. Based on Thomas Dixon, Jr.'s 1905 anti-Black novel *The Clansman*, the film showed adorative brutality against African Americans (played by white men in Blackface) and gleeful violence against African American rights and freedom.

KKK members, many of them lower-middle-class Protestants who remained fearful that non-whites would strip traditional American culture of its values, were limited to the South upon the group's formation in 1865 in Pulaski, Tennessee. By 1925, its membership had catapulted from the thousands during the post–Civil War Reconstruction South to two million nationwide.

The war, its end, and the mass migration Northward so solidified a new sense of self among African Americans, it culminated in what was later dubbed the "New Negro Movement." Yet, despite facing discrimination in all aspects of life after migrating North, Black Americans encountered fewer barriers to employment and education compared to the South. Their expansion into the workforce only created more vitriol. This would later lead Asa Philip Randolph, a rising civil rights activist of this era, to form the Brotherhood of Sleeping Car Porters—the first labor union led by Black Americans. They called attention to the increasing abuse in hiring practices and working conditions for Black workers.

The move North also meant that Black workers began earning more and starting families, so they needed bigger homes. Yet another space for discrimination emerged, leading to the rise in urban ghettos—with traces that remain today—as Black Americans were excluded from housing in neighborhoods already populated by white Americans. These communities were considered safer, with better living conditions and resources from the federal government. It's the kind of quintessential segregation and explicit racism that was already prevalent in the South and the kind that led to the Tulsa Race Massacre.

A microcosm of the prevailing racial tensions ignited the violence that erupted on that 1921 Memorial Day weekend: A white female elevator operator on South Main Street screamed at the sight of a Black man. The actual details and the sequence of events remain unclear, but the woman went on to allege sexual assault. And so ensued the deadliest racial violence in American history, as a white mob assembled and burned down the burgeoning Black Wall Street in Oklahoma's majority Black Greenwood neighborhood.

These compounding events occurred nearly six decades after President Abraham Lincoln issued the Emancipation Proclamation, declaring all enslaved people in Southern states fighting in the Civil War were to be freed. This was also a time when Ella Baker's grandparents had been enslaved themselves. And though her later years at Shaw Academy and University strengthened her resolve to drive progress for the Othered in society, as she fought for righteousness and parallelism, her school mobilizations weren't what first stoked Ella's fiery hunger for activism. That blaze was first lit by her ancestors.

We're our ancestor's wildest dreams.

When people invoke this maxim, it is to say the generation of old desired that future generations would be mightier, abounding in much, to be better than they were because they had tilled the soil, breaking through for their descendants. To say, and believe, that they'd softened the journey's tread.

This was true for Ella.

Born on December 13, 1903, her crusade story begins with her maternal grandparents, Mitchell and Josephine Elizabeth Ross, who were both born into slavery.

Mitchell, who Ella once described as tall and lean, was of Cherokee and African descent, though she was never sure of which tribe for the latter. He was a Baptist minister who not only taught about God and faith but also about freedom and oneness. He was a principled man with foresight who in 1888—twenty-five years after Emancipation—purchased fifty acres of an old slave plantation by the riverbanks of Warren County, North Carolina, where he also built a church and school. It was the same property he and his wife once labored on when enslaved.

That was the beginning of Mitchell's declaration of himself as more than a former slave.

An autodidact, Mitchell learned to read on his own. He saw knowledge as a prerequisite to social mobility. He so disassociated himself from the entrapment of slavery that he refused to eat, or allow his family to eat, foods from their enslavement, such as cornbread. He was always for his people but knew most were still ensnared in the ways of slavery, so he solidified himself as a leader of men. Mitchell's social progress became a mark of what was possible.

"He established himself, sisters and brothers, cousins, on fifty-and sixty-acre plots," Ella once recalled. "Out of it came sort of a community."

Ella was a self-proclaimed talker who engaged Mitchell often as a child. She felt she did so because of her inquisitiveness and curiosity about the world around her. This led her to tag along with him often on his routes throughout the community and to church when her family moved between Norfolk, Virginia, and Warren County during summer months. "Grandpa would hitch his horse to the buggy," she once said, "and I'd go wherever he was going."

On his property, Mitchell also ran a farm complete with wheat and corn, cattle and chickens, and an orchard. It was a vital food source for the predominantly poverty-stricken community. "You'd start off with the early peaches, and then you'd have peaches all through the summer up until the fall," Ella later remembered. "[Mitchell] had enough cows to have, say, ten or twelve gallons of milk a day, so if you came, there was plenty to eat . . . It was the business of good living. And nobody ever got turned away."

When the river would overflow the land, destroying the crops, their neighbors' needs would go unmet. As a result, Mitchell had to mortgage the property twice: once in 1889 and again in 1890. "This was the kind of background [he had]," Ella once said, "the fighting background, [it] exhibited in his attitude."

This is where Ella spent her formative years: a hallowed home that defined her calling, her point of being, her *why*. There, she was bathed in advocacy, becoming acutely aware of what an unranked society could be. One that was rooted in communal improvement and egalitarian principles, where you could involve yourself with people and their needs.

There, she witnessed her family change their world inch by inch, person by person. She saw Mitchell defend civil rights before the term "civil rights" had been widely coined. He was a devoted defender of people, of equality, and of what was right.

As a little girl, Ella would join in and lend a hand to community members who came to the land to be fed, to relish in fellowship, to sing songs of freedom, to restore their faith. She watched her grandfather preach about salvation, God, His goodness, and a living hope for tomorrow—a better one with plenty.

That idea of expectancy was most resonant in his teachings.

She often remembered her grandfather asking his congregants one stirring question, "What do you hope to accomplish?" As freedmen, many former slaves struggled with the idea of freedom: what to do with it, how to become who they could be. Many remained in that in-between place. Mitchell knew this and tried to be an example to them.

He died and was buried on his property in 1909, when Ella was six. Yet his imprint on his granddaughter was enduring. "He always called me grand lady," she said in a 1968 interview, "and he'd always talk to you as a person rather than as a child. My memory of him is pretty sharp, plus it has been accentuated by the stories that come out of the family. My mother was basically her father's daughter to the extent that she emulated much of what he did."

The foundation that Mitchell had laid in Ella flourished with his widow, Josephine. Sharing stories of resilience and resistance from her experiences of slavery, Josephine further bolstered their granddaughter's sense of purpose and empowerment.

Before their time on the farm, Mitchell and Josephine belonged to their white master, William Elams, on the Littleton plantation.

Josephine was the biological child of her master and an enslaved woman—a frequent circumstance of slavery as many enslaved women were repeatedly raped and sexually abused by their owners. Josephine's mother was fatally poisoned with calomel by the master's wife, likely out of jealousy, so Josephine was raised by her grandmother. With her fairer complexion and status as the master's daughter, Josephine was given a relatively advantageous job compared to other enslaved people at the plantation: working in the master's home cooking, cleaning, and doing childcare.

Fueled by such folklore of perseverance, Ella internalized the spirit of resilience embodied by Josephine. Josephine was indirectly instilling the act of resistance into Ella and her two siblings—an older brother, Blake Curtis, and younger sister, Margaret Odessa: no matter how oppressive a situation you find yourself in, no matter how crushing the process, stay the course, let the pruning work itself out for your benefit.

This was the case in one of the tales Ella often told about Josephine's rebellion against a foundational expectation of plantation life: the master's declaration of who an enslaved woman must marry.

When the master's wife ordered Josephine to marry a house servant, Carter, who Josephine described as "so light," she refused. Annoyed at this clear defiance, the master's wife ordered her whipped. Josephine's father—*and* master—stepped in and said instead of the whipping, she'd be banished from being a house slave to a field one. "She would plow all day and dance all night," Ella recalled of her grandmother's indifference to the punishment. It was in the fields that she would meet Mitchell. And from there came six sons and a daughter, the eldest child, Georgianna—Ella's mother.

After years of watching Mitchell teach, Georgianna followed in her father's steps and became a teacher. In 1896, she married Blake Baker, a waiter on the Norfolk to Washington ferry line—they met while students at a school in Warrenton, North Carolina.

Like Josephine, Georgianna was instrumental in sparking unshakeable determination in her children.

Ella described her mother as devout a Christian as her grandfather and just as disciplined. Knowing her family was considered middle class and representative of African Americans, writ large, Georgianna wanted her children, especially her daughters, to be polished, articulate, educated, independent thinkers.

After all, this was the early 1900s, and Jim Crow laws permeated the South. Normative conformity based on gender and race were also ever-present in this era. But Mitchell had shown his family what persevering looked like. His children and grandchildren were far from other African Americans coming up in the South; most were poor and relegated to sharecropping alongside their parents. Because of Mitchell and his journey of distinction, his descendants were rooted in education and a relentless pursuit of excellence.

Georgianna knew, by virtue of her parents and grandparents descending from and surviving chattel slavery, that for her children to have a chance at survival, education and cultural knowledge provided the best advantage.

When Ella was seven, in 1910, a year after Mitchell died, her parents permanently moved the family back to their hometown of Littleton, about 120 miles from Norfolk, Virginia. (Though her father remained mostly in Norfolk due to work, he visited often.) Before the move, Ella had attended a year of what Georgianna assessed as a subpar public school in Norfolk.

"My mother had a feeling that there was greater culture in North Carolina than obtained in Norfolk," Ella once recalled about what prompted her mom to relocate them. "Plus . . . she just didn't like the lowland-lying climate there."

In 1918, Georgianna enrolled Ella—who had been attending a local two-room, three-teacher public school—at a Baptist boarding high school run by Shaw University, a historically Black college.

"I was accepted in the first year of high school," Ella recalled, "but my mother, who did not have a very high opinion of some of the teachers [at the public school], especially in terms of the use of language, under whom I had gone, opted to have me take a year at Monroe High School [before starting at Shaw]."

At fifteen, when Ella finally set off for Shaw Academy, seventy miles south of Littleton, she entered a different America than the one her parents and grandparents knew. Much had changed in nearly every aspect of life. The most striking was the level of Black youth activism that prior generations, like Mitchell and Josephine, had paved the way for.

As social activism began to surge after the First World War, Black reformers—including activist W.E.B. Du Bois, who had been one of the founding members of the National Association for the Advancement of Colored People (NAACP) in 1909—pushed more forcefully for a federal anti-lynching law to fight the revival of the KKK. (A trying endeavor from the beginning, it would take one hundred years from when Republican congressman Leonidas Dyer introduced the first House bill for it to pass: in 2022, President Joe Biden would finally sign the anti-lynching bill into law.)

That sense of agency also spilled over into how Black students—including Ella at Shaw—took to authority across Historically Black Colleges and Universities (HBCUs), even in the face of blatant racism, while protesting Jim Crow segregation and related laws that forbade autonomy.

During the post–World War I period, there were eighty-seven HBCUs. All but four were in the South, where they were first established with the help of Northern faith-based organizations at the end of the Civil War. This ensured that Black Americans had access to education where it had previously been prohibited and where the fumes of legalized racial segregation persisted.

The four HBCU schools in the North—Cheyney University, Lincoln University, University of the District of Columbia, and Wilberforce University—were established before the Civil War through the American Freedmen's Aid Commission—a union made up of mostly philanthropists and religious groups—and the first iteration of the Morrill Land Grant College Act of 1862. Senator Justin Morrill initiated the bill to make it possible for states to use federal lands—of which about 10 million acres were tribal lands—to build colleges committed to educating working-class people.

The introduction of the law, and its signing by Abraham Lincoln, was bookended and influenced by two essential social movements: one to reform higher education and another to increase science in agriculture. Educational reformers, like those of the Working Men's Party, felt the purpose of education and upward mobility needed to move from a more traditionally focused one, where only the wealthy and privileged benefited, to a fairer one underpinned by experiential learning and inclusive of all social classes. (A still-resounding struggle today.)

As the land grant college system grew, African Americans were regularly excluded from admissions to those schools. It would take twenty-five years after the Civil War, and more educational proponents monitoring the fairness of it all, for the law to be amended to ensure Black Americans were not being discriminated against within any grant-specific higher education institution.

But the inclusion of that amendment didn't stop the subjugation of and prejudice against African Americans in higher education. Even at HBCUs.

Increasingly, students at Black colleges felt their quality of education was subpar compared to their white counterparts'. They felt, though they were *free*, control over their fate didn't belong to them, sparking an uproar that catapulted across several HBCUs where the all-white board of trustees governed student bodies that they looked nothing like, insulating their power and privilege under the guise of discipline and structure.

At the heart of the students' revolts was the authority Black students wanted over the governance of their schools and, consequently, their education and future. This post–World War I surge of deliberate consciousness and reflective action set into motion the beginning of what would be a lasting framework of organizing resistance.

Against the backdrop of the Morrill Act, one of the most influential student revolts after the end of the First World War took place at Fisk University in Nashville, Tennessee.

Founded by the American Missionary Association and the American Freedmen's Aid Commission as a Christian school, Fisk was considered one of the top HBCUs during this era, providing what notable alums like W.E.B Du Bois dubbed the best liberal arts education for African Americans.

But the board of trustees was disconnected from students. They were all white and mostly men, including the school's presidents, and were detached from students' social and cultural needs. This was a time in everyday life when whiteness was synonymous with inherent freedom, power, and dominance, and Blackness with subordination, docility, and crassness.

When Fisk was first formed, the school's grade levels ranged from elementary to college—and most of the enrollment were in the lower grades. After World War I, of Fisk's 600 students, half were listed in the college arm, which meant they had a deeper understanding of their true predicament. Gone were the days when the majority of the school was meek and unresisting.

Those college students had entered an era of thriving and coming into one's self, yet the path to agency was still controlled—socially, politically, intellectually—by a higher human power keen on keeping dominance one-sided, keen on maintaining America's budding capitalist system where only the privileged can define themselves, inhabit autonomy, and freely flourish.

The intrinsic disconnect between the student population and the board of trustees was harmful and, in its own way, subjugating, poised to indoctrinate the lie that had worked for white Americans since they first blinked: that white people were inherently greater than Black people.

Like many leaders of Black colleges founded by Northern conservative groups and private benefactors during this era, Fisk's president, Fayette McKenzie, wanted to secure even more money from those same groups as well as other rich people, aiming for a one-million-dollar endowment.

During one fundraising visit, wealthy white men and conservative groups demanded political, social, and cultural shifts on campus. They had seen demonstrations at schools like Howard University in Washington, D.C., where students were loudly organizing, screaming for equality, and roaring against Jim Crow in the South.

Fayette knew that such benefactors wanted his school—and other HBCUs in general—to teach Black students to adapt to Jim Crow and not be influenced to question or challenge it. With that in mind, Fayette had always ignored his students' tamed demonstrations and let them be—no recourse, no changes.

But once Fayette received his requested funds in full following the fundraising visit, he implemented new restrictions across campus to avoid any dissent.

Co-eds couldn't speak to each other.

Dating was forbidden.

A 10 p.m. curfew.

The only copy of the NAACP's *The Crisis* in the campus's library was censored. (Literature bans? Sounds familiar.) W.E.B. Du Bois had created the popular newspaper in 1910, one year after co-founding the NAACP. He called it a record for the "darker races."

No student chapter of the NAACP was allowed.

Dancing was prohibited.

For women specifically, the rules were stricter:

No extreme styles of dresses or dresses made with "expensive" material.

No short sleeves.

No low-neck outfits.

No silk stockings.

But most disruptive was Fayette's change to the school's curriculum.

While Fisk prided itself on being a quintessential liberal arts institution with diverse faculty, which made it stand out among other Black colleges, Fayette now steered the school's coursework toward vocational training. This shift lacked substantive real-world application and fell short of fostering intellectual empowerment.

Fayette didn't hide his attempt at indoctrination.

And students were all the wiser. Many walked off the campus in protest, returning home.

In response, W.E.B. Du Bois, Fisk's most prominent alum at the time and the target of some of Fayette's restrictions, fired back during a campus visit to watch his only daughter, Yolande, graduate, delivering his famous *Diuturni Silenti* address:

> *Discipline is choking freedom, threats are replacing inspiration, ironclad rules, suspicion, and tail bearing are almost universal. The Negro race needs colleges. We need them today as never before. But we do not need colleges so much that we can sacrifice the manhood and womanhood of our children to the thoughtlessness of the North or the prejudice of the South.*

Encouraged by W.E.B Du Bois's speech and maxims and the climate of the time, students responded to the repressive rules louder than before.

For weeks, tensions on campus mounted, with students deliberately breaking curfew in protest. Singing and chanting *"Down with the Tyrant!"* and *"Before I'll be a slave, I'll be buried in my grave!"* they pounded trash cans, broke windows, and rummaged through the school's chapel.

On February 4, 1925, students at Livingstone Hall, an all-men's dorm, sang loudly into the night. Fayette called the Nashville police.

More than fifty officers arrived.

Armed with riot gear, they stormed the campus, smashed dorm windows, and beat some of the students.

In the end, seven students were arrested and charged with felonies.

Nashville locals saw Fayette's actions as dangerous, noting that some of the students could've been killed. The next day thousands of them flooded the school in protest, alarmed that the president couldn't quell students simply protesting rules they found to be irrational. The community was still coping from Black death upon Black death. In the last year, they had watched a Black pastor shot down by a white police officer, a Black boy kidnapped from a hospital by white men and lynched without reason, and two Black women sexually assaulted in the street by a group of white men. All of that and more went without challenge and were treated as just another day in town. No laws were in place that said otherwise.

Given the community outrage, the students were released and jumped right back into organizing a community-wide strike that lasted two more months, specifically requesting for Fayette to be ousted by the board.

On April 16, 1925, he was forced to resign.

And students, relishing their victory, returned to campus.

"The fight at Fisk University is a fateful step in the development of the American Negro," W.E.B. Du Bois wrote in the spring 1925 edition of *The Crisis*, about the ongoing campus crusade. "It involves the tremendous question as to whether the Negro youth shall be trained as Negro parents wish, or as Southern whites and Northern copperheads demand."

Fisk's student demonstration success reverberated across other HBCUs, where the same traditional construction was forcefully permeating, where their institutions were controlled by white power under the masquerade of promoting academic excellence and access for Black youths.

At both Virginia's Hampton University and Washington, D.C.'s Howard University, students similarly protested against their school's white president and board, asking for student autonomy, regime change, and higher academic standards.

Students at both institutions were making strides, though the road to parity was far from over.

On June 26, 1926, Mordecai Johnson replaced Stanley Durkee, becoming Howard's first Black president.

At Hampton, the climate of civil disobedience spilled over to the local neighborhoods, with one of the earliest glimpses of white allyship. Between protests, Hampton students met with the board of trustees and members of the community. After many strikes went uncontained, the administration shut down the school and forced students to re-enroll, asking them to pledge to *know* their place on campus and not rebel.

This was met with so much community backlash that even white-run news publications, like *The Virginia-Pilot Newspaper*, covered the ordeal, calling for Hampton's president, James Gregg, to step down: "If the principal could not sympathize with the viewpoint of Negroes because he is a white man, then he ought to resign and leave the school to be run by someone who is in sympathy with their viewpoint."

In May 1929, James resigned and was replaced with another white man, George Phenix. George wasn't like the rest. He came in committed to desegregating the faculty, allowing an NAACP student chapter, and adding a more rigorous curriculum.

As such changes had been unfolding across HBCUs, Ella was

drawn into her own activism at Shaw University in the wake of new rules that took aim at controlling the female student body.

Namely, the banning of silk stockings.

The post–World War I years, later termed the Roaring Twenties, saw the first wave of feminism as well as the landmark 1920 signing of the Nineteenth Amendment, giving women the right to vote.

The Roaring Twenties was also underpinned by the whirling Harlem Renaissance, where expression through dance and clothing became an essential way for women to challenge societal norms of who they were and who they were to become.

Female performers known as flappers in the North embodied this new era of liberation and were christened the "new woman."

These "new" women were making silk stockings popular.

Flappers became a powerful symbol of women explicitly expressing their sexuality and primacy.

They were unabashed, in every sense.

They began earning their own money.

They wore their hair in bobs.

They wore makeup and sexy high heels.

Some even played sports like track and basketball.

Many smoked and drank liquor openly.

Their spirited, alluring images became a rebellion on their own.

In short, the "new woman" was a direct contrast to old-fashioned family values where women were confined to the domestic sphere, expected to be wives and mothers. She was liberated, testing her newfound, albeit limited, parity with men. There was even a song from Broadway composer Vincent Youmans's *No, No, Nanette* that pithily characterized them.

> *Flappers are we*
> *Flappers . . . fly and free*

Though the Roaring Twenties boomed loudly and introduced a momentous demographic shift, Black women didn't experience the same modern independence liberally expressed by white women. Still, it resonated.

Popularized in newspapers and magazines, flappers induced a vigorous sense of identity, of coming into one's fullness. Their influence spilled onto HBCU campuses, which were still steeped in continued demonstrations, energizing the ongoing fight for parity.

In tandem with the movement of the "new woman," Ella took on the silk stocking ban across HBCU campuses as a senior at Shaw University's Baptist boarding high school, where conservatism and traditional values were being pushed on students.

In 1923, a notice went up on campus, announcing: "Fancy, colored or silk hose . . . will not be allowed. If brought or sent, they will be returned."

During her four years at Shaw High School, the resilience that had been fermenting in Ella from her upbringing on that Warren County farm didn't take long to burst. By the time that bulletin went up, nineteen-year-old Ella had already developed a reputation around campus as a studious, unwavering, and effective communicator and leader. She had petitioned for an NAACP Youth and College Division, challenged the school on its traditionalistic dress code, questioned the school's white president's antiquated and misogynistic way of governing, and rebelled against the school's curriculum, similar to those enforced at other HBCUs. (These authoritarian rules across campuses were being documented and spread far and wide through expanding mainstream media.) Ella had also contested the closure of the school's dentistry, law, pharmacy, and medical schools. The "talker" in her never relented; even in the "little things" she raised questions, she remembered once in a 1977 interview.

Another time, when Northern white Americans visited the school—similar to when Fisk's president hosted white donors and philanthropists in hopes of securing more endowments—Shaw's president wanted Ella and other students to entertain his guests by singing spirituals, most of which had slavery ties. "I recall them asking me if I'd lead [it]," Ella remembered in that 1977 interview. "It couldn't have been 'Go Down, Moses.' I don't know what it was, but I said, 'No, Mr. President.'"

Ella's assertiveness and booming bravado voice was so palpable that one of her teachers, Benjamin Frawley, told her, "'Don't ever let anyone teach you public speaking,'" she said during that same interview. "And all that I had learned, as far as articulation—it wasn't so much oratory, because I didn't go in for that, but I had won a couple of medals speaking in contests, things like that—my mother was the one who taught us. She taught us to read before we went to school."

All of this influence and fearlessness the teen had established on campus so inspired upper-class women from the college side of Shaw that they asked Ella to lead their efforts to get the school to overturn the prohibition of silk stockings.

She agreed and penned a letter to the school deans demanding the ban be lifted.

Her request was denied.

Not only that, but the female student body were punished for their attempts. They were ordered to the school's chapel every night. This was in addition to their already required attendance at the chapel each morning. Yet another way to enforce the school's authority and conservative beliefs on its student body.

Ella's individual punishment included more prayer with the dean in her office. "I didn't seem particularly penitent," Ella once recalled, "and [the dean] was very disturbed about it. But it didn't bother me because I felt I was correct." If she continued with her protest, the dean warned, she'd be expelled. So, she acquiesced; expulsion was not an option. Not after the journey her family had survived to get her there.

Years later, Ella remembered the silk stocking demonstration as being disruptive. The news of it traveled far and wide, even to Northern states like New Jersey, as one of her cousins would later tell her. And in every retelling of the ordeal, her defiance remained clear: "I didn't have any silk stockings, but I felt it was their right to wear their stockings if they wanted to. These women were not only my seniors in terms of physical maturity—they were about to finish college and the like. But they didn't dare do the talking."

Unbowed by constraints, and with such sentiments, Ella's character shone through. She didn't care much for fashion trends or how popular the flappers were in society and popular culture, she simply felt *it was their right to wear their stockings if they wanted*. What had mattered most to her was the sheer suppression of the prohibition. Her stance on the stocking issue also sets Ella distinctively apart from the rest of the HBCU student activists during this period. She wasn't only revolting against racism and intellectual enslavement but against what would seem frivolous to many—*silk stockings*. She was fighting sexism in the shape of restriction. Most of all, she was fighting for the righteousness of others, seeking no direct benefit.

In all her efforts, her stance remained strong. It's no surprise she would rise academically to graduate top of her class at Shaw's high school in 1923 and again as valedictorian from the college in 1927—the same year the school finally and officially lifted the silk stockings ban.

While the effect of Ella's organized protest against that ban was not immediate, taking four years to see results, the mere fact that there was an eventual victory meant female students who came after her didn't have to toil in the same field she had watered.

It's also no surprise either that Ella continued to rise in the many assemblages she touched as a people builder who fostered collaboration and connection within diverse groups, a community lifter who championed marginalized voices and advocated for the least of these, and a no-nonsense activist who relentlessly pursued unity and upliftment.

In her final act of dissidence at Shaw University, Ella—armed with a pen again and backed by over fifty students—challenged the school's policy of administering a mandatory religion exam without allowing students to refer to the course's primary text: the Bible. This massive book, containing over 773,000 words and 1,189 chapters, was deemed an impossible resource to memorize for the test, prompting students to liken the situation to being asked to cram the entire library into their heads and answer questions without consulting a single book. Ella's petition argued that the exam was unfair and discriminatory and demanded that the school either revise the test format or allow students to use the Bible during the exam.

The school declined the request.

Yet another loss.

Ella didn't battle the matter further. Expulsion, again, was the recourse if she did.

Her life proved that such moments of defeat allowed for pivotal lessons in organizing. Be it with a pen, her voice, her prudence, or in assembling people, she always carried on. Because there is triumph in the battle alone. Pressing forward was its own form of resistance. It affirmed: this rejection, this defeat, was not a barometer of her value. What to many would seem a setback spurred Ella. It was redirected energy that made way for clearer foresight. The kind her grandfather had when purchasing that farm.

At Shaw, as her already sharp voice matured even more, she always maintained her civility—something that was embedded within her from watching Mitchell diligently craft his own path and later, having her mother prioritize excellence and education. Shaw is where the idea of who she was, and who she could be, cemented. Picture senior students asking you to take charge. Consider the school's president, deans, and other authority figures perceiving you as a threat due to your strong self-awareness. All because you had a clear sense that what you had to say carried a meaningful message. In all her ways, Ella preserved her truth. "I didn't break rules," she said, "but I challenged rules. And I didn't have sense enough not to do the speaking, even to groups that were older than I."

Shaw was the culmination of what Mitchell had hoped for his children's children. Ella was his wildest dream.

In between all of Ella's organizing and civil defiance, she met Thomas "T.J." Roberts during her senior year at Shaw University. In most oral histories and reports, it was clear Ella was extremely private, and her love life was, well, no one's business. All she disclosed about T.J. and their relationship is that they fell in love quickly and deeply. And though he got into the refrigeration business and traveled often for work, after graduation from Shaw, he followed Ella to Harlem, where she immediately joined the political life and community organizing, which later led to her traveling throughout the country. In 1937, after ten years of being together, they got married.

She also felt her relationship with T.J. had no bearing on her community work. She said as much during one interview in 1977: "Don't ask too many personal questions, [it] has nothing to do with the issues at hand."

Throughout the years, from battling Jim Crow through her work with the NAACP in the 1940s, to organizing Martin Luther King, Jr.'s Southern Christian Leadership Conference in 1957, to forming the revolutionary Black youth–led Student Nonviolent Coordinating Committee in 1960, Ella distinguished herself from being known as anything but herself.

Not a leader.

Not a skilled people builder.

Just a woman who did for the people what was right since her teen years, not to be named or made prominent. "I've never credited myself with a professional life," she once said. "I came out of a family background that involved itself with people."

Ella remained in Harlem until she died on December 13, 1986. It was her eighty-third birthday.

When I see young people take to institutions riddled with entrenched power, desperate for a new way, I'm reminded of Ella's foundation. They've come to grasp what it means for them to exist in freedom, the likes of which is now threatened by the thought of old. Yet, they press on, resisting the status quo, striving to restore the spirit of American democracy, and rising against opposition.

They know the fight of their ancestors. They know that even in the face of defeat or silence, they win by simply daring to challenge wrongs, just like Ella. She didn't win every battle, but she stayed the course, waging the warfare of the people. For the rights promised when freed. Rights that were not, and in some cases still aren't, fully realized in everyday America, with everyday people perpetuating everyday hate.

What most captivated me about Ella—the girl, the woman, the activist's activist, the behind-the-scenes builder—was her upbringing. I particularly drew from and zeroed in on her early years, because they epitomized the idea that our lived experiences influence who we become. They inform how we see and interact with the world. They form our ideologies, which later govern our lives. But it's the intentionality of our actions as we navigate life moments that determines our character. It dictates how far we'll go, who we'll become, how long our imprints will be felt. The legacy and purpose of it all.

Who Ella became, what I take from her is that. Our circumstances don't control our future. Our intentionality does. Those everyday things we do to make just what is wrong. To build what is broken. To restore what is rejected.

Ella's journey also mirrored Mom's immigrant grit.

Witnessing Ella's fight for others awakened a sharper appreciation for the forces that shape us in service of something greater. This understanding transported me to my childhood, to the crack-ravaged South Bronx, where Mom juggled three jobs to build a life for us against all odds.

This was in the mid-'90s. And newly in America, my dreams became tethered to the limitations of our neighborhood. But despite the sting of assimilation and otherization (bullied for my accent, stutter, clothes, hair, the cruel "African booty scratcher" taunts), I saw in Mom's relentless work ethic and calm solidity a path forward.

She spoke often of her own willful defiance: Denied education by her parents who prioritized her brothers', she carved out her own destiny as a teen in 1970s Nigeria, a time when societal expectations confined women to homemaking. In a patriarchal society where men flaunted multiple wives as symbols of power and security, families readily married off their daughters, viewing it as a transaction where cattle, kola nuts, palm wine, and other delicacies were exchanged for a man's lifetime promise of provision.

Resolute, Mom demarcated her own future. In her teens, a near-fatal motorcycle accident after which she nursed Grandpa back to health seeded a dream: to become a nurse. Grandma was impressed. Grandpa, grateful. So, Mom and Grandma—a formidable duo—forged a plan. Grandma's prized French and George lace, a status symbol at the time, were sold to fuel the dream. And that dream landed Mom in America.

Gleaning from Ella's and Mom's journeys ignited a profound belief for me: the boundless potential of young people. We are the heirs of stories like Ella's and Mom's, testaments to the resilience that resides in every yearning heart. In the face of seemingly insurmountable obstacles, we possess an inherent spark of rebellion, a relentless drive to carve our own paths. Whether it's navigating the smothering realities of a segregated America or defying societal expectations in a distant land, we inherit a legacy of resistance that whispers, "Dream, defy, build a better tomorrow."

2

A RESISTANCE RISES

The Scottsboro Nine

We have been sentenced to die for
something we ain't never done.
Us poor boys been sentenced to
burn up on the electric chair
for the reason that we is workers—and
the color of our skin is black.

THE SCOTTSBORO NINE STATEMENT EXCERPT, MAY 1932

The part of the South Bronx I came up in was the hood hood. The kind where walking home from school, barely eight years old, the sound of gunshots doesn't make you flinch. The kind with people strung out on the street. Where Corner Boys know you, look out for you, but also poke fun at you.

We lived on Freeman Street, by the 2 train. Before coming to America, we never knew what a train was, so riding on one was spellbinding. So too were paved roads, constant electricity, no rolling blackouts or noisy backup generators, and working traffic lights. Everything felt immaculate.

In retrospect, some of our everyday assimilation experiences were obscured by blinding insulation. It soon became easier to adopt the culture of those who resembled us: Black Americans. Yet, we didn't know the depths of them, of the ones who neighbored us, of the ones who would later protect and check in on us latchkey kids when

Mom worked. She toiled hard to put us in Catholic school—a symbol of excellence even within meager means—like all the Nigerians in our community, but she couldn't afford it after a year. Three jobs and all. So, off to public school we went. In. The. South. Bronx.

When you're living in poverty, it's the simplicity of life that you hold on to. When you're living in poverty and new to America and grouped into Blackness, you don't know you're also part of America's history directly tied to race as it relates to sectionalism. All you know is survival.

In between assimilating to Black culture with Air Force 1s, Foamposites, durags, oversized jerseys, Ruff Ryders, Jeezy, Jay-Z, Nas and the rest, discriminative stereotypes began for my brothers. Some talked about their encounters with New York Police Department officers. It was never an outright complaint, because we didn't know about racism or discrimination or the history of it all. We just accepted it. Even when February 4, 1999, happened, and Amadou Diallo was mercilessly killed by NYPD officers a few blocks away from us, it didn't dawn on us that this uniquely American way to die was a trend that tilted toward one race and disproportionately toward one gender.

The core of my excavation in this decade sought to know the why and the how of such encounters. Where did this disproportionate overcriminalization of Black men stem from? I remembered my brothers' experiences—some for "fitting a description"—especially as it culminated with Manny's subsequent deportation. (I wish I knew then what I know now.) An incident that forever changed the course of my family's story.

In this chapter, I focus on the Scottsboro Nine's case—and the student-led pushback that followed—because of its glaring parallel to such modern moments of outright mistreatment and abuse of power still doused in white supremacy of old. Set against the Depression Era, when folks were barely getting by, traversing poverty and just trying to try, one false accusation from two white women from a similar destitute status as the Nine caused a rippling effect still felt today. It accentuates the dangers of sectionalism, where within each class rank, race—whiteness—supersedes justice.

Theirs is a story of the hopelessness found in unrelenting inequity for all the Othered. It ascribes how in America, Black boys and men have been, and continue to be, vilified as foes. It perpetuates the lie that they have an in-built propensity for sexual aggression and criminality. The unjust arrests and killings we decry today find their roots in this very ideology. In this contemptible system of condemnation plagued with the animalistic caricature of the Black man.

MARCH 25, 1931. SCOTTSBORO, ALABAMA.

A freight train headed West. Memphis-bound, along a southern border engulfed in Jim Crow.

Aboard the steel behemoth were nine Black minors. The oldest of the nine was nineteen. The youngest, twelve. All were illiterate, all were poor.

During this time, the Depression Era had set in. The abundance Americans had reveled in during the decade of prosperity, when the economy almost doubled, came to a crash following Black Thursday on October 24, 1929. Many thought it'd surely be the end of capitalism.

Consumer spending suffered. Business investors retreated. Banks closed their doors. Mines and factories shuttered. Corporations cracked. The working class—white and Black—who had enjoyed plentiful jobs in years prior, wandered the streets hungry and desperate for a buck. Those who managed to keep their jobs saw a drastic dip in their pay or their wages completely stripped. At times, they'd receive blank pay stubs from their employers, signifying all wages were confiscated and misappropriated for the company's supplies.

The Depression also forced students to drop out of school. Many joined the millions across the nation who were unemployed. The national unemployment rate rose from 3 percent to 25 percent—about 31 million people. For Black Americans, that rate was about 30 percent more than the general population. Black adults and students alike struggled more during this era as racial tensions were very much still heightened. They were forced to work jobs they were overqualified for under hostile conditions, which allowed for more intolerance and enmity. They were usually the last hired and the first fired. As a result, many rarely had enough to eat. Some tried growing their foods or hunting and fishing.

At the peak of the Depression, around 15 million people packed sidewalks on breadlines, many of them young men, fifteen to twenty-five years old. Many were homeless transients, wandering from city to city with what they had on their backs, unkempt in their muck. These young ones, who were hired quicker than older folks, became financially responsible for their parents—for their families—forced to travel state to state in search of work. Survival was their focus.

As this hardship swept the nation, the South held its stronghold of discrimination with Jim Crow's pervasive racism and violence, rampant bigotry, lawless lynchings, and sundown towns. It was known colloquially as a white man's country, a title fiercely maintained by white residents.

This is the heat the Scottsboro Nine were confronted in.

That early Wednesday morning in March, four of the Nine hopped on the Southern Railroad Line train in Chattanooga, Tennessee.

Since the prosperity era, with advances in transportation, trains were the quickest and easiest way to go from one city to another. It was also typical to seek shelter, scour for food, while away time, or hitch a free ride as the train inched into the different stations.

That day, the open wooden cargo was crammed with unemployed, homeless drifters—Black and white—who rode in the back illegally. All were on their way to look for work in Memphis, about 330 miles away. Chattanooga was a rural area with mostly farm jobs, and those were quickly withering away. Memphis was more urban, with higher chances of industrial work.

As the train chugged along, passing over Tennessee and its rolling hills, gleaming greenery, and red soil, a group of drifters, all white teens, jumped on. As they squabbled to find space in the boxcar, somewhere in Lookout Mountain, Tennessee, one of them deliberately walked past Haywood Patterson, one of the Nine, and stepped on his hand.

Another screamed at him.

"N*gg*r bastard, this a white man's train!" he told Haywood. "You better get off! All you Black bastards better get off!"

Haywood and the three others stayed put. ("We was just minding our business," he later said.)

"You goddamn n*gg*r, I think we better just put you off!" The white teen continued with his threat.

Haywood and the other three let the intimidation slide.

This was the Jim Crow South after all—the tiniest provocation could mean someone's life.

But the two white teens' taunting continued.

The train slowed at Stevenson, Alabama.

The remaining five of the eventual Nine hopped on.

In a few blinks, the same white teen walked by Haywood and stepped on his hand again. This time, Haywood and his three friends, now joined by the five who had just boarded, had "color anger on our side," he later remembered.

And that was it; a ruckus erupted between the two groups.

Venomous words spewed, a torrent of bile as brutal as the blows. In the scuffle, the white teens threw rocks at the Nine, attempting to force them off the moving train. But the Nine fought back. They overpowered the two white teens and pushed them off the train, which was still passing through Stevenson.

Licking their wounds, the white teens dashed to the local sheriff's office to complain that they had been assaulted and wanted to press charges against the Nine.

The next stop on the train's path was Paint Rock, a small town in Jackson County, Alabama. The sheriff's office coordinated and sanctioned an armed mob to stop the train and round up everyone onboard at Paint Rock, before it made its way to the next stop in Scottsboro. This commotion happened in the span of 80 miles: The distance between Chattanooga and Paint Rock.

Pointing shotguns and rifles, sheriffs from Jackson County rummaged through the cargo, hunting for all Black Americans. The Nine were captured, tied together with a plow line, loaded up on a truck, and hauled to Jackson County jail. They were:

> **LeRoy "Roy" Wright,** twelve. Chattanooga, TN
>
> **Eugene Williams,** thirteen. Chattanooga, TN
>
> **Olen Montgomery,** seventeen. Monroe, Georgia
>
> **Ozie Powell,** sixteen. Rural Georgia
>
> **Willie Roberson,** sixteen. Columbus, GA
>
> **Haywood Patterson,** eighteen. Elberton, GA
>
> **Clarence Norris,** nineteen. Warm Springs, Georgia
>
> **Andrew "Andy" Wright,** nineteen. Chattanooga, TN
>
> **Charles Weems,** nineteen. Chattanooga, TN

Andy and Roy were brothers. Andy, Roy, Eugene, and Haywood were friends. They boarded the train first.

The rest didn't know each other. They were the ones who boarded at Stevenson, Alabama.

They learned they were all to be held on assault and attempted murder of the white teens.

Moments later, the Nine were shocked to hear of an added charge.

Rape.

Ruby Bates and Victoria Price, two white women dressed in men's overalls, had also been in the same freight car as the Nine, on their way West looking for work at cotton mills. They'd been arrested for prostitution during the raid.

Ruby was seventeen, Victoria, twenty-one.

They were from the working-class mill town of Huntsville, poorly educated, living in barren shacks with their mothers, and were similarly Othered for their extremely impoverished status. They were proud sex workers, especially Victoria, who spoke openly a few times about sleeping with various men in Huntsville and Chattanooga to supplement her textile mill work. She was twice married and had previously been in trouble with the law for adultery and being a drifter. One reportage referred to them as "*Two Huntsville Mill Girls Hobo to Chattanooga.*"

Once in custody, attempting to evade imprisonment, Ruby and Victoria accused six of the Nine of repeatedly raping them.

The weight of this accusation was heavy.

Though equally low class, these white women had soaring agency in the power of their whiteness. Whiteness being debased in any form—a look, a spoken word—by Blackness was justified cause for violence, intimidation, or even death.

The allegation from Ruby and Victoria didn't happen in a vacuum. Years earlier, in 1923 Rosewood, Florida, a white woman claimed a Black man raped her. White men swiftly responded by killing him and burning down the entire town. In Virginia, there was a local law for Black American men caught engaging in "reckless eyeballing." If seen looking at a white woman, Black men could be arrested and killed. Of the nearly 5,000 Black men lynched between 1880 and the end of this era, most were accused of sexual assault or rape against a white woman.

News of such actions typically spread fast, yet another form of intimidation for Black men who dared defy their place. Victoria knew this was the climate across the South. She was much feistier than Ruby, had street smarts, and knew Southern white men couldn't bear the thought of Black men with their women, even consensually. Ruby, who was more impressionable and shy, later admitted that she had been coerced by her spirited friend to go along with their report.

In flipping the story to their favor, they weren't poor hobo girls. They were virtuous white women desecrated by savage Black creatures. Or so their story spun.

The sheriffs eagerly believed them.

Whiteness triumphed.

An hour and a half after the alleged rapes, Victoria and Ruby, their clothes still neatly intact, were examined by two white doctors, R.R. Bridges and Marvin Lynch. The doctors concluded that the women appeared to have had sex in the last day but that there were no signs of rape. However, they added that it was impossible to rule out rape even with no physical bruises.

The allegation so disturbed the Nine that during the lineup, when Victoria—who was up first—pointed out the six she claimed raped her, Clarence yelled, "Liar!"

A guard immediately pounded the teen's hand with a bayonet.

The guard presiding over the lineup then concluded that if six of the Nine had raped Victoria, "it stands to reason that the others had [raped] Miss Bates."

And that was that. All Nine were charged with rape.

And so began the most notorious criminal injustice saga to rock the nation.

The same day of the arrest, the *Jackson County Sentinel* ran a story condemning the "revolting crime." Multiple local reports from the *Sentinel*, the *Scottsboro Progressive Age,* and the *Huntsville Times*—a paper from the women's hometown—painted Ruby and Victoria as hardworking breadwinners for their lowly families and the Nine as criminals, sex-thirsty "beasts unfit to be called human." Such slanted coverage further confirmed Southerners' public prejudice.

As a way to easily group and reference the Nine, the reporting dubbed them the *Scottsboro Boys.* This marker was a combination of the name of the tiny town—with a population of 2,000, mostly white Americans who lived in cottages against smooth lawns and towering trees—they were moved to and held in (Scottsboro housed the nearest jail, 20 miles east of Paint Rock), combined with "boys," which was a derogatory term for all Black men, no matter their age. A reminder of white America's authority over them. A reminder that they were to be servile.

The news of the arrests first spread throughout town, spurring a frenzy among white locals. Many wailed for "old Southern justice." Or, acceptable, lawless lynching. Within hours of the Nine's arrest, a lynch gang gathered at the Scottsboro jail.

"Bring them n*gg*rs outta there! If you don't bring them out, we'll come in and get them!" some in the mob shouted.

"The crowd was howling like dogs, throwing rocks and threatening to burn us out," Clarence later wrote. "All I could think was that I was going to die for something that I had not done."

The state's governor, Benjamin Meek (B.M.) Miller, authorized 120 Alabama Army National Guardsmen to step in and control the uproar and prevent what was sure to be a public execution.

On March 30, the Nine were indicted by an all-white grand jury. A week later, beginning on April 6, four separate trials were held in front of Judge Alfred E. Hawkins.

Clarence and Charles had one trial. Haywood, the second. Third was Olen, Ozie, Willie, Eugene, and Andy. And the final trial was Roy's. Given the different ages and allegations from the women, the prosecution felt separating the trials would present a fairer case than grouping them all together. That it'd reduce the chance of a mistrial or challenges for a retrial.

The trials lasted three days.

"The courthouse were full of people and they were jumpin' up out their seats with pistols," Clarence recalled, "wasn't a black person around nowhere. Everybody was white but just us nine."

The Nine's court-appointed white legal representatives, Stephen Robert Roddy and Miles Addison "Milo" Moody, presented no defense and urged them to plead guilty. Miles was sixty-nine, had not tried a case in decades, and was described in the press as scatterbrained and senile. Stephen was a real estate lawyer from Chattanooga, Tennessee, who had no license to practice in Alabama but did have a jail record for drunkenness, and would often come to court reeking of alcohol, incoherent and slurring his speech. In court transcripts and news reports, Miles and Stephen were known to be grossly incompetent and painfully unqualified and unprepared. Before trial, they spent a total of thirty fleeting minutes with the Nine.

In court, the jurors listened as the two women described being brutally raped, a knife pointed at their necks, their clothes violently ripped off.

Ruby's testimony was subdued. She appeared reluctant to speak about what happened that day, giving more mechanical responses about who she saw on the train and their visit to a cotton mill in Chattanooga.

In contrast, Victoria's testimony came across as compelling story-telling, with details changing with each retelling and straying far from what the evidence showed.

"There were six to me and three to her," she testified at trial. "One was holding my legs and the other had a knife to my throat while another ravished me. That one sitting behind the defendants' counsel took my overalls off. Six of them had intercourse with me. 'Pour it to her, pour it to her' they hollered."

At one point, she told the jury she needed to spit up between rapes, but they didn't let her. Instead, they told her and Ruby they'd take them up North and "make us their women." She said she was beaten and bruised badly. That two of the Nine waved a pistol and shot it about seven times. That they all had knives.

Reports don't mention any weapons being found on any of the Nine when they were arrested.

Though Victoria had mentioned in her testimony that the Nine forced all the white boys and men off the train except for one, several white men took to the stand, saying they'd witnessed the attack. Some even came forward to say they witnessed the flurry from a distance. One farmer, Luther Morris, said from his barn, thirty yards from the tracks, he saw the Nine "put off five white men [from the train] and take charge of two girls." Another, a passerby, Ory Dobbins, said when he saw the train pass, he could see one of the Nine throw down a white woman.

The two doctors then told the jury about their examination findings: Though there were no physical signs of rape (tearing or bruising), it didn't conclusively rule out gang rape. R.R. Bridges added that though he didn't see any physical abuse or emotional strain, he believed the women.

Miles and Stephen did not provide any closing arguments in any of the four trials.

"Within two hours, the jury had come back with a conviction," Haywood would later write. "I was convicted in their minds before

I went on trial . . . All that spoke for me on witness stand was my Black skin, which didn't do so good."

Even with contradictory statements and reports, an all-white, all-male jury found the Nine guilty and recommended that they be sentenced to death by electrocution. This was the standard sentence for Black men convicted of rape in Alabama. This was to be the fate for all except twelve-year-old LeRoy, who received a life sentence after a hung jury. Eleven jurors wanted him lynched. One sympathized with the preteen.

After the verdicts were read, locals and sheriffs described the scene inside and outside the court as a circus.

The courtroom burst into loud cheering. Armed guards stood their post inside and around the building. People from near and far—about 10,000 visitors—flocked to the town by foot, horse wagon, and car. Many were jubilant. Some even sang a popular ragtime tune, "Hot Time in the Old Town Tonight," filled with stereotypical innuendos, with religious, suggestive references.

When you hear the preachin' has begin,
Bend down low for to drive away your sin;
When you get religion you'll wanna shout and sing,
There'll be a hot time in old town tonight!

On April 27, the Nine were transferred to Kilby Prison. The executions were scheduled for the earliest date the law would allow: July 10, 1931.

The convictions buttressed interest in the case as local outlets continued their campaign to see the Nine brought to Southern justice. News stories from Scottsboro traveled north, south, east, and west. Soon, the demand for justice ran from tiny pockets of the Jim Crow South to the rest of the nation and landed at the door of the American Communist party.

In a matter of days after the Nine were sentenced, the International Labor Defense (ILD), a progressive team of lawyers funded by the Communist party, sent a telegram to the state's governor, B.M. Miller, demanding a reversal of the verdicts, dubbing the case a legal lynching. Shocked by the fast trials, the Nine's ages, and the sentences, George Maurer, one of the group's leaders who penned the note, said the ILD was determined to free the Nine and called the case an Alabama frame-up. Shortly after, George and his team began working to file a motion for a new trial with Alabama's Supreme Court.

The makeup of the ILD was mainly white men, a promising allyship for the Nine, who hoped for swift vindication. Tapped to lead the case was a tough, prominent lawyer who didn't belong to the Communist party, New York's Samuel Leibowitz. The son of Romanian Jewish immigrants, he was known for his aptitude, fiery no-nonsense approach, and investment in the "basic rights of man." He was one of two prominent criminal lawyers in America who had defended corrupt cops, gangsters, kidnappers, and rapists (the other was Clarence Darrow). In court, he relied on his showmanship and booming baritone to sway jurors. This made the ILD confident that the whip-smart defender would bring justice to the Nine.

Though it was odd for an all-white legal team to lead the defense when the likes of the NAACP usually worked on such cases, the ILD had been making a name for themselves within the Black community during the Depression. They had made efforts to recruit some to the party, pushing for labor reform and interracial job equity. They'd even defended and supported some Black men previously terrorized in the lynch-ridden South.

So, when the NAACP didn't quickly respond to the Nine's national crisis, the ILD stepped up. The newly elected NAACP executive secretary, Walter White, didn't want to associate the NAACP with the Nine—at the time, he felt they could've been guilty. He also feared that the still-burgeoning group would lose notable financial donors. Under Walter's leadership, the NAACP was all too careful to color within the lines.

In January 1932, the NAACP formally withdrew any implied or explicit association from the Nine's case.

The ILD didn't and were resolute in their fight.

The Communist party leadership argued that the Scottsboro case was an inescapable consequence of a Jim Crow system and class exploitation. Many—though not all—Black Americans agreed with the ILD's stance. So, despite being a theoretical mismatch, the Communist party's involvement didn't feel completely amiss. A team of white lawyers sympathetic to the Nine's plight teed up what most felt would be speedy justice.

Once on the case, Samuel and the other ILD lawyers met often in jail with the Nine, used publicity to garner attention, and rallied people from across the country to write letters of support, send financial aid, and stage massive protests, calling for the reversal of the verdicts.

The first attempt at a retrial failed at the state Supreme Court on March 24, 1932, but when it was sent up to the U.S. Supreme Court, on November 7 of the same year, in *Powell v. Alabama* (Ozie Powell was used as the primary plaintiff), it was successful: The Supreme Court concluded that the Nine's Fourteenth Amendment right to due process had been violated.

Though joyous news, there was still a steep climb ahead for the Nine. In May 1932, from their cells in Kilby Prison, they decided to band together to pen and send an appeal letter to the "toilers of the world" to rally on their behalf, to revolt against the grotesque frame-up.

We have been sentenced to die for something we ain't never done. Us poor boys been sentenced to burn up on the electric chair for the reason that we is workers—and the color of our skin is black. We like any one of you workers is none of us older than 20. Two of us is 14 and one is 13 years old.

What we guilty of? Nothing but being out of a job. Nothing but looking for work. Our kinfolk was starving for food. We wanted to help them out. So we hopped a

freight—just like any one of you workers might a done—to
go down to Mobile to hunt work. We was taken off the
train by a mob and framed up on rape charges.

   At the trial they give us in Scottsboro we could hear the
crowds yelling, "Lynch the N*gg*rs." We could see them
toting those big shotguns. Call 'at a fair trial?

   An while we lay here in jail, the boss-man make us
watch 'em burning up other Negroes on the electric chair.
"This is what you'll get," they say to us.

   What for? We ain't done nothing to be in here at all.
All we done was to look for a job. Anyone of you might
have done the same thing—and got framed up on the same
charge just like we did.

   Only ones helped us down here been the International
Labor Defense and the League of Negro Rights. We don't
put no faith in the National Association for the Advancement
of Colored People. They give some of us boys eats to go
against the other boys who talked for the I.L.D. But we
wouldn't split. Nohow. We know our friends and our
enemies.

   Working class boys, we asks you to save us from being
burnt on the electric chair. We's only poor working class
boys whose skin is black. We shouldn't die for that.

What's repeatedly lost in the case of the Nine, whose lives were grossly interrupted because they were Black and poor and desperate for employment, is who they actually were. Who they had hoped to one day become.

If their case happened in contemporary times, it would've surely become viral and make us endlessly scroll, scouring for every news clipping. Every angle. Every photo. Every analysis. Desperate to seek the *how* in all of it.

George Floyd.

Breonna Taylor. Eric Garner. Crystalline Barnes. Michael Brown. Tamir Rice. Atatiana Jefferson. Tyre Nichols. Amadou Diallo.

And on.

It's important to know who these young ones were—who they *really* were—before they became iconic, transformative symbols of racial injustice. To know them, to know their stories, is to know that to be poor isn't to be without value.

"While in my cell lonely and thinking of you, I am trying by some means to write you a few words. I would like for you to come here . . . I feel like I can eat some of your food."

LeRoy "Roy" Wright wrote those words to his mom, Ada Wright. At the time of their arrest, he was the youngest of the Nine at twelve. Smart and unassuming, the Chattanooga native with sad, sunken eyes, thin brows, and a short stature was on that train headed West to look for work alongside his big brother, Andrew. This was the first time he had left home, where he'd worked in a grocery store after dropping out of school—he only had four years of grade school under his belt. When the Nine were first picked up, Roy cried, so frightened of the chaos, his brother had to comfort him throughout that day. During the trial, trying to save himself, his brother, and friends Eugene and Haywood, Roy lied and said he did see nine other Black teens rape the women—that it wasn't them. The twisted tale was to no avail. Behind bars, Roy whiled away time reading the Bible, which he always kept by his side.

"I ain't got no justice here . . . It seems as though I have been here for a century."

Andrew "Andy" Wright was the second oldest of the Nine at nineteen. He dropped out of the sixth grade when his father died from an illness. Overnight, Andy, at twelve, became the man of the house and breadwinner alongside his mom. Before the pangs of the Depression, he had spent seven years as a truck driver for a produce distributor, getting paid under the table. Andy was let go when the distributor's insurance company discovered his age. He was on his way to Memphis after learning about a federally sponsored job lugging logs onto boats. While in prison, the clever and polite teen with a faint smile was regularly depressed and sick, a loner who was a steady target of the prison guards' physical aggression.

"Getting out is the main thing I think about."
Baby-faced **Eugene Williams** was thirteen when arrested. Friends with Andy and Roy, he had been a dishwasher at a local restaurant in Chattanooga. Handsome and lanky, he was rather timid and kept to himself, rarely smiling, giving him a reputation for being grim, though he was openly pious, which one interviewer called "suspicious." Because he was lighter skinned, another report referred to him as a mulatto—a common term during that time to describe someone who was half white and half Black.

"I laid on the top bunk, in a way still feeling I was on a moving freight. Nothing was standing still. I was busy living from minute to minute. Everything was rumbling. I dreamed bad dreams, with freight trains, guards' faces, and courtrooms mixed up with the look of the sky at night."
Haywood Patterson, brimming with willful pride and a brash demeanor, was surly and pitiless. Though not well read, the eighteen-year-old was vocal and not easily intimidated, and his soaring, firm stature complemented his presence. He was the fourth of ten children surviving off their father's weekly income of $28 in Elberton, Georgia, and there wasn't much to go around. He dropped out of school in the third grade to become a delivery boy. Still, the family struggled to put food on the table. So, at thirteen, Haywood took to hopping freight trains. He got so good at leaping from one to the other that he said he could light a cigarette butt in the wind from the top of a moving car. Haywood was the one whose hand the white teen repeatedly stepped on, not knowing the teen wasn't as meek as many Black men were forced to become in the face of deliberate intimidation

by white men and boys. During the trial, he always carried a horseshoe. He called it his good luck charm. When he took the stand, Haywood tried to save himself by saying he saw five of the Nine rape Victoria. But in the same testimony, he also said he never saw the women. Unapologetically rough and tough, he wasn't liked by the others or anyone else, to the extent that Clarence spoke of wanting Haywood dead. One of the guards actually paid another prisoner to kill him, but Haywood survived despite being stabbed twenty times. Soon, Haywood got his own protection: "I had faith in my knife. It had saved me many times."

"I'm just being held here because I'm a N*gg*r. That's why I'm in jail; not nothing I've done . . . I was on my way to Memphis on a oil tank by my self a lone and I was not worred with any one untell I got to Paint Rock Alabama and they just made a frame up on us boys just cause they cud."

Seventeen-year-old **Olen Montgomery** hailed from Monroe, Georgia, a small rural town forty-five miles east of the state's capital of Atlanta. While in the fifth grade, seeing his mom, Viola, support the family with a weekly salary of $1.50, he dropped out to help. He was hopping trains heading West that Wednesday, hoping to find work to buy a pair of glasses for his large, wistful eyes. Olen was blind in his left eye due to cataracts, and with only 10 percent sight in the other one, he could barely see. He typically got around by putting his hand on someone's shoulder, being led from place to place. With a fifth-grade education, he was one of the Nine who managed to read and write. During his arrest and trial, the slim and frail teen said he was riding on the far end of the train, in the oil tanker, not the gondola car where the alleged rape was said to have occurred. When he'd respond to supporters who would write him, he'd ask for money for a night with a prostitute or a six-string guitar. He dreamed of one day being the "Blues King."

"I done give up ... cause I feel everybody in Alabama is down on me and is mad with me."

Born in rural Georgia, **Ozie Powell** was sixteen at the time of his arrest. Since childhood, the well-built, tall stripling worked in a lumber company until he was fourteen, when he would straggle across states finding temporary employment at lumber camps and sawmills, working a few weeks here, a few weeks there. While his mother made ends meet tending to white families, Ozie barely completed a year of grade school, only mastering how to write his name. Reticent and bashful, during his time in prison Ozie grew increasingly frustrated and depressed to the point where he could no longer contain it. One day, when being transported from court back to jail, Ozie sliced the throat of a deputy, Edgar Blalock, with a pocketknife. Witnessing the attack, the accompanying sheriff, J. Street Sandlin, pulled over and shot Ozie in the head. Both Ozie and Edgar survived.

"If I don't get free I just rather they give me the electric chair and be dead out of my misery."

When **Willie Roberson's** grandmother died in 1930, his aunt took in the fifteen-year-old but could not afford to take care of him. He also had an IQ of 64, that of a nine-year-old, and was a lot for her to handle. (The average IQ is around 100; scores can top out around the 200s, but that kind of genius is pretty much unheard of.) She told him he'd need to go find his own money. He had already dropped out of school at twelve and had been picking up odd jobs at a hotel. Two years before that fateful Wednesday, he had been a transient, hopping from one train to another. At the time of his arrest, the sixteen-year-old had syphilis and gonorrhea, with visible swollen sores on his genitals. He could barely walk and used a cane to get around. In addition to seeking work out West, Willie hoped to find free medical care. (One of the ILD defenses later used on his behalf was that because of his sexually transmitted diseases, sex would've been painful for him, and he would've passed the infections on to the women.) Once in prison, his existing asthma worsened, and he exhibited prison neurosis, a condition where a prisoner develops claustrophobia, severe anxiety, and panic attacks.

"The lesson to Black people . . . to everybody, is that you should always fight for your rights, even if it costs you your life. Stand up for your rights, even if it kills you. That's all that life consists of."

The son of Georgia sharecroppers from the quaint city of Warm Springs, **Clarence Norris** was the second of eleven children. By the time he was seven and in the first grade, his father pulled him out of school so he could join the family trade sowing crops. Life became exponentially difficult for the quiet and shy kid. He ran away from home at fifteen to escape his father's beatings and found work in Gadsden, Alabama, working sixteen-hour days at a Goodyear plant. Life began turning in his favor: he was in a relationship and had a steady income. Before long, though, his girlfriend dumped him, and down on his luck again, he ran away with other transients and began hopping trains, moving from city to town throughout the Southeast region. This is what the strapping, imposing, tall teen was doing when he was arrested in Alabama five years later: making his way to Sheffield, Alabama, looking for work. During the trial, in an attempt to save himself, the nineteen-year-old succumbed to the fear of death behind bars and falsely corroborated the accusations by pinning the rape of Victoria on the other eight. "They all raped her," he said in court, "every one of them."

"Please tell all the young mens to try hard and not to go to prison for my sakes."

Charles Weems's deep-set eyes and weathered face reflected his life of hardship growing up in Chattanooga, Tennessee. His mom died when he was four, and only one of his seven siblings survived childhood. After his father became unable to take care of him, he was sent off to Riverdale, Georgia, to stay with his aunt. Shortly after, he dropped out of school in fifth grade, became a transient, and started hopping freight trains in search of scraps, shelter, and work. The nineteen-year-old was making his way to Tennessee to be with family and find employment when he was taken into custody.

These details from the Nine's lives did not make the papers. Headline after headline dubbed them as "black fiends," animals, over-sexualized "Negro brutes," and aggressors not to be trusted. During the trial, the prosecutor had even gone as far as to tell the jury that if the Nine were released, white women in the South would have to wear revolvers to protect the sacred parts of their bodies.

These young men were guilty of simply existing.

Almost a year after their letter went out to the world, a series of new trials for the Nine began on March 27, 1933, with Haywood's up first.

In an attempt to select a more impartial jury, hoping to reduce local bias, the trial was held in Decatur, Alabama, fifty miles west of Scottsboro, with a new judge, James Horton, Jr., who had a reputation for being equitable and impartial.

When Victoria took the stand, Samuel, the ILD-appointed defense lawyer, was determined to rip apart the stories of the two white women. His goal was to prove to the jury that Ruby and Victoria indeed had consensual sex with men they met on their journey the night prior.

SAMUEL: Did you tell a man by the name of Lester Carter that you would introduce him to Ruby?

VICTORIA: I told you, I never seen Lester Carter before.

SAMUEL: Isn't it a fact that the night before you left Chattanooga, you and your boyfriend and Ruby and Lester Carter went walking along the railroad tracks?

VICTORIA: No sir, we never have been on the railroad together.

SAMUEL: Isn't it a fact, Mrs. Price, that you had intercourse with your boyfriend on the ground while Ruby had intercourse with Lester Carter right beside you?

VICTORIA: We absolutely did not.

MOMENTS LATER, SAMUEL SHOUTED: You're a pretty good little actress aren't you?

VICTORIA: You are a pretty good actor yourself.

As Victoria remained defiant and stuck to her story, Samuel pursued another route to discredit the women. He later found the two men who had sex with Ruby and Victoria the night before. He had them testify and confirm that they did have sex, which would explain what the examining doctors reported during the trial.

LESTER CARTER: Victoria Price said she knew where we could go and see fun, take a walk, for instance.

SAMUEL: Go ahead. What happened?

LESTER: We walked up the yards 'til we came to the jungles.

SAMUEL: What occurred in the hobo jungles that night?

LESTER: We all sat down near a bendin' lake of water where they was honeysuckles and a little ditch. I hung my hat on a little limb and went to having intercourse with Ruby . . . by firelight, I saw Victoria's boyfriend had intercourse with her . . . This is what happened. It wasn't that they were raped. Victoria Price, Ruby Bates and their two boyfriends had sex. And that's all it amounts to.

And, that was that.

Meanwhile, in a private meeting with Judge James, Marvin, one of the two doctors who had examined the women told him, "I looked at both the women and told them they were lying, that they knew they had not been raped, and they just laughed at me." But then, Marvin told James he couldn't testify publicly because he feared what would happen to him if he sided with the Nine.

As Samuel continued to investigate, looking for more ways to poke holes in the women's story, the biggest bombshell of all came as a result of Ruby's conscience. A year earlier, on January 5, 1932, she confessed to one of her lovers, Earl Streetman, in a handwritten letter, that the accusation against the Nine was all made up.

Earl sent the letter to the defense during the new trial.

Jan 5 1932
Huntsville, Ala
215 Connelly Aly

Dearest Earl,

I want to make a statment too you [it] is a goddam lie about those negroes jassing me those policement made me tell a lie that is my statement because I want too clear myself that is all too if you want to believe, ok. If not that is ok. You will be sorry someday if you had to stay in jail with eight Negroes you would tell a lie two. those Negroes did not touch me or those white boys. i hope you will believe me the law don't. i love you . . . that is why i am telling you of this thing. i was drunk at the time and did not know what i was doing. I know it was wrong to let those Negrroes die on account of me. i hope you will believe me. I was jazed but those white boys jazed me. i wish those Negores are not burnt on account of me. it is these white boys fault. that is my statement. and that is all i know. i hope you tell the law hope you will answer.

Ruby Bates

P.S. This is the one time i might tell a lie but it is the truth so god help me.

With such damning evidence, Samuel convinced Ruby to step forward and recant.

She did, publicly, at trial.

> SAMUEL: You testified at each of the trials at Scottsboro, didn't you?
>
> RUBY: Yes.
>
> SAMUEL: You said you saw six Negroes rape Victoria Price, and six raped you, didn't you?
>
> RUBY: Yes, but I was excited when I told it.
>
> SAMUEL: You told at Scottsboro that one held a knife at your throat, and what happened to you was just the same that happened to Victoria Price. Did someone tell you to say that?
>
> RUBY: Victoria Price told me to say that.
>
> SAMUEL: Did she say what would happen if you didn't do as you were told?
>
> RUBY: Yes, she said we might have to lay out a sentence in jail.

On April 9, 1933—thirteen days after Haywood's trial began—within twenty-two hours, the all-white jury's verdict was unanimous. *Guilty.*

They recommended the death penalty.

Samuel called the jury "bigots whose mouths [were] slits in their faces. Whose eyes popped out at you like frogs. Whose chins dripped with tobacco juice, bewhiskered and filthy."

Judge James suspended the trial for the other eight and delayed Haywood's execution.

Outraged students nationwide rose up in response to the verdict. Their mission: ignite momentum for the Nine's right to due process.

Their resistance wielded the power of the pen.

A year before Haywood's trial, in October 1932, the editor of the *Student Review*, a publication put out by the National Student League, wrote a clarion call to students: "If we students, intellectual workers, fail to put up a strong fight for the liberation of these nine Scottsboro boys, we shall betray not only the cause of the Negro people whose desperate plight these boys symbolize but the cause of the whole working class in the U.S. and all over the world. 'Labor in the white skin cannot be liberated as long as labor in the black skin is enslaved!'"

Then, days after the guilty verdict, several letters flooded Alabama governor B.M. Miller's desk.

On April 12, a student from Elmira, New York, Eloise H. Lawrence, wrote, "I am writing to assist, if I can, in sparing the lives of the Scottsboro colored boys. I believe the boys are innocent, and as a student of criminology, it seems to me much better to devote some of the money, that state institutions of punishment require, to education in the schools—along the line of social intelligence. And until this has had sufficient time to prove its' worth, all states show consideration with criminals that are criminals because of ignorance.

"And, at the same time," her letter continued, "those states also hesitate to deal out a death sentence, where there is not certainty of guilt. My interest is real in this case and I trust it may turn out for the best."

Two days later, on April 14, a petition with more than fifty signatures was sent from Howard University calling for mercy on the Nine. The next day, another telegram arrived from the University of Chicago Student League, stating the group had "assembled in Mandel Hall on the University of Chicago campus, [to] unite in protest against the verdict of guilty entered against H[a]ywood Patterson in Decatur, Alabama. It is for you, Governor Miller, to act to exercise your executive power to free the nine innocent Scottsboro boys."

As the deluge of student letters continued to flood in, on June 22, Judge James granted the ILD's motion for another trial. (James's empathy and support for the Nine would later cost him his re-election in 1934.)

Meanwhile, the student rallies intensified, spreading nationwide, then sparking globally, from Russia to Germany to Spain. Ada Wright, the mother of Roy and Andy, did a six-month tour of Europe, ending in Moscow at a rally where she spoke in front of thousands of supporters. Statewide, Ruby joined in on the marches, even leading a few, and was seen with some of the Nine's mothers at demonstrations. Her recanting led some Southern press to change their tune on the matter too. One city paper in Virginia, *The Richmond News Leader*, ran a column that succinctly summarized the Nine's plight: *"The men are being sentenced to death primarily because they are black."*

With rising protests, the widespread uproar, and what Judge James felt was a lack of evidence for a rape conviction, he dismissed the guilty verdict. This meant the case would be sent back to trial. And with that tiny shred of hope came more demonstrations of all sizes and forms.

As mobilizations expanded in scope, the case powerfully energized young Black revolutionaries across the country to continue to rise up, take an authoritative stance against the Nine's dilemma, and join the ILD's efforts. They knew the implications of the trial were all too significant for their future too.

The Nine's plight represented America's Black youths' in many ways: Here were young people who had simply been trying to survive in an economy that crushed their demographic harder than any other group. If these Nine could seemingly be eradicated from society, what would befall all young Black people? What would become of their tomorrows, of their pursuit of one day achieving their versions of the American dream?

At HBCUs, activism against schools' racial authority and its traditional origins continued. However, with the fuel of the Scottsboro case, more students were ignited. With the ongoing Depression symptoms, HBCU students had become disgruntled with the system of wealth distribution and the widening sectionalism and social hierarchy it perpetuated. The Nine's case and the continued worsening financial realities, which exacerbated the economic disparities faced by Black Americans, unearthed the depths and persistent stain of racism in America. The once abstract notion of classism as it relates to race relations was laid bare. It renewed a fight rooted in the failing conditions for Black Americans and a desire to push the nation to its promise of a democratic republic, to its promise of the Constitution, unburdened by a rigid social, cultural, or economic caste system.

The marches and student letter-writing campaigns magnified with still more students working tirelessly to whip up a coalition for the Nine. At Alabama's Tuskegee Institute, students organizing prompted the school's president, Robert Russa Moton, to take to the pen himself, writing to Governor B.M. Miller, reminding him that "the end of the law is justice and I am confident that in this case you see that such protection as the courts can give will be meted out to the humblest, the poorest—yes the blackest member of our commonwealth."

On November 20, 1933, the third trial for Haywood began. It resembled the second. This time with a different judge, William Callahan, whose bias, Samuel and the ILD later said, was evident in how he instructed the jury on the criteria to find a defendant guilty. Samuel felt the judge intentionally omitted the complete standard, which may have confused the jury.

The case ended in another guilty verdict that December.

Death penalty.

Following yet another gut-wrenching outcome, more student letters poured in.

Up north, the National Student League City College Evening Chapter in New York sent a Western Union telegram to Governor B.M. Miller on December 7, 1933, decrying the "outrageous procedure and decision of the Alabama courts [and] demand the immediate release of [the] boys and [the] removal of Judge Callahan[.] We hold you personally responsible for their safety."

As the holiday season was in full swing, fifteen-year-old Pearl Blumkin took on the White House. "Christmas is coming. It is a night of happiness and joy," she wrote. "Yet, in seven little homes sit seven mothers who will sit alone, mourning and brooding for their sons ... Why can't these boys be given a fair trial in the Northern states where Negroes are considered as we are?"

But President Franklin Roosevelt didn't intervene, leaving the fate of the Nine still hanging in the balance—their destiny resting solely on the ILD's shoulders.

Undeterred, Samuel and his legal defense team prepared to hit harder and go as far as needed to get a fair trial.

In 1934, Samuel took the case to Alabama's Supreme Court again, seeking a new trial, saying the jury pool in Judge William's court had been tampered with by including fictitious names of people that didn't exist to give the appearance of Black Americans being considered for the jury. He argued that the actual qualified African Americans who were registered to vote—a prerequisite to be on juries—had been intentionally kept off the pool. On June 28 of that same year, the court denied Samuel's request for a new trial.

A year later, in 1935, Samuel took his fight to the U.S. Supreme Court with the same claim, arguing that the Nine would never have a fair trial, as was their constitutional right, if Black Americans were systematically excluded from the jury. The counter to Samuel's argument was that the jury pool was technically open to everyone who met the criteria, including Black Americans. So, just because they weren't selected to the pool didn't make the process less fair. (This also happened to be against the backdrop of suffrage rights being limited for African Americans. There were higher barriers to participating in local, state, and federal elections—and often outright suppression. Limitations came in the form of literacy tests, poll taxes, fraud, felony laws, grandfather clauses, and intimidation.)

On April 1, 1935, in *Norris v. Alabama*, the Supreme Court agreed with Samuel. That historic case, with Clarence as the primary plaintiff, laid the foundation for the integration of Southern juries. Systematically excluding Black Americans on a jury, the Court concluded, denied the Nine of "equal protection under the law as guaranteed in the Fourteenth Amendment."

The Court ordered yet another trial, the fourth for the Nine's case.

That December, before appearing before Judge William again, Samuel and the ILD formed the Scottsboro Defense Committee along with four other groups: the American Civil Liberties Union, the NAACP (who could no longer ignore the groundswell of support), the League for Industrial Democracy, and the Methodist Federation for Social Service.

The Court date was set for January 1936.

The jury pool of one hundred included twelve African Americans. When each of the twelve were called to the court for the typical juror screening, they were challenged by the prosecution. They were each deemed biased toward the defendants because they were the same race.

So, again, an all-white jury heard the case.

Guilty.

The sentencing included varying periods in prison for the Nine, ranging from twenty to ninety-nine years. Clarence was the only one given the death penalty.

Following the convictions, twenty-three-year-old Juanita Jackson, the national NAACP youth director, stepped up. She had been responsible for developing the NAACP Youth and College Division programs within the NAACP Youth Council. This arm of the organization formally created an NAACP presence on campuses nationwide, including HBCUs, to educate young people about the economic and civil rights challenges minorities faced, fight back against lynchings, and encourage student leadership.

With the Scottsboro Nine's case emblematic of their cause, they leaped into action.

On November 20, 1936, alongside two other Birmingham NAACP leaders, E.W. Taggart and Laura Kellum, Juanita visited the Nine in jail. She gave them her word that she and students across the nation would fight for them. That thousands of young people across the nation were all standing by them. Juanita pledged that they'd rally, march, advocate, and lobby for the Nine until they were free.

Following her visit, Juanita encouraged NAACP Youth Councils and college chapters to initiate their own letter-writing campaign to the Nine to send messages of hope.

At Fisk University, students sent greeting cards, encouraging the Nine that they were behind them, fighting for their release. Meanwhile, other NAACP youth chapters organized a monumental letter-writing campaign to Congress in protest of the all-white jury's conviction, urging representatives to intervene.

Beyond letters, the NAACP youth chapters in Houston, Montgomery, and West Virginia contributed to the Nine's legal defense fund. For Christmas that year, Laura and her Birmingham Youth Council team visited the Nine on December 22 with gift baskets packed with fruits, snacks, and stationery.

Outside of HBCUs and other college campuses, the letters and rallies surged around the world, the uproar grew louder. It was clear to many outside the blinders of Southern justice that the Nine were innocent. The case underscored, for the first time in such a definitive and seismic way, that racism wasn't just a Southern—or American—problem, it was an international crisis.

With the mounting and ceaseless public outcry, justice would finally prevail.

More than five years after that Wednesday in March on that train headed West, the prosecutor dropped all charges against Roy, Olen, Willie, and Eugene. All, except Olen were the youngest of the bunch; Olen because of his deteriorating blindness.

A year later, on July 24, 1937, all charges against those four were officially dropped.

The governor later decided to pardon Roy and Eugene because they were the youngest of the Nine. The prosecutor later wrote a statement declaring Olen and Willie innocent. In a separate announcement that year, Ozie was also declared innocent but was held in prison until 1946 for his attack on the guard with a pocketknife during the transport from court where he was shot in the head.

In October 1938, the defense committee appealed to the governor to pardon the remaining four—Clarence, Haywood, Andrew, and Charles. He agreed but controversially revoked it at the last minute, without a clear reason.

Charles was eventually paroled in 1943, followed by Andy a year later. Clarence was paroled in 1944 and pardoned in 1976. Haywood was serving his seventy-five-year sentence in Kilby Prison when he escaped in 1948. The Federal Bureau of Investigation captured him months later in Michigan, but the Northern state's governor, Gerhard Mennen Williams, refused to extradite him to Alabama to finish his sentence.

More than a decade after what was to be a mundane ride in a boxcar, the Scottsboro Nine were all officially free but barely had their lives back. Psychologically and eternally scarred, some were in and out of the criminal justice system, unable to readjust to society.

Andy settled up North, first in New York and then in Connecticut. Save for another wrongful rape charge of a thirteen-year-old girl that was acquitted by an all-white jury in New York, he managed to live a low-key life, though an emotionally unstable one that purportedly involved a domestic violence incident with a girlfriend. Willie died of an asthma attack. Charles settled in Atlanta, married, and worked in a laundromat for some time until his death. Eugene moved to St. Louis to be with his family, married, had children, and lived under the radar. Their death dates remain unknown.

Jailed for a man's death during a bar fight in Detroit, Haywood died of cancer in prison on August 24, 1952.

Olen struggled with alcoholism and moved between Atlanta and New York until his death. LeRoy went on to serve in the merchant marine and got married, but later killed his wife and himself when he learned she cheated on him. Both men died in 1959.

Following the shot to his head after he sliced the deputy's neck, Ozie suffered permanent brain damage. He lived out his adult years in Georgia and died in 1973.

Clarence died at seventy-six of Alzheimer's in 1989.

The Nine's case is the first grave glimpse of prolonged criminal injustice, of just how glaring white supremacy is sewn into policing and law. It illuminates the political history of overcriminalization and the institutionality of racism.

Many of the same hallmarks exist in today's justice system.

Did the Nine have hope of one day becoming more than their circumstance? Because that was the ultimate tragedy. Here were these young men dragged into history before their lives began. Yet, there was a courage they clung to that allowed them to survive and endure. Even when they were regularly reminded of their degradation by being called "boys."

There's power in words and the intentionality behind how we use them. The same labeling has been used in modern times by law enforcement, prominently in Southern police departments, like the Louisville Police Department, which was responsible for Breonna Taylor's 2020 death. In 2023, the Department of Justice released the findings of its investigation into the LPD, in part saying officers regularly called Black people "monkey," "animal," and "boy."

For the same degrading language that was used against the Scotts-boro Nine to remain almost one hundred years later is ominous. It's an indication of history's warnings about irrefutable dehumaniza-tion within the criminal justice system, which operates on intoler-ance and prejudice. It's a blaring signal that history has not been a reminder, rather an obfuscation, because it hasn't been made evident in everyday life. It seems foreign, and old, and irrelevant. And that's the persistent problem. One that America would encounter yet again fifty-eight years after the Nine's case in the Central Park Five.

Five Black American teens were convicted of raping a white woman in New York City's Central Park in 1989.

The parallels, unmistakable. The symptom the same.

The five young men were all exonerated years after their arrest and imprisonment when a known and convicted rapist confessed. Like the Nine, the Five had their lives interrupted for simply existing.

Each one was somebody's child.

Each one was somebody. Full stop.

"Working class boys, we asks you to save us from being burnt on the electric chair. We's only poor working class boys whose skin is black. We shouldn't die for that."

The Nine's case changed the course of American history. They became unwilling sacrificial lambs for the progress later realized during the civil rights movement—the same strides we benefit from today, though the scales of justice remain uneven.

"We shouldn't die for that."

Yet, that remains the reality for those born on the other side of America's ideals.

3

AN UPRISING COMES

The Gentlemen's Agreement
& the Bates Seven

I will not just shut up and dribble . . .
I mean too much to the youth,
I mean too much to so many kids that feel like
they don't have a way out

LEBRON JAMES

As we settled in the Bronx, a treasured family time was watching Jeopardy *and basketball. My brothers were obsessed with the New York Knicks. But these were the nineties, so everybody was a Michael Jordan superfan. Even Mom became a fan, jumping up and down at his impressive, decisive jump shots.*

My brother Anthony—we call him AO—saved up his little allowance and coins he'd get from recycling bottles at CTown Supermarket to buy the reversible Chicago Bulls windbreaker jacket Michael often sported. I still see it: The big bull on the back, one side red, the other black, with splashes of white. He only wore the black side after the Bloods tried to jump him one time for wearing their color. The corner boys had his back that day.

And sure enough, like many boys across the world, Michael inspired AO into sports.

By the time the kid hit high school, he was on nearly every team.

His basketball skills were so amazing (read this with sisterly admiration) he was invited to an all-star summer camp one year. My brother Danny—he's second after Manny—jokingly called him "All-American."

To this day, this is a family bit Danny recites. "All-American." I always smile when he does this because I think that was the point for AO, particularly the "American" part. Sports was a way for him to assimilate further. He was demarcating an identity strongly rooted in America—in Black culture.

Generally, that's what sports do. They inspire. However, the earliest expressions of sports, from baseball to basketball to football, were riddled with hate and division. Only certain people were allowed on the fields and courts. This is precisely why the focus of this chapter and decade is on the Bates Seven. The students' stance against racism in sports is a watershed moment in history that underscores the importance of exposing discrimination wherever it lurks. Underpinning that stance were the first glimpses of allyship. America boasts free speech and liberation as the foundation of democracy, a shield against totalitarianism, and a bedrock rooted in liberty and agency. But, the application of these ideals has been historically subjective. The Bates Seven serve as a stark reminder of the ongoing struggle.

The Seven were the first radical formation of young white allies. They challenged America's claim of sports as a unifier. If it were indeed so, then why were the rights of all Americans not recognized on the many fields and courts? The Seven stepped in when Leonard Bates, a Black fullback football player at New York University, was sidelined when playing Southern schools because of a racist rule dubbed the "Gentlemen's Agreement," which demanded Black athletes from Northern integrated teams not play during games with Southern segregated schools.

Unearthing this ordeal reminded me of Mahmoud Abdul-Rauf and Colin Kaepernick.

In 1996 when NBA player Mahmoud, who had converted to Islam years prior, and with what seemed a new enlightenment, began protesting the national anthem, saying the flag symbolized oppression and subjugation of all Others. So, during the anthem, *he'd shut his eyes, lower his head, and cup his hands inches away from his face in prayer. Shortly after he began expressing his religious freedom, his house was burned down in response. Reports say the arson was perpetrated by KKK members.*

Similarly, against a series of 2016 injustices—fatal police shootings of two unarmed Black men, Alton Sterling and Philando Castile; the police shooting of another unarmed Black man, Charles Kinsey; and the acquittal of police officers involved in the death of yet another Black man, Freddie Gray—NFL star quarterback Colin began taking a knee in protest during the national anthem to call attention to the perpetuated nature of racism and Black death.

Because of this, both men were blacklisted, their careers stalemated.

There remains a coordinated effort to relegate Black athletes to helots, to reduce their agency and achievements to mere spectacles within the American pastime. It's telling of America that when challenged for its failure to uphold its own founding principles, those who dare speak up are penalized for what the Constitution guarantees: freedom of speech and of agency—to simply be one's self.

This is the crux of the Seven's story.

OCTOBER 1, 1940. NEW YORK, NEW YORK.

The Second World War was in full swing after erupting on September 1, 1939, in Europe.

America joined Great Britain and the Soviet Union after Japan's bombing of Pearl Harbor, the U.S. Naval Base in Hawaii, on December 7, 1941. Together, they fought the Axis powers of Germany, Italy, and Japan.

At the same time, about 25 percent of the U.S. population—over 33 million—had been recovering from an all-time-high unemployment rate from the Depression. While that number dropped to 10 percent during this period, people still had to deal with immense inflation that caused the dollar to lose value.

Christened one of the deadliest wars in history, with almost

80 million lives lost, World War II also necessitated enormous spending and the employment of more than 12 million Americans in the military. The same went for required defense jobs. And with the draft age reduced from twenty-one to eighteen, more opportunities were available for young people who had struggled through the last decade. These positions began to lift the country out of financial despair, eventually putting an end to the Depression. Later, in 1944, Franklin Roosevelt signed the G.I. Bill, which provided benefits for World War II veterans, further helping the struggling economy.

When the guns fell silent on September 2, 1945, America and its allies claimed victory. This triumph ushered in a new chapter with the formation of the United Nations, an international organization dedicated to fostering peace and collaboration between nations. Yet, the postwar era was far from tranquil.

Devastated cities and economies demanded rebuilding, the specter of the Cold War loomed large, and the fight for decolonization raged across the globe.

Most pressing, however, was the glaring disconnect between wartime rhetoric of national unity and the lived experience of many Black Americans who continued to face racial disparities that only grew more pervasive. Discrimination and segregation, perpetuated by Jim Crow laws, remained deeply entrenched. And thanks to the wartime surge in interest in the pastime, this extended to sports, where racist policies denied Black athletes equal opportunities.

Segregation in sports was already enduring, with African American athletes often barred from competing at high levels and shunted to separate leagues and teams. The Negro Leagues, for example, were formed in 1920 in response to the exclusion of Black players from Major League Baseball. This blatant exclusion not only hindered individual careers but also perpetuated the larger social and economic inequalities facing African Americans in the nation.

This is what Leonard Bates faced upon his enrollment at New York University in the fall of 1939.

Like many Black teens affected by the Great Depression, Leonard had dropped out of high school. It took him five years to return and complete his diploma. The hefty, muscular kid was hard to miss, and a friend who knew Leonard as a skilled football player recommended him to a former coach working with NYU's team. Soon after, the nineteen-year-old was recruited and admitted to the Violets on a full athletic scholarship as the squad's starting fullback, making him the only Black athlete on the team that season.

A born-and-bred New York City kid, Leonard entered NYU's School of Education and immediately struggled to adapt to life on campus among the roughly 40,000 mostly white student body, facing discrimination both on and off the field. Racism was still rampant in the North, albeit not as explicit as it was in the South. Leonard felt this firsthand, from professors to his head coach, Mal Stevens. Mal was notoriously elitist and had no qualms about playing against Jim Crow schools, where his new recruit would no doubt be sidelined because of the "Gentlemen's Agreement" among the coaches.

That term dates back to 1890 and refers to secretive agreements among white male members of the upper class. Gentlemen's Agreements were common in sports organizations as an informal way to bar Black athletes from playing in the South, and were adopted by the National Association of Baseball Players and the National Football League. And since national leagues were seemingly open about discriminating against Black players, college athletics followed suit.

The first teams to agree to these pacts were elite, predominantly Northern white schools, such as Boston College, Colgate, Dartmouth, Harvard, the University of Michigan, and New York University. Many times, the schools even falsely documented that their Black athletes couldn't play in the Southern games due to illness or injury.

When Leonard joined NYU that fall, the campus was buzzing with protests of all kinds, from demonstrations against fascism to pro-communist marches to pacifism movements. This was the kind of progressive foundation the school was built on. But when it came to sports and the little-known but widespread practice of benching Black athletes, the school's liberal stance seemed to ring hollow. There was a clear disconnect between its ideals and its actions.

Before Leonard's arrival, NYU had already displayed its allegiance to upholding Jim Crow in sports. That habit of exclusion traced back more than sixty years prior, to 1873, when NYU's football program was founded. Though the school maintained an image of being radical, its athletic department didn't reflect this and implicitly embraced the nonbinding policy of exclusion that indisputably alienated Black athletes.

For example, in the 1920s, the football program recruited halfback Dave Myers. Upon his enrollment, NYU agreed to exclude him from a game against the University of Georgia. This sparked an outcry on campus. The students tamely demanded that Dave be allowed to play, otherwise the game should be canceled. NYU ignored the students' pleas and proceeded with the game under Georgia's segregation policies. It was seen by students as evidence that NYU was no different from its Southern counterparts when it came to racial discrimination.

This happened against the backdrop of 1920s racism, when its rigor and tenor were stronger, brewing the early stages of student uprisings. By the time Leonard donned his Violets jersey, a clear road map for resistance had been established. And so the *how* of the matter—how to organize, how to galvanize, how to amplify voices—was better understood by students. With these tactics in hand, the stage was set for a resurgence of student activism.

On October 4, 1940, *The New York Times* published a piece on Mal, the NYU football team coach, and, in a brief mention, publicly declared for the first time that Leonard, the "210-pound Negro thunderbolt," would not play against the University of Missouri in their scheduled game on November 2 at the Southern school's Columbia field.

The news traveled fast across campus. When Leonard's teammates stormed the school's student council meeting, outraged, even more students learned of NYU's decision to bench Leonard—who had become a star player the team needed to secure wins—from the Missouri game. Students en masse supported him playing and decried the Jim Crow policy, a rule most students didn't even know existed or that it was upheld by their liberal school.

As the outcry swelled, the school revealed that Leonard knew about the agreement to sideline him in Southern games. The schedule for the 1940–1941 season, the school representatives said, had already been determined and the agreement to not have any Black players on Southern fields had been finalized before Leonard arrived. The school's representatives went on to say that his coaches had informed him of this upon signing him to the Violets. They said that his coaches also let Leonard know that for the 1941–1942 season, they had worked out an agreement to have all games against Missouri played on the NYU field.

That explanation didn't sit well with the student body. The *Washington Square College Bulletin*, NYU's student newspaper, accused the administration of being hypocritical for trying to resolve a substantial, foundational race matter by simply moving the Missouri games to New York in an attempt to save face, while still being willing to continue athletic ties with Missouri, who abided by biased regulations.

But Leonard, no doubt under pressure to keep his spot on the team, agreed: If that was NYU's stance, he wouldn't play any schools in the South.

Fourteen days after the October piece in the *Times*, seven NYU students who strongly opposed the Gentlemen's Agreement and Leonard's exclusion, and who had met at different student council meetings, organized and led a mass crusade against his plight: Anita Krieger Appleby, Jean Bornstein Azulay, Mervyn Jones, Naomi Bloom Rothschild, Robert Schoenfeld, Argyle Stoute, and Evelyn Maisel Witkin. All but one, Argyle, a Black American, were white.

Later known as the "Bates Seven," they rebuked the school for being pro-segregation in the South while supporting integration in the North. NYU can't sideline one of its teammates, they declared, and let bigotry win. Instead, why not be an example?

Under Argyle's leadership, more than 2,000 students and supporters rallied. Their message was clear: placards emblazoned with the slogan "Bates Must Play," filled picketed lines outside the school's administration building. Other posters demanded an end to the Gentlemen's Agreement. In bold letters, some called for the rejection of "Nazi Games" and "Missouri Compromise." Most handbills and banners pleaded with the administration: "Don't Ban Bates," "End Jim Crow in Sports," and "End Jim Crowism at NYU."

After that, the "Bates Must Play!" student committee was officially formed. More mobilizations and petitions followed, where students chanted, "Bates must play! Bates must play!" This became the cause's spark of defiance.

On October 21, 1940, the "Bates Must Play!" committee petitioned for four demands:

1. Bates must be free of the Gentlemen's Agreement

2. NYU must state where they stand on Jim Crow and the Gentlemen's Agreement

3. NYU should not agree to such terms with any Southern schools employing Jim Crow laws

4. If the demands are not met, there will be a boycott of all NYU home games for the rest of the 1940–1941 season

The committee rigorously continued its on-campus protest over the next ten days in the lead-up to the November 2 game.

They distributed petitions requesting Leonard play or for the school to withdraw from the game altogether.

They recruited and partnered with other campus student organizations.

They created and passed around "Bates Must Play!" buttons.

They handed out flyers outlining their demands and their cause.

They organized daily demonstrations and marched around campus.

Each time, they belted out, "Bates must play!" and "Jim Crow's gotta go!"

They gathered more than 4,000 student signatures (about 10 percent of the total student body) on their petition, and some 2,000 students rallied with them on picket lines.

The Seven's efforts marked the first mass demonstration, at any school, against Jim Crow in college football. It was so stirring it received nationwide media coverage, especially from Black-owned publications such as the *Baltimore Afro-American, Chicago Defender, Philadelphia Afro-American*, and the *Pittsburgh Courier.*

Publications like *The New York Times*, on the other hand, treaded ever so carefully, interspersing mentions of the rallies within broader coverage of Mal, the coach, or the team's games.

In one such article about a match-up between NYU and Holy Cross, the first "Bates Seven" demonstration received a brief mention toward the end of the piece: "Bates was the unwitting cause of student protest yesterday at the university. Twenty undergraduate organizations circulated petitions demanding that the school cancel its game with Missouri on November 2, at Columbia, because of insistence by Missouri officials that the Negro player be kept out of the game."

The October 19, 1940, article ends by referencing a private letter that Leonard sent to student clubs, addressed to the Negro Cultural Society's president, confirming directly to students that he was aware of the agreement upon arriving on campus.

Days later, on October 30, a press conference was held by NYU's administration in response to the disruptive and persisting "Bates Must Play!" demonstrations. The school's press director, George Sheiebler, after getting his hands on the private letter, publicly read Leonard's words, hoping it would allay the student body's concerns and quell any further protesting by suggesting that Leonard himself was fine being left behind.

> *In view of the situation, which had been precipitated by the question of whether I would play in the football game between New York University and the University of Missouri at Columbia, Missouri, on November 2, I feel it necessary to clarify my position in the matter.*
>
> *When I entered New York University, it was explained to me in a perfectly friendly manner by the University Board of Athletic Control that a series of games had*

already been arranged between New York University and Missouri in which I would be unable to participate in so far as those games played in Missouri were concerned. At that time, I stated I did not wish to play in the game scheduled to be played at Columbia, Mo.

My major concern has been to gain a college education. Football is a secondary matter.

The day after the press office released his private statement, Leonard responded to its weaponization: "By playing up one part of this letter, the press succeeded in creating the impression that I do not wish to play. This, however, is false. I would like to play."

Two days later, on November 2, the NYU Violets played the Missouri Tigers as planned, without Leonard.

They lost, 33–0.

The resistance of the Bates Seven spread across campus and gained momentum weeks later when another Black athlete faced a parallel predicament.

That December, Jim Coward, a transfer basketball player from Brooklyn College, was sidelined during two games at the University of North Carolina and Georgetown University. NYU administrators said it was because Jim was not academically eligible—saying he was short a few credits—when he transferred.

The Seven, along with other student activists, who had learned about Jim's ineligibility both by word of mouth and from the student-run paper, were all the wiser by this point. Challenging the administration once more, they declared that Jim's exclusion was similarly due to the South's disenfranchising policies and its influence on college sports. If Jim was qualified to transfer to NYU's varsity athletics program, why did the school now decide to deem him ineligible?

"He felt it was unfair," Tyrone, Jim's son, later said of his father's benching, "because he had done everything he'd been asked to do."

When UNC's coach announced that Jim and any other Black

athletes from NYU could play at their games, NYU's chancellor, Harry Woodburn Chase, said he preferred to keep in line with the status quo, responding, "The time has not arrived when we can ask southern schools to play against negro players on southern campuses." This further reinforced the belief among NYU student activists that the institution was complicit in perpetuating and upholding Jim Crow practices.

Adding fuel to their growing conviction of NYU's discriminatory agenda, student protestors faced yet another blatant example in February 1941: the exclusion of Black runners from a meet. The school's track team left three of its Black athletes behind when they went to Washington, D.C., to compete against the Catholic University of America, a conservative school that participated in the Gentlemen's Agreement.

By this point, the student demonstrators had had enough: Leonard in November, Jim in December, the track athletes in February. Activism among the students soared across campus. Their focus transitioned from "Bates Must Play!" to demanding, through petitions, that NYU's administration abandon their support for Jim Crow policies once and for all and stand up against schools perpetuating such hate and division.

"I was ready to fight," Anita, one of the Seven, later recalled. "Not in a physical manner, but with words."

The Seven's persistence came to a head one day in March 1941, just weeks following the track athletes being left behind.

During lunch that day, the Seven were in the cafeteria petitioning the sidelining, "which had always been a right at NYU—a general American right," Jean, another of the Seven, later said. She saw the dean of women, the dean of student affairs, the president of student council, and the controller of student council all eyeing their demonstration table, as they gathered signatures for their petition. Some of the Seven took what they considered to be an act of intimidation to the head dean. But instead of support, they were shocked to hear the dean side with those the Seven saw as aggressors, telling them that it was in fact illegal to petition on the school's campus.

They were instructed to stop their actions.

When they refused to call off their campaign, NYU's administration began disciplinary hearings against them. In the end, it resulted in a three-month suspension and expulsion. The cited reason? Circulating petitions without permission from the university.

The Seven felt the outlandish, retaliatory sanction was a deliberate move to stifle their dissent and voice.

"We were all gung-ho," Robert remembered. "We had no idea that we were gonna get in any kind of trouble. I mean, after all, this is America, free speech, you know. And we were kids." He added that the rationale for their suspension was an "obscure rule that no one knew about that it was illegal to circulate papers in the cafeteria." Anita similarly saw it as a form of punishment, while Jean remembered feeling "absolutely numb."

Naomi couldn't fathom how the school could respond in such a punitive way, saying, "it was just incomprehensible that for wanting the school to do something right, they'd suspend us." Evelyn outright blamed their suspension on the increased publicity the Seven were receiving: "Sports columnists were writing about it in the New York papers [and] there were some administrators who were pretty vicious about it." While Jean simply framed it as "we had caused a lot of trouble."

Later, in a written statement to the Judson Hall Disciplinary Committee, most of the Seven claimed they had only received their suspension notices "three minutes" before being suspended. To fight their suspensions, they rallied on- and off-campus for support. They called newspapers, spoke with faculty members, while some sat down with columnists to tell their stories.

At a disciplinary committee meeting, the Seven pleaded their case. At the packed public hearing, more than 500 students showed up in solidarity. The Seven and their movement had even managed to get Eleanor Roosevelt, the nation's first lady, to visit the school during the hearing. The intention, Robert remembered, was to have her support their plight, but she never explicitly did so. He remembered she asked for peace and reasoning, and that she later told Anita, one-on-one, that "it takes time to bring justice between Black and white."

By the trial's end, nothing had changed for the Seven. It seemed all for show, they later said, because the same administrators who had suspended them were the same ones overseeing the hearing. Even with their suspension and their future in peril, their actions inspired other students to form yet another student petition, this time decrying the treatment of the Seven.

Stationed outside the school, thousands of student leaders and demonstrators signed on. The petition read:

> *We, the undersigned students, call for the immediate, unconditional reinstatement of the 7 students who have been suspended until June for circulating the following petitions:*
>
> *We call upon the Board of Athletic Control to send our Negro track stars to the meet sponsored by Catholic University in Washington on March 10.*
>
> *We students uphold the right of our Negro track men to participate in this meet.*
>
> *We call upon the Board of Athletic Control to halt its policy of Negro discrimination in sports which has brought dishonor to N.Y.U.*
>
> *We demand the abolition of the policy which bans Negro athletes from competing on southern campuses.*

The suspensions remained and came with personal costs.

Some of the Seven, who were seniors at the time, were forced to attend summer school to matriculate. Jean remembered how the forced three months away from classes "interrupted a couple of people getting into med school."

Despite these setbacks and while not achieving a decisive victory for Leonard and the other players they advocated for, the Seven's stalwart efforts resonated beyond their personal experiences. And like Ella Baker's grassroots organizing and the Scottsboro Nine case and galvanizations, their struggle signaled that the *third rail* of American politics and social change remained race, just as it does today. Their actions sparked a renewed wave of student-led activism, revealing a new generation's commitment to formative action. The Seven were not looking for this moment, the moment found them. Or as Anita put it, "We were not social friends. We were just decent human beings who had a cause."

Two decades before the formal civil rights movement would seize the soul of America, these seven students led a groundbreaking demonstration against discriminatory athletic policies, reminding the nation of its unfulfilled promise of racial equality enshrined in the Constitution. Their determined campaign, marked by tenacious rallies and petitions, helped shape the fight against Jim Crow in college sports.

"We just did it," Jean later said of the crusade. "It was one of these things which we had to do. When I look back now, I'm so impressed."

Each of the Seven had a story and a future temporarily interrupted when their school's administration, threatened by the students' challenge, attempted to halt their lives. The students found one another in their pursuit of righteousness for an-Other.

"For somebody who really didn't do anything more than be commendable, this was a slap . . . it was an unhappy period. It never should've been . . . I never regretted having done what I did because I still think 'Jim Crow's Gotta Go!'"

Anita Krieger Appleby once jokingly said she chose New York University over a school in Wisconsin because it had a much better, active dating scene. When the Leonard movement began, she was a senior studying social work. The anguish she once felt was still palpable during an interview decades later, as she remembered the school removing her senior picture from the yearbook. In fact, she never even got a yearbook. After completing her required semester of summer school, she went on to graduate schools at Columbia University and NYU and lectured with the City University of New York until she retired in the 2000s.

She died on September 12, 2007.

"There I was, sitting with the Chancellor at one end of the table, Mrs. Goode next to him. This is a big big Trustees meeting room, with a big big table. [The Chancellor says,] 'But Mrs. Goode, you know, NYU has this great policy; we are the most liberal university in the whole country. We hired James Weldon Johnson [a civil rights activist and Black writer]. And we were the first university to hire a Black professor, and he was a full professor.' And [Mrs. Goode] says, 'James Weldon Johnson, that Uncle Tom.'"

When Rutgers denied **Jean Bornstein Azulay's** college application for the journalism school because it had reached its "Jewish quota," she changed her major and decided to attend NYU. She quickly became active on campus, rising to become the vice president of student council. During the campaign for Leonard, the then twenty-year-old did plenty of outreach to garner outside support. At one point, her efforts landed her in a meeting with a well-known local activist and the school's chancellor, Harry Woodburn Chase. That came to be after she reached out to Paul Robeson—a famed musician, former NFL player, and activist—who was once enrolled at NYU's law school but left for Columbia after a year. Unable to make the meeting, but in support of the Seven's protest, Paul reached out to Harry to set up a meeting with Jean and his activist mother-in-law, Eslanda Goode, to discuss the Gentlemen's Agreement and how the school was failing its Black athletes in siding with the policy.

Jean died at eighty-six on June 28, 2008.

"When I was young, I was certain that the world would be socialist by 1950 at the latest. Now it's 1987, I am no longer

young and I'm left wondering what went wrong ... [The government has] failed to take account of the central place that the value of personal freedom holds in modern minds."

Mervyn Jones was one of two Bates Seven members who would never return or graduate from NYU due to the suspension. He'd moved from London in 1939 at seventeen and began at NYU that August. A burgeoning writer, Mervyn came up in upper-middle-class Regent's Park in London and attended Abbotsholme Arts Society, a progressive boarding school where he was a member of the Young Communist League. A family dispute over his higher education landed Mervyn in America. His father, Ernest, renowned psychoanalyst and biographer of Sigmund Freud, wanted his only son to go to Oxford, where he was accepted, but Mervyn, a sworn Marxist, rejected that idea, especially as the war brewed. This led his father to send him off to New York, with his mother, Mary, by his side. Focused on the arts, especially the work of Wystan Hugh Auden, a British American poet, it was Mervyn's continued focus on socialism that made the plight of Leonard most enticing. Following the suspension, during his sophomore year, he returned home in 1942 and joined the army that November. He'd go on to become a seasoned journalist and novelist, publishing twenty-four books, including his 1987 memoir, *Chances: An Autobiography.*

Mervyn died at eighty-seven on February 23, 2010.

"It colored my whole adult life—about, should I do something."

NYU piqued **Naomi Bloom Rothschild's** interest when she heard the school had a good sociology program, something she'd always been interested in. She also wanted to be close to home in New York City, where she was born and raised. A year after the demonstrations, in 1942, she graduated and completed a master's in art education. She later moved to New Jersey with her husband and son. She dedicated the majority of her life to civic duty, volunteering regularly with organizations such as the Bergen County Rape Center, the Center for Food Action, Englewood Ambulance Corps and Englewood Hospital, the Lenox Hill Neighborhood Association, and the National Council of Jewish Women.

Naomi died on November 16, 2014, two months after she celebrated her ninety-fourth birthday on September 11.

"George Barnard Shaw once said, 'If you're not a radical when you're young, you have no spirit. If you're still a radical when you're old, you're a fool.'"

Robert Schoenfeld was enrolled in NYU's unified studies, part of its liberal arts program at the time. He chose the school because his parents wanted him to stay home in New York City. He was inspired by the movements on campus and rose to become the president of the Young Communist League, which is how he became involved in the Bates protest. He called the Bates crew a "group of lefties" who wanted to do something constructive about the Jim Crow policy impacting Black athletes—that he and others in the fight "were gonna teach the school a lesson." He wrote and printed most of the fliers used during the demonstrations, remembering in a later interview that "there were many a corner that I stood on. I would write a leaflet, run it off on a mimeograph machine and stand outside and hand out leaflets. I was the leading left winger on the campus."

"It is a sad commentary that a campaign such as this is necessary to ensure the participation of a colored athlete . . . The very essence of sport is fair play."

After the Seven's suspension in the spring of 1941, the only African American of the group, **Argyle Stoute**, transferred to the University of Wisconsin–Madison. There, he earned his bachelor's and master's in psychology, eyeing a career in psychoanalysis as it relates to race and racism.

During his time at Madison, he became the first Black man to serve as president of the national honorary psychology society, Psi Chi, and president of the interracial group Negro Culture Association, whose goal was to advocate for the rights of Black Americans and preserve Black history. Argyle also organized protests in support of a Black professor, Arthur Burke, who had been promised accommodations at an exclusive university residence, but, upon his arrival in the fall of 1944, was denied when they saw he was African American. The demonstration was successful, and a year later Arthur was granted entry to the University Club as promised. After more than two decades in his field, Argyle received his doctorate at Sorbonne University in Paris. He learned to speak Spanish, German, and French and write in Latin, and once served in the all-Black infantry, Harlem Hellfighters. (During the First World War, they were the most prominent Black combat regiment and part of the New York Army National Guard.)

Argyle died on July 17, 2004, at ninety-seven.

"[The movement] changed the direction of my life."

Evelyn Maisel Witkin had a scholarship to Cornell but attended NYU instead to be closer to her family. She was an active member of the student council, which is how she became one of the leaders of the Bates campaign. A biology major and senior at the time, she was unable to graduate with her class due to the suspension and was forced to take summer school to complete her degree. She had performed so well academically that by her senior year, she had an offer for a graduate assistantship with the school's biology department. However, it was rescinded when she was suspended. "I wouldn't have wanted to stay there had it not been withdrawn," she later said. After completing her degree that summer in 1941, she attended Columbia for graduate work in biology, working under renowned geneticist Theodosius Dobzhansky.

Evelyn went on to have a celebrated career in genetics, with her research primarily focused on DNA repair. In 2002, she was awarded the National Medal for Science by President George W. Bush, and thirteen years later was the recipient of the Lasker Award—a prized award given to stellar practitioners in medicine—for her significant contribution to science.

Evelyn died on July 8, 2023, at one hundred and two.

"I remember the bogus way the athletic department tried to [frame] my letter. They made it sound like I did not want to play. I very much wanted to play Missouri."

As for **Leonard Bates**, throughout the Seven's determined push to see him play, he walked a tightrope. Despite knowing the risks of defying segregationist practices, he ultimately stood with the Seven and the students who rallied for him. His love for the game burned bright, undimmed by prejudice. Leonard went on to graduate from NYU and had a successful career in business.

He died at eighty-seven in 2006.

By the mid-1940s, fueled by escalating nationwide protests from students like the Seven, many universities, including NYU, started to abandon the discriminatory Gentlemen's Agreement. This shift garnered national and political attention, marking a significant step toward racial equality in college athletics.

That transformation began reverberating in national sports too. In 1946, three African American men from the University of California, Los Angeles, football team desegregated football and baseball. One of the men was Jackie Robinson, who became the first Black American to play on an all-white Major League Baseball team when the Brooklyn Dodgers signed him. The other two were signed to the National Football League's Los Angeles Rams: running back Kenny Washington and offensive end Woody Strode.

While the Seven's actions on their university's campus contributed to the dismantling of the Jim Crow–era sports agreement, NYU's football program shut down in 1953. The school's chancellor, Harry Woodburn Chase, pointed to its lackluster performance (in total, the team had 199 wins, 226 losses, and 30 ties) and dwindling interest in the team, saying at the time, "For the past two years football has been conducted at a considerable [financial] deficit [of $100,000], and the university cannot retain the sport any further."

As for the Seven's legacy at NYU, it wouldn't be until May 4, 2001, on the sixtieth anniversary of their activism, that they finally received due recognition at a celebratory dinner, highlighting their enduring impact of courage and perseverance in the fight for racial equality in sports.

The Seven's defiance emboldened generations to fight injustice, big and small. Their plight proves that even a few can create consequential change. Their battle spirit continues to power today's ongoing warfare against bigotry in sports.

In 2018, for example, Fox anchor Laura Ingraham chastised LeBron James for his criticism of Donald Trump's continued intolerance and prejudice. She told him to "shut up and dribble." Her comment, dripping with condescension, suggested his worth was to entertain and nothing more. The implication was clear: athletes' voices don't matter, especially Black athletes like LeBron. Yet, LeBron has defied odds upon odds, every stacked deck, to reach a pinnacle many only see in dreams.

When we shut down voices speaking against injustices, we inadvertently perpetuate these very injustices. Such dismissive responses from the Lauras of the world continue to fuel the discrimination they seek to silence. Some conveniently forget that sports, while celebrated for uniting diverse crowds, often nurture racial inequities. Once the cheers fade off the field, they are replaced by barriers limiting upward mobility for many. This "us vs. them" mentality, rooted in history, persists because it benefits those who choose to turn a blind eye.

This is a stark departure from what the Seven's journey ought to teach us: It is priceless to show empathy but costly to nourish suffering. Empathy, then, is our duty. Ignoring structural racism allows it to fester and inflict harm on today's generation and those to come. So, then, the toll of inaction is high: lost potential, shattered dreams, and continued injustice. As the Seven reminded us, respect must extend to all, and we can never honor that principle while ignoring the systemic barriers that hold so many back.

Though it didn't achieve its immediate goal, the "Bates Must Play!" campaign ignited a powerful spark of solidarity. The relentless war drumbeat of Leonard's allies amplified his voice, likely bringing him more joy than any single game. In the face of blatant oppression, their unwavering support offered him a glimmer of hope and, I believe, a deep sense of solace, knowing he wasn't alone.

Ultimately, the Seven's actions demonstrated that persistent progress demands the active participation of all. It beckons every voice, especially those cloaked in privilege, to step forward, join hands across the racial chasm, and amplify the demands for true unity until the landscape itself reflects the weight of our combined responsibility.

PART II

THE BROWN V. BOARD OF EDUCATION GENERATION & THE CIVIL RIGHTS ERA

4

THE CIVIL RIGHTS MOVEMENT

Barbara Johns

It was time that Negroes were treated equally with whites,
time that they had a decent school, time for the students
themselves to do something about it . . .
There wasn't any fear.
I just thought, "This is your moment, seize it."

BARBARA JOHNS

By the time I hit high school in the 2000s, Mom had achieved one
of her American Dreams. She bought a house in the North Bronx.
The 2 train went there too. To the 219 stop, right by the Golden
Krust on White Plains Road we frequented for some beef patties
and coco bread. Oxtails with rice and peas on some Sundays after
church.

The North Bronx wasn't safer than the South Bronx, though
I think that was Mom's push to move us there. Corner boys still
guarded territories. Bloods with their reds on one block, Crips with
their blues on the next. One time, Danny, sporting a blue Mavericks
jersey on the wrong turf, almost got jumped. Despite such assimilation challenges, we persisted, adopting Black culture in our hunger
for belonging.

Meanwhile, I was still trying to understand Blackness—trying to figure me out—in the vastness of America. This feeling only intensified when I started at Manhattan Center for Science and Mathematics High School. It was a diverse student body, and soon enough as different cultures—Asians, Hispanics, Caucasians, Black Americans and immigrants—unfolded before me, I delved deeper into my Blackness, into my identity. And for the first time, it dawned on me: Blackness wasn't singular. Black immigrants and Black Americans shared a racial experience, homogenized by the "African American" label irrespective of our diverse backgrounds. This mask only obscures our distinct stories, revealing just how fraught identity can be.

That realization resonated powerfully when AP history came around, and I began unraveling the complexities of what made America, America. While I didn't recognize it then, this exploration sowed a potent seed of belonging that heightened my craving for a home in this once-foreign land.

High school was also the first time I felt I had a civic responsibility in a country that hadn't felt like home since arriving in 1995. Discovering more about America in classes, forming genuine bonds with others, and cultivating an identity as Black, as "African American," charged a nascent sense of belonging, a possibility that America could be home.

Longing for community, I engaged more with my school and neighborhood. I ran student government. I coordinated outreach programs for those navigating food insecurity. I was part of an inaugural City Hall leadership program that partnered me with a Black female executive—a mentorship and relationship that forever changed how I interacted with America as a Black woman. In her, I saw who I could be in this country for the first time.

Everything was lining up: My agency blossomed as I developed a sense of purpose, trying to cling to this new home that was becoming increasingly familiar, a place of refuge and solace, even. I see so much of that same discovery and reconciliation in Barbara Johns.

At sixteen, she realized that her all-Black high school in her hometown of Prince Edward County, Virginia, faced substandard conditions. Compared to the white-only school with better accommodations and resources, Barbara's school was overcrowded, had no cafeteria, no gym, and no running water. Students were forced to share textbooks and sit on the floor.

Infuriated, Barbara organized a strike in protest, confronting the superintendent, demanding improvements. As the protest grew in size and influence, it made national headlines and received support from the NAACP. Her galvanization was so successful the county's lawsuit became one of the five cases used during the Supreme Court hearing of the watershed Brown v. Board of Education.

As I scoured Barbara's life and this decade, most striking was the audacity of her measures juxtaposed against the period. Here was a teen who, like me entering high school, was walking into her autonomy and confronting her identity, but all of that was interrupted when she found herself steeped in the struggle to desegregate schools. All while navigating Jim Crow in Farmville, Virginia. All while struggling to fit in, grappling with a sense of displacement in what she had always called home, wading unjust limitations. And all she wanted was a home that felt like, well, home: safe and sound.

APRIL 23, 1951. FARMVILLE, VIRGINIA.

For Black Americans, the post–World War II years were different from prior decades.

The South remained riddled with Jim Crow laws, with mounting tensions between Blacks and whites. There was also a growing social and political awareness never seen before. This was partly due to the experiences of returning Black soldiers who fought in the war.

They had served their country with distinction while enduring the horrors of racism and discrimination. When they returned home, it continued: They and their families were still denied fundamental rights. But now, these Black veterans had developed a new sense of pride and self-confidence. They were no longer willing to accept the status quo. Their new demands for equal rights and opportunities led to a new wave of activism and protests, which helped put civil rights on the national agenda.

Their stronger stance was fueled by a few factors.

The Black middle class had been growing. The burgeoning civil rights movement was advancing in varying pockets of the country. And Black students' access to higher education was on the rise. Black Americans sought—and felt it was increasingly possible to fight for—equality in *all* areas of their life from education and employment to housing and voting.

This civil rights revolution, often called America's "Second Reconstruction," was primarily led by young people who pushed for greater racial inclusion. From the organizing at HBCUs to Juanita Jackson's NAACP Youth Council, the foundation was set for yet another national movement. Primarily because the continued execution of *Plessy v. Ferguson* was still in full effect in everyday life and remained a top priority for Black student activists.

That fight against legal segregation, against "separate but equal," gained significant momentum in 1934.

The NAACP, stewarded by chief legal counsel Charles Hamilton Houston with Thurgood Marshall, the then director and later chief attorney, by his side, embarked on a campaign for better school conditions for Black children in the South. Charles felt the fight against Jim Crow, against *Plessy v. Ferguson*, must be done in the courts through constitutional change. The organization's strategy was to present lawsuits demonstrating that schools for Black children were not equal to those for white children and, therefore, illegal. The NAACP believed if the South was forced to spend the same amount of money on Black schools as it did on white schools, white citizens would realize the economic inefficiency of maintaining two separate school systems.

The NAACP wasn't prepared for the opposition they received from white communities. They pushed on anyway. By 1950, despite years of legal challenges and federal court orders, school facilities for Black and white students remained separate and unequal. School boards did not see the relevance of integration nor did they consider having two school systems wasteful or inefficient.

Still, the NAACP was laser-focused on desegregating schools. They set into motion a strategy aimed at taking legal separation to court. The plan was simple: have Black families enroll their children in all-white schools, knowing what the outcome would be.

During the fall of 1950, in Topeka, Kansas, Linda Brown, a Black third grader, was denied admission to Sumner Elementary, an all-white school in her neighborhood. In what would become a landmark case, *Brown v. Board of Education*, the NAACP successfully scouted thirteen families, including the Browns (Oliver Brown, Linda's father, served as the lead plaintiff as their family's surname appeared first alphabetically), whose children were similarly segregated and denied access to Topeka's white elementary schools.

By early 1951, as the *Brown* case prepared to be filed in the Kansas courts, the NAACP continued their search for Black families from local communities across the South willing to sue for integration. They unexpectedly came to know about a brewing effort in a tiny community in Virginia, deep in the tobacco-growing region of Prince Edward County.

During this time, life in the rural backwater of Prince Edward County, Virginia, was drenched in segregation and bigotry. Surrounded by hilly tillage and old brick warehouses, with storefronts and churches on its Main Street, Farmville was the county's seat and largest town.

Black adults in Prince Edward County faced constant discrimination in the workplace. They were paid less than white workers for doing the same job. They were less likely to be promoted. Families also faced bias in housing and were repeatedly denied real estate in what were considered *white* neighborhoods. And even when they were allowed to rent or own, they were forced to pay higher prices than white families for comparable housing. Their children attended legally separated schools that were overcrowded with substandard facilities.

Yet, the Black community was an enterprising one. Despite its bare-bones funding, the Black public school system was a great engine of achievement and ambition for students. However, further advancement was rare as students were met with relentless barriers to quality higher education, whereas the resources provided to white students were far greater. Farmville High School, for example, had libraries, contemporary heating, art workshops, locker rooms, cafeterias, gardens, nurse's offices, and atriums. Robert Russa Moton High, the *Black* school, had none of those—it barely had proper infrastructure.

Built in 1939, Russa Moton was a small brick building cradled at a fork on Route 15. Next to the school's main building were additional classrooms cobbled together from wood and covered in tar-coated paper that students referred to as "chicken coops." The school had skeletal roofs that sprang leaks when it rained. Buckets were placed around classrooms to collect the streaming water. Some students were even forced to open their umbrellas while in class.

In the face of such continued neglect, with the school's disrepair becoming ever more apparent, fed up and appalled, some Russa Moton parents banded together to appeal to the all-white school board for improved facilities.

The board's response to the petition was swift and alarming. They felt if the requests for better accommodations and resources were approved, more people would want to go to school. More people would want an education, which was, of course, the principal point of the petition. The board also stated that it was following state laws in how they were handling Farmville and Russa Moton.

Separate but equal.

The petition was denied.

It exposed the school board's intentions toward the Black community: they were not welcomed or valued. What *more people* would want education if not Black Americans? And as the Black population of Farmville grew, the school board continued to refuse to address exacerbating issues like overcrowding, let alone deteriorating facilities and repeated requests from parents for a new school building. But as parents continued to lobby the board for a better-resourced facility, as a stopgap measure to accommodate the overflow of students, the board put up more tar-paper shacks instead.

Students had to attend classes in dilapidated sheds where the only source of heat on cold days was from potbelly wood-burning stoves, which would cause so much smoke to fill the rooms. Teachers often had to interrupt lectures to tend to the fire. Conditions got so shabby that teachers were forced to hold class on school buses.

One of the students forced to learn in such deprived conditions was sixteen-year-old junior Barbara Johns. Repeatedly denied a decent education and basic needs in crumbling classrooms, Barbara and her classmates carried an invisible weight of marginalization, nursing a quiet desperation for opportunity. This struggle went deeper than any physical or economic hardship. Grappling with it, they also faced a message parroted from birth: that they were less than deserving, breeding self-doubt, low self-esteem, and a fear that this could very well become their life sentence.

But Barbara saw it differently.

"We wanted so much here and had so little," she later recalled. "We had talents and abilities that weren't really being realized and I thought that was a tragic shame, and that was basically what motivated me to want to see some change take place."

Barbara was frustrated by the refusal of the school board to build a new school for Black students. She also knew her school was built to contain 200 students but had twice that amount, and the classes that were meant to be held temporarily on school buses and in the auditorium were now permanent arrangements. Their futures, in effect, were in peril.

Barbara decided the students could no longer passively accept mistreatment. A revolution was in order. Though she anticipated resistance from the white community and school board, she knew inaction meant accepting continued inequity. Students needed to force change, to shake the authoritarian structures that perpetuated their disenfranchisement, to demand the respect and resources they deserved as equal members of the community, and to garner attention from those who held the power to change their circumstances.

In the fall of 1950, Barbara first took her concerns, specifically about the conditions of the shacks they were being taught in, to one of her teachers she had come to confide in, Inez Davenport.

She compared the all-white and highly resourced Farmville High School to theirs, decrying the injustice.

"I'm sick and tired of it all," she told Inez.

"Why don't you do something about it?"

Inez's simple charge to the teen would prove profound.

Though her family had roots in Virginia, Barbara was born in New York City on March 6, 1935, after her parents, Robert and Violet, migrated north looking for work during the Depression Era. While they lived in Harlem, Robert did odd jobs, and Violet was a domestic homeworker. More than a year later, the Johnses moved back south to Farmville.

For some time, they lived in the back room of Robert's older brother's home. He was the renowned activist Reverend Vernon Johns. The Johnses paid their way by working at Vernon's country store, one of two in Darlington Heights, a small unincorporated community fifteen miles south of Farmville. By 1942, in search of better opportunities and resources for their family, the Johnses moved out of Vernon's place and on to Washington, D.C., where Violet had found clerical work for the Navy. This was during the heat of the Second World War, and shortly after, Robert was drafted into the army.

With her husband gone, the weight of the family's upkeep overwhelmed Violet. So once again, she decided to move the family back south to her hometown in the small county of Prince Edward, with its rolling hills, pine forests, and farmland. They lived with Violet's mother, Mary Croner, in a house with no electricity, lit by kerosene lamps. Mary once said Barbara wasn't stuck-up like other young girls because she "didn't have a lot of put-on airs about her—she was a country girl, not some flirty thing worrying about clothes." Barbara was serious and hardworking right from the time she was a little girl. She'd work out on the farm picking tobacco, feeding chickens, collecting their eggs, fetching water, and cutting down timber to sell.

Once they settled in on Mary's farm, Barbara attended a nearby one-room segregated schoolhouse for elementary school, which doubled as a Sunday school. Mary would send her grandchildren to light the potbellied stove in the schoolhouse to make sure the children were warm when they came for class.

During the workweek, Violet still worked as a clerk for the Navy in D.C. When she was gone, Barbara, as the eldest, assumed the role of caretaker of her four younger siblings. A quiet but spirited girl, Barbara stewarded her three brothers and sister, cleaning and cooking and ensuring they got to and from school.

One time, when Robert briefly returned from the war, he moved the family again, this time to his mother's, Sallie Johns, home. Vernon and his family lived there too since he had taken to traveling to preach and lecture, leaving his wife, a teacher at Russa Moton, and children behind. Sallie's home put greater emphasis on studying than chores. And whenever Vernon was around, he'd lecture all the kids about the importance of education, with special attention to African American history.

When the war finally ended in 1945, Robert returned to Prince Edward County for good. Looking to plant permanent roots, he built a wood-framed home on a hilltop in Darlington Heights close to the woods, where Barbara would ride her horses. He then set up a farm, where he toiled long hours, tending to their cash-cow crop of tobacco, soybeans, watermelon, sunflowers, and corn.

In 1947, Vernon, who had now gained prominence as a militant minister and renowned member of the Black community, became a controversial figure. He moved from his mother's home to serve as the pastor of Dexter Avenue Baptist Church in Montgomery, Alabama. While at Dexter, he was a vocal critic of segregation and racial inequality. He urged his congregation to take action against injustice and helped lay the groundwork for the Montgomery bus boycott.

In 1950, a year before she would be inspired to rise up against conditions at her school, Barbara witnessed Vernon organize a boycott of a local grocery store that refused to hire Black employees. His fiery sermons and teachings and denunciations of white supremacy and Black subservience ignited anger on both sides, but his message of action never wavered. This, layered with the stories she'd heard from Mary and Sallie about the brutality of slavery, the raw terror of lynchings, and the daily struggle of living under oppression, powered a deep fear of white power in Barbara. Yet, a still-whispering of curiosity made her wonder, what if all people could share the same power? This foundation of hope profoundly shaped Barbara's outlook, setting her on an uncharted path.

"As I lay in my bed that night, I prayed for help," Barbara remembered of her talk with Inez. "That night, whether in a dream or whether I was awake, but I felt I was awake, a plan began to formulate in my mind. A plan I felt was divinely inspired because I hadn't been able to think of anything until then."

Some days after her conversation with Inez, she went for a walk in the woods behind their home. It had become a hobby she'd come to find respite in. As she strolled, the charge from Inez churned in her mind. She thought about what it would look like if she were to *do something about it.*

Lost in the dappled daylight filtering through the trees, adrift in the sea of green, a tender memory flashed: Years prior, she and one of her neighbor friends, a white girl, would sneak off into the woods to play. They did so because the girl's parents disapproved of her associating with any Black Americans. But in the woods, no separate but equal rules could keep them apart. There, the two girls existed innocently, simply, in their youth.

Another not-so-distant snapshot swirled: One recent morning in October 1950, when she had been getting her siblings ready for school and out the door in time to catch the bus, in the rush, she forgot her lunch at home. As her brothers and sister waited for the bus, Barbara ran home to grab the bag. But by the time she made it back down the hill, the bus had taken off. She was stranded with no means to get to Russa Moton. She had to wait for someone, anyone, to drive by who could take her to school, since it was fifteen miles south. An hour later, as Farmville High's half-empty bus approached, knowing it would pass Russa Moton on its way, she signaled for a ride.

It kept going.

"Right then and there, I decided something had to be done about this inequality," Barbara later said of that moment. "But, I still didn't know what."

But a plan would later come to Barbara after she scoured her thoughts for the *hows,* knowing all too well the *why* was greater than herself.

The strategy finally formed for the teen, and it was simple: organize the students against their deplorable conditions. They would boycott classes, march with signs on the school grounds, command the attention of the school board and community, and precipitate the change they desperately needed.

However, the execution and outcome, Barbara knew, could be grave.

Barbara's vision began to take shape shortly after the school bus incident in October.

At school, Barbara started secretly enlisting a student representative from each grade. That person would then be responsible for telling other students in their grade about the upcoming strike. Her pitch to potential recruits was also simple: Concerned faculty and parents had tried to advocate on students' behalf, but who better than the students themselves to rise up against their unfair conditions?

Among those Barbara assembled were seniors and twins John and Carrie Stokes, who served in student government as vice president and president, respectively. Barbara then tapped football player and member of the debate team John Watson. These three would become core leaders in executing Barbara's plans.

At their first meeting, it was decided that Barbara and her three leads needed to be shrewd with their campaign. Springtime, they agreed, made the most sense to execute their blueprint because it was right around finals and graduation, which could command more attention and urgency. So, they decided to strike in April.

In the meantime, Barbara, Carrie, John Stokes, and John Watson would focus on streamlining their tactics. Meanwhile, each continued to recruit students from all grade levels and attend school board meetings to assess whether progress from the existing community push about building a new facility was being made.

Given that there were about six months before their demonstration was to take place, the plan also called for utter secrecy, especially for the uprising to be kept from parents and faculty. The group feared if the board or local leaders were to find out that parents and faculty knew about their course of action and were complacent in the matter, it could very well mean loss of jobs and livelihood. For Barbara, she thought about her siblings too. She wanted the full weight of the fallout, if there were to be any, to fall solely on her.

In February 1951, with students anxiously awaiting news on their school's future, a board meeting announcement revealed plans to purchase a new building. Nothing concrete was divulged, and board leaders told the community and faculty they didn't need to come to future meetings to receive updates on the plans.

Months passed with no further mentions of the new building. Barbara knew something was needed to push the needle.

It was time to strike.

After months of mobilizing, the core leaders had recruited the entire student body population: 450 students.

"We were taught to be obedient and respectful," Edwilda Allen, an eighth grader at the time and the selected representative for her grade, remembered, "and there [Barbara] was, asking us to be disobedient. It was shocking."

On Monday, April 23, 1951, everything was set in motion.

The students were ready.

The student leaders had planned for the strike to begin at eleven, during the regularly scheduled morning assembly run by Principal Boyd Jones. But they knew that would present a problem because Boyd would never allow the students to take over the assembly. So, the first step in their plan was making sure he was off the premises.

Barbara tasked John Watson with distracting Boyd.

John's family was one of the few in town with a private phone at their house, which also had a good view of the school. That Monday, John ducked out of school right before the assembly time and placed a call to Boyd. Putting a handkerchief over the phone and altering his voice, John pretended to be a local white business owner complaining that some of Boyd's students were downtown being disruptive. They knew this would get the principal's attention because he had received a similar call weeks earlier. And when that incident happened, Boyd promised business owners that instead of calling the police on any student, they should instead call him, and he'd tend to such matters personally. So, this call from John meant Boyd would have to go off campus.

The plan worked.

Just as the assembly was set to start, Boyd received the bogus call and immediately dashed out of Russa Moton.

The second step in Barbara's plan required her to forge the standard assembly announcement note from the principal to each teacher and classroom. It was simple enough, as students had previously handled the distribution of them throughout the school. It was even a task Barbara had seen done before, so she knew each letter was only signed with Boyd's surname initial, "J."

The moment Boyd left school, Barbara instructed students to pass out the notice. As they did that, she made her way to the auditorium and remained in the wings of the stage, waiting for the entire student and faculty body to arrive and fill the hundreds of foldable metal chairs.

As everyone trickled in, Barbara readied herself, looking to her committee leaders who were now by her side. Once the hall was filled, she and her team emerged from behind the purple and gold curtains. They began by reciting the Pledge of Allegiance, as they had done before, followed by the Lord's Prayer. Then, Barbara ordered the teachers to leave the assembly, declaring what they were there for, saying this fight was the students' cross to carry, emphasizing that their allegiance with the students could very well endanger their lives and could lead to dismissals from their jobs.

The teachers left.

Barbara passionately began her appeal to a stunned crowd, her eyes flashing with determination.

She explained why she and her committee had to keep the extent of the demonstration a secret, knowing retaliation in the form of suspension or expulsion, or worse, was likely. She reminded them of the cramped classrooms, the leaking ceilings, the inhumane conditions, telling them that the only way change was coming was if their voices roared louder than the fear whispering in their ears. That they would no longer be silenced. That their anger would be their anthem, their solidarity their weapon.

"Are we going to just accept these conditions or are we going to do something about it?" she asked them before launching into a call-and-response, urging the student body to "Strike the school!"

"What do you want to do?"

"We want to strike!"

"When do you want to strike?"

"Today!"

Meanwhile, Boyd had realized the phone call was a hoax and returned to the auditorium, shocked to see what was taking place. He attempted to quell the riled-up students, saying the school board had promised a new building and better conditions and though it hadn't materialized yet, such things take time. He then ordered them back to class.

Barbara resisted.

She told Boyd *he* needed to leave. That the assembly was *their* time.

The adults had tried it their way. Now, it was time the students tried something new.

"She put into words what needed to be said," one student later said of Barbara's unflinching will. "I was glad someone had the courage to stand up and say it."

As fear mounted among students, they stared at Barbara, as if to say: *Now what?* Her mandate to them remained simple: We stick together to the very end. "The jail isn't big enough for all of us," she told them. Barbara then marshaled the students outside to peacefully march on the school grounds with the handmade signs she and her committee had on the ready. If that felt too radical for some students, she instructed them to go back to their classrooms.

They were to sit in silence and not do any classwork or participate in activities or lessons.

Joan, Barbara's sister, later remembered not only the marvel that shot through her like a fever as she sat front row during the assembly and afterward, but the fear: "I thought, oh my goodness, what's going to happen to us now?"

Outside the assembly hall, Barbara's friends, who she'd also kept in the dark for their protection, asked her why she had done such a brazen thing.

She told them, "We have to make a change."

Later that Monday, word of the strike spread across Farmville.

It eventually reached the head of the only local NAACP chapter, L. Francis Griffin. He was already on his way to the school's library to observe where the students had marched when he received a call from one of the student committee members asking him for help to further their cause at the school.

He obliged.

The students were struggling with dissenting voices among themselves. Once on campus, L. Francis taught them to democratically vote on whether they should continue their fight. Most of the students voted in favor of it. Seeing their resolve, Barbara itched for more support beyond L. Francis's help. She called the Richmond NAACP. It was a larger chapter since it was located in the state's capital, which had more than 60,000 Black Americans, compared to Farmville's roughly 4,000.

Barbara spoke with the chapter's lawyer, Oliver Hill, and asked if they would represent the students and provide continued assistance until the school board acted in their favor. Oliver dismissed the teen's request and told her to return to class. Barbara continued to plead with him. Over her exuberant insistence and in an attempt to get her off the phone, Oliver told the teen she could write the chapter a formal letter if she wanted, thinking that would deter her.

Barbara and Carrie penned a letter immediately and mailed it out that same day.

Gentlemen:

We hate to impose as we are doing, but under the circumstances that we are facing, we have to ask for your help.

Due to the fact that the facilities and building in the name of Robert R. Moton High School are inadequate, we understand that your help is available to us. This morning, April 23, 1951, the students refused to attend classes under the circumstances. You know that this is a very serious matter because we are out of school, there are seniors to be graduated and it can't be done by staying at home. Please we beg you to come down at the first of this week. If possible, Wednesday, April 25, between nine A.M. and three P.M.

The next day, students continued their strike.

When their request for the county's white superintendent, Thomas McIlwaine, to meet them at Russa Moton was denied, Barbara, her committee leaders, and a small group of students marched downtown to his office. They pushed past his secretary and into his office. As the room filled quickly, he redirected them to a larger room.

Once there, one of his workers took down all their names and asked for their parents' names. Thomas warned them to end the strike, otherwise their parents would be the ones to pay with their jobs, or they would be jailed.

The very thing Barbara had feared.

Thomas went on to substantiate his threats, telling the teens he felt their parents had put them up to the strike since they hadn't been successful in convincing the county for a new school building. He also said Boyd, their principal, was equally responsible, rebuking him for not instantly squashing the students' efforts. In Thomas's eyes, it was unfathomable that a group of teens—Black teens at that—could come up with such an elaborate plan on their own.

Despite being frightened at the thought that she had dragged her family and others' into her protest, Barbara ignored Thomas's threats and questioned him about school integration and why the new building plans had made no progress. Thomas, dismissing her, told Barbara the former was illegal and the latter was in the works.

By the third day of the strike, Oliver, the NAACP southeast regional counsel, and his colleague, Spottswood Robinson, stopped by the Farmville NAACP chapter.

Both were also lead lawyers working to bring the federal lawsuit against *separate but equal* in schools. Oliver and Spottswood first felt the Russa Moton students' demonstration, being in a small county, wouldn't be a good case study for their larger efforts. This is what had led Oliver to dismiss Barbara's initial phone call because such areas that were highly segregated meant more opposition from white locals and less amenability and empathy. In larger cities, however, they had seen more chances for allyship, which had furthered their cause.

Even with their doubts, Oliver and Spottswood agreed to meet with the students at First Baptist Church, where L. Francis was a pastor. The men told the students, given the circumstances of the matter—an apathetic school board most of all—it was pointless to continue their strike. That they should go back to class.

Barbara dissented.

She argued that if they all continued with their protest, it would become an issue for the county. It would force the hands of the board to act. The lawyers, with all their experience in such matters, countered, firing off questions, ending with one simple one: *What if the school board continues to say no?*

The students said they'd stay out of school until the board acts.

The lawyers contended that doing so would mean they were delinquents.

The students, all in agreement, recited Barbara's charge to them during her assembly on day one: *The Farmville jail is not big enough for all of us.*

Their unbreakable spirit moved Oliver and Spottswood. In the teens' compelling idealism about America and their painful understanding of the realities before them, the two men felt the students' budding actions were formidable—a David versus Goliath matchup. An unlikely fight, yet these wide-eyed crusaders were keen on slinging all the shots, determined to see it through.

Finally, Oliver and Spottswood agreed to help only if the students were willing to sue the county for integrated schools, not only for equal conditions.

The students eagerly accepted, which meant two things.

First, in enlisting the lawyers' help, their case would join the NAACP's larger effort to end legal segregation, not just at schools. Second, since they were all minors, each of the students' parents must come on board to be the plaintiff of record, similar to the *Brown* case.

Barbara accepted the challenge.

"It never entered my mind at that time that this would turn out to be a school desegregation suit," Barbara later said in a 1959 interview. "We didn't know of such things. We were thinking that the school would be improved, or at best, that we would get a new school."

On the fourth day of the strike, Thomas ended all bus services to Russa Moton. Barbara and her committee leaders, looking to continue their demonstration at school, began a carpool system, after securing cars and trucks and drivers from supporters, to transport students.

Frustrated, but emboldened by the superintendent's retaliatory actions, Barbara and her crew also organized a community meeting at L. Francis's church. They canvassed the neighborhood, spreading the word about the meeting while petitioning Black residents for support, as Oliver and Spottswood had instructed them. They explained to parents that to take their issue to the next level, they needed the adults to see the importance of their fight.

That evening, of the roughly 4,000 Black residents in town, 1,000 attended the meeting. Oliver and Spottswood had intended to host the meeting but abruptly left town to tend to another issue, so the NAACP's Virginia State Conference executive secretary, Lester Banks, ran it.

Once the students and Lester presented the crux of the case to parents, a select fearful few opposed the lawsuit. They worried about the pushback from the county's white leadership. Barbara tried to quell their concerns and spoke to the grand scale of the suit, how their tiny locale could cause a significant precedent. Lester then spoke to the urgency not only for parity in schools, but for Black Americans across the nation.

"The problem is that a new colored high school will not bring you equality, even if it is built brick for brick, cement for cement, like the white school," Lester said. "When colored people are separated, we're stamped with a brand of inferiority. As long as we accept separate schools, we accept a caste system that says we're unfit to sit beside whites. This segregation must not be allowed to continue."

In the end, parents at the meeting, inspired and expectant for a just outcome, all overwhelmingly supported the strike.

As anticipated by many that Thursday night, the meeting caused a stir in the white community. So much so that the next day, town council member and *Farmville Herald* publisher Joseph Barrye Wall ran a scathing editorial calling the protest reckless, convinced that it was simply the students' attempt at skipping school.

By the following Thursday, on May 3, the momentum of the strike had caused enough public attention it summoned Oliver and Spottswood back. They held another meeting that day at L. Francis's church. With the ongoing vitriol against Black citizens from white community members, news of the gathering prompted state troopers to set up checkpoints across town.

At the meeting, on what was now day 11 of the strike, a similar crowd of more than 1,000 Black residents filled the space. Oliver and Spottswood opened with "My Country 'Tis of Thee": a symbolic, patriotic song that speaks of the promises of America and the limitless freedom it harbors. Spottswood then assured the crowd that the NAACP was fully behind them, that soon enough, they would file papers to sue the county for segregation. He told them this move was an emblematic one, emphasizing that Black people in the county were no longer going to accept or be subjected to second-class citizenship.

At this, a joyous chorus of "Amen!" echoed throughout the room.

Spottswood then encouraged the crowd some more, instructing parents, "If you're really ready to back [the students], then you have to sign this petition."

Just then, the dissenters in the hall, including the former Black principal of Russa Moton, Joseph Pervall, spoke up. Joseph especially felt Oliver and Spottswood were using the Black residents as pawns in their larger schemes. "I was under the impression the pupils were striking for a new building," Joseph said. "You are pulling a heavy load, Mr. Robinson, coming down here to a country town like Farmville and trying to take it over on a nonsegregated basis."

A battle of words ensued between attendees. As Spottswood and Oliver tried to soothe anxieties by explaining the weight of the suit and the debate crescendoed to a fever pitch, Barbara took to the stage. Her presence brought the screaming match to a halt and her words quieted the restless: "Don't let Mr. Charlie, Mr. Tommy, or Mr. Pervall stop you from backing us," she said, speaking directly to the parents. "Don't let any *Tom, Dick, or 'Harry'* Pervall stop you from supporting us." She reiterated that this was no longer about desegregation in schools, but equality. The crowd loudly cheered her on. Some had tears in their eyes, while others looked on, shocked and in awe at the "courageous pupil, unafraid to speak her mind," as the *Richmond Afro-American* newspaper described her the following day.

As Barbara stepped down, she was immediately embraced by her parents. She later recalled that her parents "were at first bewildered by it all—but they attended the meetings in full strength. . . . They stood behind us—timidly at first but firmly." L. Francis then took to the podium and gave the final push: "Anybody here who won't fight against racial prejudice is not a man."

The meeting closed with another unifying anthem, "God Bless America."

Two days later, on Saturday, May 5, the movement climaxed when a cross was burned outside Russa Moton, a vile and chilling warning symbol of hate popularized by the KKK since its inception almost a century earlier. Barbara and her student leaders rallied and steadied the nerves of their peers, who feared for their lives.

That Monday, May 7, the strike finally ended when the NAACP officially filed the lawsuit against the school board. Immediately, the students returned to the classroom.

Days later, Prince Edward County denied the petition.

On May 23, 1951, the NAACP filed the *Dorothy Davis et al. v. County School Board of Prince Edward County* lawsuit in federal court. That case was then consolidated with the organization's existing marquee one, *Brown v. Board of Education*, which they were prepping for the Supreme Court. The Prince Edward County case joined four others: Kansas's *Brown v. Topeka Board of Education*, South Carolina's *Briggs v. Elliott*, Delaware's *Belton (Bulah) v. Gebhart*, and Washington, D.C.'s *Bolling v. Sharpe*.

In all cases, about 177 students (one suit only lists the number of parents)—of which 117 were from Prince Edward County—had sued their local school boards, arguing that the segregation of public schools was unconstitutional.

The fallout from Barbara's strike and the resulting lawsuit came quickly.

The school board maintained that Boyd, the school's principal, had a hand in the strike. He was fired and replaced with an out-of-towner.

The town's Black community continued to face economic and social oppression. Some lost their jobs and many were unable to find new ones. Others, including L. Francis, were denied lines of credit at stores. For the Johnses, as Barbara had been the face of the movement, the intimidation was more personal and relentless.

They were threatened constantly. Banks and stores also denied them credit, which stifled their livelihoods. Now only surviving on the yields from their farm, the Johnses didn't see a way forward if they stayed in Prince Edward County. Barbara was unable to return to Russa Moton. When she received a death threat that summer, her family sent her to Montgomery, Alabama, to live with Vernon and his family. The family didn't publicly share the details of the harassment, but it terrified them enough that they relocated the sixteen-year-old.

Barbara began her senior year at Alabama State Laboratory High School, where she graduated in the spring of 1952. She then went on to Spelman College. During her sophomore year, the NAACP Legal Defense and Educational Fund, led by Thurgood Marshall, officially brought the consolidated five cases and a culmination of the organization's twenty-year legal campaign before the U.S. Supreme Court in *Brown v. Board of Education*. Thurgood argued that segregation had a detrimental effect on Black children and violated the Equal Protection Clause of the Fourteenth Amendment, which guarantees everyone the same treatment under the law.

On May 17, 1954, after two rounds and two years of arguments—the first in December 1952 for three days, the second, another three-day debate, on December 7, 1953—the Court supported the students' claim and unanimously said segregation in schools was unconstitutional.

This was a full three years after Barbara led the Russa Moton student strike.

Speaking on behalf of the Court, Chief Justice Earl Warren declared, "In the field of public education, the doctrine of 'separate but equal' has no place." The Court further concluded that "separate educational facilities are inherently unequal" and "separate educational facilities do not provide equal educational opportunities." In effect, the ruling overturned the "separate but equal" dogma established in the 1896 *Plessy v. Ferguson* case.

Shortly after the decision came down, life remained in turmoil for Black residents of Farmville.

One time, while the Johnses were away in Washington, D.C., their Darlington Heights home was burned to the ground. This escalated assault forced the family to permanently relocate to D.C. The same bullying tactics were equally devastating for other residents who faced ongoing intimidation and struggled to rebuild their lives in the face of the strike's fallout. Though the landmark case bellowed throughout the nation, it served as a stark reminder that the road ahead was long and arduous. Implementing the decision and bridging the chasm of existing racial division wouldn't be easy.

A year after the decision, the reality of widespread bigotry remained a harsh truth.

On August 28, 1955, Emmett Till, a Black fourteen-year-old,

vanished while visiting his great-uncle's home in Money, Mississippi, swallowed by the darkness of racial hatred. Days turned into agonizing nights for his family. Then, news ripped through the community like a shotgun blast: Emmett's body, mutilated beyond recognition and weighed down by a cotton gin fan fastened with barbed wire around his neck, had been pulled from the Tallahatchie River. The gruesome scars of unspeakable cruelty he bore on his body weren't just physical, they were etched with the searing reality of animus. His murder, fueled by an unfounded accusation, stood as a brutal testament to the depths of prejudice that still festered. The perpetrators of this heinous crime, two white men, faced no legal consequences. Yet, the ripples of Emmett's murder permeated the South. More atrocities against Black bodies persisted—a grim reminder of racism's stranglehold.

Later that year, on October 21, eighteen-year-old Mary Louise Smith refused to give up her seat on a city line bus to a white passenger. She was arrested.

Three months later, on December 1, Rosa Parks also refused to give up her bus seat and faced the same outcome.

On March 29, 1958, twenty-two-year-old Jeremiah Reeves was executed by electrocution in Alabama after police tortured him into giving a false confession to raping a white woman in 1952 when he was sixteen.

On March 5, 1959, sixty-nine Black boys were padlocked and set on fire while in their dorm at Negro Boys Industrial School, a run-down, neglected Arkansas reform school in the predominantly Black town of Wrightsville. Twenty-one of them burned to death, the rest escaped. No one was ever held responsible.

Layered with such compounding series of oppression and persecution was the persisting fight for and against school integration. Across the South, school boards and legislators carried out measures to thwart it altogether.

In Virginia, the state's white governor, James Lindsay Almond, Jr., was so firmly against the Supreme Court's decision that he went so far as to shut the doors to all public schools. After yet another legal battle, on January 19, 1959, four years after the *Brown* case was decided, the Virginia Supreme Court ruled that such closures in Virginia were unconstitutional and ordered all schools to reopen. Though James acquiesced to the ruling, he gave counties what was called a "local option." Essentially, local leaders had two choices: reopen with mandatory integration or remain closed.

Most counties chose to integrate (some needed more legal battles than others before fully doing so), but in Prince Edward County, the school board refused to integrate and permanently shut its doors to all students. When the decision was announced, the Department of Justice intervened and tried to prevent the school closures by filing a motion in the federal district court. But the closure would carry on for five years, garnering national attention and launching several more litigations.

During the public school system-wide closure, white students attended Prince Edward Academy, a new kindergarten through twelfth grade private school built thanks to segregationists, state grants, and private donations. As for the others—the roughly 1,700 Black and lower-income white students—they tried to find schooling in neighboring counties or stayed home waiting for integration to take root in their county.

Meanwhile, an effort to maintain segregation in Prince Edward County had been brewing thanks to Robert Crawford, a dry cleaner and school board member. He spearheaded the formation of the Defenders of State Sovereignty and Individual Liberty. This white supremacist group set out to defy integration, further intimidating Black families and escalating the already charged atmosphere.

As the shutdown continued, demonstrations for desegregation for Prince Edward County Black students boomed. Leading civil rights leaders like Asa Philip Randolph and Bayard Rustin joined in on the action. They organized rallies that brought attention to the students' plight culminating in the historic Youth March for Integrated Schools—two demonstrations held in D.C. in 1958 and 1959 under Martin Luther King, Jr.'s leadership. It demanded integration and equal education and united young voices in the fight against segregation.

While such powerful calls for racial justice mounted, the South remained unwavering in its resistance against integration. It grew so pervasive in places like Prince Edward County that Robert F. Kennedy, the then attorney general, commented on its explicit unconstitutionality during a March 1963 address commemorating the centennial of the Emancipation Proclamation: "We must achieve equal education opportunities for all children regardless of race . . . We may observe with much sadness and irony that, outside of Africa, south of the Sahara, where education is still a difficult challenge, the only places on earth known not to provide free public education are Communist China, North Vietnam, Sarawak, Singapore, British Honduras—and Prince Edward County, Virginia."

Soon after, Robert F. Kennedy came forward with a practical expression of hope: funded by the likes of the National Education Association and private, sympathetic donors, he spearheaded a free school program specifically for Prince Edward County students.

The schools opened that fall in privately rented buildings with teachers from across the country. This influx of support injected a surge of hope into a community battered but not broken.

Soon, resistance bloomed anew. That summer, a group of young and not-so-young Black protesters flooded Farmville's side roads, while some sang on the steps of the whites-only Farmville Baptist Church, demanding equal job opportunities and entry to local shops. Though they were met with opposition from police and arrested for demonstrating without a permit, several businesses began hiring Black residents again: a promising sign of progress and a ray of reassurance to Black residents uncertain about their fate.

Then, finally, in September 1964, after a thirteen-year legal battle and the movement that Barbara had sparked, Prince Edward County public schools were reopened and ordered to be integrated under Supreme Court order. Black students returned to their now legally integrated school, which remained mostly underfunded, under-resourced, and Black.

The whites-only private academy that had been built during the shutdown remained open and continued discriminating against Black Americans until 1985, when it was finally integrated.

After the consequential strike, Barbara remained out of the public eye and the civil rights fight. On January 1, 1955, having dropped out of Spelman, she married Baptist minister William Powell and had five children: four daughters and a son. She later earned her bachelor's in library science from Drexel University in 1979 and worked as a Philadelphia school district librarian for more than twenty years.

Barbara lived a quiet life in Philadelphia until she died at fifty-six from bone cancer on September 25, 1991.

_____

As I mined this era and Barbara's tussle, I came to understand that there are three layers of equality: biological, civil, and social.

Though we're born with inherent (biological) rights like freedom from undue restrictions (or, liberty), achieving true equality is a complex journey in everyday life.

"We hold these truths to be self-evident, that all men are created equal, that they are endowed by their Creator with certain unalienable Rights, that among these are Life, Liberty and the pursuit of Happiness."

The Declaration of Independence's principle of "all men are created equal" is muddied by regional interpretations. This was the case in Prince Edward County. While civil equality—the legal rights defined by law—existed on paper, access to resources and opportunities remained unequal in practice.

The law said one thing, but reality spoke differently.

Today's educational disparities juxtaposed against the wealth gap emerge as a contemporary example of a persistent, structural social inequality that memorializes the cycle of disadvantage.

So then, it is not just about the laws that govern the land but the existence we, the people, create together.

So then, it's really about the majority embracing its responsibility to dismantle these systemic inequalities.

Until then, students of color will continue to face limited opportunities.

Because though we now have lawful desegregated schools, in considerable ways, they are still socially segregated. You can almost assess the quality of one's education by the zip code or neighborhood they attend that school in. This has come to be yet another layer of division when someone feels they can define your ability, your character, your future, simply by your zip code. And still, it remains a matter of resources, of the privileged and deprived. And in many instances, it clips the wings of the Othered's potential.

When you can't see beyond your immediate lefts and rights, beyond your circumstances and social sentence, you become blind to the vastness of the future. You become consumed by the urgency of mere endurance, thinking, "Let's survive today to survive tomorrow." Your possibilities feel left to chance. Growing up in 10459, in the heart of the South Bronx, I toiled with this myself. It consumed my already fragile identity, especially given my school's condition: Dilapidated walls. Peeling paint and exposed cinder block. Rusty gym equipment. Clumpy free lunch. The library, with its tattered, barely bound books, resembled a neglected roost.

But that was my normal. That remains the normal for so many from places like 10459.

But yet, from their perches of privilege, some don't see us, instead they condemn us as lazy or unintelligent. They harp on about our supposed lack of reading, preaching its gospel for success and freedom. But where are the resources? Where are the books? Where are the vibrant, diverse stories, the windows to other worlds? A child empowered by a single book doesn't just read for a day or a year, they embark on a lifelong odyssey of learning. Give us the tools and watch us soar.

But even when faced with such shortcomings then, I can't imagine ever mustering half the boldness Barbara did, to dare think I could speak on the conditions I found myself in. There are parts of life we often feel powerless to, in a "Who am I that I should speak?" kind of way. As I looked back on my school years, going from 10459 to 10029, this decade made me relish, more than ever, the lives of these young ones I knew nothing of—of Barbara and her quiet force— whose journey changed mine.

5

THE REVOLT CEMENTED

SNCC & Charlie Cobb

When you're in Mississippi,
the rest of America doesn't seem real.
And when you're in the rest of America,
Mississippi doesn't seem real.

BOB MOSES

*Not long after Mom secured her American dream in the North
Bronx, it began to fray. Our new "home" contorted to a nightmare.
For all of us, given Manny's deportation.*

*While at Northeastern University, I began researching how to
bring him back to America, leading me to request his case records
through the Freedom of Information Act. After reading the 622
pages, I confirmed my fears: my brother had been caught in a storm
of prejudice, from being given an inadequate public defender (read
this with sisterly rage) to the escalation from a probation recom-
mendation to felony. I wished to rewind time.*

*This is where my journey into storytelling began. After years in
corporate America, Columbia University launched me into a world
I longed for, teeming with freedom of the press, a reality I was
keenly aware was suppressed in Nigeria. I came to it with reverent
awe. It's a responsibility I don't take for granted. As an independent reporter, I've honed a beat focused on the vulnerable and marginalized. It's allowed me the privilege to serve as a documenter*

and conduit to amplify voices who may not know that their voices are indeed valid and worthy. I've been able to interview remarkable everyday people and some not-so-everyday folks.

I once wrote about a young Black hairstylist who, looking to expand her business, had saved up money to buy land in Salisbury, North Carolina. She was only seventeen when the dream cemented for her, and she leaped into action to make it happen. By the time she was twenty-one, she had done it. What she didn't know was that the area her purchased land was on was once a sundown town with remnants of blatant racial animus. She was met with prejudice even before moving in. An older white man verbally attacked her and vandalized her property, all in an attempt to intimidate her out of her land. She fled and never looked back.

Her story stuck with me. In the course of our interview, dejected and stunned, she scoured her memory when I asked her what her experience had taught her about contemporary race relations. After a long quiet beat, she said, "Racism has only gotten worse. It's honestly just hidden—racism is thrown under the rug . . . Like, we know Martin Luther King made a speech about it, but still, nothing has changed."

Racism is thrown under the rug.

That rang in my ears for days: It's simple in its expression yet poignant in its connotation. Her reference to King's "I Have a Dream" speech was similarly resonant. That, sixty years later, "the bank of justice" he spoke passionately about remains mostly "bankrupt" for us, the Others.

I remembered that young woman as I researched this decade because her words are what the civil rights movement, at its root, aimed to expose: that though Black Americans had been freed almost a century prior, the everyday battles endured by those Othered was a persistent war for recognition, respect, and the basic rights promised that remained unrealized.

I zero in on Charlie Cobb in this chapter because in his "I-didn't-plan-to, then-one-day" (as he once put it) journey to the front lines of the civil rights fight, I saw semblances to my own stumble into journalism. In his journey to self, of beginning to understand himself within the context of history, I saw his vigor in wanting to lay down for the cause, specifically the Mississippi Movement, which saw the rights of Black Americans even more stifled than the rest of the country.

Above all, his mission to educate young minds drew me most to his story.

AUGUST 28, 1963. AMERICA'S CAPITAL.

At the break of dawn, they surged into Washington, D.C. They were Black, they were white. They came from the East and West, the North and the South. They came by air, bus, and train. They came in the thousands—more than 250,000, to be exact—to condemn racial inequities. They came seeking to sway Congress to pass a sweeping civil rights bill that would end the decades-long attack on Black bodies and minds.

Two months prior, on June 21, 1963, President John F. Kennedy had met with the leaders of this march, including the multigenerational core organizers, known as the Big Six: seventy-four-year-old labor leader Asa Philip Randolph; Bayard Rustin, the march's fifty-one-year-old director; forty-three-year-old James Farmer from the Conference of Racial Equality; twenty-three-year-old John Lewis of the Student Nonviolent Coordinating Committee; thirty-four-year-old Martin Luther King, Jr., head and co-founder of the Southern Christian Leadership Conference; and the National Urban League's president, forty-one-year-old Whitney Young, Jr. For an hour, they discussed the demonstration's strategy and some of the president's concerns about the crowds.

That August day, as sunlight peeped through the clouds, casting a warm glow, the tame crowd began singing songs of hope, courage, and comfort before the march on Washington for jobs and freedom was to kick off around noon. Soon, they were making the one-mile walk from the National Mall to the Reflecting Pool of the Lincoln Memorial, resonantly singing "We Shall Overcome." The hymnal had become an anthem of the civil rights movement, which had found its rhythm and strengthened at this point, through protests, marches, boycotts, and civil disobedience. It had come to signify the political, legal, and social campaign to achieve equal citizenship rights for Black Americans while denouncing segregation and prejudice.

That Wednesday in America's capital was also eight years to the day when Emmett Till was murdered, underscoring the plight and peril for the more than two million African Americans nationwide. However, that historic day of reckoning didn't come as a surprise to those following the movement, because a symphony of dissent had been playing out across the land, as waves of escalating attacks against Black bodies continued.

Part of this surge in brutality came despite, or perhaps in response to, the massive Children's Crusade on May 2, 1963, when more than 5,000 children in Birmingham left their classrooms and marched for nine days protesting segregation in public places. The demonstration energized people across ages, mostly bolstered by the increased participation by the likes of nine-year-old Audrey Faye Hendricks, who boycotted her school, marched for four days, and was arrested, making her the youngest known demonstrator to be arrested during the movement.

Even with such dangers, undaunted, young people kept rising as leaders in the movement, propelled by the *Brown* case, fighting fiercer for equal education and integration. They began staging sit-ins throughout the South. The first student sit-in in the nation happened on February 1, 1960, when four Black college students—David Richmond, Ezell Blair, Jr., Joseph McNeil, and Franklin McCain—from North Carolina Agricultural and Technical State University sat down at an all-white lunch counter at a Woolworth's department store in Greensboro, North Carolina. In the end, more than 50,000 students who participated in sit-ins nationwide were arrested. The sit-ins drew thousands more young Black people into the movement.

Soon, a challenge presented itself: There was no unified place for young Black activists to organize. They also received less support and encouragement from the movement's senior leadership, who were used to nonviolent tactics, whereas students were seemingly more willing to risk arrest and violence. Ella Baker, who had built a reputation as a firebrand grassroots organizer, recognized the need for a dedicated space where students could strategize and learn from each other. She had already been impressed by their fight for equality, especially in schools.

On April 15, 1960, Ella formed the Student Nonviolent Coordinating Committee for young Black leaders. It gave them a centralized place to organize and assemble. When it came to SNCC's membership and leadership, she instructed them that a top-heavy approach to organizing was ineffective and preached about how power belonged at the level where people are, that "up here does not direct down here—down here directs up there." She told the nascent SNCC leadership and members, including Diane Nash, Bob Moses, John Lewis, James Bevel, and Marion Barry, that though they were leading the way, they were to be accessible activists focused on local issues. Another one of Ella's maxims that underpinned SNCC's mission was: "The day has come when racism must be banished." That charge inspired SNCC members to operate at an unparalleled level.

Before the March on Washington, SNCC members had been laying the groundwork for one of their largest efforts yet, scheduled to take place a month after the D.C. demonstration—Operation Mississippi: One Man, One Vote Campaign. A voter registration project in Greenwood, a small city between Jackson, Mississippi, and Memphis, Tennessee, SNCC's goal was to increase voter registration among African Americans. Or, as Ella put it: "We're trying to figure out how to get Black people registered to vote without getting them killed."

SNCC began their initiative in Mississippi because it was widely known as one of the nation's most viciously racist, segregated states. Its Black residents had been restricted from voting since the turn of the century due to increased barriers to voter registration and cruel enforcement of Jim Crow laws. By this time too, the state had come to be wholly defined by the barbaric slaying of Emmett Till in its Sunflower County. Soon, SNCC's efforts extended statewide, to similarly register as many African American voters as possible, starting with the Mississippi Delta area. There, half the population was Black and mostly sharecroppers, but, in most counties, just one percent of eligible Black voters were registered. In Leflore County, for example, of the 39,000 Black residents able to vote, only 26 were registered. As SNCC's plans amplified in the Delta area, members were met with death threats. Some were shot, others severely beaten, arrested, or firebombed. Most times at the hands of police officers.

Before Operation Mississippi was conceived, the Delta had also been the site of several key demonstrations that inflamed the March on Washington. On March 27, 1961, nine college students at Tougaloo College, dubbed the Tougaloo Nine, in Jackson, were arrested for entering a segregated library to complete their schoolwork. They were imprisoned for a month and fined $100. Medgar Evers, the renowned civil rights activist and first field secretary for Mississippi's NAACP chapter, rallied to bail them out, later getting the case dismissed. That same spring, organized by the Congress of Racial Equality to challenge segregation on interstate buses, the first Freedom Riders traveled from Washington, D.C., headed to New Orleans, Louisiana. While passing through the Delta they were met with violence and arrests orchestrated by white supremacists. (Freedom Rides helped bring national attention to endemic segregation in the South and put pressure on the federal government. In September 1961, John F. Kennedy ordered the Interstate Commerce Commission to desegregate interstate buses and bus terminals.)

Then, a year later in October 1962, with the help of Medgar Evers, now the head of Mississippi's NAACP chapter, twenty-nine-year-old James Meredith successfully enrolled as the first Black American student at the University of Mississippi. He had twice been denied admission to the still-segregated school. His registration sparked a riot, causing John F. Kennedy to send federal troops to restore order. (Two months before the march in D.C., on June 12, 1963, Medgar Evers was assassinated in Jackson.)

So, on that blistering Wednesday in D.C., beneath the marble gaze of Abraham Lincoln's statue, as many climbed trees and stretched their necks to see beyond the throng holding signs that reflected their angst, the weight of the fight laid heavy. They also saw a most poignant panorama: A hundred years and some 240 days earlier, Abraham Lincoln signed the Emancipation Proclamation that freed enslaved people, yet the idea of liberty for the thousands in that crowd had yet to be realized.

The monumental day culminated with Martin Luther King, Jr.'s acclaimed "I Have a Dream" oration.

After about three hours, at 4 p.m., the day ended with a meeting between the march leaders and John F. Kennedy at the White House's Oval Office. The leaders focused their conversation on the pending civil rights legislation in Congress and its urgency for securing Black Americans' equality. The president told the Big Six and the other civil rights leaders, including Roy Wilkins, Whitney Young, and James Farmer, that he was impressed at the size and spirit of the march and vowed to continue to work for civil rights.

Even after such a seismic day, violence against Black Americans and their allies raged on. Before morning service on September 15, 1963, the 16th Street Baptist Church in Birmingham, Alabama, was bombed, killing four young girls and injuring several others. One month later, on October 7, Alabama troopers attacked hundreds of Black Americans trying to register to vote in Selma. And three months after the march ended, John F. Kennedy was assassinated, on November 21, 1963.

Newly sworn-in President Lyndon Johnson, formerly Kennedy's vice president, signed the Civil Rights Act a year later on July 4. The legislation ended the nation's apartheid, making segregation officially illegal.

Yet, many remained dismayed at the government's inaction at its execution locally with the continued assault on Black lives. In response, a coalition of local and national civil rights organizations, including Congress for Racial Equality, NAACP, SCLC, and SNCC, under the umbrella of the Council of Federated Organizations, decided to organize a voter drive and education campaign in what they anointed the Mississippi Freedom Summer.

The push built on SNCC's Operation Mississippi and had two simple goals: register as many African American voters as possible in the state and replace the state's all-white delegation for the upcoming Democratic National Convention. But one young visionary who joined SNCC and Freedom Summer sparked a third objective: create a learning environment to empower the state's Black youths.

Charles "Charlie" Cobb, Jr., was born in Washington, D.C., on June 23, 1943, to middle-class parents, Charles and Martha, who were active in the civil rights movement. Martha was an educator with a terminal degree in her field who had studied at Sorbonne University in Paris and taught at Classical High School in Springfield, Massachusetts, the same school Charlie later attended. Charles was a Howard University alum and a prominent minister who was friends with Malcolm X. Like his wife, he pursued his academics to the highest, earning a master's and doctorate degree. They raised their son and two daughters, Adrienne and Ann, to be strong advocates for justice. Charlie described his upbringing as "open, educated, and politically active."

As a kid, Charlie came up in Frankfort, Kentucky, where his father ministered at an AME church. Later, when the family moved to Springfield during Charlie's teen years, Charles pastored St. Johns Congregational Church, a well-known, politically active faith community with historical significance: it was one of the stops on the Underground Railroad.

During Charlie's eleventh-grade year at Classical, the 1960 Greensboro sit-in flared and soon reverberated throughout the South and onto national headlines. When the sit-ins spread to other cities like Nashville, where there were accompanying protests led by the likes of SNCC's Diane Nash, it received even more attention and reached wider audiences nationwide. Its reach spilled into the Cobbs' home. "We were seeing people more or less our own age involved in, and actually leading, civil rights struggle," Charlie later remembered. "[It was] kind of a first in the sense of realizing that you didn't have to be a grown-up to engage in serious civil rights struggle." This marked his first consequential taste of activism. Compelled by the leadership of youths and rooted in a politically engaged home and community, he began joining picket lines in support of the sit-ins.

That level of impact was felt by many young Black people. They saw their peers get involved, and it caused a domino effect across the country, stirring up more and more youths to the front lines. And it wasn't limited to Black youth, either. "There was a kind of sympathetic resonance," Charlie later said, "on college campuses and high schools attended predominantly by white people toward the sit-ins and the freedom rides and the civil rights struggle." This level of allyship ballooned the more young white Americans witnessed the government struggle to improve the rights of Black Americans. Bathed in the fever of the movement for Black lives, white students were also seeing firsthand the grave mistreatment of Black people and recognized its deep immorality, which only fueled their involvement. This was the first era where demonstrations, sit-ins, and marches were more diverse. It caused the culture around protesting to shift to where it stands in contemporary expressions.

By the time Charlie was set to enroll in college, there was no doubt in his mind that he'd attend a historically Black college. His father had all but planted this seed in him since he was young. "These kinds of things were a part of the conversation at the dinner table," Charlie once said. "My father was encouraging students, Black students—because we lived in a Black community and the church was predominantly Black—to go to college and was taking them on trips to historically Black colleges and universities in the South."

Charlie ended up at his father's alma mater.

During his freshman year at Howard, in the fall of 1961, the teen plunged deeper into activism. The eighteen-year-old became a member of Howard's Nonviolent Action Group and SNCC's campus cohort.

On a trip with other NAG members, going from D.C. to Baltimore, Maryland, they stopped at a pizza eatery in Annapolis. In a blink, the stop turned into a sit-in. Still inexperienced at demonstrating, Charlie followed the pack, many of them slightly older with more rallying mileage. "Instead of setting up a picket line as I expected," Charlie later remembered, "they entered the restaurant, sat down at tables, refused to leave when asked, were arrested . . . I just held on to the biggest person in the group as we were dragged out of the eatery."

All NAG members were arrested.

While locked up in Anne Arundel County Jail for four days, speaking to other detained protesters, Charlie heard about SNCC's initiatives in Mississippi. "Almost everyone I know in my generation who became deeply involved with the Southern civil rights movement has an I-didn't-plan-to, then-one-day story of [their] first involvement," he said of that moment. "The sudden leap into direct action was like plunging into the ocean for the first time."

And so it went. After his release, something in him was activated. Back on campus, in between classes and exams, he'd sit in at establishments and stand on picket lines. By 1962, he became so known and recognized at demonstrations that he was invited by CORE to attend a civil rights workshop for students in Houston that August.

He jumped at the chance.

On his way to Texas, solo, during a pit stop in Jackson, Mississippi, he ran into another student and one of SNCC's field secretaries, twenty-three-year-old Lawrence Guyot. When Lawrence learned about Charlie's destination, he scolded the teen for going to *learn* about civil rights organizing.

"'Civil rights workshop in Texas?'" Charlie once remembered Lawrence chiding him. "'Tell me, just what's the point of going to Texas for a workshop on civil rights when you're standing right here in Mississippi?'"

Charlie never made it to Houston.

He didn't return to Howard to finish his degree, either.

Instead, he remained in Mississippi. Inspired by Lawrence's charge, he had found himself in an *I-didn't-plan-to, then-one-day* moment.

Charlie quickly advanced within SNCC and was appointed as one of its field secretaries posted at the Delta office alongside the other twenty-two organizers in the state.

Shortly after his appointment, one day, as Charlie canvassed Sunflower County (the same one where Emmett had been murdered) with two other SNCC members, the mayor of Ruleville, Charles Dorrough, pointed a gun at them and forced them into his hardware store, where he threatened them and ordered them to leave because he felt they were only there to cause trouble. At one point, as Charlie later tells it, he instructed them, "Best you get out of town."

The mayor's actions and words revealed firsthand to Charlie the kind of repeated intimidation and fear Black residents felt, even at the hands of local leadership. "I remember thinking," he said, "Leaving now, I thought, would be flight, not continuation of a planned journey."

Fear-stricken but purpose-driven, Charlie pressed on and emerged as an assertive and proactive leader within SNCC.

Before Charlie arrived in Mississippi, the state's white leadership had a campaign of their own: To drive out African Americans by replacing their livelihood of sharecropping, mostly at the Delta cotton plantations, with an automated system. This way, Black residents would be deemed irrelevant and out of work and be forced out of the state, lessening the already scant Black vote and any chance of African Americans gaining political power.

Knowing this and realizing that simply registering Black voters wasn't going to be enough to address such systemic oppression, in the fall of 1963, SNCC leaders broadened their Freedom Summer plan. They had come to recognize the need for Black political representation at the state level, especially with rising threats from the White Citizens' Councils.

Similar to Robert Crawford's segregationist group, Defenders of State Sovereignty and Individual Liberty in Prince Edward County, which formed in opposition to the *Brown* decision, the White Citizens' Councils, a collective made up of supremacists, had emerged around the same time, spearheaded by Mississippi judge Tom P. Brady. Their goal? Preserve racial hierarchies and white dominance and privilege in the South. Their influence quickly spread across the region, and they gained legitimacy through funding from the all-white, all-men Mississippi legislature's Sovereignty Commission. (The Commission was meant to desegregate the state; instead it became the architect of deeper division.) To evangelize their segregationist agenda, the WCC used intimate home meetings, media programs, and state-sponsored propaganda and regularly employed intimidation tactics to suppress efforts for integration, targeting both Black and white Americans who dared challenge the established racial order.

In response to the rise of the WCC's gatekeeping tactics, especially preventing Black people from accessing political power, and inspired by John Lewis's "Where Is Our Party?" speech at the March on Washington, Bob Moses, SNCC's Mississippi project director, in addition to ideating Freedom Summer, proposed forming the Mississippi Freedom Democratic Party to challenge the all-white delegation at the Democratic National Convention. This move would also call into question the legitimacy of the existing Mississippi Democratic Party and its systematic exclusion of Black voters.

This was all underpinned by a time when 45 percent of the state's population were Black Americans, but less than 5 percent were registered to vote. That percentage was much worse in rural counties with an even higher Black population, like Marshall and Tallahatchie (where Emmett's body was dumped), where the percentage registered to vote was less than one and sometimes zero. Those were the counties that Freedom Summer's ten-week initiative, to begin June 1964, planned on zeroing in on. It was also a use case SNCC leaders pointed to when recruiting volunteers.

By the time planning ramped up ahead of those consequential weeks, Charlie was tasked with recruiting and training volunteers from across the country. Recruitment efforts on college campuses and within religious groups surpassed SNCC leaders' expectations. In the end, in addition to the recruits from individual civil rights groups under COFO, more than 1,000 young white students joined African American youths in Mississippi.

At the same time, Charlie had also been familiarizing himself with the project's primary goals. The further he delved, the more he sensed something was amiss. He felt if the summer plan was to uproot the state's cruel cycle of oppression, the focus should equally be on the children—after all, they were to be its future. And the steel instrument to breaking those bolted chains was equal access to quality education.

Even though segregation in schools had technically been outlawed, education for Black Americans remained unequal. It'd been much more glaring and deeply rooted in Mississippi than other parts of the nation. Long before the *Brown* decision and the burgeoning of the civil rights movement, the state simmered with compounded social and political unrest.

In the early 1900s, for example, the state's economy was largely agricultural. Many Black Americans worked as tenant farmers and were subjected to harsher expressions of Jim Crow. The same was felt within the state's segregated educational system. Black schools were grossly underfunded, overcrowded, and starved of resources.

The other thing Charlie confronted, as Bob had done too, was the fact that the state's Black population held little to no representation in the state legislature (at one point, though, in 1930, they had roughly 5 percent of the seats), the judiciary, or the police force. This meant they held little to no say in their future, let alone the future of their children. It dawned on him that it was a political system dominated by white supremacists. Extremists who made up the minority yet regularly used violence and intimidation to keep African Americans from registering to vote, voting, and participating in civil rights protests.

In December 1963, after months on the ground in Mississippi, seeing the impact of the state's history and the current limitations on the future generation, Charlie began penning a proposal for what he called Freedom Schools. He explained that it was impossible for Black children to have any chance at a future as long as their schooling was another layer of suppression, and "repression is the law; oppression, a way of life—regimented by the judicial and executive branches of the state government, rigidly enforced by state police machinery, with veering from the path of 'our way of life' not tolerated at all . . . [Students] have learned the learning necessary for immediate survival: that silence is safest, so volunteer nothing; that the teacher is the state, and tell them only what they want to hear; that the law and learning are white man's law and learning."

The situation, as Charlie presented it, was dire.

Children were encountering enslavement of a most dangerous kind: the locking up of their minds. Their ability to construct self-identity, obtain a worldview, and conceptualize social relations was limited. Charlie felt that developing an independent education program built on the premise of resistance and grounded in the principles of the civil rights movement would become the manifestation of the Black community's stand against the over-politicization and subjugation by segregationists. Black students would no longer be made to believe in the Southern way of life for them and their families: That to be Black is to be forgotten, isolated, forever subservient, and undervalued. Through education, these young minds would reclaim their rightful place of self-governance in society.

Charlie's final proposal for Freedom Schools summarized the urgency of the program.

He divided it into six main parts: the core description, the curriculum, the target student body, the target staffers, the schedule, and the costs.

The meticulous plan underpinned that "the State of Mississippi destroys 'smart n*gg*rs'" and expanded on the ways Freedom Schools would "supplement what [Black students] aren't learning in high schools around the state."

Charlie then went into communities to introduce the idea and scout locations. He knew that, as he later put it, "if you're going to organize in a community, you have to find a consensus that you can work with that will commit people to what you're trying to do."

He immersed himself in neighborhoods and congressional districts across the state, speaking with organizations about partnering with the school for what he had established as two core cohorts: a day program and a boarding school–type setup.

His outreach was successful, and he returned with an actionable approach of twenty-five schools in twenty-five towns. The day programs could accommodate 50 students, while two overnight programs could take about 200 students per location. The boarding schools were pitched as more rigorous. Since that cohort would be on campus with the ability to delve deeper into curricula, he crafted it for students with budding leadership qualities who could handle the added intensity.

The program continued to take shape.

The curriculum was developed in partnership with the National Council of Churches during a conference with educators from across the country. They focused on leadership development with an emphasis on Black history and the continued fight for justice and a restorative academic module that aimed to improve students' overall academic performance in areas like world history, math, reading, and writing. The syllabus also centered around current issues to give students an understanding of organizing, while the social skills element of the coursework helped students develop a sense of agency through hands-on fieldwork, student government, theater, and open classroom dialogues.

When it came to the target demographic, Charlie narrowed his focus to primarily high school students because of the limited capacity of the secured locations. To recruit them statewide, he partnered with churches, educators, and other local organizations. To attract teachers to the program, Charlie looked to existing SNCC volunteers, many of them white, and capitalized on their elite education and connections. He tapped some to be in charge of enlisting student teachers and training them on the curriculum. Among those recruited to teach were advanced high school students from Chicago with high-level skills who had Black history education and professional educators who were sponsored by the National Council of Churches and the Presbyterian Church. All of them were white.

The choice to have white people teach Black students anything, let alone Black history, was a point of contention that was met with dissonance from SNCC organizers—even with Charlie. He felt that "part of what we were trying to do [was] show and persuade people that they could take control of their lives. And if you brought all these white people into the state, it just becomes another example of white people reaching down to uplift the downtrodden Negro." But Bob, who had been frustrated dealing with repeated death and violence among his volunteers and organizers, had reached a point of exhaustion while trying to maintain hope in a hopeless situation. Bob felt that getting white allies on their side, in whatever capacity, could be the best way to amplify the gravity of Mississippians' experience out into the world.

In one conversation, during a planning session, Charlie remembered Bob saying, "'Enough, we've got to get the country to pay attention to Mississippi, and I'll bring these [white] students—I want these students here because I know if we bring the children of America to Mississippi, the country will pay attention.' And he was right on that."

White allies were both a strategic and practical choice for the programs at Freedom Summer. That's how most SNCC senior leadership came to see it. That's precisely how the group's twenty-three-year-old chairman, John Lewis, saw it too. He felt focusing on students from predominantly white and elite schools during volunteer recruitment meant money. Money that SNCC barely had and needed to execute their plans. Many of the white students came from affluent homes, some with parents in positions of power. The more white young allies found purpose in the movement, the better for organizations like SNCC. (For example, in the end, the total cost to execute both the day and boarding programs for Freedom School was $114,100—or $1,169,716 today. Monies raised because of such allyship.)

Though Charlie finally acquiesced to the idea of having white teachers lecture Mississippi's Black youth, in a letter he wrote to the educator recruits, he reinforced the urgency of the program, reminding them that this was not to be merely another summer fling.

"There is hope and there is dissatisfaction—feebly articulated—both born out of the desperation of needed alternatives not given," he penned. "This is the generation that has silently made the vow of no more raped mothers—no more castrated fathers; that looks for an alternative to a lifetime of bent, burnt, and broken backs, minds, and souls. Where creativity must be molded from the rhythm of a muttered 'white son-of-a-bitch'; from the roar of hunger bloated belly; and from the stench of rain and mud washed shacks."

In June 1964, as Freedom Summer kicked off, so too did Freedom School. Anticipating resistance, SNCC leaders persevered as they faced white opposition.

The larger intiative was divided into about forty-four smaller projects based on the targeted rural counties such as Pike, Panola, and Le Flore, areas where the Black population was high, but voter registration was virtually zero. Each smaller project operated as a packaged deal. It included an arm that focused on voter registration. Another focused on developing and recruiting for MFDP in that district, and building community centers that provided cultural and educational programs for the community, like adult literacy courses.

The last arm was Freedom Schools.

The first set of schools opened on June 16, 1964. Though communities where the schools were located were largely supportive, many schools were met with increased harassment from police and threats from segregationists and white locals. Public libraries were unwilling to allow Black students in their doors, and resources were scarce. Teachers were forced to request books and materials from Northern organizations who would then ship donated books and supplies.

The most haunting expression came when three volunteers, twenty-one-year-old James Chaney, twenty-year-old Andrew Goodman, and twenty-four-year-old Michael Schwerner, were tasked with training new recruits at the Western College for Women. They learned that one of the Freedom Schools Michael had helped launch at Mount Zion Methodist Church in Philadelphia, Mississippi, had been firebombed by the KKK. The trio decided to travel from their training site in Oxford, Ohio, to the church's location to investigate.

On June 21, 1964, with assistance from the county's sheriff deputy, Cecil Price, they were stalked, arrested, and then killed by more than a dozen KKK members. James was a Black American from Mississippi's Meridian who had participated in the Freedom Rides demonstrations and was a volunteer with the local CORE group. Andrew and Michael were well-known white allies from New York City. Michael led a local CORE group on the Lower East Side of Manhattan, and Andrew had been active in the effort to integrate schools. (Their kidnapping and death, investigated by the FBI under code name Mississippi Burning, were later portrayed in the 1988 film of the same name.) What makes the death of the trio even more tragic is its connection to Charlie's revolutionary education plans. It puts into perspective just how terrifyingly dangerous it was to fight against Southern racism.

Throughout the summer project, the brutal violence that met James, Michael, and Andrew escalated. There were 35 recorded shootings, 6 documented murders, roughly 84 volunteers beaten (of which 4 were critically wounded), and over 1,000 unjust arrests.

With such intimidation tactics and barriers, fear permeated the program. Unbowed, the more than 3,000 enrolled students carried on throughout forty-one schools held at churches, community centers, and other public institutions. What Charlie and many Freedom School teachers did not expect was the surge of students who actually showed up. They ended up ranging from school-aged children to those in their eighties.

Beyond the classroom, Freedom Schools ignited liberating journeys for its students. Many counted their experience as one that forever recast how they viewed themselves and the circumstances before them.

Then fourteen-year-old Jacqulyn Reed Cockfield, who attended classes at the Meridian, Mississippi, location, called it "a life-changing event for me, a poor, Black youngster. While I attended Catholic school all my life, the first white adults, other than Catholic school nuns, to say a kind word to me were Freedom School teachers. The experience awakened an abiding desire in me to become more knowledgeable of the entire civil rights movement." The program catapulted her into activism. She went on to work for the National Urban League and volunteer with the NAACP.

Freedom Schools similarly influenced its volunteers. Pam Parker was one of the program's white teachers and an exchange student from Spelman College. That summer marked the beginning of a life dedicated to social justice.

"There was never the assumption that the teacher was smarter," Pam later remembered. "That [the teacher] is better than the students. Rather, the teacher shared what she or he knew and was respected for her expertise and knowledge, and the students were also respected for what they knew, including what they had experienced and what they thought. In Mississippi, that meant that the students knew much more than the Northern freedom school teachers about the violence and discrimination and what it meant to be a Black person in Mississippi."

In the spirit of the program, Pam went on to form a women's liberation school in 1970 called Breakaway, teaching the principles and origins of racism and white supremacy. She continued teaching in other programs that emulated the Freedom School framework, like the existing one developed, with the same name, in San Francisco in 2005 by the Children's Defense Fund.

By all measures, Freedom Schools exceeded expectations, from higher recruitment counts to a surge in student engagement, and made a lasting impact on participants. After the program ended, about 200 volunteers remained in Mississippi, abandoning their jobs or dropping out of school to continue fighting for Mississippians. The state had, in effect, become the linchpin of the civil rights fight.

Charlie walked away with three lessons from that summer.

The first goes back to the mother of SNCC herself: Ella Baker. To what she had enabled them to accomplish. It was because of Ella that "for the first time, you begin to see young people taking on leadership roles," Charlie said of this period. First through "the development of SNCC and then through the transformation of student protesters into grassroots organizers. This has a lot to do with the influence of Ella, one of the great figures of twentieth-century political struggles. [She] taught us to organize from the bottom up, rather than from the top down."

It also goes back to what Ella had reminded SNCC members at the very beginning, about the "voices of people who were usually spoken for by other people," Charlie said. But now, because of the efforts by the likes of him, those voices, he remembered, "began to speak for themselves in a way which you could not ignore them. And what the movement did was continually cultivate those voices."

It was all a symbol of how substantive change can take root in communities.

The second lesson? Charlie realized and saw firsthand the power young people had when they turned out and dedicated themselves to a cause. The civility and clarity in their fight made all of it possible. "You don't have to be a grown-up," he simply said, "to begin working for change."

The greatest of all truths from that summer was that it only takes a few to begin a movement for change. "It was four students who sat in Greensboro," he said, "not the entire student body of North Carolina A&T. And while you can't predict that the action of a few will always trigger a movement, you can say that almost all movements have been triggered by the actions of a few."

Despite the violence, setbacks, and intimidation experienced during the summer project, it achieved one of its most pressing goals: More than 17,000 Black residents were inspired to register to vote, though only 1,600 were successful. That surge in participation and the ultimate blatant exclusion helped raise national awareness of the discrimination faced by Black Americans in Mississippi and, by extension, in the South.

However, Southern racism was still an unrelenting, formidable force.

On March 7, 1965, when a similar effort began in Alabama, carnage erupted. Led by John Lewis, about 600 protestors marched from Selma to Alabama's capital, Montgomery, in hopes of securing voting rights for Black Alabamans who were subject to unfair obstacles like literacy tests and poll taxes. As the marchers crossed the Edmund Pettus Bridge, a wall of state and county officers awaited, ready to pounce. The mobilization, later dubbed Bloody Sunday, halted and turned violent when state troopers and local police attacked the peaceful demonstrators. The officers used tear gas, billy clubs, and nightsticks to assault the marchers, causing injuries to sixty people, including John.

Two days later, Martin Luther King, Jr., brought 2,500 marchers back to the bridge, but obeying a court order, they were forced to turn back.

Then, on March 21, protected by the national guard ordered by Lyndon Johnson, thousands jumped in and out of the third fifty-four-mile Selma-to-Montgomery march.

On March 25, 25,000 demonstrators had successfully participated in the trek when they reached the state's Capitol building and delivered a petition of grievances to Governor George Wallace.

The events in Selma ultimately led to the passage of the Voting Rights Act of 1965. Signed by Lyndon Johnson on August 6 of that year, the legislation aimed to eliminate discriminatory voting practices and protect the voting rights guaranteed by the Fourteenth and Fifteenth Amendments. In Mississippi, the law contributed to a significant increase in Black voter registration, particularly in the Delta region where the summer project had focused its efforts. By 1968, over 60 percent of Black residents in Mississippi were registered to vote, compared to the previous 6 percent.

Despite these achievements, the Voting Rights Act did not fully address the underlying issue of systemic racism or the everyday oppression faced by Black Americans. So, the fight continued, with young activists from SNCC still at the forefront.

On June 6, 1966, James Meredith, the young Black man who had first integrated the University of Mississippi four years prior, was critically injured during his one-man march from Memphis, Tennessee, to Jackson, Mississippi, to promote Black voting rights. The attack galvanized SNCC, now led by twenty-four-year-old Stokely Carmichael, to march in James's honor, with the support of Martin Luther King, Jr.

Though committed to nonviolence, SNCC leaders like Stokely recognized the limitations of nonviolence tactics against persistent violence. They began advocating for more assertive, even radical, methods of resistance.

Ten days after James's attack, at an SNCC rally at Stone Street High School in Greenwood, as part of the "Meredith March Against Fear," Stokely delivered a rousing speech about the daily mortal danger Black Americans endured. It happened after he was freshly released from prison that same day following a brief intimidation arrest for trespassing at Stone Street.

Stokely rallied a crowd of over 600 demonstrators.

In his speech, he revived the slogan once used by Alabama's Lowndes County Freedom Organization, a political party supported by SNCC, which he had helped organize in 1965 and 1966: *Black Power for Black People.*

He told the crowd, "We have been saying 'Freedom Now' for

six years, and we ain't got nothing. What we're gonna start saying now is: 'Black Power!' 'Black Power!' 'We want Black Power!' 'Black Power!' 'We want Black Power!' 'Black Power!'"

"What do we want?" He asked the crowd.

"Black Power!"

They knew now.

"That's right!"

After Stokely's speech on Black Power, moderate leaders within the civil rights movement, like Martin Luther King, Jr., criticized the term. They feared its potentially militant connotations would alienate white allies. However, many, particularly younger generations, resonated with the Black Power message of raising awareness of social inequalities, instilling dignity in Black heritage and culture, and highlighting issues like voting rights suppression and police brutality.

It fueled a distinct crusade within the broader fight for equality.

When Martin Luther King, Jr., was assassinated on April 4, 1968, it triggered nationwide riots and the passing of the Fair Housing Act days later, on April 11. While the legislation was a definitive response to his tragic slaying, his death also served as a stark reminder that the fight for equality was far from over.

In the aftermath, the Black Power movement gained significant momentum. Fueled by the ideals of racial pride, self-determination, and economic empowerment for Black Americans, budding youth-led organizations, community initiatives, and cultural collectives began championing these goals, reinvigorating the fight for civil rights.

After Stokely's electrifying "Black Power" address, he further solidified the movement's message in a speech he gave at the University of California, Berkeley: "Every civil rights bill in this country was passed for white people, not for Black people."

This reminded me of the question that plagued me after George Floyd's death: Who is this country really for?

Stokely's words underscored a crucial reality of this country: Laws cannot change hearts. Unless the majority among us understand the need for them and adopt them, true equality remains an endless pursuit. When we've seen landmark victories like the Voting Rights Act come under attack, it only amplifies the question: who truly benefits from these laws? It only reveals the limitations of legal change.

Despite all of that, I choose to celebrate the breakthroughs of this decade. If not for the sacrifices and efforts of Charlie and the thousands of young people who stood up in the face of hostility, powering the political momentum, the passage of the Immigration and Nationality Act of 1965 would never have happened.

Mom would never have made it onto American soil.

During the heat of the civil rights movement, legal measures to challenge racial bigotry nationwide shared the same fighting spirit as the yearslong push by immigration reform advocates to end racial quotas in immigration laws. It became a top issue for the president that year. Both efforts aimed to dismantle discriminatory practices. Just like laws eventually banned segregation, that landmark Immigration and Nationality Act abolished the national origins quota system. It led to increased immigration from regions like Asia, Latin America, and Africa, contributing to America becoming one of the most diverse countries in the world.

The way I've come to see it, the civil rights movement proves a continuum, a nexus, for the majority to really see us. Many will grow weary doing the work needed for lasting equitable societal participation, but someone always benefits.

Someone like Mom gets to realize her American Dream.

And no matter the challenges still faced by all of us Othered, Mom gets to be here. Mom gets to be part of this still-fragile yet resilient and widely respected democracy.

That says something.

That's been enough.

6

BLACK POWER RISES

The Wilmington Ten & the Students Against Apartheid Movement

My very first political action,
the first thing I ever did that involved
an issue or a policy or politics,
was a protest against apartheid.

BARACK OBAMA

The trauma of Manny's deportation began to impact how I engaged with America.

At Northeastern, I regressed to my days of deep insecurity and introspection. I felt lost in all of it: the separation, the worry, the existential question of Who am I?

I was conflicted about my skin, especially attending a predominantly white institution. Never had I been one of the few like this, where in any given class, I was the only one, maybe two. Never had I been this conspicuous raisin in a supersized basin of milk. It felt like grade school again where I'd get knots in my stomach because I didn't fit in with them.

I began to experience firsthand that society grouped all Others into good versus bad minorities. I became calculated about whom I spoke to and hung around, how I carried myself, and how I interacted with the majority white student population and the second majority Asian population. I reclaimed the Nigerianness I had shied away from all those years ago when I preferred to go by Rita, my second first name, instead of Abiemwense, my first first name. (It means I was born at the right time.)

Now, with the rising awareness that this skin can be so problematic in this country, I looked for ways to announce my heritage. "How do you say that?" professors and students would ask. "I love it! It's so different!"

I'd offer more context without being asked, "Ah-be-em-when-say Oh-mocha. I'm Nigerian."

I wondered if it would've made a difference if the officers who stopped Manny knew he was Nigerian. Was all they saw his skin and nothing more? I grew anxious of what could happen if those on campus judged me for my skin, for being Black.

This led to my struggle with the model minority complex. Did I now have something to prove? To whom? Was my identity forever tied to my academic excellence and performance? My Nigerianness? My Blackness?

The better I performed, the more I became an unwilling Black token and grew exhausted trying to remain one. I lost myself contorting to the ideals of how I was perceived instead of living my truth—whatever that was.

My college years taught me that identity is complex and influenced by several factors. Our relationships, personal experiences, and culture are most prominent, layered by our social groupings (like religion, ethnicity, and so on), which provide insights into how others view and treat us. This is why I feared being typecast. I had come to understand what my identity meant within the context of America's "race." But, most of all, it taught me that identity is something we create and negotiate throughout our lives.

Over time, new elements are developed and blended into who we are. It's ever-evolving, shaped by interactions and different settings. Who I am in one setting versus another can necessitate a transformation for the sake of the situation itself or for survival's sake. Like the mindset shift I had at Northeastern with Manny's circumstances constantly churning in my mind. Or even now, in adulthood, the freedom I've walked in, no longer trying to bend to this or that ideal.

The other insight about identity, and in turn, belonging, that I uncovered is that it can be individualistic or within a group. Group relationships lead to a sense of community and acceptance and help us find our place in this big, big world.

The Black Power Movement that swept the nation was deeply rooted in this very reality. After Stokely rekindled a sense of racial pride in African Americans' pursuit of self-governance, that idea began chipping away at the negative stereotypes associated with Blackness that many had struggled with. The same perception that still existed all those years later that I navigated.

The movement urged people to reclaim their identities and destinies, rejecting the limitations imposed by the dominant white perspective. Aware of the challenge, many Black leaders and groups championed self-determination and empowerment, offering diverse interpretations of how to achieve that change within their communities. This spirit of self-reliance and cultural affirmation is what powered a new tide of Black activism and the founding of the Black Panther Party.

JANUARY 25, 1971. WILMINGTON, NORTH CAROLINA.

As a warm breeze wafted through Wilmington, a coastal city nestled on the Cape Fear River, another student uprising crackled in the air.

At New Hanover High School, a school in the throes of slow integration, tensions spilled over during lunch as students rushed the Wildcat, a popular chill spot. A fight had broken out between white and Black students.

As the brawl brimmed back onto the school grounds, police officers pulled the teens apart, but not before a white male student, who was never identified, attacked a Black tenth grader, Barbara Swain, with a knife. When Barbara reported the attack to her school's principal, he chose not to pursue her attacker and instead suspended Barbara and four other Black students for the fight.

Several Black students were frustrated at the flagrant injustice. Three days later, on January 28, a united front of student leaders found a central hub to organize against the suspensions. More than a hundred Black students flooded the Gregory Congregational Church that Thursday to discuss the fight, the suspensions, and what had underpinned it: the ongoing racial warfare that had taken hold of their community and was now putting Black students in peril at newly integrated schools.

At the meeting, twenty-one-year-old Connie Tindall, one of the student organizers, declared that the following day they'd boycott school in what would be dubbed Liberation Day, protesting unfair treatment and calling attention to systemic barriers to advancement.

During this period, students across the nation had increased their organizing and protesting efforts. They had a problem-solving approach to activism and took up many issues, from the ongoing crisis of campus inequality, to women's rights, to overarching civil rights and racial justice issues, to the draft and Vietnam War, which had begun in 1955. And coming off the heels of that landmark *Brown* decision, school integration was also experiencing a powerful push. Hearing about James Meredith, for example, defiantly and successfully integrating the University of Mississippi after suing, Black students became increasingly energized and ready for changes in their own cities.

In Wilmington, desegregation had been a long and arduous process.

In 1969, five years after the passing of the Civil Rights Act and one year after Martin Luther King, Jr.'s assassination, the city was still largely segregated, with Black students attending Williston Industrial High School and white students attending New Hanover and Hoggard high schools.

Williston was prestigious, ranking high academically in the state. After the federal requirement to integrate, the school board shut down Williston at the end of the 1968 school year and forced its students and teachers to New Hanover and Hoggard. The school board's white chairman, Emsley Laney, rationalized the closure by saying "it would be very difficult to integrate Williston High

School and send white students there. It was in a Black neighborhood, and this was never discussed a great deal, but we felt that for the benefit of the community as a whole and the school system, the best thing to do was take the Black students from Williston and split them between the two white high schools." Most of the Williston teachers were fired. Newly integrated Black student athletes couldn't participate in their sports, and those who had held student government positions were not allowed to run for office.

The early years of integration at New Hanover and Hoggard were marred by constant tension for Black students. Racially motivated bullying, intimidation, and even violence became their daily reality. White locals opposed to desegregation often infiltrated the schools, specifically targeting Black students with provocation and aggression. Fights erupted frequently, so much so that a day without one felt like an anomaly. And when fights did break out, school administrators, heavily biased against Black students, readily concluded they were the instigators, leading to harsh punishments like expulsions and suspensions. In more extreme cases, local police were called, further escalating the hostile environment.

This climate of fear and injustice culminated in the melee that Monday at the Wildcat. It was first just *another* day in Wilmington for Black students who endured daily taunts and violence.

This time, though, students had had enough.

On Liberation Day, students executed their plan: boycotting New Hanover and Hoggard, demanding an end to the discriminatory environment, insisting that white school administrators stand with them in allyship, and for the curriculum to reflect Black history and pay homage to Martin Luther King, Jr.

And so it began.

On Friday, January 29, 1971, the boycott was in full swing. The Gregory Congregational Church remained their organizing headquarters. Students and their allies reconvened and strategized when they weren't taking to the streets, marching and chanting and decrying their repressed education and liberties.

Days into the boycott and protesting, the church's white reverend, Eugene Templeton, who had granted the students access to his building, noticed they were in over their heads, struggling to structure their outreach. So, he sought assistance from the United Church of Christ in Raleigh—about a hundred miles north of Wilmington. At this point, too, Eugene had already been subject to intimidation and death threats for his allyship to the cause. He had become accustomed to it, though, but he grew fearful for the students, who lacked organizing experience and the ability to protect themselves.

On February 2, the UCC, led by Charlie Cobb's father, deployed twenty-three-year-old Benjamin Franklin Chavis, Jr., a rising star within their Commission on Racial Justice. Benjamin, a persuasive orator and minister, was a protégé of Martin Luther King, Jr., and was known for his skillful and strategic approach to activism.

Benjamin had come from a family of educators and activists who were involved with the civil rights movement, particularly the NAACP. His grandfather was John Chavis, the first African American to attend Princeton University. By thirteen, as a student at segregated Mary Potter High School in his hometown of Oxford, North Carolina, Benjamin was an organizer with the Southern Christian Leadership Conference. Shortly after, he organized a protest to desegregate his town's all-white public library. His attempt failed, but he pressed on and became the first Black person in town to get a library card.

By the time Benjamin finished college at St. Augustine's, thanks to the charge of "Black Power," he'd found a calling for cooperative organizing and formed a strong belief in the superiority of Black Americans layered with a desire to radically change society in that pursuit. He became SCLC's youth coordinator, working closely with Martin Luther King, Jr., as one of his advance team members.

He went on to continue his bachelor's education in chemistry at the University of North Carolina–Charlotte, where he remained socially engaged. He graduated in 1969 and was appointed southern regional program director for the UCC's Commission on Racial Justice, which meant overseeing and responding to racialized and systematic efforts to suppress Black progress in the region.

When hatred met his family back home, he turned his mourning into a powerful call for justice. In 1970, his cousin, twenty-three-year-old Henry Marrow, a Vietnam veteran, was murdered. He had been shopping at a store owned by a white grocer, Robert Teel. As Henry grabbed a Coke, he exchanged a few words with a white woman. Some say he said those words to Robert's wife. Robert and his son were so enraged by Henry's actions, they chased him from the store, pounded him, then fatally shot him—blowing out his brain with a shotgun. Others say they heard Robert tell his son, "Shoot the son of a bitch," before Henry was executed. With the help of SCLC, Benjamin organized a large boycott of white-owned businesses. But despite his efforts, the outcome mirrored the Emmett Till case: the perpetrators went unpunished.

With the specter of Henry's case serving as a grim and persistent reminder of the challenges Black Americans faced, Benjamin led desegregation efforts for the UCC across North Carolina before arriving in Wilmington with a clear mission: empower the students to organize their boycott effectively.

Once on the scene, Benjamin forcefully and tactfully reiterated the students' demands to the school board and accused them of racism. He pledged to students that he'd be by their side until the fight was won. His no-nonsense approach combined with his unique sense of style—he often sported a bright El Dorado top hat, fur coat, and oversized Afro—caught the eyes of local white leaders, and soon he became a prime target of law enforcement and other white extremist vigilantes.

As the boycott continued, it wasn't long before Benjamin and the student demonstrators faced mounting obstacles. The school board suspended and expelled Black students en masse. A well-known white supremacy citizen militia group, the Rights of White People, joined the police and city officials to stunt protesters' efforts by shooting into the Gregory Congregational Church every night. On one of those days—on Friday, February 5—nineteen-year-old Marvin Patrick was shot and injured by an RWP member. No arrests were made even though police were stationed at the church that day for surveillance.

By this point, with the rising threats from white citizens, groups, and officials, the protesters formed their own militant response to protect themselves and the church. They recruited locals who were either veterans or serving at nearby military bases like Camp Lejeune and Fort Bragg. Some of them began taking more radical tactics to combat the suppression efforts of the RWP, including arson and property damage.

Overnight, Friday into Saturday, the tension came to a head.

Around 10 p.m. on Friday, as students and their allies took to the streets, a white-owned shop, Mike's Grocery, one block from Gregory Congregational Church, was firebombed.

A ruckus ensued.

Police deployed.

Tragedy struck when seventeen-year-old Black student and co-lead organizer Gibb Stevens Corbett was fatally shot by police while checking on the store, which officers had secured, and its perimeter.

As chaos and violence erupted, continuing into the wee hours, a fifty-seven-year-old white man, Harvey Cumber, breached police barricades and charged the church, which was guarded by the Black defense team.

Fearing for their safety, they opened fire, fatally shooting Harvey.

No one specific person was identified as the shooter.

As sirens flashed and ambulances arrived, some Black protestors claimed they were shot at by snipers, who had somehow infiltrated the roof of the church, escalating the already tense atmosphere. This tragic chain of events pushed the already divided community closer to the brink, deepening the well of mistrust and simmering anger that choked the air, further suffocating the already divided region.

About a century before that day, in 1898, Wilmington was an integrated port city. While it boasted a diverse population of about 25,000—58 percent white and 42 percent African American—political power wasn't equally shared. The city was highly segregated, with separate neighborhoods, schools, and public spaces.

The Black population was concentrated in the Second Ward, the city's most densely populated area. This ward housed a majority of Black businesses and churches, while the white population, though more dispersed, was concentrated in the affluent First Ward. This reflected the prevalent racial segregation of the South at the time, when Black residents faced systematic exclusion from political and economic life and often encountered violence and discrimination for stepping outside their designated roles.

Only thirty-five years after Emancipation, and within a context of escalating political disenfranchisement and rising white supremacy, this systemic oppression ignited a violent massacre. It all began on the morning of November 10, 1898.

Enraged by the growing political power of Black Republicans in Wilmington, a group of white supremacist Democrats embarked on a violent coup d'état. This occurred just a few years after the start of the Reconstruction Era, a period following Emancipation when Black Americans made significant progress in achieving social and political equality. They gained citizenship, the right to vote, and increased representation in local governance. However, as the proceeding years tragically demonstrated, this progress was illusory, overshadowed by ongoing intimidation, violence, and murders that effectively nullified any sense of true equality. With the end of Reconstruction in 1877 and the introduction of Jim Crow laws, Black people were subjected to heightened and explicit segregation.

The white supremacists grew frustrated with sharing social power with those they did not deem to be equal. They had been witnessing the significant, albeit slow, change for Black Americans that seemingly disrupted their power structure.

So, on that Thursday, a mob of white men began their attack at the offices of the *Daily Record*, a Black-owned newspaper. The mob then went on to attack Black homes and businesses, killing at least sixty Black people.

The coup successfully overthrew the city government, replacing the newly elected Black leaders with white supremacists, just two days after the election.

The coup, in effect, annulled the voting power of Black citizens. This was the stifling environment that underpinned Black lives in

Wilmington until the sweeping changes of the 1960s, with the civil rights movement and its domino effects. And yet, all those decades later, the unhealed wounds of that era would resonate again, felt by the young Black students from New Haven and Hoggard high schools, echoing the same yearning for justice that culminated in the destruction of Mike's Grocery on February 6, 1971.

That Saturday, following the bombing, the National Guard took over Wilmington.

A curfew from 7:30 p.m. to 6 a.m. was put into place.

Order was restored.

Damages were estimated at $500,000.

Several arrests were made, including ten of the protestors, who, without evidence, were jailed for setting fire to the shop and shooting snipers. Many maintained that the arson was started by white locals looking to further incite the unrest.

The detained demonstrators came to be known as the "Wilmington Ten."

The Ten were Benjamin, the UCC minister; Marvin, the young man injured during one of RWP's drive-bys; Connie, the student leader who called for Liberation Day; nineteen-year-olds James McKoy, Jerry Jacobs, and William Wright, Jr.; and eighteen-year-olds Reginald Epps, Wayne Moore, and Willie Vereen. All were Black except the tenth member, a white ally: thirty-five-year-old social worker Ann Shepard, who had dedicated her career to antipoverty and racial justice.

Support from white allies like Ann was no longer an oddity. It had become a cultural norm after being popularized and grounded during the civil rights movement, as interracial student demonstrations flourished on the grounds of academic autonomy, intellectual freedom, and school integration.

Meanwhile, on the other side of the country, the burgeoning Black Power Movement had been brewing a different kind of activism, the likes of which had influenced Benjamin and his spirit of empowerment. In West Oakland, California, the Black Panther Party were gaining prominence as a powerful force for Black liberation. This rising national consciousness around Black activism, both through self-protection and self-determination movements, would ultimately play a role in the Wilmington Ten's case.

A potent mix of inspiration and frustration spurred the founding of the Black Panther Party by twenty-four-year-old Huey Newton and twenty-nine-year-old Bobby Seale while attending Merritt College.

The son of longshoreman Walter Newton and domestic worker Armelia Johnson Newton, Huey was born in Monroe, Louisiana, on February 17, 1942. One of seven siblings, he grew up in Oakland, California, and experienced the bleak realities of poverty, racial segregation, and police violence. He witnessed discrimination during school integration efforts and the brutal treatment of Black Americans by law enforcement. These experiences ignited a deep-seated sense of justice in a young Huey, leading him to participate in protests and organize youth groups, demonstrating his early commitment to activism.

Similarly, Bobby was born in the predominantly African American neighborhood of Liberty, Texas, on October 22, 1936. His father, George Seale, a carpenter, and mother, Thelma Seale, a homemaker, struggled to provide for their family in an era rife with racial segregation and economic hardship. The Seales moved to Oakland when Bobby was eight, where his upbringing continued to be characterized by the grim truths of poverty and discrimination, experiences that shaped his worldview and energized his later activism.

These shared experiences of racial discrimination and a hunger for justice gelled Huey and Bobby's bond at Merritt College. Both found themselves deeply moved by the message of Malcolm X, particularly after his assassination on February 21, 1965. His ideas of Black autonomy and armed resistance resonated deeply with them, finding further echo in Stokely Carmichael's gripping "Black Power" speech the following year, on June 16, 1966. This ignited their escalating desire for parity and fueled their urgent desire to act.

The simmering pot of tensions finally boiled over for them with the compounding brutality carried out by the Oakland police that fall. In early September, during the arrest of a Black teen boy, his sister was severely beaten by officers. When hundreds of young people flooded the streets in protest, the police response was swift and heavy-handed, with over sixty officers arresting a dozen of them. Then, on September 27, tragedy struck again. When another Black teen, sixteen-year-old Matthew Johnson, was pursued by police for alleged grand theft auto, he was fatally shot in the back while fleeing. Left to bleed on the ground for over an hour, his death ignited the predominantly African American Hunters Point community into days of protests and looting.

Witnessing the ceaseless pain, desperation for justice consumed Bobby and Huey. They felt the mainstream nonviolent tactics of the time were insufficient. They wanted a new approach that emphasized self-reliance and directly addressed the challenges faced by Black communities. Fueled by this conviction, they decided to form the Black Panther Party for Self-Defense on October 15, 1966.

Later, Bobby and Huey shortened the name to the Black Panther Party, dropping "for self-defense" to emphasize their broader social and economic change vision. This concept centered around several core principles:

—Arming Black communities for self-defense

—Organizing and empowering communities

—Ending police brutality

—Securing the release of political prisoners

—Redistributing wealth

—Obtaining reparations for centuries of slavery and exploitation

—Achieving economic empowerment for Black Americans

These demands were formalized in their Ten Point Program, outlining the path forward for their revolutionary organization. Artie

McMillan, formerly Artie Seale—Bobby's partner at the time—was tasked with typing the list of aspirations. With her experience as an office worker, she was able to transcribe the handwritten notes from the men. She worked on it through the "wee hours one of those October mornings in 1966," she told me. After many revisions by Bobby and Huey, it took Artie about a week to finalize the document.

Once finished, Artie said it "was printed off utilizing a mimeograph machine—a stencil duplicator—and then distributed" at the next meeting.

The Ten Point Program handout laid out a pointed mission:

1. **We Want Freedom. We Want Power to Determine the Destiny of Our Black Community.** We believe that Black people will not be free until we are able to determine our destiny.

2. **We Want Full Employment for Our People.** We believe that the federal government is responsible and obligated to give every man employment or a guaranteed income. We believe that if the White American businessmen will not give full employment, then the means of production should be taken from the businessmen and placed in the community so that the people of the community can organize and employ all of its people and give a high standard of living.

3. **We Want An End to the Robbery By the White Man of Our Black Community.** We believe that this racist government has robbed us, and now we are demanding the overdue debt of forty acres and two mules. Forty acres and two mules were promised 100 years ago as restitution for slave labor and mass murder of Black people. We will accept the payment in currency which will be distributed to our many communities. The Germans are now aiding the Jews in Israel for the genocide of the Jewish people. The Germans murdered six million Jews. The American racist has taken part in the slaughter of over fifty million Black people; therefore, we feel that this is a modest demand that we make.

4. **We Want Decent Housing Fit For The Shelter of Human Beings.** We believe that if the White Landlords will not give decent housing to our Black community, then the housing and the land should be made into cooperatives so that our community, with government aid, can build and make decent housing for its people.

5. **We Want Education for Our People That Exposes The True Nature Of This Decadent American Society. We Want Education That Teaches Us Our True History And Our Role in the Present-Day Society.** We believe in an educational system that will give to our people a knowledge of self. If a man does not have knowledge of himself and his position in society and the world then he has little chance to relate to anything else.

6. **We Want All Black Men To Be Exempt From Military Service.** We believe that Black people should not be forced to fight in the military service to defend a racist government that does not protect us. We will not fight and kill other people of color in the world who, like Black people, are being victimized by the White racist government of America. We will protect ourselves from the force and violence of the racist police and the racist military by whatever means necessary.

7. **We Want An Immediate End to Police Brutality and the Murder of Black People.** We believe we can end police brutality in our Black community by organizing Black self-defense groups that are dedicated to defending our Black community from racist police oppression and brutality. The Second Amendment to the Constitution of the United States gives a right to bear arms. We therefore believe that all Black people should arm themselves for self-defense.

8. **We Want Freedom For All Black Men Held in Federal, State, County and City Prisons and Jails.** We believe that all Black People should be released from the many jails

and prisons because they have not received a fair and impartial trial.

9. **We Want All Black People When Brought to Trial To Be Tried In Court By A Jury Of Their Peer Group Or People From Their Black Communities, As Defined By the Constitution of the United States.** We believe that the courts should follow the United States Constitution so that Black people will receive fair trials. The Fourteenth Amendment of the U.S. Constitution gives a man a right to be tried by his peer group. A peer is a person from a similar economic, social, religious, geographical, environmental, historical, and racial background. To do this the court will be forced to select a jury from the Black community from which the Black defendant came. We have been, and we are being, tried by all-White juries that have no understanding of the "average reasoning man" of the Black community.

10. **We Want Land, Bread, Housing, Education, Clothing, Justice And Peace.** When, in the course of human events, it becomes necessary for one people to dissolve the political bands which have connected them with another, and to assume, among the powers of the earth, the separate and equal station to which the laws of nature and nature's God entitle them, a decent respect of the opinions of mankind requires that they should declare the causes which impel them to the separation.

The pamphlet closes with an excerpt of the preamble of the Declaration of Independence: "We hold these truths to be self-evident, that all men are created equal; that they are endowed by their Creator with certain inalienable rights; that among these are life, liberty, and the pursuit of happiness . . . But, when a long train of abuses and usurpations, pursuing invariably the same object, evinces a design to reduce them under absolute despotism, it is their right, it is their duty, to throw off such government, and to provide new guards for their future security."

The pursuit of happiness.

This pursuit, for millions of Black Americans, had for too long remained a distant dream bolstered by coordinated systemic racism and discrimination.

After penning their vision for a more just society, Bobby and Huey went to work, engaging with the community and nurturing the empowerment they imagined.

Huey, known for his directness and uncompromising commitment to righteousness, quickly became a polarizing figure. His brilliance and riveting speeches earned him admiration from many, while his impulsive behavior and involvement in violent confrontations raised concerns among others. Bobby, similarly, captivated audiences with his charisma and ability to unite people behind the movement's cause. While their approaches differed, their shared devotion for liberation was unmistakable.

Externally, their leadership began to face scrutiny, particularly due to their stance on open gun-carrying as a means of self-defense for Black communities. This posture, while controversial, stemmed from the very real and ongoing experiences of police brutality faced by Black residents. In response, the Party evolved into an unofficial armed community defense group, patrolling their neighborhoods, dressed in all black, their guns visible and ready. They'd greet each other with a pumped fist, a mark of solidarity. This gesture was already a symbol of unity and resistance that gained prominence during the civil rights and Black Power movements. The Party popularized it, making it synonymous with Black Power.

The Party's stance was visually represented by the black berets they wore, evoking the anti-fascist resistance spirit of French fighters against Nazi occupation during World War II. Drawing inspiration from these figures, the Party aligned itself with the broader struggle against oppression. The Party also embraced the Black Liberation flag developed four decades prior by Marcus Garvey, the Jamaican-born leader of Pan-Africanism and Black Nationalism. The red represented the strength and resilience of Black people—the bloodshed and sacrifices made in the fight for liberation; the green for prosperity; and the black for unity. The flag was often displayed at Party rallies and protests, serving as a powerful embodiment of hope and solidarity.

As the Party evolved, so too did its political framework. Influenced by Maoism, Marxism, and the writings of social philosopher Frantz Fanon, it solidified into revolutionary intercommunalism, which was underpinned by the idea of building solidarity between oppressed communities. Doing this distinguished the Party from other Black cultural nationalist organizations as they came to recognize the exploitation of the Black working class by Black capitalists and elites. They also began making a clear distinction between racist and nonracist whites.

Their ideology began to ferment.

Huey and Bobby believed that traditional forms of nationalism were ineffective in the face of global capitalism and imperialism. To that end, they started fundraising and investing in over sixty social programs, known as community survival programs, including free breakfast for children, medical clinics, and voter registration drives. These programs gained popularity among African Americans, leading to the explosive growth and influence of the Party.

However, their radical stance also created tensions with established civil rights leaders. Before his assassination, Martin Luther King, Jr. acknowledged the frustrations animating the Black Power Movement and some of the Party's tactics. He expressed reservations about their use of violence, fearing it would escalate the cycle of violence and ultimately hinder progress. For example, in his April 30, 1967, "Why I Am Opposed to the War in Vietnam" speech, he said: "As I have walked among the desperate, rejected, and angry young men, I have told them that Molotov cocktails and rifles would not solve their problems. I have tried to offer them my deepest compassion while maintaining my conviction that social change comes most meaningfully through non-violent action." He felt resorting to violence risked alienating potential allies and ultimately harming the very communities the likes of which Huey and Bobby sought to empower.

Despite their community programs and growing influence, the Party, whose clarion call had come to be "power to the people," grappled with internal contradictions.

One glaring example was the disconnect between their outward message of oneness and the patriarchal leadership within the Party itself, which struggled to live up to its own ideals of equal power for all people. Artie recalled several times when women in the Party, who were supposed to be empowered alongside the community, were silenced and relegated into the shadows. (As a result, their vital contributions have often been left out of historical accounts of this period.)

"It was proper to be seen and not heard by your spouse," she told me. "Married women to [the] leaders were beaten and taught to know their place. We cooked breakfast for school children. Sold newspapers, kept offices clean, and if we were not artists and worked diligently on the upcoming newspapers, we drove, passed out leaflets, marched for exercise, and manned telephones. The men were the leaders, and the women remained silent. Women were not readily welcomed into the fold and were treated as second-class. The equality jargon was for the public to hear and not practiced within the Party." She said there was always the undertone of, "Change everything but the way we treat our women." Still, in the face of these internal struggles, Artie made it clear that the Party's work for the community remained unrelenting.

Though plagued with its ills, the Party continued to blossom into a dominant force and global symbol of the Black Power Movement. Their chapters spread across American cities like Charlotte, Philadelphia, Los Angeles, and, notably, Chicago. That prominent branch was founded by the acclaimed twenty-year-old Fred Hampton in 1968.

The Party swamped colleges too, with chapters on campuses such as the University of California—Berkeley, Lincoln University, and many HBCUs, including Howard, Texas Southern University, and North Carolina Central University.

Its influence even spread internationally, with affiliates popping up in countries like the United Kingdom, Cuba, Germany, France, and Algeria. In South Africa, the Party's ideology and activism served as a roadmap for the burgeoning anti-Apartheid student movement.

* * *

Three years after Bobby and Huey founded the Black Panther Party and months before the Wilmington boycott, two South African student activists formed the Black Consciousness Movement, demanding an end to the dominance of the white establishment and championing Black self-determination and self-reliance.

Co-founded in 1969 by twenty-three-year-old Steve Biko and twenty-five-year-old Barney Pityana, the BCM was inspired by the Black Power Movement and the Party, replicating and adopting its foundational principles of Black pride, educational liberty, and community organizing.

Barney hailed from the Eastern Cape, the second-largest province in South Africa, home to diverse tribes like Xhosa and Thembu. In 1966, he began at the historically Black school, University of Fort Hare, to study law. In the throes of Apartheid, Barney was a founding member of his school's chapter of Southern African Students' Organization to promote Black consciousness and self-determination. SASO was formed by Steve Biko, who had campaigned across the country around that time, galvanizing students to create exclusively Black student governments at their campuses.

Born December 18, 1946, Steve grew up in a politically charged family in King William's Town, South Africa, about 300 miles south of the capital city, Cape Town. His father, Mzingayi Mathew Biko, was a police officer who died when Steve was just four. In the face of abject poverty under the oppressive Apartheid regime, his mother, Alice Nokuzola Biko, a domestic worker at Grey Hospital, became a powerful force in Steve's life. He had three other siblings: two sisters and a brother, Khaya, who joined the local chapter of the Pan-Africanist Congress, a national liberation movement inspired by figures like W.E.B. Du Bois and Marcus Garvey. (The PAC later became a lasting political party in South Africa.) Steve's outspoken nature and involvement in activism, however, led to his expulsion from grade school, forcing him to attend a private one afterward.

He went on to study medicine at the University of Natal, where he remained heavily involved in student politics. Meanwhile, as the SASO frontman, he began teaching and popularizing the idea of Black Consciousness as the Black Panther Party's influence fastened. The term had come to pithily encapsulate the effort to empower Black people through reclaiming their identity, building self-reliance, and uniting against oppression.

In 1969, after Barney was expelled from Fort Hare for his political activism, he connected with Steve to form BCM.

By this time, they had both been equally supercharged by Nelson Mandela.

The prominent freedom fighter who had become a global symbol of resistance against oppression had been imprisoned for seven years already, serving a life sentence for his anti-Apartheid activities. Since the 1940s, Nelson had been organizing campaigns through the nation's social-democratic political party, the African National Congress. One such demonstration was the 1952 Defiance Campaign, where protesters marched to white-only areas.

Nelson had laid the groundwork and energized many Black South African youths toward a more profound, more intentional activism. His defiance and resilience in the face of brutality instilled in Steve and Barney a steely resolve to continue the fight for justice and equality. Building on Nelson's decades-long struggle against the nation's oppressive regime, the duo's grassroots efforts began clicking into place.

They recruited students to BCM. They circulated and drew inspiration from the Party's Ten Point Program, emphasizing its self-defense and armed tactics. The social services framework enforced by the Party also influenced how BCM wanted to address the needs of the Black community.

On its face, BCM's formation was a brazen act of defiance. This boldness becomes even more striking when considering the suffocating reality of Apartheid had gripped South Africa since 1948. The term "apartheid" itself, derived from the Afrikaans word for "apartness," speaks volumes about the systematic segregation and oppression that Black South Africans endured.

Fueled by a legacy of colonial segregation, the Apartheid system, like America's "separate but equal" doctrine, mandated racial separation and denied Black South Africans basic rights and opportunities, effectively confining them to a permanent underclass. This system was enforced through laws like the Population Registration Act, the Group Areas Act, and the Bantu Education Act, which, respectively, classified people by race, designated separate living areas, and aimed to restrict and inferiorize Black education.

It was rooted in white supremacy by the National Party, a minority government that came to power in 1948. Ruling over a nation where reports estimate demographics during this period at 18 million people of color and 4 million whites, they imposed a strict racial hierarchy that privileged the white minority and systematically silenced the majority non-white population, including Black Africans, Coloureds, and Indians. ("Coloureds" is a term used in South Africa to describe people of mixed racial heritage. Their ancestry can include indigenous African, European, and Asian origins, such as Indian, Malay, Indonesian, or Sri Lankan.)

The National Party's justification for Apartheid was to preserve their white culture and colonial heritage, safeguard resources, and prevent interracial relationships. In effect, to suppress Black empowerment of any kind. Black South Africans were not allowed to live in the same areas as white South Africans. They were prohibited from using the same public facilities, such as schools, hospitals, and restaurants. They were not allowed to vote in elections.

Separate but equal.

Many who began standing up against Apartheid, like Nelson Mandela, were either imprisoned or exiled. This systematic oppression fueled the rise of the Black Consciousness Movement. As the group gained popularity among Black South Africans, Steve emerged as its eminent leader and a vocal critic of the segregationist government. His emphatic speeches and poignant writings on Black Consciousness, like "Black is Beautiful," compelled and propelled the South African liberation struggle, especially among students. His rising profile and growing influence also made him a target for the government, who viewed him as a threat to their regime.

In 1973, Steve was banned by the government, prohibiting him from public speaking, attending political meetings, and even leaving his home district. Undeterred, he continued to be a vigorous opponent of Apartheid, wielding his pen as his weapon. It was during this time that he wrote the seminal manuscript "Black Consciousness and the Quest for a True Humanity." In it, he argued that Black Consciousness should be embraced as a positive mindset, a way of life that empowers Black people to unite and find pride in their shared identity and cultural heritage. He rejected the notion of imitating white culture and instead emphasized liberation from external control, urging Black people to strive for freedom and true humanity on their own terms.

While Steve's voice continued to be suffocated by oppressors within South Africa, the fight against Apartheid began to resonate internationally.

Inspired by Nelson's tireless campaigning against injustice, even from behind bars since his imprisonment in 1962, and the growing momentum of BCM, local chapters of the Black Panther Party began providing crucial support to the anti-Apartheid movement. They used their newspaper, *The Black Panther*, and educational events to raise awareness about Apartheid and garner international support. They donated essential supplies (like food, clothing, and medical aid); organized rallies and protests across America at South African embassies, consulates, and businesses; and spoke out against the oppressive regime. Some leaders even formed alliances with global anti-Apartheid organizations and established connections with political groups like the ANC and PAC.

Such allyship only added fuel to the burgeoning global movement for Black liberation, which began to crescendo in 1974.

The South African minister of Bantu Education, responsible for the segregated school system for Black students, imposed a new discriminatory rule. The policy mandated that all education be taught in English and Afrikaans, the Dutch colonized language spoken by the white minority.

Founded and funded by the Apartheid government in 1953, Bantu schools were already designed to offer Black South Africans inferior education. They were poorly equipped, lacked qualified teachers, and followed a curriculum designed to limit advancement opportunities. Previously, students had learned in their own indigenous languages, like Xhosa, Tswana, and Venda. This new directive was another attempt to suppress their progress and erase their cultural identity.

In response, BCM students decried the blatant attempt to stifle Black South Africans' cultural identity and disadvantage them educationally. Their stewing outrage reached a boiling point on Wednesday, June 16, 1976. In protest of their poorly funded education that was severely constrained by Apartheid, students walked out of Morris Isaacson High School and marched about four miles to the South African Police Service station in Orlando, South Western Townships (colloquially known as Soweto).

The police were like gods in the Johannesburg township, terrorizing Black citizens at any opportune turn. So, this act of defiance by the students, in and of itself, indelibly conveyed an unmistakable message.

And in a forceful display to assert their power, the peaceful student demonstrators were met with immediate violence by SAPS officers. They opened rapid fire on the marchers, fatally gunning down hundreds, including twelve-year-old Hector Pieterson.

The photo of Hector's lifeless body being carried by eighteen-year-old Mbuyisa Makhubo with Hector's horrified sister, Antoinette Sithole, by his side turned this moment of protest into a globe-organizing crusade. Soon coined the Soweto Uprising, it led to a formalized and systematic campaign to overthrow the South African government. (Hector's life and the Soweto Uprising are honored annually on June 16 in South Africa as "Youth Day.")

Days of ceaseless protesting ensued, spreading to other parts of Soweto.

On June 17, as demonstrations continued across Soweto and other townships, so did the death toll and property destruction (including school buildings), forcing the government to declare a state of emergency.

By that Friday, June 18, protests had spread to other parts of South Africa, including Cape Town. The protest grew so massive, the government was forced to deploy the army to quell students.

By the formal end of the demonstration that Friday, more than 20,000 students had walked out of their schools.

The tremors of the unrest were immediate and lingered long after.

Though he hadn't organized the uprising, the government blamed Steve Biko, who was already under close surveillance, and the BCM for the rise in political consciousness among Black South Africans. They saw BCM as a key factor in students' continued protests and refusal to return to schools.

A year later, on August 18, 1977, Steve was arrested and detained in Cape Town. He had violated his prior arrest release terms to not travel to certain regions and was taken to the Port Elizabeth police station. There he was interrogated, severely beaten, and tortured. Steve was denied medical attention and died on September 12 from injuries sustained during his interrogation.

Steve's death was a tragic blow to the movement.

Yet, his sacrifice, and that of Hector Pieterson and the resulting iconic image, became evocative symbols of the fight against Apartheid.

The violence and uprising showcased the country's systemized racial oppression and sparked international outrage. Before the uprising, many outside of South Africa knew little about the plight of Black South Africans, let alone its similarities to the struggles for racial justice and equality occurring in America. The brutality of Apartheid resonated with American activists, including thousands of students. The Black Panther Party's existing solidarity with Black South Africans bolstered the emerging student anti-Apartheid movement.

Soon, Black students and their allies across the globe began to mobilize, becoming a powerful force against the South African oppressive regime.

HBCUs became incubators for anti-Apartheid activism across American campuses. These schools and their students, who had a storied history of social justice, knew all too well the sting of racial oppression. They had not only been actively supporting the Black Power Movement, they also provided platforms for intellectual discourse, seeking lasting and actionable solutions, through think tanks like the Institute of the Black World. They also addressed the growing issue of gun violence within Black communities in America. So, this existing commitment to equity naturally extended to the fight against Apartheid. With their established networks and experience, HBCUs and their students began raising awareness, organizing protests, and advocating for international sanctions against the South African government.

HBCU students also crystallized the critical values of the anti-Apartheid movement in America, drawing upon campaigns from leaders such as Randall Robinson and Mary Frances Berry, who founded the Free South Africa Movement.

Students from Spelman and Morehouse to Howard University and Tuskegee University organized protests, strikes, teach-ins, boycotts, and similar divestment campaigns: They called for their school administrators and American businesses to withdraw their billions in investment from companies tied to South Africa, hoping to cripple the nation's economy, which would then force the end of Apartheid.

They disrupted speeches when South African politicians visited America.

They barricaded schools and other business buildings.

They sent letters of solidarity to South African activists, raised money for the ANC, and organized concerts and other events to benefit them.

On campus lawns, students constructed shantytown replicas that reflected the debilitated conditions of Black South Africans and attracted national media attention. Much like slums, South Africa's shantytowns, hastily constructed with scrap materials, bore the grim reality of poor sanitation, limited access to essential services, and high crime rates, all due to their unplanned and unregulated nature. They often sprawled onto land never meant for habitation.

HBCU students also formed a national coalition to better coordinate student activism against Apartheid and raise awareness across all campuses. Other campuses followed suit: the University of California formed the Campuses United Against Apartheid and Washington University founded Action Against Apartheid. These coalitions organized impactful nationwide protests, like the boycott of South African goods, and lobbied the government to impose economic sanctions on South Africa.

A similar student movement had been taking root for the Wilmington Ten as they faced a daunting legal challenge: their trial began on February 14, 1972, almost a year to the date after Mike's Grocery was burned down. Benjamin and the nine others were now charged with arson for the firebombing and with conspiracy for allegedly shooting at responding firemen. If convicted, they faced long sentences ranging from 20 to 34 years, for a combined total of 282 years.

Like the Scottsboro Nine's case, the Ten's ordeal drew national and international attention to what many deemed wrongful arrests and charges.

In South Africa, anti-Apartheid activists, including Nelson Mandela—still imprisoned—and Archbishop Desmond Tutu, expressed solidarity with the Ten, drawing parallels to their own fight. British trade unions, like the International Defense and Aid Fund for Southern Africa, condemned the trial and called for the immediate release of the Ten.

Stateside, as student activists held rallies outside the South African Consulate in New York, they likened their condemnation of Apartheid to the battle for justice for the Ten, the demonization on both ends glaring. Students at HBCUs like Howard and North Carolina Central were ceaseless in their fight, mobilizing and organizing protests, sit-ins, and marches, demanding the Ten's release.

Celebrities joined in, too, amplifying the student rallying voices. Singer and civil rights activist Harry Belafonte used his influential global platform to keep the Ten's names front and center. On February 20, 1972, in Wilmington, actor and activist Ossie Davis gave a speech at a rally in support of them, emphasizing the importance of standing up against injustice.

The New York Times, *The Washington Post*, and other local and major newspapers provided extensive coverage of the Ten's case, highlighting the racial dynamics and controversies surrounding the case. Television networks such as CBS, ABC, and NBC aired news segments and reports on the trial, helping the plight of the Ten reach a wider audience.

As the trial kicked off, it was initially scheduled to take place in New Hanover County. However, persistent protests and growing media attention prompted officials to move the proceedings twenty-five miles north to Pender County Superior Court that June. There, a jury composed of ten Black Americans and two white Americans was selected.

Just as the trial was about to begin, the white prosecutor, twenty-nine-year-old Jay Stroud, complained of stomachaches, causing a delay that raised suspicion about the legitimacy of his claims. Ultimately, a mistrial was declared. Another trial was set for that September.

During jury selection for the second trial, Jay revealed a deeply concerning level of racial bias. He systematically challenged and excluded most of the Black Americans, leaving the final jury with a disproportionately skewed composition: ten white, two Black. It later came to light that while claiming illness during the initial selection process, Jay had kept a disturbing tally on a legal pad. Next to six white potential jurors, he had scrawled "KKK Good!" in bold letters. Beside the name of a Black woman, he simply wrote "NO." The back of the pad revealed a chilling calculation: the pros and cons of forcing a new trial, with one clear motive scrawled—"mistrial."

When the trial finally began, it quickly shifted into high gear.

Provided by the UCC's Commission for Racial Justice, the defense's James Ferguson presented evidence showing that the charges were politically motivated and orchestrated by the state, who targeted the Ten for their activism.

The prosecution countered with questionable witness testimonies, like that of seventeen-year-old Allen Hall. Offered a deal for his own conviction in the Wilmington protests, Allen claimed he saw some of the Ten participate in violent actions and arson that day. He specifically said he heard Benjamin egg on the others to set fire to the store.

During cross-examination, James effectively challenged Allen's credibility, highlighting contradictions in his testimony.

To bolster Allen's story, the prosecution presented additional witnesses, including twelve-year-old Eric Junius and seventeen-year-old Jerome Mitchell—both seemingly vulnerable at the hands of the white prosecutorial office due to their young age and backgrounds. Jerome was a convicted felon and Eric hadn't completed middle school.

In the end, neither of their testimonies identified any of the Ten.

The trial concluded on October 12, 1972, with the conviction of the Ten. All were high schoolers except Connie, Ann (the white social worker), and Benjamin.

> **Ann Shepard**, sentenced to fifteen years, convicted on a reduced charge for being an accessory to the crime
>
> **Benjamin Chavis**, sentenced to thirty-four years
>
> **Connie Tindall**, sentenced to thirty-one years
>
> **Jerry Jacobs, James McKoy, Marvin Patrick, Wayne Moore, William Reginald Epps**, and **Willie Lee Vereen**, each sentenced to twenty-eight years
>
> **William Wright**, Jr., sentenced to twenty-nine years

The verdict was further marred by the revelation that Allen only served one of a twelve-year sentence for his role in the protests, raising serious questions about the motivations behind his testimony.

Determined to overturn the injustice, James appealed the convictions. However, in 1974, the North Carolina Court of Appeals upheld the decision, leaving the Ten's future uncertain.

Two years later, in March 1976, a bombshell dropped: in a signed sworn statement, Allen recanted his testimony. He confessed that Jay, coercing him with threats and violence, had forced him into falsely implicating Benjamin and the others. The gravity of his words hung heavier in the air as his disclosure went deeper: Allen admitted harboring personal animosity toward Benjamin due to his popularity and activism, even plotting to kill him at one point. This shocking confession exposed the corrupt heart of the Ten's case. The excerpts from his recantation offer a disturbing glimpse into the fabricated testimony:

> ALLEN: And so then, like, they told me what to say in Court because I had gotten mad, and I had said that for them to just give me a gun, that I would kill Chavis, you know. And so Stroud said, No, uh, you couldn't kill him because if you kill him, they would investigate because he is in a civil rights movement. And so then they said that the best way to get him is through, by law. He said, because law has so many quirks and turns in it and so like, I went along with that. So like, then after they had told me how to make Molotov cocktails and they had showed me what dynamite was, you know, and blasting caps.

> JAMES: Did you know anything about Molotov cocktails and dynamite before they told you about them?

> ALLEN: No, because I had never been involved in nothing like that before.

> JAMES: You hadn't seen Chavis or any of the other people who were on trial making any Molotov cocktails or bring dynamite into the church or anything like that?

> ALLEN: No.

> JAMES: Okay, go ahead and tell us what else happened.

> ALLEN: Well, then Mr. Walden, [ATF—Alcohol, Tobacco and Firearms—agent] Bill Walden, he said here's some dynamite and blasting caps, claiming it was electric dynamite. He said he found it in the church basement and asked if I'd seen it. I said no, I hadn't seen any dynamite in any church basement. So, he said, "No, you don't say that because you're looking at the dynamite now, right?" I said yes. He said, "Well then, that's the dynamite that came out from under the church. You're supposed to say you saw the dynamite in the basement of the church." So, I said, "Okay then."

. . .

JAMES: Where was Ben when Mike's Grocery was burned?

ALLEN: In Reverend Templeton's house. To the best of my knowledge, Ben didn't know anything about it. Half the time, whenever the gas was there, Ben wouldn't even know because they kept it hidden.

JAMES: Okay, so are you saying then that Ben didn't tell anyone to burn down Mike's Grocery Store?

ALLEN: No.

JAMES: And he wasn't out there when Mike's Grocery was being burned?

ALLEN: No, he wasn't out there when it was being burned.

Benjamin was interviewed in Central Prison after Allen's confession. He felt the teen was "as much a victim of the state justice system as we are. I have nothing but compassion for him."

That unwavering optimism and perspective also colored his view of their predicament. Because even in the face of their harsh reality, Benjamin continued clinging to hope. In another interview, he said, "If there will be any justice in the Wilmington Ten case, it will be through federal intervention . . . The justice system in North Carolina is racist to the bone."

In January 1977, the Department of Justice launched a probe against the prosecutors, and the results were damning. Their investigation uncovered a shocking conspiracy: the prosecutors had paid witnesses in some fashion, including Allen, Eric, and Jerome, to falsely identify Benjamin and the other nine defendants for arson and conspiracy.

These discoveries, along with the added recantations of Eric and Jerome, fueled a firestorm of controversy and international attention. Civil rights organizations, activists, and public figures, outraged by the blatant racial bias and potential political persecution, rallied even harder for the Ten's release.

Closer to home, in North Carolina, news of the Department of Justice's investigation reverberated deeply. Winston-Salem, home to the state's most formalized Black Panther Party chapter, became a crucial center of action. Their proximity and active engagement made them a key pillar of support. The chapter's regular active rallies and Black consciousness classes amplified the movement, while their satellite center twenty miles south, in nearby city High Point, extended their reach in the state. While details of their full contribution remain murky, their established infrastructure, including the free breakfast for children program, free clothing distribution, and ambulance services, undoubtedly provided essential logistical support to the Ten and their families.

Beyond local support, the broader Black Panther Party network proved instrumental in the case. Through their Legal Defense Fund, they provided ongoing financial support for legal appeals. Additionally, they mobilized public pressure, fought to overturn the convictions, and demanded a fair trial, collaborating with civil rights organizations to amplify their efforts. This included continuously leveraging their newspaper, *The Black Panther*, and organizing rallies, speeches, and public appearances.

In April 1977, these sustained efforts reached Amnesty International. Recognizing the Ten as prisoners of conscience arrested for their political activities, not the alleged crimes, the global human rights group took on the Ten's case.

The growing pressure began to bear fruit.

On January 23, 1978, North Carolina governor James B. Hunt, Jr., reduced the sentences of the Ten, making most eligible for parole later that year, except Benjamin, who had a harsher sentence, making him eligible in 1980.

Outraged by this continued injustice toward the UCC minister, the movement gained renewed momentum.

A month later, Bobby Seale addressed a D.C. rally organized by the Wilmington Ten Coalition, a new coalition of local organizations formed to combat racism and political oppression. Though he had officially resigned from the Party around 1974, Bobby still had political influence, which he used to rally on behalf of the Ten. During the protest, he connected the Ten's circumstances to ongoing injustices faced by Black Americans and called for their immediate release.

"We want their feet out here on the bricks," he declared to the roaring crowd that February 5 day, echoing the sentiments on some placards that read "Human Rights Begins at Home, Free the Wilmington Ten."

"I've been a political prisoner, so to speak," Bobby added, speaking to *The Washington Post*, "[so] I understand."

Even though the Party had been fizzling out since Bobby's resignation—primarily because members had struggled with internal conflicts, rising government repression, and FBI efforts to disband them, including the murder of Fred Hampton in 1969—his involvement in the Ten's case and the continued legal battles stoked still more public pressure.

Months after the D.C. rally, a judge dismissed the defense's motion for the Ten's conviction relief, deeming the recanted testimonies unreliable. However, the defense persisted, filing a federal appeal that ultimately succeeded in December 1980. The judge ruled that the prosecution had withheld crucial evidence.

After years of struggle, the Ten's convictions were overturned, leading to their official release: nine that December, and Benjamin in January 1981.

The prosecution never retried them.

Upon his release, Benjamin immediately resumed his activism, later becoming the NAACP's executive director.

With the Wilmington Ten finally released, marking a significant milestone in their battle for justice, students across college campuses didn't lose momentum. Inspired by the Ten's resolve, they shifted their focus to their ongoing commitment to dismantling Apartheid in South Africa.

By the early 1980s, activists and officials in America and South Africa had formed the South African Education Program to prepare South African students to be leaders in a post-Apartheid society. The program, which saw over 1,500 students graduate in less than a decade, was vital in building capacity for future leadership.

Even with the SAEP in place, students continued their activism at HBCUs. Some wrote letters to elected officials, urging them to take more decisive action against Apartheid. Others organized rallies and spoke out at public events, raising awareness and galvanizing support for the movement. Similarly, at private colleges and universities, from Dartmouth, Smith, and Wellesley to Harvard, Barnard, and Occidental, students became pivotal to the scale of the movement in America, organizing divestment campaigns, hosting educational events, and building pressure on institutions to take a stand.

On February 18, 1981, in response to Nelson Mandela's continued imprisonment and the ongoing fight against Apartheid, nineteen-year-old sophomore Barack Obama took the stage at an anti-Apartheid student protest outside Occidental College's Coons Hall. In his first-ever public speech, Barack echoed what had become a moral imperative for students nationwide: calling on America to impose economic sanctions on South Africa, boycott South African goods, and support the ANC in their fight for liberation. He argued that America had an ethical responsibility to dismantle Apartheid, a system of racial oppression he deemed fundamentally unjust. Silence, he said, was not an option, as it would only embolden the South African government. Before he could finish his speech, two students, seemingly embodying oppressive Afrikaaners, carried him off the stage, adding a touch of unexpected satirical interruption to the charged atmosphere.

This marked Barack's first foray into the political arena. The echoes of his words lingered long after the rally ended. Energized, he continued his efforts, moving beyond words to action. He printed flyers and penned letters to the school's faculty urging them to take a stand against Apartheid. He even reached out to the ANC party, inviting representatives to speak at Occidental, and strategized with other students to organize further protests and demonstrations.

Outside of coordinated campus events, the student movement against Apartheid continued to gain momentum. It became a global cultural phenomenon, inspiring celebrities, the likes of tennis star Arthur Ashe and prominent musicians Stevie Wonder and Mary Travers, to attend protests. Some were even arrested by police for their participation.

Far and wide, students kept on.

Formed in 1983, the D.C. Student Coalition Against Apartheid and Racism, a powerhouse alliance of student organizers from Howard, Georgetown, George Washington University, Johns Hopkins, and University of Maryland College Park, successfully pressured their universities to divest from corporations supporting South Africa's Apartheid regime.

In 1985, the Morehouse Anti-Apartheid Rally electrified 2,000 students as civil rights titans Andrew Young, Julian Bond, and John Lewis, alongside family members of Martin Luther King, Jr., and Bishop Desmond Tutu, addressed the profound connections between the struggles for racial justice in America and against Apartheid in South Africa. Their powerful message urged students to stay the course with renewed vigor.

The following year, pressured by the ongoing demonstrations, Congress passed the Comprehensive Anti-Apartheid Act, calling for an end to Apartheid and placing economic sanctions on South Africa. The bill prohibited the import of South African goods, the sale of arms and military equipment to the nation, and any new investment in the country. The legislation also demanded the release of political prisoners, a lifting of the state of emergency, and the establishment of a non-racial democracy.

Spelman students, who had become a vanguard for anti-Apartheid activism, continued their seven-year firestorm of campaigning against their own school's financial ties to South Africa. The student newspaper had amplified the voices of South African students, and campus events brought the fight for justice closer to home. Though lacking a large endowment, the school's board finally bowed to the pressure in April 1986, divesting from the oppressive regime.

On September 11, 1987, a student identified simply as "Ms. Taylor" addressed the United Nations, decrying the Apartheid system, during a hearing on South Africa. This was three years after she had co-led students from Fisk, Tennessee State, and Vanderbilt to the state Legislative Plaza in similar protest.

As nationwide pressure and boycotts intensified, major companies began withdrawing from South Africa, contributing to significant economic strain on the Apartheid regime. While international factors and domestic resistance also played a crucial role, the Comprehensive Anti-Apartheid Act undoubtedly served as the critical turning point.

As the South African government transitioned into negotiations over the future of their nation and its existing system, Nelson Mandela, the long-standing icon of the struggle against Apartheid, was finally released on February 11, 1990, after twenty-seven years in prison.

His release sparked jubilant celebrations across the world and marked a significant victory for the anti-Apartheid movement.

Following Nelson's release, his forceful rebuke of his imprisonment and unwavering calls for democracy inspired further momentum, fueling more companies to divest from South Africa in 1991 and 1992.

Two years later, on April 27, 1994, Nelson led the ANC party to victory in the country's first free election, marking the official end of Apartheid.

He became the nation's first Black president.

Reflecting on the late South African leader's unrelenting compassion in embracing his oppressors after his release, in pursuit of unity for his country, in a June 27, 2013, speech given three days after Nelson's death at ninety-five, Barack Obama, America's first Black president, said, "it gave me a sense of what is possible in the world when righteous people, when people of goodwill, work together on behalf of a larger cause."

While separated by borders, the anti-Apartheid movement and the Wilmington Ten, both of which saw galvanizing involvement from the Black Panther Party, were united by a common thread: the pursuit of educational freedom. From Soweto to Wilmington, young people ignited movements demanding equal access to quality education, a right denied them due to systemic racism and oppression—a testament to the power of *righteous people working together on behalf of a larger cause.*

The Black Panther Party, though officially disbanded in 1982, left a lasting impact beyond their role in the fight for Black liberation, community empowerment, and survival social programs. Bobby and Huey successfully transformed Stokely Carmichael's cry of "Black Power" into a way of life, and their influence continues to be felt in various aspects of American life. From pop culture to community programs, their legacy serves as a reminder of the power of collective action and the fight for justice.

Huey died on August 22, 1989. He was fatally shot in West Oakland during a confrontation with drug dealer Tyrone Robinson.

Bobby's last known location was Oakland.

As for the Wilmington Ten, it wasn't until May 2012 that they received official pardons, declaring their innocence.

In a statement about their exoneration, Governor Beverly Perdue said, "New evidence was made available to me in the form of handwritten notes from the prosecutor who picked the jury at trial. These notes show with disturbing clarity the dominant role that racism played in jury selection. The notes reveal that certain white jurors believed to be Ku Klux Klan members were described by the prosecutor as 'good' and that at least one African American juror was noted to be an 'Uncle Tom type.' This conduct is disgraceful. It is utterly incompatible with basic notions of fairness and with every ideal that North Carolina holds dear."

"People that are more educated are less racist," Artie told me one afternoon as we chatted. "People who are less educated are more ignorant. They don't pick up books to read, they don't try to understand different cultures . . . People need to get out and vote. People need to be more educated—constantly inundated with facts."

We were discussing the upcoming sixtieth anniversary of Martin Luther King, Jr.'s "I Have a Dream" speech and the state of contemporary America in terms of race relations.

This was also days after the Supreme Court eviscerated race-conscious college admissions from Affirmative Action. In a blink,

I tried connecting the dots of her simple yet weighty assessment of education. One I found to be revelatory, thinking back to my own experience at a predominantly white institution, intermingling with mostly white students, who for some I was their first Black friend. I was part of their social education. And through them, I learned there is an ingrained belief of Black intellectual inferiority.

Artie's perception is also what's most glaring about the Soweto Uprising and the Wilmington Ten.

It boils down to education.

Who controls it.

Who has it.

Who needs it.

Who gets it.

Because education is everything.

All over the world, it's the one commodity that remains a prized portal to independence. An agent of autonomy. Yet it is the one stock those in power who know its capacity remain keen to suppress. What the Supreme Court did that June 2023 day, in shunning reality, was tell the millions of Others that our racialized experiences don't count.

The Court didn't repeat history.

They repressed progress.

Access to education remains a potent weapon against ignorance and prejudice. To truly honor the legacy of Soweto and Wilmington, the fight for educational equity cannot be isolated from the broader struggle for racial equality. We must amplify the voices of our young, dismantle systems that funnel them into underfunded schools and limit their opportunities, and eliminate biases that deny their talents and potential.

Imagine a future where the education system recognizes the inherent worth of every child, regardless of their zip code. A future where classrooms hum with the vibrant exchange of diverse perspectives, where mere brilliance, absent of race, absent of skin color, is nurtured and celebrated, where the dreams of young people transcend limitations set by generations past.

That is the true promise of educational freedom: a liberation of minds, a dismantling of barriers, and a paving of the path toward a world where "I Have a Dream" is not just a stirring ideal but a lived reality for us and our descendants.

PART III

THE TRAYVON MARTIN GENERATION & A NEW WAVE OF YOUNG REVOLUTIONARIES

7

TOUGHER ON BLACKS

The Jena Six

We have predators on our streets that society has,
in fact, in part because of its neglect, created . . . It does not
mean because we created them, that we somehow forgive them or do not
take them out of society to protect my family and yours from them.
They are beyond the pale many of those people—beyond the pale.

JOE BIDEN

"Akata" in our Nigerian Pidgin translates to Black American.

"Oyinbo" translates to white American.

*Akata is an uncomplimentary term. The American stereotype of
"Black American" is embedded within the literal Yoruba word for
wildcat. As a Nigerian, if you're anointed akata, it means you're the
caricatured Black American in speech, dress, mannerisms, and the
like. You're seen as having pledged allegiance to "that" side. Your
Nigerian card is, in effect, revoked.*

*Oyinbos, on the other hand, are seen as superior. A remnant
of colonialism. There's priority and authority thrown their way.
It comes from the Yoruba word for red skin, first used to describe
those of European descent. Over time, it took on a meaning of for-
eigner, white, and, more commonly now, white American.*

*I was christened akata when I visited Nigeria years after Man-
ny's deportation. Family and locals laughed at my Pidgin. It had
lost its twang. There was a stark difference in my enunciations and*

inflections. The richness and thickness of the locals' were melodic and heavy and smooth.

I was home but no longer one of them.

It revived my plight of belonging, to be seen for me without pleasing this or that gaze or contorting to this or that ideal. Home became lost for me. It was at once the Bronx and my motherland's Ekiadolor Village, but also nowhere.

That Othering of akata is a paradoxical reflection of our deep-seated desire for connection. We seek common ground through shared dialects, music, politics, or socioeconomic status, hoping to find affinity. However, when these attempts at connection fail, some people resort to constructing rigid explanations that categorize and exclude others. Often fueled by prejudice and fear, these explanations can have far-reaching and detrimental consequences, as exemplified by the 1994 crime bill's disproportionate targeting of minority communities and its lasting impact on the justice system.

Driven by America's impenetrable societal structure, the bill ostracized and punished those on the margins. Its complicated legacy of cyclical victimization reflects a system neglectful of the many Othered while penalizing them for its own failures.

For example, think about the education system.

Public schools, often underfunded in predominantly Black and brown communities, have systematically failed students of color. This lack of investment leads to larger class sizes, fewer resources, and, ultimately, a higher likelihood of students dropping out.

In turn, many turn to the streets for a different kind of education.

Some end up incarcerated.

Others die. At the hands of gun or gang violence.

Many more just get left behind.

This rinse and repeat of neglect year after year leads to still more marginalization, perpetuating a cycle of poverty, violence, and further incarceration across generations. Trapped in this loop, these targeted communities never realize they are being persecuted for their sheer existence, unaware of how to challenge the very system harming them. The same one their ancestors survived. The same one rooted in division.

Akata. Oyinbo.

Black. White.

Inferior. Superior.

All distinctions. All categorizations.

Instead of fixing the underlying problems in areas deemed "high-crime neighborhoods" (often communities of color), the 1994 crime bill introduced and championed by then-Senator Joe Biden focused on locking those on the margins up. This meant jailing more minorities, who already faced unfair policing and neglect. Historian Michelle Alexander dubbed this the "new Jim Crow" because it creates a system of racial control that, like the Jim Crow laws of the past, disproportionately disadvantages African Americans. Black men and boys were found to be especially targeted, stuck with criminal records that hinder their ability to find employment, housing, and education, perpetuating a cycle of disadvantage.

Ultimately, the bill offered no real solutions but unjust punishments. All because of a fundamental disconnect and misunderstanding of the Othered. One that comes with a steep price, and one that felt inescapable for six Black teens in Louisiana. Their case tragically exemplifies contemporary prejudice in the criminal justice and education systems, revealing how racism is concealed under "law and order."

AUGUST 31, 2006. JENA, LOUISIANA.

In the morning light, three nooses hung ominously from a giant oak tree's leafy branches outside Jena High School.

There had been an unspoken rule.

A privilege, really.

Only white students were allowed to sit under the oversized tree. Until Wednesday, August 30, 2006, when Kenneth Purvis, a Black sophomore, asked administrators during a school-wide assembly if he, too, could sit under the tree's shade. The answer was *yes*.

The next day, the nooses appeared.

The Black student body immediately felt the pang, the racial friction sparking. They saw the nooses as a threat. A Jim Crow intimidation tactic. A message for them to know their place.

A symbol of hate.

"The first thing that came to mind was the KKK," Robert Bailey, one of the Black teens there that morning, later said. "I don't know why, but that was the first thing that came to my head. I used to always think the KKK chase Black people on horses, and they catch you with rope."

Something had to be done.

"Y'all want to go stand under the tree?" Kenneth asked other Black students in the courtyard that Thursday.

"They said, 'If you go, I'll go. If you go, I'll go.' One person went," Kenneth said as he remembered the launch of their sit-in. "The next person went, everybody else just went."

During their impromptu demonstration, Reed Walters, the town's district attorney, unexpectedly showed up flanked by armed police officers. Their arrival, a chilling symbol of authority, cast a long shadow over the peaceful gathering. "See this pen in my hand?" Reed yelled at the baffled teens. "I could end your lives with the stroke of a pen."

In the end, six Black teens were expelled from school for their sit-in.

Furious at the blatant display of bigotry and the unconscionable outcome, Scott Windham, the school's white principal, demanded the expulsion of the three white teens found to be responsible for the nooses. However, the white superintendent of the 2,700-student LaSalle Parish School District, Roy Breithaupt, denied the request. Instead, he doled out a slap-on-the-wrist punishment for the three white students: a nine-day alternative school program followed by a two-week in-school suspension. Unable to condone such an egregious mistreatment and display of inequity, Scott resigned in protest.

In the 1990s, race relations in the piney woods of Louisiana were complex and strained. By the time the 2000s came around, demographic shifts led to a growing Black population and continued public school integration, fueling anxiety among white residents.

This was especially true in Jena, where 90 percent of the 4,000 residents were white. Like many places in the American South,

Jena had long grappled with a nuanced history of racial bias and discrimination. The demographic shift only exacerbated existing tensions and disparities, exposing deep-seated fears rooted in the town's segregated past.

By 2006, the integrated student body of 521 at Jena High was primarily white, representing about the same racial split as the district, which was about 85 percent white.

When news of the nooses began to trickle out of small-town Jena, Billy Wayne Fowler, a white member of the LaSalle Parish School District Board, said that Jena was being unfairly painted as racist. He called the actions of the three white teens a prank, saying it was blown out of proportion.

"This is the Deep South. Black people know the meaning of a noose. Let me tell you something—young people don't," he said. "You can't overlook the seriousness of hanging the nooses, but I don't think our young people understood the significance of that symbol" as an explicit reminder of the prolonged history of lynchings of Black Americans.

Further infuriating the community, who were demanding answers, the Black teens' appeal of their expulsion to the school board was met with a wall of secrecy. The district conducted an investigation but never shared its findings with the board or the public. The lawyer acting on the board's behalf was Reed Walters, the same district attorney who had threatened the Black students during their sit-in.

Of the investigation findings, Billy said Reed was the "legal authority" who told the board "it was a violation of something" to show the findings to the board or community members. To bolster his claims, Reed said it wasn't a crime in Louisiana to hang a noose, because no criminal statute existed. So, the board was forced to vote on the teens' appeal without the investigation findings. All but one, the sole Black board member, Melvin Worthington, voted to uphold the Black students' expulsion, which only exacerbated festering racial tensions.

Incensed, some Jena residents reached out to the FBI to investigate. Federal authorities, including FBI agents and officials with the

Department of Justice civil rights division, descended on Jena. After looking into the case, they were unable to prosecute the white teens for hate crimes because they found that the three minors acted alone, without any coercing from adults or hate groups. They also said juveniles were rarely prosecuted in federal court. Since the school had already penalized them, they felt that was sufficient.

By late fall, the racial tension remained palpable on campus, leading to a series of confrontations. At every turn, each gaze seemed a threat.

In the early morning of November 30, Jena High was set ablaze, damaging major parts of the two-story building. It was later determined as an act of arson, but no one was identified as the perpetrator.

The next day, Robert Bailey, one of the students from the sit-in, and his friends dropped by a private all-white party outside a local community center, Fair Barn. When the host, a white woman, asked them to leave, a fight broke out. Robert was hit over the head with a beer bottle by a twenty-two-year-old white man, Justin Sloan.

The brawl escalated to the point where the cops were called.

Justin was arrested on simple battery charges. He pleaded guilty and paid a $250 fine. Given the nature of the confrontation, many Black residents considered the attack extremely serious and the punishment a mere slap on the wrist.

Then, on December 2, while at a Gotta-Go Grocery store, an eighteen-year-old white teen, Matthew Windham, threatened Robert and two other Black teens with a 12-gauge sawed-off shotgun.

Another fight broke out.

The three Black teens were able to wrestle the gun to the floor and bolt to the police station, where Matthew would claim Robert and his friends jumped him and stole his gun. The Black teens ended up being charged with assault and robbery—their version of what took place, dismissed.

Matthew faced no consequences.

"I know they were in fear of their lives," Caseptla Bailey, Robert's mom, later said of the incident. "They were afraid that

[Matthew] was going to shoot them, you know, especially in the back, running away from the scene."

It all came to a head two days later, on Monday, December 4, the first day students were back on campus following the school's fire.

After months of escalating racial tension, the drama spilled out into the schoolyard that afternoon, and blows were hurled between white and Black students.

In the tussle, a white seventeen-year-old junior, Justin Barker, was injured and taken to the hospital. He suffered a concussion and multiple bruises. He was released the same day, after less than three hours in the hospital, and went back to hanging with friends. He also appeared in good spirits at the school's class ring event that evening.

Later, several accounts about what really landed Justin in the hospital began to surface.

Some students said Justin had bullied Robert during lunch, teasing him about getting beat up at the party three nights before. Justin, others claimed, had called Robert the n-word before walking out of the gym and onto a covered walkway. Many white students said that's where they saw Mychal Bell, a Black student, punch Justin from behind, knocking him to the concrete. Others mentioned that at that point, a group of Black students began stomping on Justin, kicking him in the face and head as he was on the ground.

Disputing the sequence of events, Kenneth Purvis, the teen who originally asked to sit under the tree during assembly, said, "If any fight would have popped off, Black and white, everybody would have been fighting."

As rumors swirled about Justin's attack, legal repercussions began to take shape.

DA Reed Walters, despite conflicting accounts and continued community uproar over racial profiling, deemed Robert and five other Black students to be the perpetrators. Once they were arrested, and though no investigation had been conducted, the local newspaper, the *Jena Times*, covering the alleged attack positioned the case's evidence as irrefutable—solely based on the DA's office. It was also reported that LaSalle Parish Sheriff's Department officials commented that the Black students had beaten Justin unconscious.

In a statement to the paper, Reed addressed the Black teens, saying, "I will not tolerate this type of behavior. To those who act in this manner I tell you that you will be prosecuted to the fullest extent of the law and with the harshest crimes that the facts justify. When you are convicted I will seek the maximum penalty allowed by law. I will see to it that you never again menace the students at any school in this parish."

Further inflaming the already tense atmosphere, Reed went on to charge each of the teens with attempted second-degree murder and conspiracy to commit murder and sought the maximum sentence. They each faced up to one hundred years behind bars without parole. Their bail was set between $70,000 and $138,000 in a town where the average Black household income was about $35,000.

> **Robert Bailey's** bail was set at $138,000. He was seventeen and a junior.
>
> At the time of his arrest, fourteen-year-old freshman **Jesse Ray Beard** was listed as an unidentified minor; most of the details surrounding his case were (and are) sealed.
>
> **Mychal Bell,** $90,000, sixteen, and a sophomore. He was the only one charged as an adult since he was the one who allegedly first hit Justin.
>
> **Theo Shaw,** $130,000. He was seventeen.
>
> **Carwin Jones,** $100,000. He was eighteen.
>
> **Bryant Purvis,** $70,000. He was seventeen and was Kenneth Purvis's cousin.

All but Jesse were on the football team, the Jena Giants. Their coach, Mack Fowler, felt Mychal, an academically successful sophomore football running back, had the most to lose, given the heightened charges against him and his all-star status that had merited attention from Division I colleges nationwide.

Most of the teens could not make bail for nearly a year, so they awaited their trial date in jail. With each passing day, the severity of the charges against the group, dubbed the Jena Six by local papers, galvanized the community. Many, from locals to the parents of the Six, argued that the charges were excessive and disproportionate to the offense, particularly compared to how similar incidents involving white students were handled.

"The DA is a racist DA," Marcus Jones, Mychal's father, said of Reed. "The reason we is taking a stand for our kids for what he's not doing is right . . . Somebody has to take a stand now. If not, he's going to continue to fill the prisons up with Black people more and more."

Marcus told his son, "You know what it is to be Black now . . . if this don't teach him what it is to be Black now, I don't know what will. But he's seventeen now. You know, he's got a lot of life left ahead of him."

Caseptla, Robert Bailey's mom, shared a similar sentiment.

"They want to take these kids, my son, as well as all these other children, lock them up, throw away the key," she said, "That's a tradition for Black males. So they want to keep that tradition going because they want to keep institutionalized slavery alive and well."

Robert spent more than two months in jail until Caseptla managed to gather enough money for his bond by leveraging three properties from various family members. Once home, Robert felt victimized. Steeling himself for what the future possibly held, given the minimum twenty-five years behind bars, he said the case against him and the others had nothing to do with anything that actually happened. He felt the facts were being ignored.

"I ain't got no criminal record, nothing," the seventeen-year-old said at the time. "I ain't got no probation, community service or nothing—nothing like that. The DA, he ain't after finding the truth. That's what a DA's for, [to] find the truth of the case. He's just trying to put me up in a jail cell for life. Twenty-five to a hundred years."

"You can just say, 'Forever.' Twenty years is forever to me."

On November 18, 1993, fifteen years before the Jena High clashes, Senator Joe Biden took to the Senate floor and admonished the nation's rising violent crime rate, pointing squarely at one subset of the population. He warned, "It doesn't matter whether or not they're the victims of society. The end result is they're about to knock my mother on the head with a lead pipe, shoot my sister, beat up my wife, take on my sons."

America was experiencing an agonizing surge in crime, particularly in violent categories like homicide, robbery, and aggravated assault. The FBI, responsible for tracking such statistics, reported roughly 9.5 homicides per 100,000 people in the United States, which had resulted in an estimated 24,700 homicides in 1993, when the American population was about 260 million.

That same year, violent offenses, which consists of homicides, rapes, robberies, and aggravated assaults, soared to a rate of 747 per 100,000 residents, translating to a staggering 1.9 million instances nationwide. This marked a nearly eightfold increase compared to 1963.

Similarly, property crime (burglary, larceny-theft, motor vehicle theft, and arson) in 1993 mirrored the escalating and troubling trend, peaking at 4,296 offenses per 100,000 residents, resulting in 11.2 million total incidents.

These grim figures represented a stark contrast to previous decades, when violent crime averaged about 10,000 *total* offenses per year.

While the crime spike had multifaceted causes, poverty played a prominent role in the initial upsurge during the sixties and seventies. Rapid urbanization—as people migrated from rural areas to cities—contributed to scarcer resources in certain parts of the country, which created a pressure cooker environment. The absence of access to quality education, decent housing, and essential resources crucial for social mobility further heightened the risk of criminal behavior. This perpetuated a cycle of limited job prospects, lower income potential, increased generational economic disadvantage, and a higher likelihood of engaging in street life. This social and economic upheaval created a breeding ground for the surge.

Those glaring and rising disparities in poverty and unemployment ignited a powder keg where crime flourished. Desperation drove people to criminal activity, seeking survival. The alarming ease of obtaining guns and drugs only further weakened the already vulnerable communities, making them easier targets for gangs to exploit. All of this engendered a cycle of crime that seemed impossible to escape and led to a drug epidemic.

Law enforcement's response, often heavily focused on aggressive tactics, further strained relations with minority groups disproportionately affected by poverty. Addressing the root causes of poverty and inequality became essential, yet these very issues fueled social disorganization, weakened community ties, and eroded social institutions, making it even harder to tackle the very problems they perpetuated. This created a vacuum where criminal activity thrived, escalating year after year.

It was against this backdrop that Joe Biden sponsored the Violent Crime Control and Law Enforcement Act. The proposed bill seemed a desperate antidote for a country unable to zero in on a resolution that was at once tough yet readily applicable. It also included the Violence Against Women Act, which funded programs to combat domestic violence, sexual assault, and stalking.

President Bill Clinton signed the legislation on September 13, 1994. It called for more police officers, allocated $9.7 billion for prisons and $6.1 billion for prevention programs, and expanded the government's authority to deal with "criminal aliens." On that immigrant front, it provided $2.6 billion to the FBI, the Drug Enforcement Administration, the Immigration and Naturalization Service, the U.S. Attorneys, the Federal courts, the Treasury Department, and other Department of Justice arms.

This historic bill had been Joe Biden's signature initiative since becoming the youngest senator at twenty-nine in 1972, after unseating Republican senator Caleb Boggs.

Joe Biden came up in Scranton, Pennsylvania, and moved to the suburbs of Wilmington, Delaware, in 1953 when he was ten. He had a front-row seat to a period of compounding heightened racial unrest, agitation, and turbulence. His Senate win came just four years after Martin Luther King, Jr.'s 1968 murder, and Wilmington had been undergoing a reckoning of its own. In the aftermath of Martin Luther King, Jr.'s assassination, the state's governor, Charles Terry, had to deploy the National Guard and placed a nine-month dusk-to-dawn curfew.

A year before Joe Biden was elected to the Senate, Black students would successfully file to desegregate their public schools. In the landmark *Evans v. Buchanan* case, the Delaware chapter of the NAACP filed a lawsuit against the state and its governor, Russell Peterson. They argued that the public school system was racially segregated and that the system had violated their constitutional rights.

As he campaigned for Senate, seemingly welcoming and charismatic, Joe Biden allied himself with such causes plaguing African Americans. One of his slogans was "Joe Biden: He understands what's happening today." He evangelized being the senator for the people, unlike the two-term Caleb Boggs, who was sixty-three and seen as the "establishment." Joe Biden characterized his opponent as out of touch with the younger generation. He explained that he was a different kind of politician who cared about everyday people, especially those who had been systematically forgotten and silenced for decades.

Above all, Joe Biden wanted to bridge and unite across races. In his 2007 memoir, *Promises to Keep: On Life and Politics*, he put it this way: "I knew blacks and whites weren't talking to one another." (The autobiography came out months before the 2008 presidential race where he mulled what was his second run for president, the first being in 1988. He later sidestepped for Illinois senator Barack Obama, who at the time he anointed "the first sort of mainstream African American who is articulate and bright and clean." When he dropped out of that race, he was named Barack Obama's vice presidential candidate.)

Upon entering the Senate, Joe Biden established himself as a Democrat who prioritized being tough on crime. He criticized President George H. W. Bush for not taking sufficient action to address the rising violent crime rates. In response to the president's 1989 drug policy address, where the president proposed allocating $50 million to combat crime in housing projects and $1.5 billion to prevent drugs from entering America, Joe Biden accused him of being lenient, of not funding prisons or putting more police officers on the streets. He went on to emphasize the alarming rise in violent drug offenders, arguing that the president's plan lacked the necessary resources to effectively combat the uptick.

Four years later, his crime bill proved tough in the areas previous administrations had overlooked. After the bill became law, providing funding for state and local law enforcement agencies, prisons, and crime prevention programs, many argued that an unspoken directive emerged: focus on criminalizing communities of color. Or, as then senator Joe Biden put it in his 1993 speech to Congress, it targeted "predators on our streets." As the law launched across the nation, different states adopted varying interpretations, leading to concerns about uneven application and potential for bias.

Within a year of its rollout, The Sentencing Project found that the number of young Black men incarcerated or on probation increased from 23 percent to 32 percent. Black Americans were imprisoned at a rate five times higher than white Americans, with one in about eighty Black adults serving time in prison. In a quarter of states, more than half of the prison population was Black, and around seven states had a Black-white disparity greater than nine to one. These statistics, coupled with racial profiling and the overcriminalization of nonviolent drug offenses, contributed to the rise of mass incarceration.

Consequently, this trend continued.

Year after year, the makeup of prisons nationally was becoming increasingly younger and more racially skewed.

In 1997, about 68 percent of state prison inmates had not

completed high school, and the majority of new juvenile detainees were from communities of color. Black youths without prior criminal records were six times more likely to be incarcerated than white youths for the same offenses.

By 1999, the prison population kept on exploding, grossly overrepresented by Black and brown boys and men. And still, communities of color remained under siege by excessive policing.

The tragic death of Amadou Diallo happened in the throes of this, exemplifying the deadly effects of such flagrant bias.

The twenty-two-year-old Guinean immigrant was fatally shot by four New York City police officers on February 4, 1999. This happened during a period when New York's mayor, Rudolph Giuliani, was implementing his response to the tough-on-crime legislation through stop-and-frisk policies. The plan involved plainclothes officers—like the ones involved in Amadou's shooting who later claimed they believed he was reaching for a gun. No weapon was ever found on Amadou. His death sparked protests and demands for reform within the NYPD. The officers were ultimately acquitted, leading to still more protests.

Amadou's seismic slaying wasn't an isolated cataclysm. It was a chilling manifestation of pervasive racial profiling in policing. At its peak, stop-and-frisk resulted in more than 100,000 low-level police stops. Despite the high number of stops, during the program's run (it officially ended in January 2014), most didn't result in fines or convictions, and a significant proportion of those stopped were Black and Hispanic boys and men.

The same was true in Louisiana.

Law enforcement used funds from the crime bill to hire more officers, acquire new equipment, and implement their version of stop-and-frisk called the Community Oriented Policing Services (COPS) program. This approach similarly led to over-policing in communities of color.

This is the cross fire the Jena Six found themselves caught in.

During the 1990s and early 2000s, studies show that Jena had the highest rate of hate crimes in all of Louisiana. They also reveal that Black residents were disproportionately targeted, stopped by police more frequently than white residents, and faced higher arrest and conviction rates.

Jena only served as a microcosm of a larger, persisting problem. With the continued enactment of the crime bill, a disturbing national trend emerged: minorities were being incarcerated at vastly disproportionate rates, and they kept getting younger and younger.

By 2003, Black youths were being locked up at a rate four and a half times higher than their white counterparts. Similarly, youths of color accounted for 61 percent of all young people detained, despite comprising only about one-third of the nation's youth population.

This unfettered climb in harsher punishments for those on the margins ties back to the dominant punitive approach to crime reduction ushered in by the crime bill. A precedent that played a considerable role in the arrest and charges against the Jena Six. It also led to the first glimpse of young people organizing in a new way than before. Because as the inequities against communities of color ballooned, emerging technologies began to likewise engulf the nation, particularly social media, which allowed for a new medium of dissent.

Each case of police brutality against Black people became an indictment of the crime bill's implementation. It began to trigger widespread protests and marches by young activists.

There'd been the Million Youth March in Harlem of the late nineties, demanding an end to police violence, more funding for education and jobs, reparations, and self-governance for Black communities. Then several more followed with the alarming deaths of still more young people of color at the hands of mostly white police officers. Like the fatal shootings of nineteen-year-old Tyisha Miller by Riverside police officers in California on December 28, 1998, and that of Timothy Thomas on April 7, 2001. Each time the agony cut deeper for those who saw themselves in each act of dehumanization. Each, in its own way, an insidious act of erasure.

Then came the early 2000s and the emergence of digital media. At once an uncharted battleground and a promising leveling frontier.

The growing online platforms allowed users to create, share, and connect with content and engage in virtual communities. It began to shape the landscape of communication.

Launching on March 22, 2002, Friendster was one of the earliest online social platforms. The site introduced the concept of digital "friends," which became a cornerstone of online social networking and influenced subsequent platforms. MySpace, with a similar ethos, followed, going live for the first time on August 1, 2003, quickly gaining popularity with its focus on user-generated content. It allowed users to customize their profiles, connect with friends, and post photos.

A year later, in February 2004, while at Harvard, nineteen-year-old Mark Zuckerberg and his co-founders launched Facebook, a network initially exclusive to Harvard University students. Then, in 2005, although primarily a video-sharing platform, YouTube was created and evolved into a social media platform. (Instagram would later come out on October 6, 2010.)

As social media platforms began safely bringing people together and building online communities, Black and brown communities continued to face the harsh reality of police brutality.

In February 2005, Devin Brown, a Black thirteen-year-old, was shot and killed by Los Angeles police officers. The officers pursued him in a vehicle Devin had allegedly stolen, and when he drove toward them, they opened fire. The incident led to more public outcry and calls for transparency and reforms in the Los Angeles Police Department.

A year after Devin's fatal shooting, Twitter launched on March 21, 2006.

Mobilizing on social media—whether through text, videos, or images—began to be a mainstream way to decry such atrocities and better organize.

That September, Facebook opened to the general public, quickly expanding to become a global phenomenon.

Social media, writ large, steadily evolved. Soon, it became transformational to social movements.

However, the rise of social media denouncements wasn't accompanied by a decline in police brutality. In fact, the 2006 shooting of Sean Bell tragically illustrates the cruel paradox of being killed by those sworn to protect, and how online outrage can't erase offline injustices.

In the early morning of Thanksgiving Day, the twenty-three-year-old unarmed Black man was on his way home from his bachelor party with two friends, Trent Benefield and Joseph Guzman. Sean was set to get married to Nicole Paultre, the mother of his two daughters, later that day, but he was fatally shot fifty times by three NYPD officers in plainclothes, in Jamaica, Queens.

Joseph and Trent survived but were injured.

Given the undeniable brutality, Sean's death became a global high-profile case. In turn, it was one of the first such incidents to incite widespread discussion across traditional and online mediums, including on blogs, Facebook, and MySpace. This was before virality became a mainstay in digital media.

Social media sparked a new wave of activism, allowing people—most of them young people—to raise their voices against police brutality from the comfort of their screens. Digital platforms connected on-the-ground movements with global audiences and supporters, amplifying a united chorus of condemnation that reverberated across the country and beyond. It allowed for simultaneous demonstrations to erupt across large cities, small towns, and even remote corners, a testament to the unifying power of online activism.

The Jena Six case happened in the thick of this: a generation of young Black activists mustering for change, brimming with righteous indignation. Injustice had hung heavy in the air for them, animating a collective demand for accountability and an end to police brutality against Black bodies.

By the time the Six were indicted with unduly harsh charges, the response was swift. The movement's call for justice thrummed farther and wider.

The Jena Six's separate trials kicked off six months after their December 2006 arrests.

On June 25, Mychal Bell was up first. In an unexpected move, likely due to the ongoing community uproar, DA Reed Walters reduced the charges against the football star, who had pending athletic scholarships to several universities, including Louisiana State University, Southern Miss, and Ole Miss.

The charges were reduced from attempted murder to aggravated battery and conspiracy, which carries a maximum of twenty-two years in prison. However, the condition for that charge requires a lethal weapon to be involved. Reed argued that Mychal's sneakers constituted a lethal weapon, as they were allegedly used by a "gang of Black boys" to beat Justin.

Mychal declined the plea deal.

"Whenever a Black man is offered a plea," his father, Marcus Jones, later said, "he is innocent. That's a dead giveaway here in the South."

Mychal was represented by a white court-appointed public defender. His parents, Marcus and Melissa Bell, were not allowed at trial because they were listed as potential witnesses for the prosecution. Though they fought this order, they were denied entry. The court also ordered them to stop speaking to the press. However, Justin Barker, the alleged victim who was also a witness for the prosecution, was allowed to be in the courtroom during the trial.

The prosecutor called seventeen witnesses: eleven white students, three white teachers, and two white nurses.

Some claimed they saw Mychal kick Justin.

Others said they didn't see him do anything.

Justin, while on the stand, said he didn't know if Mychal hit him.

Mychal's public defender didn't challenge any of the all-white jurors during the selection process and presented no defense. After resting his case without calling any witnesses, he told the *Alexandria Town Talk* that he didn't "believe race is an issue in this trial. I think I have a fair and impartial jury."

"I know for a fact that he was getting railroaded," Melissa later said of the representation her son received.

On June 28, 2007, the jury deliberated for less than three hours and found Mychal guilty on the highest possible charges of second-degree aggravated battery and conspiracy: it carried a maximum of twenty-two years in prison. (Two jury members were later found to be friendly with the DA, and another was a friend of Justin's father.)

Outside the courtroom, Jena Six parents kept the pressure on.

Caseptla Bailey, Robert's mom, had taken to regularly protesting outside the school with other parents and residents to call attention to the unfairness of the trial. She had written letters to local, state, and national agencies, like the Department of Justice, hoping they'd see the inequity in the charges and intervene.

"No justice!" she called out one afternoon, pumping a placard sign.

"No peace!" locals responded.

"No justice!"

"No peace!"

(That call-and-response seemed so simple: where there was no justice, there could be no peace. The poignant assertion—a profound observation, really—goes back to Martin Luther King, Jr., who many say coined the term. The January before he died in 1968, speaking out against the Vietnam War, outside Santa Rita Rehabilitation Center in California where anti-war protestors were imprisoned for resisting the draft, he said, "There can be no justice without peace. And there can be no peace without justice.")

In July, following the highly publicized verdict in Mychal's case, national attention shifted to Jena. Journalists from across the country descended on the town to interview locals and photograph what had been deemed the "white tree." To escape the unwanted attention, city officials had the oak tree chopped down to its stump.

As the embers of local protests fanned into a national inferno, on September 4, a state judge overturned Mychal's charge of conspiracy to commit aggravated battery because he was a juvenile. That same day, the DA reduced the attempted murder charges against two of the Six—Carwin and Theo—to aggravated second-degree battery and conspiracy. Robert's reduction came on September 10.

Days later, on September 14, the appellate court threw out

Mychal's aggravated battery conviction and said the case should be heard in juvenile court. He remained jailed as prosecutors prepared an appeal of the court's ruling.

As the fate of the Six remained shrouded in uncertainty and local protests kept Jena engaged, a nationwide wave of support for the teens swelled. Students, empowered by a powerful blend of traditional activism and the burgeoning power of social media, mobilized.

Offline, they organized demonstrations, rallies, and walkouts, their voices resonating. Online, platforms became battlegrounds—rallying cries for the Six reverberated across the digital landscape. This mighty mix of conventional and modern engagement invigorated a broader movement, keeping relentless pressure on local and national authorities.

The Six's case, catapulted by this unwavering support, transcended its local roots, morphing into a powerful contemporary symbol of hate and injustice that struck a chord across the nation. Blogs, radio waves, social media feeds, and national publications like *The New York Times* became its megaphones.

Los Angeles–based Black activist Jasmyne Cannick, a popular online blogger at the time, dedicated extensive coverage to the case, summoning support and encouraging her visitors to join in. Her efforts helped spread the word about an online petition for the Six's release. It gained significant traction after her involvement, garnering nearly 400,000 signatures. YouTube creators like ConsciousL similarly contributed to larger online campaigns like Jasmyne's by sharing news footage and creating original content to air their opinions and rally support. In one protest video, ConsciousL rapped, "Jena Six Louisiana, it's so clear—racism still alive and kickin' down there."

Meanwhile, on the ground, college students pounded the pavement. Four days after Mychal's conviction was overturned, as he waited to find out whether he'd be charged again as an adult or juvenile by Reed, more than 200 students from Morehouse College, Spelman College, and Clark Atlanta University took to the streets in Atlanta.

They stomped for two miles, from Atlanta University's Center campus to Centennial Olympic Park. Their placards read, "Stop the racist prosecution of the Jena 6!"

They chanted, "Until the Six are free, neither are we!"

They thronged the pavements along the way, decrying the injustice of the arrests and drawing parallels to their own lives.

"Things like this happen all the time," Tammy Timbers, a senior at Spelman College, said, calling the arrests a violation of the Six's Fourteenth Amendment rights. "Jena Six is just getting a lot of publicity."

"We're here to make sure our voices are heard," Reginald McKinley, a senior at Morehouse and one of the rally organizers, said, "and to make sure they see support from their peers."

"They represent us," Morehouse sophomore Koree Hood added. "We see an injustice in Jena, Louisiana. It's gone on for too long, and very few people knew it was happening today."

Inspired by the college students' organizing, Atlanta's Southern Christian Leadership Conference organized buses to drive droves of multigenerational supporters to Jena to join forces with locals on Thursday, September 20, 2007, on what was to be a massive show of solidarity for the Six.

As word spread of the Jena protest, student leaders from NAACP's Youth Council chapters quickly mobilized young people across their campuses.

Online, Jasmyne, the blogger, did likewise, urging her followers to descend on Jena. Inspired by the ethos of the Black Panther Party, she told them to wear black in solidarity, and even if they couldn't physically attend, everyone everywhere, she insisted, should gear up.

Facebook was especially essential in organizing people in lightning speed for the rally. It allowed organizers to create a group called *Free the Jena 6*, which instantly became the primary information hub where people turned to for event details and updates.

The comprehensive outreach online and in traditional outlets moved thousands to attend the Jena rally.

In addition to the many young activists, most of them from high schools and HBCUs, social and cultural pillar figures also joined.

From celebrated rapper Yasiin Bey (formerly Mos Def) to Reverend Jesse Jackson, from state legislators to rally organizers, to civil rights activist Al Sharpton and radio personality Michael Baisden, who said of the case, "if you're poor and white in this country, you get involved in the legal system, you're in trouble. But if you're poor and black, you're in hell."

After riding on all-night buses, protesters began clogging Jena's tiny roads by 5 a.m. that Thursday.

"This is the first time something like this has happened for our generation," twenty-four-year-old University of Louisiana at Lafayette senior Eric Depradine said that day. "You always heard about it from history books and relatives. This is a chance to experience it for ourselves."

"When I first heard about [the charges against the Six], I thought it was obscene, so I felt I had to come," Eric's schoolmate, twenty-two-year-old Charley Caldwell, said. "When we got here, there's nothing but white people, and they aren't used to seeing this many people of color."

"I just feel like every time the white people did something, they dropped it," seventeen-year-old high schooler April Jones, who came with her parents from Atlanta, said of why she was stomping for the Six. "And every time the Black people did something, they blew it out of proportion."

The march began at 7 a.m.

The route passed Jena High, past the oak tree's stump.

The march inched forward along a two-mile route, flooding the two-lane highway through downtown and residential streets, where people poured over onto the sidewalks.

State officials said the crowd swelled and spread so far across their small town that they were unable to get a concrete head count, estimating that at the protest's peak, there were more than 50,000 protestors. Their presence forced the closure of schools, local businesses, and even the courthouse.

Their sheer force was loud and booming.

Many donned black tees and held placards that read, "Free the Jena Six" and "Enough is Enough."

One man initiated: "No justice!"

"No peace!" the crowd responded.

"Free the Jena Six!"

The roaring crowd didn't miss a beat: "Free the Jena Six!"

"In the 20th century, we had to fight for where we sit on the bus," Al Sharpton said when he addressed the crowd. "Martin Luther King, Jr. and others faced Jim Crow. We come to Jena to face 'James Crow, Jr. esquire.'"

Jesse Jackson echoed Al Sharpton's sentiments, adding that it was a historic protest akin to those in Montgomery and Selma, Alabama. He said the fight must continue, insisting, "There is a Jena in every town, a Jena in every state."

At one point, he leaned into the crowd and prayed for a solution to "this crisis without the madness of confrontation."

Al Sharpton, who had previously met with Mychal and his parents, said he was partnering with House representatives William Jefferson from Louisiana, Maxine Waters from California, and Sheila Jackson Lee from Texas, all Black Democrats, to push the House Judiciary Committee to order DA Reed to explain to Congress why he had arrested the Six.

Al Sharpton called Reed's actions a launchpad for Black America's fight for twenty-first-century justice.

On that same Thursday, news of the thunderous protest reached Washington, D.C., even before Al Sharpton could follow through on his plans. Responding to the demands of the protesters, George W. Bush voiced concern about the racial tensions in Jena and announced that federal law enforcement agencies, such as the Department of Justice and the FBI, would monitor the situation.

"The events in Louisiana have saddened me, and I understand the emotions," he said. "And all of us in America want there to be, you know, fairness when it comes to justice."

The protest's reach didn't stop there.

Grassroots civil rights organizations such as Color of Change raised money for the Six's defense. Fortified by this support, the Southern Poverty Law Center stepped in to provide the teens with a proper defense.

On September 27, as public support grew, having spent nearly a year behind bars since his arrest, Mychal was released on $45,000 bail. This milestone in the teen's case served as a springboard, propelling the rally's impact forward.

On October 16, witnesses presented impactful testimony to Congress about the urgent need to address hate crimes and racially motivated violence in public schools. Prominent figures like Al Sharpton and J. Richard Cohen, president of the Southern Poverty Law Center, were among those present.

Harvard Law School Professor Charles J. Ogletree, Jr., director of the Charles Hamilton Houston Institute for Race and Justice, delivered a compelling testimony that captured the essence of the Jena Six's plight and this era so marked by the crime bill.

He argued that failing public schools were a root cause of worsening social issues hampering communities of color.

As an example, he presented data demonstrating racial disparities in school suspensions, highlighting the long-term harm they inflict: Black students nationwide were 2.6 times more likely to be suspended than white students. These disproportionalities were only exacerbated by zero-tolerance policies. Suspended students are then three times more likely to drop out by tenth grade. This triples their likelihood of future incarceration.

Zeroing in on Jena High School, the findings were equally egregious. In 2003, Black female students were about five times more likely to be suspended than white females (22 percent vs. 4.8 percent). For Black male students, the suspension rate was 20 percent, while for white males, it was 15.5 percent.

Charles's findings stressed an undeniable fact: these vast differences translated to real-world consequences. A child suspended from school may face academic setbacks, social isolation, and an increased risk of entering the criminal justice system. His testimony also underscored the urgent need for reforms that ensure fair treatment and dismantle discriminatory practices in school discipline.

Meanwhile, back in Jena, DA Reed, facing escalating local and national pressure, dropped his effort to try Mychal as an adult and moved the case to juvenile court. On December 9, Mychal was sentenced to eighteen months in juvenile detention, which many, even those within the justice system, still considered harsh.

Instead of going to trial, the other five opted for a plea deal.

They had to plead "no contest" to misdemeanor simple battery, a minor offense involving physical contact without serious injury. This did not constitute an admission of guilt or involvement in the incident. As part of the agreement, they each received a $500 fine and seven days of unsupervised probation, avoiding any jail time. Additionally, Justin Barker received $29,000 in damages from all except Theo and Mychal.

After their release, the Jena Six kept a low profile. Some went on to college. Others chose to go directly to the workforce.

All cut ties with Jena.

"When people ask me where I'm from, I don't like to say Jena," Robert once said. He graduated from Shaw High School in Columbus, Georgia, and moved on to Grambling State University, where he joined the football team as a wide receiver. He later joined the Reserve Officers' Training Corps and then the military.

Carwin kept strictly private after the incident.

Bryant got his bachelor's in criminal justice from Grambling and later penned a memoir, *My Story as a Jena 6*. He went on to become a motivational speaker and criminal justice activist.

"Carry yourself in the right manner, and don't let one situation define who you are," Bryant once said, addressing Black youths during an interview. "Things are gonna happen to you, but it's not about what happened—it's how you respond."

Jesse, the youngest of the Six, finished high school at a private boarding school in Connecticut before attending Hofstra University, where he studied law and business on an academic scholarship. While there, he played on the lacrosse team.

Mychal, the heavily recruited football star and the central figure in the Six's case, went on to play cornerback at Southern University. (In 2009, navigating a mental health crisis, he reportedly tried to end his life by shooting himself in the chest.)

While incarcerated, Theo read and used legal publications to navigate filing court papers, sparking his interest in law. He earned a political science bachelor's from Louisiana State University before attending University of Washington and Georgetown University law schools on a full scholarship. After graduating, he served as a staff attorney for D.C.'s Public Defender Service.

Tempered by his time in jail and the small-town firestorm that not only ravaged his community but engrossed the nation, Theo remained resolute. He once told New Orleans's local newspaper, the *Times-Picayune*, "I was forced to be hopeful. To not be hopeful would be to give in to their belief of who I was."

In 2009, Louisiana created a criminal statute specifically prohibiting the "public display of a noose on property of another or public place; intent to intimidate."

As I reflected on the lasting effects of the crime bill, whose full impact on communities of color may never be fully understood, I couldn't help but notice the irony.

The same stereotype Joe Biden used to demonize and criticize Black and brown men, a broad brush stroke that painted them as dangerous and criminal, could have easily applied to the very president he later served under. That's the danger of seeing the world solely through the lens of your lived experience: it limits perspective (until you become intentional about ridding yourself of your insulation).

"Things have changed drastically," Joe Biden said during one of his 2020 presidential town halls in Philadelphia, responding to criticism over the crime bill. He admitted the bill was a result of a different way of thinking.

"But here's where the mistake came," he added. "The mistake came in terms of what the states did locally."

Did Joe Biden specifically want communities of color targeted or want the interpretation of the bill to have been so lethal for Black Americans, especially young Black men? No one can answer that.

But as I processed Joe Biden's about-face, I was reminded of another realization from the previous chapter: self-development is a journey of discovering new ways to become better versions of ourselves. And as our identities are shaped over time, so too is our perspective. Our ability to refine our beliefs and values influences our perception.

We see the world anew.

I believe that Joe Biden once viewed a segment of the population in one way. But as his perspective evolved, so did his empathy. Perspective breeds empathy, and empathy nurtures understanding.

Another eye-opener while unpacking this era was recognizing the pitfalls inherent in American exceptionalism, the belief that America possesses unique qualities and virtues that make it superior to other nations.

This idea suggests that America has a divine role in the world, and to protect its image, those in power often exploit that role to justify the mistreatment of Others. From the Manifest Destiny, which powered the conquest of Native lands on the fallacy of white superiority, to Jim Crow laws to Japanese internment camps during the Second World War, these actions came from a belief in exceptionalism that often shuns the humanity and rights of minority groups.

Though seemingly disparate, the Jena Six case and the persistent belief in American exceptionalism share a common root: oppressive beliefs poisoned by prejudice. This has warped perspectives and undergirded institutional racism. Law enforcement officers, under the influence of such biases, easily adopt a "soldier" mentality, leading to discriminative actions and excessive punishments for disproportionately young Black people. This has eternalized a cycle of injustice within the court system, contributing to undue incarceration.

Unfortunately, such systemic blindness extends beyond the legal system. That unwavering conviction in exceptionalism, deeply rooted in the same poisoned well of bigotry, causes aversion to anything foreign and unfamiliar. This, in turn, creates a society where differences are not embraced but ostracized, deepening the cycle of marginalization and injustice.

That's the burden of America.

8

A RESURRECTION OF BLACK LIBERATION

Johnetta Elzie

I can't breathe.

ERIC GARNER, JULY 17, 2014

Reeling from the stench of the crime bill, Barack Obama's "hope" and "change" 2008 presidential campaign and victory was a balm for generations of pain.

He revived a new kind of politics. The kind that saw young voters turn out in historic droves, in part because of the widespread use of social media. It was the first time a presidential campaign was taking place after platforms like Facebook and Twitter had become a dominant force. They allowed his message to reach more voters, especially younger ones, in a way that had never been possible before.

I still remember the day he won.

It was Tuesday, November 4, 2008.

It was a special day for me too. I was in college, and it was my first time ever to the polls, my first time understanding the gravity of politics and public service.

That semester, I was in Cleveland, Ohio, doing one of two six-month college apprenticeships with General Electric. I was at a watch party with people from all walks of life as results came in. All of us, the young and not so young, cried when Barack Obama's victory against Senator John McCain was announced at 11 p.m. on CNN.

We embraced each other and the momentous juncture.

I think we all shared a common belief that, surely, a change had come. His victory was our victory. In Barack Obama, we saw the "Dream" attained, the possibilities of America fulfilled. The romanticized version packed with prospects.

During his victory speech, we listened as he spoke of the "young and old, rich and poor, Democrat and Republican, Black, white, Latino, Asian, Native American, gay, straight, disabled and not disabled," about unity, about shifting from adversity to abundance.

The air the next morning even felt different, brimming with the hope and change he embodied, overflowing with renewed pride.

Here was a Black man who had dispelled notions of the demonization of what the likes of him represented in America. Here was a Black man with the stirring oratory skills of Nelson Mandela and Martin Luther King, Jr., to still quivering minds and spark revolutionary thinking. Here was the son of a Kenyan man and a Kansas-born white woman who dared say, rising from obscurity, I shall and will overcome. Even when faced with grave opposition in victory—like the birtherism movement inflamed by Donald Trump, which claimed the Hawaiian-born Kenyan American was not American—he persisted. His campaign catchphrase, "Yes, we can," became a thunderclap for the disenfranchised.

Many evangelized it. Many more clung to it.

As Barack Obama's term began, parts of the country remained buoyed, inhaling the optimism of democracy. For another segment, he stained American exceptionalism; his presence in the White House seemed heretical. The progress made in decades past, culminating with his consequent election, was undoubtedly significant. Yet, it wasn't enough to silence the deep-rooted prejudice that had permeated society. It became clear that his presidency, paralleling the seminal reach of Martin Luther King, Jr., couldn't single-handedly reconcile a nation or uproot systemic issues.

This became tragically evident when, one after another, more Black bodies turned up, killed at the hands of police or vigilantes. The rise in these deaths was a clear indication of how deeply ingrained the pathology of the crime bill had become in societal understanding of all Others, in marking certain people as "beyond the pale."

The chilling figures paint a dire picture: Between 1999 and 2019, 10,650 Black and brown men, women, boys, and girls, ages one to ninety-three, were killed as a result of police violence. (The total number of deaths due to police violence reported in this period was 27,415; 9,312 were white. The rest were unspecified.)

Glaring still was the alarming rate of fatal police encounters with young Black people. Between 2010 and 2019, 1,181 Black and brown boys (out of 6,471 total Black and brown men killed) and 152 Black and brown women and girls (out of 601 total Black and brown women killed) between one and twenty-one years old were killed by officers.

Each life, prematurely quenched, triggered grief and outrage, flaring a surge in Black youth-led activism. Groups like the Dream Defenders, the Million Hoodies Movement, and Campaign Zero sprouted, leveraging the power of social media to amplify their voices and demand change.

It was in this heat of scorching activism that Johnetta Elzie, co-founder of Campaign Zero, realized her calling.

FEBRUARY 26, 2012. SANFORD, FLORIDA.

Around 6 p.m., sporting a dark gray hoodie, white Air Jordans, and beige jeans, seventeen-year-old Trayvon Martin left a town house at The Retreat at Twin Lakes.

He was visiting from Miami, where he lived with his mother, Sybrina Fulton. He was to spend a few days with his father, Tracy Martin, and his father's girlfriend, Brandy Green. Tracy would visit Brandy from Miami about twice a month—the two had met two years earlier at a Masonic convention. Tracy and Sybrina, who had married on June 11, 1994, separated in 1999 when Trayvon was five, sharing custody. He spent most of his time with his mother and was with Tracy on weekends.

This particular season, The Retreat had been reeling from fore-closures and burglaries left and right—there had allegedly been eight break-ins in the last year. The gated community was located in Sanford, a north-central city in Florida. With a population of roughly 53,000 people at the time, Sanford was about 65 percent white and 25 percent Black. After the rise in crimes, a neighborhood watch team of volunteers and unarmed security guards formed to patrol the community. The protocol was, whenever they saw anything out of the ordinary, they were to immediately call Sanford Police Department.

Trayvon arrived in Sanford that Wednesday, February 22, after a five-hour Greyhound bus ride. Time away from home was a punishment of sorts for the seventeen-year-old. He'd been suspended for ten days from Dr. Michael M. Krop Senior High School in Miami after he was caught scribbling "WTF" on a locker in an unauthorized area. When he was searched by the school's security, they found a screwdriver and women's rings and earrings in his backpack. They labeled the screwdriver a burglary tool, and because he'd refused to say who the jewelry belonged to, he was sent home.

Though Sybrina busied Trayvon with odd jobs around the house during his time away from school, his parents didn't want him spending his suspension dilly-dallying with friends, so a trip north seemed appropriate. It was also perfect timing because Tracy had a convention—the same Masonic convention he and Brandy had met at—in Sanford that weekend.

That Sunday evening, Tracy and Brandy left Trayvon and Brandy's fourteen-year-old son Chad at home while they attended the third conference day at Orlando's DoubleTree Hotel, about thirty minutes south of The Retreat. Still grounded by his parents, Trayvon begged his dad to go to the store. His dad relented.

At around 6:20 p.m., Trayvon walked into a 7-Eleven, hood over his head.

It was a pleasant seventy degrees, typical for a Florida evening in February. No matter the temperature, though, Trayvon loved making a fashion statement with his hoodies. His mom once said he would cycle through black and gray ones.

Once in the convenience store, Trayvon grabbed a bag of Skittles that Chad had asked for and a can of Arizona iced tea, the watermelon kind. At the counter, he reached deep into his jeans' pockets, paid the cashier, and walked out, the Arizona can tucked in the center pocket of his hoodie.

Like many that day, Trayvon was excited to return home to watch the NBA All-Star Game, which was being played just miles away in Orlando. It was a big day for basketball heads. It featured NBA megastars like Kobe Bryant, LeBron James, Kevin Durant, Dwyane Wade, and Dwight Howard from the Western Conference going up against the Eastern Conference. That past Friday, Brandy had even bought Trayvon and Chad tickets to watch the NBA second-year players from the West (Shaquille O'Neal's "Team Shaq") and East (Charles Barkley's "Team Chuck"), like Jeremy Lin and Kyrie Irving, duke it out.

On his way back to The Retreat, at around 6:55, he called his girlfriend, Rachel Jeantel, who was back in Miami. Throughout that day, they had talked for about seven hours, on and off, and this call would last about twenty minutes.

He re-entered the gated community at around 7:10.

Five minutes later, the Sanford Police Department received a phone call. Sean Noffke, an SPD dispatcher, answered. The caller was a twenty-eight-year-old Hispanic man who'd been driving through The Retreat, patrolling the grounds.

Sanford Police Department, the line's being recorded. This is Sean.

Hey, we've had some break-ins in my neighborhood, and there's a real suspicious guy—it's Retreat View Circle. The best address I can give you is 111 Retreat View Circle. This guy looks like he's up to no good, or he's on drugs or something. It's raining, and he's just walking around, looking about.

Okay, and this guy is he white, Black, or Hispanic?

He looks Black.

Did you see what he was wearing?

Yeah. A dark hoodie, like a gray hoodie, and either jeans or sweatpants and white tennis shoes. He's [unintelligible] he was just staring—

Okay, he's just walking around the area—

—looking at all the houses.

Okay.

Now he's just staring at me.

Okay, you said it's 1111 Retreat View? Or 111?

That's the clubhouse.

That's the clubhouse, do you know what the—he's near the clubhouse right now?

Yeah, now he's coming towards me.

Okay.

He's got his hand in his waistband. And he's a Black male.

How old would you say he looks?

He's got button on, his shirt, late teens.

Late teens, okay.

Something's wrong with him. Yup, he's coming to check me out, he's got something in his hands, I don't know what his deal is.

Just let me know if he does anything, okay?

How long until you get an officer over here?

Yeah, we've got someone on the way, just let me know if this guy does anything else.

Okay. These assholes, they always get away—When you come to the clubhouse, you come straight in and make a left. Actually, you would go past the clubhouse.

So, it's on the left-hand side from the clubhouse?

No, you go in, straight through the entrance, and then you make a left—you go straight in, don't turn, and make a left. Shit, he's running.

He's running? Which way is he running?

Down towards the other entrance to the neighborhood.

Which entrance is that, that he's heading towards?

The back entrance—fucking punks. These assholes, they always get away . . .

Trayvon was like any seventeen-year-old in the in-between phase of boyhood and manhood. He was tall and lean—6'0" and 140 pounds—and loved playing football. He once thought maybe the NFL would be where he'd end up.

He'd played football since he was five, coached by his father and his local high school coach, Jerome Horton. They'd play at Forzano Park in Miramar, Florida. After reaching the maximum age for the local youth league, Trayvon remained involved, volunteering at the concession stands, sometimes going there straight from school to help out until late at night.

During his freshman year at Miami Carol City Senior High School, Trayvon developed a deep love for airplanes and pivoted from his football aspirations. Recognizing their son's budding passion, his parents enrolled him in a seven-week "Experience Aviation" program in Opa-Locka, Florida. The program was founded by Barrington Irving, the first Black pilot and the youngest person to ever fly solo around the world. Upon completing the program (two summers before that fateful Sunday), Trayvon returned the following summer to assist with new students.

Looking for a better environment for Trayvon to thrive, especially considering his budding love for math, Sybrina transferred him from Carol City to Dr. Michael M. Krop Senior High School for his junior year. He had also decided on a clear career path, aviation mechanic or professional pilot, and was setting his sights on the University of Miami or Florida A&M.

His friends and football coach, Jerome, called him shy. He never liked attention. Always with a hoodie on and his headphones plugged in, listening to some R&B hits, which friends say were his favorite. They called him "Mouse," a nickname that eventually grew on him. Some felt it was because he wasn't afraid of anything, while family members attributed the moniker to his ability to fit in anywhere and his quiet, calm demeanor.

And just like any other teen, after school and on weekends, Trayvon would hang out with friends—at the movies, at the skating rink. Go to parties. Spend time with Rachel. Collect Jordans. When it came to kicks, though, he had the kind of dedication that led teens to wait outside sneaker stores like Foot Locker at six in the morning, hoping to be among the first to cop the latest and greatest. Trayvon always tried to keep up with what was in. So much so that when his mom couldn't handle the frequency of the new releases, he'd take on odd jobs for extra cash: washing cars and trimming hedges here, pulling weeds, cutting grass, and babysitting there.

But beyond Trayvon's youthful exuberance, there was a deeper, steadfast love: he was a mama's boy. He used to call Sybrina "cupcake." He'd tell her, "you're so sweet." Whenever she was sick, he'd pretend to be her doctor. When she was tired from work (at one time she worked for the Miami-Dade County Solid Waste Management, where she met Tracy, and later for the Miami-Dade County housing agency), he'd want to cook for her or offer to carry grocery bags or clean the house or wash her car. Sometimes, Sybrina would pretend she was too tired to do something just so she could ask her son to do it. Eager, he'd jump at the chance. He'd tell her, with a big smile, "I've got it, Cupcake."

Are you following him?

Yeah.

Okay, we don't need you to do that.

Okay.

All right, sir, what is your name?

George. He ran.

All right, George. What's your last name?

Zimmerman.

…

All right, George. We do have them on the way. Do you want to meet with the officer when they get out there?

Yeah.

All right, where you going to meet with them at?

If they come in through the gate, tell them to go straight past the clubhouse. And uh, straight past the clubhouse, and make a left. And then they go past the mailboxes, that's my truck—

What address are you parked in front of?

I don't know. It's a cut-through, so I don't know the address.

Okay, do you live in the area?

Yeah, I—

What's your apartment number?

It's a home. It's 1950—Oh, crap. I don't want to give it all out, I don't know where this kid is.

Okay, do you want to just meet with them right near the mail-boxes, then?

Yeah, that's fine.

All right, George. I'll let them know to meet you around there, okay?

Actually, could you have them call me and I'll tell them where I'm at?

Okay, yeah, that's no problem.

Should I give you my number, or you got it?

Yeah, I got it. [redacted]?

Yeah, you got it.

Okay, no problem, I'll let them know to call you when you're in the area.

Thanks.

You're welcome.

During the call, George had kept on Trayvon, tailing him as the teen quickened his steps. George's call with the dispatcher ended around 7:13. Trayvon's call with Rachel ended one minute earlier, right as George inched closer.

In a later testimony to prosecutor Angela Corey, Rachel said she told Trayvon to run, but he refused:

And what, if, if anything, did Mr. Martin say?

He said no, he's almost right by his daddy fiancé's house. And then he said, "That n*gga is still following me now." I asked him how the man looked like. He just told me the man looked "creepy. Creepy, white"—excuse my language—"cracker. Creepy ass cracker. Now the creepy ass cracker is following me." And then I just told him to run. And he said "No."

You told him to run?

Yes. He said, "Why are you following me for?" Then I heard a hard-breathing man come and say, "What are you doing around here?" Then I started saying, "Trayvon, Trayvon, what's going on?" Then I heard a bump. Then I started hearing wet grass sounds. I start hearing a little bit of Trayvon saying, "Get off, get off."

Then what did you hear?

Then suddenly the phone hung up.

The tussle was loud enough to stir neighbors, who began calling the police. One said the commotion sounded like people arguing. When another called, a male's voice is heard in the background saying "Help" and "Help me" about fourteen times in under forty seconds. An analysis done by the FBI later said it was hard from the audio to distinguish who was yelling given the heightened emotional state.

While on the phone with Sanford Police Dispatch, another unidentified neighbor heard the final, bleak moment. It all went down behind her home.

9–1–1, do you need police, fire, or medical?

Um, maybe both. I'm not sure. There is just someone screaming outside.

. . .

Okay. Does he look hurt to you?

I can't see him. I don't wanna go out there. I don't know what's going on, so. (Female caller)

Call the cops. (Male voice inside home with female caller, in the background)

They're sending—(Female)

So, you think he's yelling, "Help"?

Yes. (Female)

All right. What is your—number?

(GUNSHOT)

Just, there's gunshots. (Female)

You just heard gunshots?

Yes.

How many?

Just one—Get down. (Female)

I know. (Male)

The shot rang out at about 7:14.

A single bullet from George's black KelTec PF9 9mm semiautomatic handgun nestled into the left part of Trayvon's chest.

Three minutes later, the officers George had summoned arrived and found the teen face down in the grass. A sergeant checked for his pulse. There was none. Still, he and another police officer performed CPR for the next six minutes. As the scene buzzed with activity, a neighbor brought them a plastic bag, which was used to seal Trayvon's chest wound.

Firefighters and EMS from the Sanford Fire Department arrived at 7:27 and immediately began their lifesaving protocols.

Three minutes later, Trayvon was pronounced dead.

Shortly after, George, his face swollen, his back wet and soiled, was taken into custody by officers for interrogation. He told them Trayvon attacked him, punched him in the nose, and knocked him to the ground. Fearing for his life, he said he took out his gun and shot at him. (When Trayvon's body was later examined, there was a slight scratch on his finger, but there were no scrapings from underneath his nails that suggested the prolonged struggle George had described.) At 1 a.m., after five hours of questioning, without any other evidence to rebut George's claims of self-defense, the Sanford Police Department let him go.

After returning from their conference, long after the shooting scene cleared, Tracy and Brandy grew anxious when they hadn't heard from Trayvon. Around 8:30 that morning, they filed a police report, telling officers that the teen hadn't come home after going out the night before.

Connecting the dots, officers presented Tracy with a photo of Trayvon from the crime scene, his bloodied body laid out on the grass.

Tracy confirmed that was his son.

He then called Sybrina.

"Trayvon is gone."

Trayvon's death cast a long shadow over Barack Obama's presidency. Many who had seen him as a savior-type, a bridge to racial harmony, were left disillusioned as atrocities against the marginalized persisted. Yet, he remained determined to traverse divides and enact change, even if the path wouldn't be easy. He understood, perhaps more than anyone, the urgency of addressing the systemic inequalities that plagued America: He, too, had walked the razor-thin paths and felt the sting of prejudice, the constant vigilance it demanded.

He once said, "Trayvon Martin looked like I did at the age of fifteen, sixteen, seventeen. There were many times I'd get on the elevator, and women would clutch their purse. Or I'd walk by a car, and suddenly, you'd hear the locks go down. And maybe the only thing that separated us was luck."

Despite continued racial tensions and accompanying disenchantment, Barack Obama ushered in a new era in politics, marrying hope with pragmatism. His administration prioritized inclusivity and policies like the American Recovery and Reinvestment Act, which created millions of jobs and helped lift many out of poverty. It exemplified the focus on problem-solving over partisan gridlock. He also championed individual rights, signing the Affordable Care Act into law and repealing Don't Ask, Don't Tell, demonstrating his commitment to equality for all. These actions, reflecting his promise of change, made significant progress toward addressing pressing challenges.

And yet, in the face of his efforts to address generational poverty and structural inequalities, the deep stench of entrenched racism remained unchecked and pervasive. These biases reinforced stereotypes and created a harmful cycle where limited access to quality education and economic resources perpetuated systemic issues, further clouding perceptions of the Othered. This stigma was signified by the unconscionable death of Trayvon, where even what he wore—his hoodie, which made George Zimmerman find him "suspicious"—made him a target.

Overnight, the teen's hoodie became a symbol of unrestrained racial profiling, a shared burden that catalyzed protest and solidarity. Across the nation, people of all ages along with cultural icons like LeBron James and Dwyane Wade of the Miami Heat donned hoodies. LeBron even took to social media, posting a photo of his team in hoodies with hashtags like #WeAreTrayvonMartin. It underscored the chilling reality: the hoodie, a simple piece of clothing, had come to embody generations of stereotypes, reducing young Black men, especially, to mere targets based on their appearance, daring to exist as they are.

Trayvon's death exposed a still fragile democracy where power and privilege remained in the hands of a select few. Yet it revived a new form of Black youth activism, one that, despite persistent inequalities, was resolute and resilient. These young ones were tired of being tired and demanded to be heard. Energized by a rekindled desire for justice, this generation of young activists stepped out with a powerful message: enough is enough.

For far too long, their communities had endured a cycle of violence. Forced to navigate a world rigged against them, they called for a dismantling of systemic racism and a complete overhaul of the institutions that perpetuated it. Their fight wasn't just for themselves, but for future generations, a future where hoodie-clad teens wouldn't be seen as threats, but simply as kids making their way home.

Enough was enough.

Unlike previous waves of activism, this new breed of crusaders leveraged not only social media but the widespread availability of smartphones to build the twenty-first-century civil rights movement and further their reach.

Soon after that fateful Sunday, they quickly assembled and began taking to the streets with outsized protests, rallies, and demonstrations. Organized by youth-led groups like Black Youth Project 100 in Chicago and The Gathering for Justice in New York, they were clamoring for accountability, specifically for George Zimmerman's arrest.

Many more protests followed.

Days following Trayvon's slaying, South African American Daniel Maree, a recent graduate of American University, founded the Million Hoodies Movement for Justice in New York. He felt he had to "do something . . . Trayvon could have easily been me or my little sister." Starting as a YouTube video and blog, it quickly grew into one of the largest internet protests. The twenty-four-year-old uploaded over 300,000 photos of supporters wearing hoodies, and the movement gained over 50,000 committed members nationwide, with college chapters across the country. They played a significant role in collecting more than two million signatures on a Change.org petition advocating for the arrest of George Zimmerman.

On March 13, 2012, about two weeks after Trayvon was gunned down, Sanford Police Department homicide detective Chris Serino filed an affidavit for George to be charged with manslaughter. Chris argued that George's failure to identify himself as a community patrolman made Trayvon's death avoidable. He believed that if George had done so, the encounter wouldn't have escalated to the point where Trayvon was shot. He also disputed George's claims of injuries sustained during the altercation, stating they were not consistent with a life-threatening situation. Furthermore, Chris emphasized that there was no evidence of Trayvon's involvement in any criminal activity at the time.

A week later, on March 21, Daniel gathered more than a thousand people in New York City, all in hoodies, all mobilized on social media using the hashtag #millionhoodies. The event's Facebook page declared: "A black person in a hoodie isn't automatically 'suspicious.' Let's put an end to racial profiling!" The date for the march was equally significant. It was the annual United Nations International Day for the Elimination of Racial Discrimination, a day dedicated to raising awareness about combating prejudice and intolerance and promoting inclusion and equality regardless of race, ethnicity, or background.

During the rally, Sybrina and Tracy addressed the crowd.

"My heart is in pain, but to see the support of all of you really makes a difference," Sybrina told them. "We need this kind of support. Our son is your son. I want you guys to stand up for justice and stand up for what's right."

"George Zimmerman took Trayvon's life for nothing," Tracy said. "George Zimmerman took Trayvon's life profiling him. My son did not deserve to die, but I'm here today to [ensure] that justice is served and that no other parents have to go through this again."

The day after the demonstration, on March 22, Department of Justice officials met with Sybrina and Tracy in a closed-door meeting, likely to discuss whether there were any federal civil rights violations.

The following day, in the White House Rose Garden, Barack Obama delivered a searing speech, castigating the teen's death and calling for an end to systemic injustices. Standing before a somber audience of activists, community leaders, and grieving family members, his voice trembled with sorrow and determination.

"This is a tragedy," he said. "I can only imagine what these parents are going through, and when I think about this boy, I think about my own kids, and I think every parent in America should be able to understand why it is absolutely imperative that we investigate every aspect of this . . . But my main message is to the parents of Trayvon Martin. You know, if I had a son, he'd look like Trayvon. And I think they are right to expect that all of us as Americans are going to take this with the seriousness that it deserves and that we're going to get to the bottom of exactly what happened."

A day later, thousands flocked to Freedom Plaza in D.C. for the Stand Up for Trayvon rally. Many in the crowd were young. Many sported a hoodie. Some pumped their fists to the tune of countless cycles of calls and repeats.

SAY HIS NAME.

Trayvon Martin!

On April 11, after months of ceaseless rallying, George was indicted for second-degree murder.

Meanwhile, former Florida A&M University students, led by Phillip Agnew, launched the Dream Defenders that same month. The group's aim was to mobilize young people, utilizing Facebook as their primary medium of organizing and connecting.

Embracing this new fervent spirit of activism, Phillip later said of their movement, "With every time you raise up your voice, a chapter is being written. With every time you stand inside an area with someone who doesn't look like you and see humanity in someone across the aisle, a chapter is being rewritten in the history of our country."

A year later, on June 13, 2013, George's trial kicked off.

Activists like Daniel and groups like Dream Defenders kept on, sustaining a thundering wave of online and offline resistance.

On July 13, after four weeks of testimony, the jury delivered an acquittal.

While the prosecution argued that George had profiled, pursued, and confronted Trayvon without justification, the defense pointed to Florida's "Stand Your Ground" law, which allows people to use deadly force if they reasonably believe it is necessary to prevent death or great bodily harm to themselves or others. Ultimately, the six-member jury, composed entirely of white women, agreed. (The Department of Justice later decided not to press any federal civil rights charges.)

Outraged by the acquittal, three Black women organizers in their late twenties and early thirties—Patrisse Cullors, Alicia Garza, and Opal Tometi—took to Facebook. Lamenting the verdict, they declared what seemed spiritual, a sacred psalm in three simple words preceded by a hashtag: #BlackLivesMatter. This succinct phrase went on to embody the struggles and aspirations of a people, becoming a passionate, unifying plea for justice, equality, and empowerment.

Those three words, often abbreviated "BLM," became a seed of revolution for the global Black community. BLM's main goal was to get justice for unarmed Black Americans killed at the hands of police, as convictions for such cases were rare. Also, the movement wanted to see an end to racialized police violence.

Similar to the civil rights movement, this new crusade for Black lives began to have a profound impact on the national discourse surrounding racism, discrimination, and police brutality. But, it wasn't until a year later, on August 9, 2014, when a white Ferguson police officer in Missouri fatally shot eighteen-year-old Michael Brown (who some onlookers said had his hands up at the time he was gunned down) that the BLM movement gained widespread attention.

Michael's death was just five days after twenty-two-year-old John Crawford III was shot and killed by a white officer in a Dayton, Ohio, Walmart for holding an unpackaged BB gun he had picked up while shopping. A fatal end that had gripped the nation, then Michael's unbearable blow happened. The compounding nature of what seemed targeted yet unavoidable deaths became all-consuming.

The exhaustion of a people was laid bare by still more protests, many led by high school and college students flooding streets across the nation.

Roaring, "Black lives matter."

Chanting, "Hands up, don't shoot."

Their raised placards declaring the same.

Many still donned hoodies in remembrance of Trayvon.

This was a watershed moment for the ongoing movement against police brutality and racial injustice.

This was the air that spurred twenty-five-year-old Johnetta Elzie to action. Michael's death was personal to the St. Louis native.

It activated a purpose within her.

"The first I even heard about [Michael's shooting] is because a woman named April, who I've been following on Twitter since 2009, messages me this guy, Young Pharaoh God's Twitter feed," Johnetta told me about that August Saturday. "And she's like, look at this picture. And it's a picture of [the shooting officer's] feet standing over Mike Brown's body . . . and she's like something just happened in your city."

The Twitter account was that of @TheePharoah, a local rapper in St. Louis, who saw it all go down.

Michael's shooting happened about one minute after noon.

At 12:03 p.m., the rapper tweeted, "I JUST SAW SOMEONE DIE OMFG."

Seconds later—still 12:03—he tweeted again: "Im about to hyperventilate."

Twenty minutes later, he posted yet another message: "dude was running and the cops just saw him. I saw him die bruh."

Remembering that message from April, Johnetta told me, "It just changed my entire life."

It was a scorching Saturday.

Michael Brown and a friend, twenty-two-year-old Dorian Johnson, were walking from Ferguson Market and Liquors, a convenience store, when they were stopped at 12:01 p.m. near the

Canfield Green housing complex on Canfield Drive by a white police officer, Darren Wilson.

Shortly before noon, there had been a call to the police from the market that there was a robbery in progress. Surveillance footage shows Michael grabbing a handful of cigarillos before walking out of the store. Dorian later said before entering and after exiting, they'd been talking about life and faith, about "the Bible and God, how you're supposed to be as a human going through life."

About the stolen cigarillos, Dorian acknowledged it happened, but that he didn't know how to address it head-on with Michael.

"I was being a real good friend and staying with him," he said, "even though I know he committed a crime . . . It wasn't like he robbed the store like he held it at gunpoint or anything. So, I didn't think the guy [at the store] was really gonna call the police."

On his way to a lunch date with his wife, Barb, Darren received a dispatch from the Ferguson Police Department, alerting him of the theft with a description of two suspects.

"Do you guys need me?" he radioed back.

The dispatcher told him the suspects were no longer in sight.

Darren continued driving west on Canfield Drive in his police department Chevrolet Tahoe, windows down.

He spotted Michael and Dorian jaywalking in the middle of the busy road and asked them to go on the sidewalk.

"Fuck what you have to say," Darren later said Michael responded.

"Get the fuck on the sidewalk," Darren yelled back.

The duo allegedly ignored his commands.

Darren then figured, given the dispatch and the proximity to the store, Michael and Dorian had to be the suspects mentioned on the radio call. He immediately called for backup and angled his car to barricade the roadway to stop them from leaving.

What followed next, in under two minutes, has been heavily contested.

Some eyewitnesses said Darren was the aggressor. Others, including the Department of Justice report based on Darren's account, said Michael initiated the altercation by reaching into the Tahoe's open window and punching Darren. Dorian later disputed

Darren's account and simply classified their stop as racial profiling. (The Department of Justice report also mentioned there were traces of Michael's DNA inside the driver's side door. It also found the FPD often abused its power, racially profiled people, and other evidence pointed to their discrimination and bigotry. An example referenced was of FPD officers sending racist emails to each other like one from November 2008 about Barack Obama that read, "What black man holds a steady job for four years.")

Darren said he only drew his gun because he feared for his life. And at that point, Darren said that's when Michael tried to reach for the weapon and allegedly told him, "You are too much of a pussy to shoot me." (Both Michael and Dorian were unarmed. Darren later told investigators that he had no Taser on him—only his gun, baton, and mace—and that when the situation turned intense, his gun was the only weapon he had readily available.)

Eyewitness accounts confirm that at some point after Darren drew his gun, Dorian ran and took cover behind a car. It was around this time—perhaps after the alleged ongoing scuffle with Michael that Darren later detailed to investigators—that the officer began firing at the teen. It was the first time he'd ever fired his weapon on duty in his six years on the force.

As the bullets began to fly, from eyewitness accounts, Michael began to run away, his back to Darren. One onlooker, Tiffany Mitchell, said when Michael's body appeared to be shot from the back, as he fled from Darren, she saw his body jerk. She then saw him put his hands up in surrender. This was when Dorian said he saw Michael turn to face Darren, his hands raised and now at a farther distance from the officer.

Dorian heard Michael say, "I don't have a gun. Stop shooting."

Michael was shot at repeatedly.

Of the twelve bullets, six struck his 6'4" 292-pound frame, with two hitting his head, four striking his right arm.

As more dispatches went out and more FPD officers flooded the scene, Michael's body, face down on the pavement, blood streaming from his temple, remained in the street for four hours, under the torrid heat.

"It was tragic," Duane Foster, Michael's former teacher, told me. "That was so traumatic. And I don't think we realized the magnitude of how it affected young people."

Eight days before that summer day, Michael had graduated from Normandy High School. He'd begun his educational journey within the Normandy Schools Collaborative District at Pine Lawn Elementary, receiving special education support because "he had some struggles," his mother, Lezley McSpadden-Head, once told me. When she decided to move away from the Normandy area, Michael pleaded to stay nearby so he could continue attending his school and be with friends. She acquiesced and moved him in with his grandmother, just five blocks from Normandy High and where he had been walking back to from the grocery store that Saturday.

Though labeled withdrawn and shy by friends and teachers, Michael started blossoming in seventh grade, testing the waters with theater. Duane, who was head of the program, directed him as Bobo in *A Raisin in the Sun,* but by his senior year, he noticed that Michael had lost his "jovial personality . . . he wasn't the same." So, recognizing the teen's academic and personal struggles, Duane, who also led the choir and had a makeshift music studio, gave Michael unlimited access to the space, nurturing his burgeoning creative spirit.

"One thing that [Michael] did have was life in music and producing music," Duane told me. "He was a silent leader, especially in regards to the studio. [He] established the rules for the studio: 'People don't leave stuff on. Don't come after school trying to smoke. Don't go home and smoke weed and come back to the studio because Foster gon cancel the program' type of thing. The kids listened to him."

Michael's mom also fondly remembered all the songs Michael had been writing and producing.

"He made the beats and he recorded it. And he did not have a microphone," she told me. "He had no studio, and he didn't pay for studio time . . . He used a headset from some earphones and an old computer that my brother gave him. And somehow, he was able to speak into this handset to record himself and put this stuff on SoundCloud. It's still out there, and it's really lovely to listen to it and hear his voice."

This infectious enthusiasm for crafting beats made the teen redirect his focus toward becoming a music producer instead of going into the HVAC business, like his dad. He even enrolled in Vatterott College, set to begin his journey just days before his death.

"I had never let my son do anything over the summer as far as being away from home," Lezley remembered of Michael's final day. "But why not? He went to school, he graduated. Hey, yeah, you can go hang out in the neighborhood with some guys that you know. What's wrong with that? Well, little did I know."

"Little did I know," she repeated, her voice cracking this time. "Never did I think that would be my son. Never. Never, ever in a million years ever, because he could go anywhere and he could communicate with anybody. My son didn't belong to a gang. You know how you get with people and they do what they do? But you not into that? But you can still can have a conversation with them—y'all alright, you know?"

"Yeah, I get you," I told her.

"When you live in areas like this, that are urban areas that [have] drug activity, gang activity, and different things go on, but it doesn't mean you are always a product of your environment. And my son was not that. He was not that. But he knew how to mix and mesh with people. And that was Michael. And so for August 9 to just snatch my dreams away . . ."

Through tears, she trailed off.

We sat in silence.

As Johnetta scrolled on Twitter that Saturday, she was already experiencing what she described to me as the worst year of her life "ever." Her mother, a fierce matriarch and entrepreneur who ran a hair salon for decades in St. Louis, had died that January.

"That hurt me," she said, "I was deeply depressed."

Then, three weeks later on February 12, 2014, her best friend, a twenty-seven-year-old Black man, Stephon Averyhart, was fatally shot in an alley during a foot chase by police officers. The St. Louis Metropolitan Police Department never launched a full investigation, leaving Stephon's family with a gaping hole and unanswered questions. Stephon's death seemed to fade into obscurity, met with deafening silence from the public. There was no outrage, no demand for justice, as if his life never mattered.

"I couldn't process that kind of grief while still grieving my mother," Johnetta told me, her voice still thick with pain.

Throughout Johnetta's life, education had been paramount. Her mother and grandmother had ensured Johnetta and her younger sister had access to the best resources and opportunities. So when Johnetta's mother passed away, the twenty-four-year-old knew she had to continue this legacy. After taking a break from Southeast Missouri State University, Johnetta stepped up as her sister's primary caretaker, diligently prepping her for high school at Francis Howell North, a predominantly white public school in the suburbs of St. Charles, Missouri.

Francis Howell School District had gained national attention when the Normandy Schools Collaborative District lost its accreditation in 2012 and was taken over by the state. A Missouri Supreme Court decision authorized students from failing districts like Normandy to transfer to better-performing schools, leading many Black parents from those communities to bus their children to affluent districts like Francis Howell. However, some parents in Francis Howell objected to the busing program, citing, in part, resource allocation.

Johnetta, who herself had faced challenges with identity and colorism in predominantly white academic spaces, saw this experience as a powerful revelation about societal inequalities.

"What was really crazy is [that] Mike Brown's high school, Normandy, was on the same street as my [private] high school, Incarnate Word Academy," she said. "So [it's disheartening] to even know that this school that we paid a lot of money for me to go to, that has greatly impacted my work, my network, my social life—*everything*—and just right down the street are hundreds and hundreds of Black kids who are just passing through with low GPAs and graduation certificates that mean nothing."

She went on to say that the busing ordeal and the pushback from white parents, especially the mothers, showed her the complicity of white women in how they contribute to the preservation of privilege, discrimination and sexism. (This led her to later believe that "Hillary Clinton was not gonna win that [2016] election [against Donald Trump].")

Descendants of a multigenerational household shaped by the Great Migration, with roots tracing back to Mississippi and Arkansas, Johnetta and her sister began attending town halls alongside their grandparents ahead of the 2014 fall semester. Parents from Francis Howell were making their case against busing, and the prejudice and racism underlying their arguments became painfully clear to Johnetta.

"White people were saying, 'No, we like the nigg*s we already have,'" she remembered of the objections. "'We don't want new nigg*s from across the way. They're not the same as these Black people we already got.' Black people at my sister's school, me, my family, [we] were in the town hall scene like—'We hear how you are talking about Black people period. We hear how you are talking about us.'"

And as if the air wasn't thick enough with racial tension and aggression, "Boom! Mike Brown is killed. And I'm like, Jesus. Like, you can't make 2014 up."

She had reached her boiling point.

From the first shots to when Michael's body laid out in the sun for hours, people began flooding the streets, snapping and posting, lashing out at Ferguson Police Department on Twitter and Facebook for their disregard and negligence.

Meanwhile, a video on YouTube and a photo on Twitter and Facebook of the teen spread out on Canfield Drive, blood oozing from his body, went viral. It was around this time that April messaged Johnetta on Twitter, and "immediately after that, my best friend and I at the time we drove down," Johnetta told me, remembering still with intense fervor. "That was the beginning of everything."

Once at the scene, Johnetta began taking photos and videos, tweeting what she saw.

In one tweet that night, at 11 p.m., she wrote, "It's still blood on the ground where Mike Brown Jr was murdered. A cone in place where his body laid for hours today. #STL #Ferguson."

Her tweets went viral as she was one of the few on-the-ground citizen journalists capturing every moment for the world. She quickly became a trusted source of information, crystallizing the notion of social media activists.

She remembers the urgency she felt going out there that night. It wasn't the compounding of moments from the year she'd endured but a deep passion for her Blackness. Though she had come up in the suburbs and attended all-white private schools at her mother's behest, it was in her single mom's hair salon, being around Black barbers and hairdressers, that "shaped [and] complete[d] my love for Black people."

"I [saw] it every day," she said. "Even though I'm separated from my community when I go to these white schools, I still leave these white schools and get loved on when I go back home around these positive examples of Black folks. So that is what really made me want to go out—is just hearing the details . . . I thought about Stephon, and I was just like no one knew Stephon Averyhart was shot and killed right down the street." As if to add insult to injury, she said Stephon was killed on the same road as Michael. Just two miles down, in fact, on the very street where her mother used to work. The coincidence felt deeply personal, an echo of her loss.

"I was just like maybe this is an opportunity to try to like bring what happened to my friend also to the forefront."

One of the most haunting moments for Johnetta that first night was seeing the spread of Michael's blood. She had watched as officials tried to wash it away with water, but it seemed impenetrable.

"When I got down there, it was so incredible," she said. "There was still a vibrant pool of blood on that ground." The blood, she felt, called to her. It was a powerful symbol that took her back to her grandmother's Christian faith and the many religious private schools her mother had enrolled her in. It was biblical. An ethereal encounter.

"I know about the power of the blood," she continued, her voice thickening. "It was just something about seeing his blood still there even after they tried to wash it. In my mind, it was like the blood is working. The blood is still speaking. The blood is still talking. Like, the blood will not be washed away. That's just what made me feel that this was something different. It was vibrating through my body. Staring at that blood. It was like making silent agreements with God." Spiritual agreements that made her realize this was a moment she couldn't ignore.

At a candlelight vigil for Michael the next day, among pumped fists and roars of "Black lives matter" and "Hands up, don't shoot," swarms of officers stood guard.

A QuikTrip convenience store on West Florissant Avenue, a stone's throw from where Michael was shot down, was looted and burned down.

Several other businesses were destroyed.

On August 11, as simmering tensions and days of unrest continued, the FBI opened an investigation into Michael's death. That night, police escalated their tactics and came out in riot gear, firing tear gas and rubber bullets, an attempt to disband demonstrators.

Many nights of outrage persisted.

Each time, it seemed thousands more resisted.

Each time, they wailed those three simple words, now their anthem: *Black lives matter.* This ongoing wave of dissent, with many iterations nationwide, helped solidify the BLM movement.

The entire time, Johnetta was immersed in the bubbling cauldron of protest, feeling the heat and energy on all sides. Still at the forefront, leading the charge, she was telling locals—and the world through social platforms—how to help. Where to drop off food donations. What was needed for care packages. She directed the hundreds of thousands that flooded in and out of the city. When police would throw gas canisters at protesters, she was there washing them off. She witnessed people decry the systematic brutalization of Black bodies.

"I saw Black women yelling and screaming and crying literally at the Ferguson Police Department because they had brought the German Shepherd dogs out and everybody was just losing it. But Black women were like you killed this person, you killed that person. Y'all killed this person. You took me. Y'all tried to take my kids. Just all the ails of what happened, [of] being a Black woman. All I could do was to be a witness."

Johnetta vowed to amplify those cries of the unheard, her grief morphing into a global fire for change. Recognizing the movement couldn't sustain itself on sheer momentum, she joined forces with other young leaders she'd met on the ground (like the twenty-nine-year-old executive director of St. Louis's Teach for America, Brittany Packnett Cunningham, and twenty-nine-year-old Minneapolis school administrator DeRay Mckesson), determined to figure out how to maintain the explosive crusade gripping the nation and channel its raw energy into concrete action.

As she looked for ways to strategize what was to come next, Johnetta remained intentional about keeping her message simple and pure. It had to always be about the blood being shed, not about her.

"I just kept telling God, if you take care of me, I will say what I've seen," she remembered thinking after the movement began skyrocketing. "I will try to keep that at my core the whole time. I just wanted to be a witness. It really felt like, that's what his blood—that's what the message was when I was staring at it. It was just like, 'Please tell what you see.'"

She began by challenging mainstream media accounts of what was happening on her streets.

"The news was getting it wrong in the early hours," she told me.

So, encouraged by fellow activist and law scholar Justin Hansford, she decided to begin disseminating her message beyond social media and launched a citizen journalism newsletter that also served as a nonviolent civil rights campaign she aptly called This

Is the Movement. She focused on keeping people informed about nationwide police brutality cases and protests. At one time, it had more than 15,000 subscribers.

When the Ferguson protests grew more heated that November after the St. Louis County grand jury decided not to indict Darren, she was still there. The jury had heard testimony from both sides, but the evidence, they felt, was inconclusive. The news prompted still more protesting that erupted into rioting and looting.

More buildings were set ablaze.

More police descended with riot gear.

Five days after the announcement, on November 29, Darren resigned from the FPD.

In between all of this, Johnetta and other local activists pressed on, forming national community networks.

There was the Don't Shoot Coalition, an alliance of organizations, locals, lawyers, and professors focused on police reform at varying sites and levels. Johnetta said it consisted of pockets of "literally everyone who was involved and cared."

Then, shortly after, she partnered with DeRay and twenty-five-year-old Samuel Sinyangwe (who joined the movement after being a Twitter follower of DeRay) to launch Mapping Police Violence. They had discovered an untapped void of information: there was no encyclopedic database tracking such deaths nationally. Their initiative would gather sweeping statistics surrounding police-related fatalities across the country, with a specific focus on incidents involving the death of minorities at the hands of police.

This data gap was particularly egregious since, in 1994, Congress had mandated that Attorney General Janet Wood Reno carry out a similar project, but it was never executed. Without seeing the magnitude of the numbers, the trio felt, it would be impossible for people to understand the gravity of the epidemic or be able to have solution-driven discussions about it.

Samuel, a political science graduate from Stanford and a data scientist by trade, spearheaded the project. By late fall 2015, the website was live. He sourced data from private databases specializing in police-related deaths, including the FBI's Supplementary

Homicide Reports, the National Violent Death Reporting System, and the National Vital Statistics System. He also cross-referenced with police reports and newspaper articles, sometimes consulting social media accounts to build a fuller narrative and confirm the victims' identities. The award-winning tool remains effective and influential for researchers, journalists, and scholars. (Months after Mapping Police Violence debuted, *The Washington Post* launched a similar tool, Fatal Force Database.)

The initiative was similarly personal for Samuel.

Growing up in a predominantly white neighborhood in Orlando—26 miles north of Sanford, Florida—he had experienced the sting of racial prejudice firsthand. He was used to being called the n-word, bullied for his darker skin, and, at one time, even frequented the same convenience store Trayvon had spent his final moments in.

"[Trayvon] could have been me," he once said. "It really could have been anyone who looked like me."

Samuel went on to develop another database, The Police Scorecard, the nation's first and largest public database of comprehensive assessments of American policing. His team of data experts and scholars delve deep into each municipal and county law enforcement agency, gathering and examining factors like racial disparities in police stops, use of force compared to other departments, and accountability measures. This exhaustive analysis draws on data from multiple sources, providing a clearer picture of police practices across the country.

On March 4, 2015, the Department of Justice cleared Darren of any federal civil rights violations in Michael's death. This decision extinguished the sliver of hope many held for accountability. Yet, the tragic reality continued: between August 2014 and March 2015, approximately 270 Black people died at the hands of police, seemingly unaffected by the national outcry in the wake of the teen's unspeakable death.

Further illustrating the abiding mistreatment of communities of color, when peaceful demonstrators assembled on a "day of resistance" sit-in, they were unduly confronted by law enforcement. Taking place at the St. Louis Justice Center on August 10, 2015, the staged occupation was to mark Michael's one-year remembrance. As police presence soared, all in riot gear, Johnetta, who was present alongside DeRay, took to Twitter: "If I'm arrested today, please know I'm not suicidal. I have plenty to live for." (This was one month after a twenty-eight-year-old Black woman, Sandra Bland, died by suicide in police custody in Waller County, Texas. Many found the circumstances around her death suspicious, calling for an in-depth investigation that never came.)

Johnetta's post continued, "I did not resist, I'm just black."

Johnetta, DeRay, and fifty-five others were hauled into custody, inflaming the seething anger in a community already reeling from the fallout of a system that seemed hell-bent on stifling dissent and perpetuating racial imbalances.

They were released shortly after.

In response to this unrelenting assault on Black lives, Johnetta and her team began strategizing how to systematically organize and formally address these inequities. Haunted by the unyielding drumbeat of racialized violence, irrefutable proof now meticulously compiled and documented by the Mapping Police Violence project, they craved a war room. This stark reality exposed yet another critical gap: the movement lacked a central hub, a digital and physical space to effectively unify and share their message, synchronize efforts, and engage a broader audience.

Meanwhile, as their movement continued to balloon, they had been facing intense scrutiny from notable figures seeking a new Martin Luther King, Jr.–like leading figure. Unlike previous Black Freedom movements, this new wave of young leaders fighting for Black lives lacked a clear mandate or identifiable leadership. There was no single leader who could be easily recognized as the face of the revival.

So as their crusade swelled, so too did the searing scrutiny.

Months after the Ferguson protests erupted, media mogul Oprah Winfrey shook the movement when she questioned their aim.

"I think it's wonderful to march and to protest, and it's wonderful to see all across the country, people doing it," she said. "But what I'm looking for is some kind of leadership to come out of this to say, 'This is what we want. This is what has to change, and these are the steps that we need to take to make these changes, and this is what we're willing to do to get it.'"

Similarly, Hillary Clinton, then the 2016 presidential candidate, said these contemporary youth-led movements were shortsighted and muddled in their goals. Without a plan, she felt, their cause wouldn't move the needle much on the racial injustices they were condemning.

"The next question by people who are on the sidelines, which is the vast majority of Americans, is, 'So, what do you want me to do about it?'" she said. "'What am I supposed to do about it?' That's what I'm trying to put together in a way that I can explain it, and I can sell it because in politics if you can't explain it and you can't sell it, it stays on the shelf."

Longtime activist Al Sharpton, who had marched on the front lines of countless civil rights battlefields, pointed out what he saw as shortcomings in this new wave of Black youth activism, urging them to learn from the past and adapt their strategies. He even labeled some of them as angry and cautioned that "there's a difference between an activist and a *thug*." This loaded word choice, a byproduct from what many considered the *tougher on Blacks* era, alienated him (and other traditional activists like Jesse Jackson, who had also attempted to calm tensions) from many young activists, who saw it as a continuation of harmful stereotypes.

When Al Sharpton's National Action Network organized a march in D.C. the winter after Michael's death, thousands gathered in honor of those slain by police violence. As he declared it a "history-making moment," Johnetta leaped onto the stage, her voice ringing out, "We started this!"

In the crowd, a sign held aloft declared: "We, the youth, did not elect Al Sharpton our spokesperson. Have a seat."

This fiery exchange became a stark reminder of the generational divide within the now-multigenerational fight for justice. The chasm, already a well of simmering discontent beneath the surface, widened with every heated word, leaving its mark on the movement's uncertain future.

Johnetta and her peers viewed their older, more traditional counterparts as disconnected from contemporary and local activism. They understood that true power and influence went beyond simply taking the stage and speaking passionately. It went beyond appearing authoritative without producing tangible results.

They had discovered their own unique power and voice, which they found through the transformative possibilities of social media, with its ability to instantly unite and mobilize people. It was a new era of collective agency. These young activists had come to prefer a participatory, leaderless, and evenly distributed framework that empowered an all-hands-on-deck mentality—an Ella Baker type of activism. They rejected relying on a charismatic few and instead formed strong alliances of interconnected activists who operated based on consensus.

But as mounting criticisms poured in, Johnetta, Brittany, DeRay, and Samuel, now key voices within the movement, felt pressure to address concerns about having a definitive plan. They decided to answer the call by establishing a central organization to coordinate efforts and amplify their message. This led to the birth of Campaign Zero in August 2015. They believed they could formalize their strategy without sacrificing the grassroots approach that had fueled their movement.

Campaign Zero emerged with a simple yet powerful mission: to achieve better policing and end systemic abuses of power.

Now, armed with loads of data Samuel had been compiling, what most powered Campaign Zero was the idea of, "How do we marry data and people?" Johnetta told me. "The initial thing that brought us together was trying to figure out, 'Okay, we have all this information that's either untapped because the police have never been asking questions.' Or it's hidden because they've never FOIA [Freedom of Information Act]-requested this information.

Or it just doesn't exist because nobody's brain has thought about, 'Well, hey, can you track certain metrics with police violence and people?'—A lot of that [data gathering] was Sam. And the people part was me."

One of Campaign Zero's primary goals was to put an end to broken-windows policing: a strategy that focuses on maintaining order and preventing serious crimes by cracking down on minor offenses and visible signs of disorder in communities, often targeting communities of color.

Through their advocacy and vision, they emerged as a prominent activism group, gaining recognition from various organizations and notable media as one of the leading policy-driven groups working toward police reform in America.

With their unparalleled experiences as on-the-ground protesters and leaders, they were able to effectively evangelize and transform their firsthand knowledge into specific, measurable goals, utilizing the force of social media to persuade politicians to embrace their vision.

There was finally a clear leadership with a tangible mission people could conceive.

Shortly after Campaign Zero launched, endorsements flowed in from Barack Obama, Oprah, and several other influential figures. The group was invited to the White House. Magazine interviews followed. They were on various celebrated lists and won awards. In 2016, with a company net worth of more than $40 million from donations and partnerships, they were anointed one of the most influential tech-driven political organizations in the country by *WIRED* magazine.

Along the way, though, Johnetta remained cautious.

She began discerning an issue in this new formalized format. "The minute people try to make a structure and put a name to it, that's when all hell broke loose," she told me. Campaign Zero, she felt, began to stray from the bottom-up, community-based, hands-on dynamic they had envisioned.

Now, it became about establishing and reporting to a board. It became about getting their name out there and responding to this or that media request, making this or that appearance, meeting this or that celebrity, attending this or that White House function, rather than disrupting the status quo. Instead of staying faithful to the blueprint they had pioneered—to lead the way *their* way—it became about following traditional structures and bureaucratic processes.

Soon, the organization lost its spirit and passion. The leadership conundrum that had plagued youth-led new-era movements reared its head.

Johnetta exited the group in 2016 (Brittany and Samuel both left too) when she felt DeRay became more focused on building his name than the cause. (DeRay has denied such allegations.) She felt he obscured the role he was playing at Campaign Zero publicly when he became the de facto face of the movement for a time. She said it felt like he erased her contributions as a Black woman leader, increasingly silencing her and others' voices. All of which, she felt, reflected poorly on their collective mission of Black liberation.

With her matriarchal upbringing, she told me she knew her worth and work—she knew why she had started in the fight in the first place. It was all too personal to trade for magazine spreads, TV spots, endorsements, and hierarchy.

This is the movement.

The grassroots, ten toes to the pavement, was the work.

That was real for her.

Johnetta dove back to what fed her soul: being a fiery voice on social media and a relentless advocate for her St. Louis community. She remains dedicated to the work she began there, still a proud local, fighting for justice however she can, clinging to bits of progress.

"The fact that Tishaura Jones is the [first Black female] mayor in the city [is significant progress]," Johnetta told me, taking stock of her community now, "she's battling the police . . . She is also getting reparations for the city—that is important work that definitely came and is rooted out of the movement that happened in Ferguson.

"There's a lot to be celebrated and a lot to be devastated and sad about. I just think that's life as a Black person in America."

Trayvon was buried dressed in all white.

White suit.

White shoes.

It was March 3, 2012, at the Antioch Missionary Baptist Church of Miami Gardens. The "Home Going Celebration" program included another nickname: Trayvon "Slimm" Martin.

Underneath his name: February 5, 1995–February 26, 2012.

Close to a thousand people showed up to pay their respects.

He laid in a baby-blue casket, his name engraved on the side. His hair freshly cut. His skin smooth. His mom said it looked like her baby boy was about to attend his high school prom.

"The child I lost was a son, a boy who hadn't yet crossed the final threshold to becoming a man," his mom later wrote in the book about her son's life. "He had been seventeen for only three brief weeks, still in the beautiful and turbulent passage through childhood's last stages, still on his way to becoming. Instead, he will be remembered for the things he left behind. The bullet that pierced his heart. The blood that stained the ground.

"The crime-scene photographs of his corpse. And the famous hoodie picture."

Trayvon was laid to rest in a mausoleum in Dade Memorial Park in Miami.

A day after the two-year mark of Trayvon's death, on February 27, 2014, Barack Obama established the My Brother's Keeper Task Force. A federal program that united various government agencies, local communities, philanthropic organizations, and other stakeholders, aiming to address the opportunity gaps for boys and young men of color, who statistically face disproportionately higher rates of school suspensions, incarceration, and unemployment.

It emphasized that all young people—regardless of background—can reach their full potential and "have a chance to go as far as their dreams will take them," Barack Obama said during the program's launch. "In every community in America, there are young people with incredible drive and talent, and they just don't have the same kinds of chances that somebody like me had. They're just as talented as me, just as smart."

The program also zeroed in on promoting education and career advancement, reducing negative interactions with the criminal justice system, and encouraging community engagement.

"Hopefully, the legacy of this tragedy is not just outrage but something constructive," Barack Obama later said during the ten-year mark. "And that doesn't fill the hole that Trayvon's parents feel. But hopefully, it's viewed by them as a testament to the fact that we care and that what happened was unacceptable, and that this country can do better. My hope is that we look back on what happened with Trayvon and are able to say that was the start of America looking inward, in fits and starts, coming to terms with what has always been our original sin."

Michael—his mom used to call him "Mike Mike"—was buried on August 25, 2014.

More than 4,500 people flocked to where the funeral was held at the Friendly Temple Missionary Baptist Church in St. Louis, including three White House aides sent by Barack Obama to represent him.

Two supersized posters of the teen's round, plump face flanked his brown coffin, his "STL" black-and-red St. Louis Cardinals baseball fitted on top.

His full name in large script print on another rug-material poster: Michael Orlandus Darrion Brown, Jr.

Underneath: May 20, 1996–August 9, 2014.

He was the eldest of his siblings, a brother and three sisters that his mom said he adored. Their last vacation together had been the year prior, an annual fishing trip billed as a family ritual.

On that hot summer day, the family arrived by the riverside on the outskirts of town around noon.

By five, no one had caught any fish.

"Mom said, 'Okay, let's go, I'm hot. Now I got a headache.'"

Lezley remembered. "And Mike Mike went and said, 'But I ain't caught no fish yet.'"

"I said, 'Oh, Ma, Mike Mike didn't caught no fish. We gotta wait.'"

Michael asked to use his mother's and grandmother's poles before settling on a cane pole.

"He was holding it, and all of a sudden, he said, 'I got one! I got one!' We all looked over at him, and he pulled the hook up so fast the fish flew back and over his head and went back into the grass. And we all looked and said, 'Oh okay, he got it! We can go now!'"

"All he wanted to do was catch one fish," Lezley continued. "He didn't want to take it off. He didn't want to take him home. He just wanted to know he could catch a fish."

Michael's grave site, St. Peter's Cemetery, is less than a mile from his alma mater, Normandy High School.

The deaths of Trayvon, Michael, and countless more continue to haunt America.

Each tragedy, a spark, erupting like a geyser, spewing a torrent of protests and social media outrage. The demand for justice only intensifies each time, a deafening roar that grows ever more insistent.

And at every turn now, Black and allied youths stand as a defiant surge, armed with their phones and the power of a connected world, sounding the alarm.

And every time, a wave of unrest washes over America.

It happened after twenty-five-year-old Freddie Gray was severely injured in the custody of Baltimore police on April 12, 2015, and succumbed to his injuries seven days later.

And again on July 28, 2016, when eighteen-year-old Paul O'Neal was fatally shot by Chicago police.

And again and again when Donald Trump began as the forty-fifth president of America on January 1, 2017, his bigotry and xenophobia fanning the flames of racial tension, deepening divisions and animosity.

Rinse. Repeat.

Alas.

One promising and lasting change this era brought was the giant leap in closing the gap on police accountability with the ideation and execution of police violence databases, notably the ground-breaking Mapping Police Violence. With many new iterations since then, including The Police Scorecard and *The Washington Post*'s Fatal Force Database, access to such data has proven critical in understanding the magnitude of the epidemic, making for a robust and informed national dialogue and framing policy discussion.

When Joe Biden signed the "Advancing Effective, Accountable Policing and Criminal Justice Practices to Enhance Public Trust and Public Safety" executive order two years to the date of George Floyd's murder, it echoed the work Johnetta, Samuel, and countless others were tirelessly pursuing: transparency and improved community policing. The directive included a critical provision for a national accountability database, or as succinctly summarized in the order, a "centralized repository of official records documenting instances of law enforcement officer misconduct."

This presidential decree was a monumental ripple reflecting the fight of those young visionaries who stomped day and night—a testament to the enduring power of their work and urgent need to press on.

This chapter was the hardest to pen.

Mostly because I have spoken to too many mothers who have lost their babies to police violence.

Adrienne Hood. Constance Malcolm. Darlene Cain. Dionne Smith-Downs. Flora Shorter. Gwen Carr. Guerlyne Felix. Kadiatou Diallo. Kim Thomas. Kimberly Davis. Lezley McSpadden-Head. Pamela Fields. Rahimah Rahim. Toni Taylor. Valerie Bell. Vickie Williams. Wanda Johnson.

And so many more.

I remembered the times I asked some of the mothers what it was like to be pushed to the center of the world stage overnight. What it was like to see your child's name in magazines and on airwaves, seemingly losing all control of the narrative. Media outlets tend to focus on these women in relation to their dead children, overshadowing what life has been like following their intractable losses. About what happens when the cameras and viral moments fade. When the tragedy is not our own, it's painless to turn away, but survivors bear the burden for a lifetime.

That's why this became my central focus whenever I spoke with them.

Just a simple, "How are you today?" can bring forth so much.

In response to that very question, Lezley once told me there were days she thought about not waking up.

"Anytime you feel like you are happy or you're thinking about something other than your child, you feel guilty, and sometimes you catch yourself not even breathing. You're holding your breath. It's traumatizing. It's aging. It's tiresome. It's a journey.

"And on journeys, you feel all kinds of emotions," she continued. "And very seldom do we feel happy. Like, you'd never find a happy spot again. You may smile, but you're never fully happy. And it's this—it's just a sad way to live your life because, I'm married, I have three other children, my parents are still alive . . . I have brothers and sisters. And they want to see me happy, Rita. But it's so hard for me to be. It's so hard for me to enjoy just the sun, you know? Meaning that my eyes have opened, and I'm seeing the sun again. It's hard for me to even enjoy that. It's like, did I even want to wake up this morning? I want to be with my son. I want him back with me, but I don't want to leave my other kids. You're conflicted. You're confused. It's everything that PTSD describes. So pray for all the mothers and the fathers. All of them because we definitely need it."

And while the stench of injustice lingers from these conversations, I remain hopelessly optimistic that someday soon, the tears and anguish of all mothers, of all fathers, of all guardians, of all surviving siblings, will be replaced by anthems of joy and justice.

That someday soon, it will have been enough.

"The blood is working.
The blood is still speaking . . .
The blood will not be washed away."

Johnetta's words stuck with me for weeks.

As a Christian, it was doubly striking.

The blood carries great significance throughout the Bible. In part, the shedding of blood represents the cost of sin and the need for a sacrifice to restore a right relationship with God.

It represents both life and death.

It also reminded me of the unseen and abundant blood that covers this nation.

From Colfax to Wilmington. From Tulsa to Ferguson. From Selma to Sanford. From the 1600s to the 2000s. Each instance exemplifying the cost and sacrifice of too many Black and brown bodies. Many of them young.

Enough is enough.

Dale Graham. John Crawford III. Ashley McClendon. Fanta Bility. Walter Scott. LaShawn Thompson. Jordan Davis. Ronnie Lee Shorter. Natosha McDade. Oscar Grant. Alexica Stevenson-Gates. James Rivera, Jr. Ramarley Graham. Mya Hall. Cary Ball, Jr. Donte Jordan. Tinoris Williams. Canisha L. Staten. Kimoni Davis. Earl Shaleek Pinckney. Etoyce Johnson. Matthew Felix. Usaamah Rahim. Natasha Renee Osby. Darnesha Harris. Nizah Morris. Henry Green V.

"The blood will not be washed away."

9

THE MATTER OF GEORGE FLOYD

Darnella Frazier & the Twenty-First-Century Freedom Fighters

I opened my phone, and I started recording because I knew if I didn't, no one would believe me.

DARNELLA FRAZIER

"*What were your thoughts?*"

"*I just cried so much,*" *she told me about watching George Floyd's final moments.* "*I was aware of, like, disparity, but I hadn't opened myself up to watching people just like die. It just felt like the harsh reality of it all. And it felt very desensitizing. I understand why they were showing it on the news, but at the same time, why are you showing it on the news when we know it's wrong and nothing's going to happen from it.*"

That's what led sixteen-year-old Laila DeWeese to start the youth-led organization PDX Black Youth Movement in Portland. I met her on September 30, 2020, during my cross-country trip. Laila and her team had organized a massive protest to memorialize another Black man killed at the hands of police. He was shot nine times in the back.

It also happened to be my first time at a protest. Ever.

When she shared those thoughts with me, we were catching up for a Teen Vogue *piece I was working on, where I spoke to young Black organizers nationwide about their organizing efforts for democracy on the heels of George Floyd's one-year memorial. I told her I had also been reawakened to the perils of this country and its disregard for all Others after George Floyd. And that, like her, I felt I needed to do something to make sense of the moment.*

As she delved into why she had to break from "the older generations" and start her own group and do things the "new way"—the way that was needed for the time before her—I wrote down something in Pidgin: Na man na know himself pass. It translates to: We have the deepest understanding of ourselves. Essentially, our truest mirror reflects the soul within. It's a maxim I've tried to embody since returning from that Nigerian trip that left me feeling more like an outsider. The trip that had christened me akata and left me wondering if Abiemwense and Rita could ever coexist.

Na man na know himself pass.

It's those quiet moments we have with ourselves. Those quiet thoughts of who we are, who we are becoming, or who we desire to become. Those internalizations and introspections. That's who we are or striving to be. All finding our way to living life with purpose, on purpose.

This I had learned. This, it seemed, Laila—so young, so wide-eyed—was blossoming into. She had tapped into a special kind of enlightenment that I believe the collective Othered, especially young ones, were uncovering, asking themselves: What is the alternative to this life of racialized state violence? Who are we in all of this? How do we become who we were meant to be in spite of this while fighting it?

Unlike previous generations, these young activists know their power stems from a deep, intentional commitment to service, bolstered by the ubiquitous presence of cell phones and social media. These tools have become weapons, readily exposing systemic injustices all the while underscoring societal rifts and fueling polarization. This double-edged sword presents both immense potential and significant challenges. To navigate this complex landscape, they must deconstruct outdated political strategies and forge new paths.

Their goal?

To build a formidable grassroots movement that can reshape the very fabric of American society, ensuring a future where righteousness prevails.

As I connected the dots between Laila and the wave of global protests that erupted after George Floyd's death, I recognized that this entire awakening, this surge of a new generation of freedom fighters, all traced back to one act of extraordinary courage by one resolute teenager: Darnella Frazier.

MAY 25, 2020. MINNEAPOLIS, MINNESOTA.

Around 7:30 p.m. on Memorial Day, a towering Black man entered Chicago Unbeatable Prices (CUP) Foods.

A staple in the community for more than thirty years and owned by Palestinian immigrant Samir Abumayyaleh, CUP had just about everything, from sandwiches, cigarettes, and chips to fresh produce and electronics. In the back, customers could add minutes to their cell phones or fix their iPads. It also had a notary public and MoneyGram service. A true one-stop shop. The kind of place oozing with familial bliss, where clerks know their customers' orders by heart, their mamas' birthdays, and laugh at recycled jokes.

The Black man staggered through the store in a loosely fitted black tank top and dark blue sweatpants. He spoke to staff as he made his way through the aisles.

He grabbed a banana, held it in his right hand, and returned to the front of the store.

With his left hand, he dug through his pants pockets, pulled out some bills.

He swayed intermittently, unsteady, as if the ground under him were moving. As he waited in line, he was increasingly unstable, unable to stand still. He chatted with CUP staffers and customers around him, laughed, scratched his stomach, placed both hands on his head, switched hold of the banana, left hand, right hand, rubbed his head, did a hobbling skip dance, then danced as if to a specific tune.

Left-right.

Right-left.

He moved from the cashier's line he had originally stood in to another, to where CUP's newest employee, eighteen-year-old Christopher Martin, was standing.

They chatted a bit about sports.

The soaring man asked Christopher for some cigarettes from behind the register in a dedicated tobacco section. The teen walked over, the man followed.

Christopher later said though the man was friendly and approachable, he quickly sensed that it "took him a little long to get to what he was trying to say, so it would appear that he was high."

Christopher reached over to his left, grabbed a pack of menthol cigarettes, and handed it to the man, who then paid with a twenty-dollar bill. The teen immediately noticed a blue pigment on the bill, the kind a hundred-dollar bill would have. This struck him as odd.

While the man waited, looking out into the street, Christopher raised the bill to the light with both hands, quickly glancing at it before completing the transaction.

The man walked out of the store and across the street to a parked car.

Around 7:45, Christopher held the bill up to the light again. Analyzed it. Over and over. Studying all sides. The store's policy, as Christopher was recently made aware, was if any cashier took payment with a counterfeit, the amount was deducted from their paycheck.

After his many inspections, he deemed the bill to be counterfeit.

At that point, the teen recalled the man had already visited the store earlier in the day when he came in with a friend. The friend had tried to use a similar kind of bill, but his demeanor seemed suspicious, like he knew he was giving a fake.

Christopher had refused that bill. The friend didn't fight it and left.

But with this man in the black tank, Christopher genuinely felt he didn't know he had handed him a fake. So, he accepted the bill initially, feeling he'd "be doing him a favor." But after thinking about it some more and knowing if it was, in fact, discovered to be counterfeit, the amount would be deducted from his pay stub, Christopher reported it to one of the managers, asking what to do. The manager instructed him to go tell the man to come back inside.

Solo, Christopher attempted to get the man to come back inside. Twice.

No luck.

Minutes later, alongside two CUP employees, he returned to confront the man as he sat in the driver's seat of an SUV at the intersection of East 38th Street and Chicago Avenue. They told the man to return to CUP to resolve the matter, or for him to give them back the cigarettes. The man ignored them.

Once back inside, reporting the man's refusal, another employee was instructed by the store manager to call the police.

911, what's the address of the emergency?

This is, ah, 3759 Chicago Avenue.

How can I help you?

Um, someone comes our store and give us fake bills, and we realize it before he left the store, and we ran back outside. They was sitting on their car. We tell them to give us their phone, put their [inaudible] thing back and everything, and he was also drunk and everything and return to give us our cigarettes back and so he can, so he can go home, but he doesn't want to do that, and he's sitting on his car cause he is awfully drunk and he's not in control of himself.

Okay, what type of vehicle does he have?

And, um, he's got a vehicle that is ah, ah he got a vehicle that is ah. One second, let me see if I can see the license. The driver license is BRJ026.

Okay, what color is it?

It's a blue color. It's a blue van.

Blue van?

Yes, van.

Alright blue van, gotcha. Is it out front, or is it on 38th Street?

Ah, it's on 38th Street.

On 38th Street. So, this guy gave a counterfeit bill, has your cigarettes, and he's under the influence of something?

Something like that, yes. He is not acting right.

What's he look like? What race?

Um, he's a tall guy. He's like tall and bald, about like six, six and a half, and she's not acting right, so and she started to go, drive the car.

Okay so, female or a male?

Um—

Is it a girl or a boy?

[Talks to somebody]—He's asking (inaudible)—One second. Hello?

Is it a girl or a boy that did this?

It is a man.

Okay. Is he white, Black, Native, Hispanic, Asian?

Something like that.

Which one? White, Black, Native, Hispanic, Asian?

No, he's a Black guy.

Alright. [Sighs.]

How is your day going?

Not too bad.

Had a long day, huh?

What's your name?

My name is [redacted].

Alright [redacted], a phone number for you?

[Redacted]

Alright, I've got help on the way. If that vehicle or that person leaves before we get there, just give us a callback. Otherwise, we'll have squads out there shortly, okay?

No problem.

Following the call, two police dispatches went out.

20:02:13 NCIC Plate Check: BRJ026, MN, 2020 [Shared] OTS ON 38 ST-RPT'G THAT THERE IS A MALE PROVIDED A COUNTERFEIT BILL TO THE BUSINESS-SUSP IS BM / 600+ [The National Crime Information Center is a centralized database, like a law enforcement–grade search engine, that aids in criminal investigations, missing person searches, and stolen property recovery.]

20:03:46 SITTING ON TOP OF A BLUE MERCEDES ML320 SUV LIC/BRJO26 (CLEAR TO 2419 ILION AV N)—ALSO APPEARS THIS PERSON IS UNDER THE INFLUENCE [Shared]

At 8:08, Minneapolis officers Thomas Lane and J. Alexander Kueng arrived on the scene.

Upon approaching the SUV, Thomas immediately drew his gun, ordering the man to put his hands on the steering wheel.

MAN: Hey, man. I'm sorry!

THOMAS: Stay in the car! Let me see your other hand.

I'm sorry, I'm sorry!

Let me see your other hand!

Please, Mr. Officer.

Both hands!

I didn't do nothing.

Put your fucking hands up right now! Let me see your other hand.

All right. What I do, though? What we do, Mr. Officer?

Put your hand up there. Put your fucking hand up there! Jesus Christ, keep your fucking hands on the wheel.

Startled, the man complied. Thomas returned his gun to his holster, yanked the man out of the car, and handcuffed him. The man appeared still, but his eyes flickered with fear.

Thomas and J. Alexander walked him away from his SUV and ordered him to sit on the sidewalk against the wall of Dragon Wok, a Chinese restaurant at 805 East 38th Street, on the corner opposite CUP. The man thanked the officers, still appearing nervous. At one point, he cries and pleads with them, "Please don't shoot me."

Moments later, the two officers walked the man across the street, to the front of CUP where their squad car was parked. The man, his hands cuffed behind him, tells them he doesn't want to be put inside the back seat of the car.

J. ALEXANDER: Stand up. Stop falling down! Stand up! Stay on your feet and face the car door!

I'm claustrophobic, man, please, man, please.

. . .

I just want to talk to you, man. Please, let me talk to you. Please.

THOMAS: No.

J. ALEXANDER: You ain't listening to nothing we're saying.

I know.

J. ALEXANDER: So, we're not going to listen to nothing you saying.

. . .

I'm claustrophobic.

J. ALEXANDER: I hear you, but you are going to face this door right now.

THOMAS: Listen up, stop!

I'll do anything. I'll do anything y'all tell me to, man. I'm not resisting, man. I'm not! I'm not! You can ask him, they know me.

THOMAS: Check that side.

God, man, I won't do nothing like that. Why is this going on like this? Look at my wrist, Mr. Officer. I'm not that kind of guy.

The back-and-forth go on for about ten minutes. The officers continued to try and get the man, who loomed over them with his 6'6", 225-pound frame, into the squad car's back seat. During the deadlock, another squad car with officers Derek Chauvin and Tou Thao pulls up.

It's now about 8:17.

Derek and Tou step out and approach the standoff. Derek outranked the three officers. He immediately took over the scene.

Man, let go of me, man. I can't breathe. Can't breathe.

THOMAS: Take a seat.

Please, man. Please listen to me.

DEREK: Is he going to jail?

. . .

Please listen to me.

J. ALEXANDER: He's under arrest right now for forgery.

As J. Alexander struggled to get the man into the back seat of the squad car, the man continued to plead with him.

Tou stood guard.

Derek went to the other side of the car where J. Alexander had been trying but failing to secure the man. He began to pull the man across the back seat. After a few moments of struggle, the man is completely ripped from the passenger side of the backseat and tossed onto the concrete on his stomach.

> **DEREK:** Do you got your ah, restraint, hobble?
>
> I can't breathe. I can't breathe. I can't breathe.
>
> **THOMAS:** Jesus Christ.
>
> I can't breathe.
>
> **J. ALEXANDER:** Stop moving.
>
> Mama! Mama! Mama! Mama!

A few storefronts away from CUP, nine-year-old Judeah Reynolds was on a mission. She had three dollars to burn and craved some Skittles or sour gummy worms. At such a tender age, she couldn't go outside alone, especially because of the crime-plagued neighborhood they lived in. For years, residents had long complained about drug activity and violence gripping the area.

So, Judeah needed to be accompanied to their corner grocery store. But she had one problem. Everyone in her family's apartment she had asked kept telling her, "no." Finally, after begging her big cousin, seventeen-year-old Darnella Frazier, who had the day off from working at the mall, she got a "yes."

As they strolled down the block on what would normally be a lazy holiday Monday—Judeah, sporting a bright yellow "LOVE" T-shirt with jeans, and Darnella, a multi-athlete (basketball and volleyball) at Roosevelt High School, in her flip-flops, blue sweatpants, and gray sweatshirt—the teen noticed a handcuffed Black man being forcefully pulled from a police squad car by a white officer. In a blink, she saw three more officers subduing him.

As Darnella edged forward, she noticed the struggle's intensity. Judeah continued into CUP while the Minneapolis native remained outside. She immediately took to her phone, scrolled to the camera app, and hit record. She began filming from different vantage points before stepping even closer for an unrivaled, unobstructed view.

It's now around 8:20.

Tou continued to stand watch over the crowd that was slowly forming.

J. Alexander held the man's back.

Thomas secured his legs.

Derek put his right knee in the thick nape of the man's neck.

As the three officers continued to pin down the man, Tou grabbed a hobble restraint from the squad car to secure the man's ankles to his handcuffs, but the officers decided against it.

The man lay restrained on the pavement, his chest on the ground.

> DEREK: You're under arrest, guy.

> All right, all right. Oh my God. Can't believe this. I can't believe this.

> DEREK: So you're going to jail.

With every passing minute, more onlookers gathered. The air became thick with tension as many of them began to call out to the officers to ease up on the already shackled and subdued man, who now appeared to be struggling to breathe, at times speaking, mumbling, pleading.

> I can't believe this man. Mom, I love you. I love you . . . Tell my kids I love them. I'm dead.

> THOMAS: Mine's in my side, it's listed, it's labeled. It says hobble; it's in the top.

> I can't breathe or nothing, man. This cold-blooded man. Ah! Ah! Ah! Ah! Ah!

> DEREK: You're doing a lot of talking, man.

> Mama, I love you. I can't do nothing.

> J. ALEXANDER: EMS is on their way.

> TOU: Well, do you want a hobble at this point, then?

THOMAS: Um, okay, all right.

My face is gone. I can't breathe, man. Please! Please, let me stand. Please, man, can't breathe.

As the officers continue to ignore the man's pleas, Christopher, the employee from CUP, joined onlookers. He increasingly grew anxious as he heard the screams and saw Derek and the other officers atop the man. The teen put his hand over his black durag-covered head. He later said he felt "disbelief" and "guilt," thinking: "If I had not taken the bill, this could've been avoided."

DEREK: Just leave him.

THOMAS: All right. Hopefully, Park's still sitting on the car. They were—he was acting real shady like something's in there.

TOU: He high on something?

THOMAS: I'm assuming so.

J. ALEXANDER: I believe so. We found a pipe.

THOMAS: He wouldn't get out of the car. He wasn't following instructions. Yeah, it's across the street. Park's watching it, two other people with him.

Please, I can't breathe. Please, man! Please, man!

TOU: Do you have EMS coming—code three?

THOMAS: Ah, code two, we can probably step it up then. You got it?

Please, man!

TOU: Relax!

I can't breathe.

J. ALEXANDER: You're fine. You're talking fine.

THOMAS: You're talking. Deep breath.

Throughout the commotion, Darnella stood steadfast, phone in hand, and, though shaky at times, she continued to film.

"It wasn't right," she later concluded. The man on the ground was "in pain. It seemed like he knew—like he knew it was over for him. He was terrified. He was suffering. This was a cry for help."

She described Derek as impassive and vexed by the crowd's pleas to the officers to get off the man. She even sensed that Derek kneeled harder in response. Then, when Genevieve Hansen, an off-duty firefighter in the crowd, repeatedly begged the officers to check the man's pulse, Darnella said Derek remained unfazed.

"He just stared at us, looked at us," she said. "He had like this cold look, heartless. He didn't care. It seemed as if he didn't care what we were saying. It didn't change anything he was doing."

She also remembered that no one in the crowd could do much to help the man. Any time someone attempted to get close, the officers "put their hand on their mace," she said. "I can't remember if they actually pointed it at us, but they definitely put their hand on the mace, and we all backed [away]."

Darnella felt Derek's reach for his was even more threatening.

"He seemed like, how do I word this? I felt like I was in danger when he did that," she said. "It rubbed me the wrong way. I didn't understand why they would do that . . . That's why I felt threatened."

THOMAS: He's got to be on something.

TOU: What are you on?

Can't breathe. Please . . . l can't breathe. Shit.

CHARLES MCMILLIAN (EYEWITNESS): Well, get up and get in the car, man. Get up and get in the car.

Well, l can't move.

CHARLES: Let him get in the car.

THOMAS: We found a weed pipe on him. There might be something else—there might be like PCP or something. Is that the shaking of the eyes right? Is PCP?

My knee, my neck.

THOMAS: **Where their eyes like shake back and forth really fast?**

I'm through, I'm through. I'm claustrophobic. My stomach hurts. My neck hurts. Everything hurts. I need some water or something, please. Please? Can't breathe, officer.

DEREK: **Then stop talking, stop yelling.**

You're going to kill me, man.

Shortly after, around 8:24, the man's desperate gasps for air became shallower and farther apart. With every passing moment, his breaths grew weaker, until his chest stilled. Then he stopped moving. Thomas noticed.

THOMAS: **Should we roll him on his side?**

DEREK: **No, he's staying put where we got him.**

THOMAS: **Okay. I just worry about the excited delirium or whatever.**

DEREK: **Well, that's why we got the ambulance coming.**

THOMAS: **Okay, I suppose.**

Seconds later, Thomas questioned his superior again, asking if they should ease up. He attempted to sound cool, but his concern seemed evident.

THOMAS: **Should we roll him on his side?**

Derek did not respond. The crowd's roar intensified as the man now appeared lifeless.

DONALD WILLIAMS (EYEWITNESS): He's not responsive right now, bro.

GENEVIEVE HANSEN (EYEWITNESS, THE OFF-DUTY FIREFIGHTER): Does he have a pulse?

DONALD: No, bro. Look at him, he's not responsive right now, bro. Bro, are you serious?

THOMAS: **You got one?**

GENEVIEVE: Let me see a pulse.

J. Alexander checked the man for a pulse. He couldn't find one.

DONALD: Bro, he was just moving when l walked up. Bro, he's not fucking moving! Bro.

UNIDENTIFIED EYEWITNESS: Get the fuck off of him. What are you doing? He's dying, bro. What are you doing?

At 8:27, as the EMS team approached, Derek removed his knee from the man's neck. The unconscious man was laid on a stretcher and loaded into the ambulance.

This is where Darnella's video comes to an end.

In the ambulance, the man went into cardiac arrest. The paramedics called firefighters to meet them on the corner of 36th Street and Park Avenue for assistance. Upon arrival, they found the man still unresponsive and without a pulse.

Moments later, they reached the Hennepin Medical Center.

Emergency room staff and first responders tried reviving the man. At 9:25 p.m., the man was pronounced dead.

Quickly, news circulated about the man. Eyewitnesses were spreading the word.

That night, social media erupted with residents' suspicions about the police department's handling of the fatal encounter. Concerns about potential bias and lack of transparency mounted on social platforms adding to the firestorm of tensions.

In response, at 12:41 a.m., the Minneapolis Police Department put out a statement:

Man Dies After Medical Incident During Police Interaction

On Monday evening, shortly after 8:00 pm, officers from the Minneapolis Police Department responded to the 3700 block of

Chicago Avenue South on a report of a forgery in progress. Officers were advised that the suspect was sitting on top of a blue car and appeared to be under the influence.

Two officers arrived and located the suspect, a male believed to be in his 40s, in his car. He was ordered to step from his car. After he got out, he physically resisted officers. Officers were able to get the suspect into handcuffs and noted he appeared to be suffering medical distress. Officers called for an ambulance. He was transported to Hennepin County Medical Center by ambulance where he died a short time later.

At no time were weapons of any type used by anyone involved in this incident.

The Minnesota Bureau of Criminal Apprehension has been called in to investigate this incident at the request of the Minneapolis Police Department.

No officers were injured in the incident.

Body worn cameras were on and activated during this incident.

The GO number associated with this case is 20–140629.

After the press release went out, unable to shake what she had witnessed, at 1:46 a.m., Darnella posted her footage, all ten minutes and nine seconds, on Facebook.

She captioned it: "They killed him right in front of cup foods over south on 38th and Chicago!! No type of sympathy #POLICE-BRUTALITY."

The recording showed Derek had his knee on the man's neck for nine minutes and twenty-nine seconds.

It showed the man's eyes swelling at some points.

It showed the man screeching for air.

It showed the concern of passersby as they loudly begged officers to let the man sit up.

It showed it all. A raw portrait of undeniable human suffering.

The video swiftly made its way around all social media platforms, immediately disputing the version of events laid out by the MPD.

The outcry sparked by the viral footage finally made its way to the police chief, Medaria Arradondo. He received it from a local who was questioning him about the death of the man.

Medaria quickly informed Mayor Jacob Frey that something had to be done, knowing now, with such irrefutable evidence, this was no "medical incident." To call it one, Medaria said, was "an insult."

At 3:11 a.m., the MPD announced the FBI would be part of the investigation.

Three hours later, at 6:45 a.m., Medaria and Jacob held a press conference.

"What we saw was horrible," Jacob said, referencing Darnella's video. "Completely and utterly messed up."

And from there, a collective grief coalesced, a tide of sorrow washing over every corner of the country. It began with local, state, and federal officials condemning the unthinkable act that same morning.

The video of a Minneapolis police officer killing a defenseless, handcuffed man is one of the most vile and heartbreaking images I've ever seen. The officer who stood guard is just as responsible as his partner; both must be held fully accountable. This must stop now.

—St. Paul's mayor, Melvin Carter, 8:46 a.m. on Twitter

We heard his repeated calls for help. We heard him say over and over again that he could not breathe. And now we have seen yet another horrifying and gutwrenching instance of an African American man dying . . . There must be a complete and thorough outside investigation into what occurred, and those involved in this incident must be held accountable. Justice must be served for this man and his family, justice must be served for our community, and justice must be served for our country.

—Minnesota senator Amy Klobuchar, 9 a.m. on Twitter

The lack of humanity in this disturbing video is sickening. We will get answers and seek justice.

—Minnesota governor Tim Walz, 9:45 a.m. on Twitter

No one knew the man's name when he was sprawled out on the street, the fight draining from his lungs. Even in the immediate aftermath, he was simply *the suspect*. But by 10:30 that morning, a name would be etched into the world's conscience, forever marred by the brutality it represented. The family, their grief a heavy mantle, turned to attorney Benjamin Crump, seeking answers in the fight for justice.

This abusive, excessive and inhumane use of force cost the life of a man who was being detained by the police for questioning about a non-violent charge. We will seek justice for the family of George Floyd, as we demand answers from the Minneapolis Police Department. How many "while black" deaths will it take until the racial profiling and undervaluing of black lives by police finally ends?
—**Excerpt from Benjamin Crump's statement, 10:27 a.m. on Twitter**

The forty-six-year-old man was George Floyd.

"Nobody deserves to die because they have a past," Darnella later wrote on Facebook. "That man was begging for his life and Chauvin did not care."

As the days passed, Darnella's recording continued exploding across social media and local and major TV channels, reaching millions of viewers. In what seemed a blink, thousands flooded nationwide streets, condemning the heinous brutality.

In Portland, Oregon, sixteen-year-old Laila DeWeese, a sophomore at Jefferson High School, saw the video and was immediately enraged. The months leading up to that moment had already filled her with frustration—the footage was a breaking point.

Two months before George Floyd, on March 13, 2020, Breonna Taylor, a twenty-six-year-old Black woman, was gunned down inside her Louisville, Kentucky, home as plainclothes police officers executed a no-knock warrant just after midnight. Before that, on February 23, 2020, there was Ahmaud Arbery, a twenty-five-year-old

Black man fatally shot while jogging in Glynn County, Georgia, by a white father-and-son vigilante duo.

The suffocating grip of the relentless coronavirus, a constant reminder of isolation, loss, and the Black community's heightened vulnerability, added another layer to Laila's weariness. Relegated to remote learning, she found herself glued to the cold glow of her computer screen, a poor substitute for the warmth and camaraderie of a physical classroom. The silence of her room pressed in, intensifying the gnawing discontent that threatened to boil over.

The pandemic growled through Black and brown communities, leaving behind a trail of empty chairs and hushed sobs. It laid bare deep-rooted health and socioeconomic disparities caused by systemic racism in healthcare access, education, and employment. Crowded living conditions and the need to work in essential jobs, like grocery stores, made social distancing difficult for many already living on the margins. This crisis highlighted the urgent need for policies that address social determinants of health—factors like income, housing, and education—and the dismantling of racism to achieve equitable health outcomes.

This was also year four of Donald Trump's presidency. His inflamed rhetoric against all Othered (he once referred to countries like El Salvador, Haiti, and many African nations as "shithole countries") stirred young activists like Laila to press for significant change.

George Floyd's death served as the ultimate trigger, inspiring a swell of demonstrations and policy advocacy.

Though she had been around organizing before because her godmother, an educator, was a longtime community activist, Laila had never been politically or socially engaged. Before George Floyd's murder, she'd noticed that "there weren't a lot of Black Lives Matter protests even going on in Portland at the time."

Although the city had witnessed similar deaths at the hands of police, not many demonstrations were happening. "It was [just] a lot of climate strikes and women's marches."

One of those marches was on September 20, 2019, which also happened to be Laila's first-ever protest. She joined student activists and supporters from Portland, Milwaukie, and Beaverton to ditch their classrooms and spill onto downtown streets before making their way over both lanes of Hawthorn Bridge. Spearheaded by sixteen-year-old Greta Thunberg, the Swedish youth climate change activist, the demonstration was part of the Global Week for Future. It featured a series of international strikes and protests demanding action to address climate change.

"Seeing how big that protest was," Laila told me, "and seeing how small the Black Lives Matter ones are [in comparison] it really makes me think that people don't care. People built full-on floats for [the climate protest]. Like, when have you ever seen a float at a Black Lives Matter event? When are people actually going that hard? When is it ever liberation for all people and not just, can we do the work together?"

Reflecting on this salient distinction, Laila and some of her friends began conceptualizing the PDX Black Youth Movement. (PDX is what Portland is colloquially called; it's the airport code for their international airport.)

"We all started meeting at protests," she said, "and we were all wanting to be in the front and yell and get people super excited, and make people hear us. And the adults weren't serving us and they weren't allowing us to do that. So we left and built something that was entirely us. And we started saying whatever we wanted. We threw events when we wanted. It was fun and it was family."

While Laila and her newfound group were laying the groundwork for their movement, Minneapolis was still pulsating with raw, visceral expressions of loss and anger.

Flowers, candles, and protest and remembrance signs sprung up around CUP Foods after Benjamin Crump released George Floyd's name that morning. Tensions continued to mount as calls for the arrest of the officers spread on social media, and news outlets flocked to Minneapolis.

By noon, the ACLU called for a transparent investigation.

Two hours later, Medaria announced the firing of all four officers, their names withheld.

The following morning, George Floyd's autopsy revealed injuries consistent with restraint and neck compression. The medical examiner's twenty-page report ruled it a homicide, concluding George Floyd died from cardiopulmonary arrest. "That's really just fancy medical lingo for the heart and the lungs stopped," Andrew Baker, the examiner, later testified. "No pulse, no breathing. And, in my opinion, the law enforcement subdual, restraint and the neck compression was just more than Mr. Floyd could take, by virtue of that—those heart conditions."

The day after the autopsy was completed, on Wednesday, May 27, the names of the four officers involved were released. Derek was confirmed to be the officer who had his knee to George Floyd's neck.

Public tensions worsened when Hennepin County Attorney Mike Freeman appeared hesitant to press charges against the four officers, saying he needed to be sure there were sufficient grounds to proceed.

"I will just point to you the comparison to what happened in Baltimore in the [Freddie] Gray case. It was a rush to charge. It was a rush to justice. And all of those people were found not guilty," the six-term white attorney told reporters during a press conference that Thursday. "I will not rush to justice. I'm going to do this right. And those folks who know me in the African community know I will do my very level best." (Freddie Gray was the twenty-five-year-old Black man who died in Baltimore police custody in 2015; his death was attributed to a serious spinal injury and led to charges against six officers but no convictions.)

"That video is graphic and horrific and terrible, and no person should do that," he continued. "But my job in the end is to prove [Derek] violated a criminal statute. And there is other evidence that does not support a criminal charge. We need to wade through all of that evidence and come to a meaningful decision, and we are doing that to the best of our ability."

From coast to coast, Mike's remarks drew scathing condemnation from community leaders and activists. The ongoing street demonstrations surged, growing more fervent, many of them led by young Black people.

In Oakland, two students and childhood friends added their rallying cry to the nationwide protests. Xavier Brown and Akil Riley, both nineteen-year-old Black Americans, called each other while home from college break (Xavier from UCLA and Akil from Howard) and made a plan to "disrupt the peace" because they felt, after seeing George Floyd's death play out on their screens, that society deemed Black lives as disposable.

On May 27, Xavier took to Instagram to share an image he made to publicize their planned protest with hashtags: #JusticeforGeorgeFloyd, #Socialrevolution, and #Dosomething.

He captioned the post, in part, "We are disrupting the normality of hatred against black people in this country."

Meanwhile, as the teens strategized and mobilized, the mounting pressure from the escalating activism across the country seemed to be yielding progress in Minneapolis. On May 29, Derek Chauvin was arrested and charged with third-degree murder and third-degree manslaughter.

On June 1, Xavier and Akil successfully organized more than 15,000 multigenerational demonstrators to flood Bay Area streets in a march to the Oakland Police Department.

Two days later, on June 3, Minnesota's first Black attorney general, Keith Ellison, took over the case from Mike Freeman and Hennepin County. That same day, he upped Derek's charges to second-degree murder and manslaughter and arrested and charged the remaining three officers with one count of aiding and abetting second-degree murder and one count of aiding and abetting second-degree manslaughter.

The demand to see justice fulfilled kept protesters on the streets.

A similar spirit from Oakland was felt by fifteen-year-old Zee Thomas in Nashville, Tennessee. The then rising sophomore at Nashville School of the Arts watched as people from other cities united to protest and wanted the same for her city. She took to Twitter and assembled five others to join her.

"I was like, enough is enough. We're going to do something. I got on social media," she said about her recruitment strategy. "Social media was like my best friend."

The interracial group of teens from different cities in Tennessee—sixteen-year-olds Nya Collins and Mikayla Smith, fifteen-year-olds Emma Rose Smith and Jade Fuller, and fourteen-year-old

Kennedy Green—dubbed themselves Teens 4 Equality and created an Instagram page (@teens.4.equality) that received thousands of followers within days, including Barack Obama.

Teens 4 Equality didn't meet in person until their first organized protest on June 4. (Due to the pandemic, many cities and schools remained closed.)

Using Twitter, Instagram, and Discord (an instant messaging platform launched in May 2015 that allows users to create communities using text, voice, or video), the teens got their word out. They felt Nashville was diverse enough to resonate with their message of social change and hoped at least 800 people would show up.

On that Saturday, they were surprised when more than 10,000 protesters came out to Bicentennial Park and marched to the state Capitol and City Hall.

"We didn't have a podium or anything, we were standing on water coolers to speak," Zee later remembered. "I'm an introvert, and when I got up there I was like, 'Oh my God, what am I doing?' But I kept going." They marched for more than five hours that torrid day, roaring, "Not one more," "Black lives matter," and "No justice, no peace."

Two days later, on June 6, the fervent flame of justice continued to burn brightly as more demonstrations emerged. In Washington, D.C., about a dozen college students from Freedom Fighters DC organized a march from the Dirksen Senate Office Building to the National Mall, with stops in front of the Smithsonian's National Museum of African American History and Culture and the Lincoln Memorial.

The group was created by two students, twenty-three-year-old white American Jacqueline LaBayne and twenty-two-year-old Black American Kerrigan Williams. Jacqueline was a graduate student at Florida State University, and Kerrigan attended Georgetown University, also pursuing a graduate degree. Like Teens 4 Equality, the two met on Twitter.

"We spotted each other via a mutual friend's thread on Twitter immediately following yet another police-executed murder," Kerrigan said at the time. "Now, we organize together in real life to help other first-time activists get involved in local responses to injustice."

Hours after watching Darnella's viral video, the duo established the group on Twitter (@FFDC202) and Instagram (@freedomfightersdc), which amassed thousands of followers within days.

"White allies need to become accomplices in the fight against racism toward Black people," Jacqueline once said about encouraging others like her to not keep silent. "Embracing this cause is the only way to have meaningful impact in 2020—the only way justice is served."

Like the Oakland and Nashville marches, thousands—mostly Gen Z—flooded Capitol Hill that Saturday. Organizers, who wore black shirts with their organization's name, estimated there were more than 100,000 in attendance.

They chanted and roared, and the air vibrated with a groundswell of righteous anger.

"We are the voice of the voiceless!"

"Hands up!"

"Fight back!"

"Hands up!"

"Fight back!"

In addition to decrying George Floyd's murder and racially biased police brutality, they called for action from Mayor Muriel Bowser and the D.C. government on police reform.

Angus King, a senator from Maine who was there that day, said the size of the crowd and the vigor of their voices reminded him of the 1963 March on Washington. He had been a nineteen-year-old college student when he witnessed Martin Luther King, Jr.'s "I Have a Dream" address, and he felt like these young ones were carrying the torch lit by marchers years ago.

"Nobody's asking for anything special," the senator said. "They're only asking for what America has promised: Freedom and justice for all, brotherhood from sea to shining sea, our basic creed. That's all people are asking for . . . This is what America is all about. First Amendment rights of people to peaceably assemble and petition the government for the redress of grievances. This is a 400-year-old grievance."

Drawing strength from the growing cacophony of voices

demanding change, young Black activists and their allies continued to march on, their will unyielding. This was true in San Ramon, California. Seventeen-year-old Tiana Day spearheaded a demonstration on the Golden Gate Bridge after connecting with nineteen-year-old Mimi Zoila on Instagram. Initially expecting around fifty attendees, they were shocked when thousands showed up.

Similarly, in Chicago, eighteen-year-old Shayla Turner spent her high school graduation week organizing demonstrations for the removal of police officers from public schools—a first step, she called it, to fixing racial inequities burdening kids in her city.

With nothing more than her smartphone and the familiar walls of her childhood bedroom in St. Louis, nineteen-year-old Brianna Chandler led a digital teach-in for local students, seeding vital conversations about racial justice.

The call for systemic change following George Floyd's murder also resonated with young people far beyond America's borders—from Europe to Africa. In Berlin, defiant chants outside the U.S. embassy called for an end to such senseless deaths. Across London, Cardiff, and Manchester, thousands marched under the chorus of "No justice, no peace." While in South Africa, young people echoed a similar cry, calling for an end to police brutality in their own country, a reality exacerbated by the pandemic.

Young people all over were finding ways to express solidarity, highlighting the universality of the fight for righteousness.

With megaphones in hand, Laila and her PDX Black Youth Movement were now at the forefront of rallies demanding racial justice across Portland. They challenged the deep-rooted legacy of discriminatory practices that had choked the life out of communities of color for generations in their city. Redlining in the 1930s, for example, had funneled Black and brown families into segregated neighborhoods, far from economic opportunities.

Even in supposedly *equal* spaces like public schools, students of color faced underfunded classrooms, limited resources, and a segregated curriculum, leading to disparities in graduation rates and perpetuating a cycle of disenfranchisement. This, in turn, disproportionately impacted young Black men, who faced increased biased policing and harsher sentencing laws, exacerbating mass incarceration.

So, the fight for Laila and the PDX Black Youth Movement was much more layered.

They were not just highlighting such injustices—they demanded reforms in education and the criminal justice system. And it seemed the wrinkles of disparity that had long stoked fear and distrust among residents of color came to a crescendo that 2020 summer. Protests across Portland drew up to 10,000 people.

Many times, demonstrators belted, "Black lives matter."

By this time, the BLM movement experienced yet another surge as groups embraced its powerful, succinct message. It cemented itself as the people's gospel, attracting widespread support and media attention.

However, as it catapulted some more into people's consciousness that summer, many from far ends of the political spectrum weaponized those three words, calling them divisive and exploitive. To address concerns about polarization aggravated by a lack of unified messaging and organizational structure, the movement decided to establish national headquarters and local chapters with public-facing leadership.

This centralization wasn't without its challenges. The new structure came under scrutiny, and some investigations later arose into some of its prominent leaders. Some BLM followers and official chapter members felt those leaders had strayed from the grassroots principles and instead were prioritizing personal gain over community needs.

Despite the turmoil, the maxim had made its palpable imprint across the nation.

By September 5, that war cry had electrified protesters in Portland to take to the streets for one hundred consecutive days.

On September 30, Laila and her team would be one of those central groups to bring out thousands to rally against police brutality, specifically calling attention to the killing of twenty-seven-year-old

Patrick Kimmons. Exactly two years to that date, in 2018, Patrick was fatally shot in the back nine times by two Portland Police Department officers who were cleared of wrongdoing by a grand jury.

As Laila had envisioned when she first formed the PDX Black Youth Movement, that Wednesday evening, the teens kept the demonstration upbeat and humming, complete with a drumline to accompany the marchers' rhythmic chants. It was the type of melody that burrowed into your brain, refusing to leave, yet somehow felt like a holy mantra.

B! I got your B, I got your B.

L! I got your L, I got your L.

M! I got your M, I got your M.

During lulls in the drumming and belting, Laila yelled into a bullhorn, "What does that spell?"

"Black lives matter!" demonstrators responded.

"What does that spell?"

"Black lives matter!"

The crowd made their way to the parking lot on Third and Harvey Milk, where Patrick had been gunned down.

"What's his name?" Laila's words, burning as fiercely as her red hair, boomed through the megaphone as the petite powerhouse led the march down Yamhill Street.

"Patrick Kimmons!" the crowd shouted back.

"I. Can't. Hear. You!" Laila screamed, her neck craning left and right as she punctuated every word.

"Patrick Kimmons!"

She continued, fearlessly commanding the crowd of more than 1,500 people.

The teen owned every chant. Every step. Every liberating dance move.

Some walked with a tightly clenched fist hoisted in the air.

Others raised placards high to the sky.

"WHITE SUPREMACY IS TERRORISM."

"BLACK LIVES MATTER."

"SAY THEIR NAMES."

When the crowd reached the lot where Patrick was killed, the drumline dropped again. Louder, this time. Someone took to the megaphone and riled the crowd with another call-and-response. Another sonic earworm.

"This is not a riot!"

Without a beat lost, the crowd knew: "It's a revolution!"

This had been their liberation song all along.

"This is not a RIOT!"

"It's a REVOLUTION!"

Moments later, I watched as Laila delivered an impassioned speech. I watched as hundreds of young ones, Black, Hispanic, white, and Asian, all hung by her every word.

"If you don't think about Black and brown children every morning when you wake up, you are doing the bare fucking minimum," Laila told us, her voice cracking, the mic in her right hand, her left underscoring every word. "If you are not constantly thinking, how can I help her? How can I create opportunities for these children? You are doing the bare fucking minimum! And people like you disgust me."

The crowd roared louder.

"Get rid of this nasty system," she continued, "that is tearing Black individuals down. I fear going outside. I fear leaving my dad's side. Because me, as a light-skinned woman, could protect him. I fear that he'll get pulled over, and a cop will shoot him fucking dead. I'm tired of being scared. So I come out here every fucking chance that I get. I am not doing the bare minimum, am I?"

"No!" the crowd wailed.

"I'm tired of walking in their white spaces."

At this point, the teen sounded tired too. Seemingly exasperated and overwhelmed by it all. Perhaps stewing in the very thought she would later articulate during our catch-up call that March 2021 day.

"We know it's wrong and nothing's going to happen from it."

As the prominent perpetrator in George Floyd's death, Derek Chauvin's forty-three-day trial was closely watched and scrutinized.

In the course of the proceedings, it came to light that Derek had been a repeat offender when it came to excessive force since joining

MPD in 2001: He had a record of thirty-two complaints filed against him, including indifference to the pain of residents.

One incident involved the shooting of Latrell Toles during a domestic abuse call in 2008, when Derek claimed self-defense but was contradicted by eyewitnesses. In 2013, Derek inappropriately escalated a traffic stop with LaSean Braddock. In 2015, he handcuffed and kneeled on Zoya Code, causing her head to forcefully hit the ground. The same tactic was used on John Pope in 2017.

Derek's pattern of excessive force, particularly targeting people of color, led to millions in settlements for Zoya and John. Despite such civilian complaints, most cases were closed without him ever being disciplined, and only a few resulted in oral reprimands.

As the trial unfolded, Darnella was one of forty-five witnesses to testify. She spoke softly as she recounted what she saw that Memorial Day and its impact on her life: "When I look at George Floyd, I look at—I look at my dad. I look at my brothers. I look at my cousins, my uncles, because they are all Black . . . I have a Black father. I have a Black brother. I have Black friends.

"It's been nights I stayed up apologizing and apologizing to George Floyd for not doing more and not physically interacting and not saving his life. But it's like, it's not what I should have done, it's what he should have done."

There wasn't much more the teen could've done. There wasn't much more anyone could've done. Derek and the other officers stood like an impassable wall, their uniforms a chilling reminder of the power held and the help denied. All the teen could do, restrained but resolute, was bear witness. And all the teen could see was a Black man struggling for each agonizing breath, lungs desperate for air that wouldn't come—recognizable in every way. He *could've* been her father, her brother, her uncle, or her friend. And George Floyd was all those things and more.

George Floyd came up in Houston's Third Ward, in Cuney Homes. Born on October 14, 1973, he was one of seven siblings, three sisters, Bridgett, LaTonya, and Zsa Zsa, and three brothers, Philonise, Rodney, and Terrence. By the time he was at James D. Ryan Middle School, he was exceptionally tall. When he reached Jack Yates High School, he was a multi-sport star athlete playing basketball as a power forward and football as a tight end. His football team christened him a gentle giant. Because of his extra large size, he was aware some saw him as threatening before anything else. Friends said he was shy, humble, and friendly. The kind of person that would shake you with two hands. The kind of person that liked hugging on you.

After graduating high school in 1993, he made a go at college, attending South Florida Community College on a basketball scholarship. He left before his first year was done—he didn't like it there. He was later recruited by Texas A&M–Kingsville to play basketball. He dropped out before the end of sophomore year.

Ultimately, college just wasn't for him.

At the same time, he had been falling more and more in love with music—it'd always been a passion of his. This was the nineties, and "chopped and screwed" hip-hop music had been popping off in Houston, so George Floyd found his way onto the scene. Soon, he took to rapping with the Screwed Up Click, a crew led by Houston local legend DJ Screw. Everyone called him Big Floyd, and on one of their tracks, "Sittin' on Top of the World," on the *Chapter 324— Dusk 2 Dawn* album, he handles the third verse, his drawl distinct.

> *On the grind, true South Sider*
> *Watch me crawl low on my motherfuckin' spiders*
> *Welcome to the ghetto, it's Third Ward, Texas*

In the end, rapping didn't stick, either.

After that, he struggled to find his footing. Soon, adrift, he clung to his vices. There were some drug uses. Some time behind bars. Eventually, he found God and, soon, craved a new beginning.

His move to St. Louis Park, Minneapolis, in 2014 was for a fresh start after his release from Diboll Unit private state prison in East Houston for aggravated robbery. Once there, he started a ninety-day drug rehab program at Turning Point and found a job working security at a Salvation Army in downtown Minneapolis.

Before his murder, he had been working security at Conga Latin

Bistro on East Hennepin Avenue while grieving the death of his mother, Larcenia Jones Floyd, who died on May 30, 2018, in their hometown. But as the pandemic and unemployment overwhelmed the nation, he lost his job at Conga and a second one as a truck driver.

His former manager at Conga, Jovanni Tunstrom, said George Floyd was always cheerful. "He had a good attitude," he said. "He would dance badly to make people laugh. I tried to teach him how to dance because he loved Latin music, but I couldn't because he was too tall for me. He always called me 'Bossman.' I said, 'Floyd, don't call me Bossman. I'm your friend.'"

The night before that fateful Memorial Day, George Floyd and his childhood friend Christopher Harris were talking about temp agencies. They were talking about trying to get back on track, about forging ahead. They were talking about expectancies often extinguished by a society that has long classified them as *beyond the pale* and relegated them to the margins. For George Floyd, those plans remain forever unfulfilled, whispered with desperate hope, shattered in the face of a system that offered no second chances.

"He was happy with the change he was making," Christopher said. "He was doing whatever it takes to maintain going forward with his life."

George Floyd had five children; three have kept out of the public eye, but two are more publicly known: a son, Quincy Mason Floyd, who was twenty-two when his father died, and Gianna Floyd, who was six.

On June 9, 2020, thousands descended to a memorial service for George Floyd in his hometown at the Fountain of Praise Church. A horse-drawn carriage took his gold casket to Houston Memorial Gardens cemetery in Pearland.

He was buried next to his mom.

Derek's trial came to a close on April 20, 2021, when, after ten hours of deliberation, the jury of four white women, three Black men, two white men, two mixed race women, and one Black woman—in their twenties to sixties—reached a verdict.

It had been 330 days since George Floyd died.

And, at long last, the scales of justice tipped.

Derek Chauvin was found guilty of all charges.

Accountability, it seemed, was now a line in the sand.

On June 25, Derek was sentenced to 22.5 years. He was the first white police officer in the state to be convicted of the murder of an African American.

To mark one year since George Floyd's death, Darnella took to Facebook and Instagram and posted, in remembrance of him:

A year ago, today I witnessed a murder [and] it changed me. It changed how I viewed life.

It made me realize how dangerous it is to be Black in America. We shouldn't have to walk on eggshells around police officers, the same people that are supposed to protect and serve. We are looked at as thugs, animals, and criminals, all because of the color of our skin. Why are Black people the only ones viewed this way.

A part of my childhood was taken from me . . . Having to up and leave because my home was no longer safe, waking up to reporters at my door, closing my eyes at night only to see a man who is brown like me, lifeless on the ground. I couldn't sleep properly for weeks. I used to shake so bad at night my mom had to rock me to sleep. Hopping from hotel to hotel because we didn't have a home and looking over our back every day in the process. Having panic and anxiety attacks every time I see a police car, not knowing who to trust . . . I hold that weight.

A lot of people call me a hero even though I don't see myself as one . . . Behind this smile, behind these awards, behind the publicity, I'm a girl trying to heal from something I am reminded of every day. Everyone talks about the girl who recorded George Floyd's death, but to actually be her is a different story.

We forget the cost of courage. We forget the price of a revolution awakened. We forget the invisible scars of a truth-teller. The burden Darnella carried, and continues to shoulder, the toll it took on her life, we can never fathom. And yet, what the unflinching teen did has reverberated, its consequence still felt in every pocket around the world.

She has left an abiding legacy in the fight for racial justice.

Her lawyer at the time, Seth Corbin, said she was "just a seventeen-year-old high school student, with a boyfriend and a job at the mall, who did the right thing. She's the Rosa Parks of her generation."

Markeanna Tyus, Darnella's friend at the time and a junior at Roosevelt High School, two miles from where George Floyd died, said, "She set the stage for girls like me looking up to her . . . She's a hero—I go to school with a revolutionary."

Since that day, Darnella and her family have moved from their Minneapolis neighborhood and kept a low profile. She has also intentionally stayed out of the media spotlight. Her legal team said she's still healing. They told me countless local, national, and international news outlets have requested interviews and specials with her. She's been offered full scholarships to universities. She's been honored by many organizations, including the Pulitzer Prize Board and PEN America, both organizations that celebrate and spotlight exceptional journalism.

It was never about any of that for Darnella, who had just wanted to take a lazy stroll to the corner store. But for righteousness' sake, she did what she knew was right upon seeing one of the world's gravest atrocities. She donned the mantle of witness. She became the enduring chronicler of that moment. She became the living lens through which history was written. And because of her, justice triumphed.

Because of her, goodness finally prevailed.

Her cousin, Judeah, has also been healing. The then third grader told the jury she was "sad" and "kind of mad" as she watched George Floyd die.

In 2022, she penned a children's book about her coping process, which included hugs from her mom. Before her family moved away from the neighborhood, Judeah made her way back to CUP to see it one more time.

In remembrance of George Floyd, she saw that many had continued leaving candles, flowers, and signs in front of the grocery store where it all began.

Judeah left a sign too.

It read: IT CAN BE BETTER.

After Derek Chauvin was found guilty, Christopher, the teen who spotted the twenty-dollar bill, returned to CUP. He and his family had moved away a week after the murder.

He went to the very spot where George Floyd spent his final moments, crying and screaming and begging. The nineteen-year-old took to Instagram, uploaded a photo of himself against a mural of George Floyd, and tapped "share."

The caption read: "Miss you brother."

"Why, in this nation, do Black Americans wake up knowing they can lose their life just for living their life?" Joe Biden, the then presumptive Democratic presidential nominee, said during George Floyd's June 9 funeral.

That question has long tormented America.

However, this system—this fence of oppression—began to show cracks, trembling under the weight of truth from the lips of the young. Because innocence speaks. Innocence uncovers. And in this unforgettable year, when the world was thrust into a state of upheaval, it seemed reconciliation would remain distant. (Even the symbolism of a white man on a Black man's neck—a haunting embodiment of the yearslong struggle examined in previous chapters—radiated oppression.)

But Darnella showed us all that what you reveal, you heal.

Derek Chauvin's verdict was a start.

It seemed an immediate healing for a people long relegated to invisibility.

George Floyd's death wasn't just a moment, it was history's grim echo. It wasn't history repeating but our failure to learn from it. We are the actors in this ongoing drama. When we ignore the past, we condemn ourselves to repeat its mistakes. We must connect the dots of injustice, looking back to understand why it happens and how to break the cycle. Only then can we truly learn and create a future free from the burdens of the past.

Through their defiant voices and tireless actions, young Black changemakers encapsulated this very understanding and fought against oppression. From the fight for empowerment at HBCUs to Freedom Summer to the George Floyd Justice Movement, their protests have always challenged the walls of injustice, cracking them open with demands for equity. Their refusal to be silenced, their commitment to humanity, and their belief in collective action remind us that progress is possible.

And since Darnella's catalytic ripple, America has witnessed a growing number of young people of color engaging in political activism and seeking elected office.

Khaleel Anderson. New York State legislator. At twenty-four, he began his first term on November 12, 2020.

Alex Lee. California State legislator. At twenty-five, he began his term on December 7, 2020.

Jasmine Blackwater-Nygren. Arizona State legislator. At twenty-five, she began her first term on February 9, 2021.

Chi Ossé. New York City council member. At twenty-three, he began his first term on January 1, 2022.

Arturo Alonso. Oklahoma State legislator. At twenty-three, he began his first term on November 23, 2022.

Zaynab Mohamed. Minnesota State legislator. At twenty-five, she began her first term on January 3, 2023.

Maxwell Frost. Florida congressman. At twenty-five, he began his first term on January 3, 2023.

Nabeela Syed. Illinois State legislator. At twenty-three, she began her first term on January 11, 2023.

And many more.

The torch of resistance hasn't just been passed down, it burns bright in the hands of future generations. They are not simply inheritors of the struggle but architects of a path toward liberation, redefined and fought for anew.

EPILOGUE

It Continues, in Retrospect

You've got to be taught to hate and fear . . .
You've got to be taught to be afraid
Of . . . people whose skin is a diff'rent shade

RICHARD RODGERS AND OSCAR HAMMERSTEIN II

Make history personal.

Those three words were my anchor as I penned this book. A reminder of the lessons since returning from my road trip in search of the *how* that made my *why* possible in America.

Resist is the book I would've turned to upon my return—a starting point—as I questioned who came before Laila DeWeese and those of the PDX Black Youth Movement in Portland. This journey began with that very simple question: What other young voices had challenged the systems of old?

History isn't only about the past. It's a compass for the present. To grasp the logic of "why," we must understand the mechanics of "how." "Why" questions the rationale, "how" dissects the process. Just as a machine depends on its inner workings, understanding today's problems requires knowing how our complex present came to be. By delving into the past, we unveil the forces that molded our world and the challenges we now face.

Understanding the history of Black youths isn't about remembering names and dates. It's about recognizing the ongoing legacy of their shadowed resistance. Their overlooked fight for equality, their pursuit of justice, and how their indubitable creativity in action have shaped the very fabric of this nation. From the enslaved ancestors who toiled in the fields to the freedom fighters who challenged segregation to the 2020 activists who demanded police accountability, young Black reformers have consistently pushed the boundaries of what's possible, forcing America to confront its contradictions. By witnessing their unwavering struggle, we awaken to our own capacity for change, confront the unfinished quests for justice, and ignite the possibilities for a more liberating dawn.

What we must remember, what we must honor, is that the story of America is incomplete without acknowledging the profound influence of young Black torchbearers and their allies.

Throughout generations, they haven't only endured the challenges of systemic oppression, they've actively redefined the nation's social, cultural, and political landscape. The Ella Bakers and the Darnella Fraziers each pushed the boundaries of possibility. Their zeal powered cultural revolutions, while their fighter spirit and tireless engagement offer invaluable lessons for navigating today's labyrinth, laying the groundwork for present-day strides: from voting rights and economic justice to environmental activism, LGBTQ+ visibility, and the ongoing fight against systemic inequality. In charting their rich constellation, we seed their enduring imprint of resilience. Their stories illuminate not only the struggles overcome but the steadfast commitment that ignited lasting change, each strand whispering stories of triumph against formidable odds.

Their stories teach us that America's devotion to white exceptionalism has nurtured the stigma of Black inferiority, denying Black people their rightful place. Yet, this reality has been and continues to be disproven by the adeptness of young changemakers and their efforts to challenge unjust power hierarchies and walls of oppression. Their consistent actions demonstrate that being Black should be—*is*—synonymous with brilliance, with tenacity.

Journeying through these decades was revelatory.

Growing up, when I left our home, I always returned to our little Benin City and Ekiadolor Village in the South Bronx, separated from the outside world of race, racism, and discrimination. There was no discussion of any of that, let alone what young kids like me did to make me possible in this land. At home, we spoke our dialect. We played our music. We ate our foods. We lived in our bubble.

Most people, though, never get the opportunity to break from their bubbles and intentionally ask questions about history that isn't their own—or about history, period. Instead, they remain comfortably isolated and, at times, develop unconscious biases that can often morph into intolerance and extremist views. They lack the *why* and the *how*, instead clinging to cherry-picked information that reinforces their existing beliefs and social group, fostering a harmful us vs. them mentality.

Religious vs. non-religious.

Hetero vs. non-hetero.

White vs. non-white.

And so on.

A mentality that says if *those* people are not like us, we exclude them, we berate them, we make them know their place. A mentality that America methodically constructed and nurtured with racial divisions, assigned individuals roles within those divisions and enforced segregation based on such distinctions.

Studies have shown that people, regardless of age, are naturally inclined to hold a more positive disposition toward people they consider to be like them. And similarly, with the inverse, people treat those unlike them as outsiders. This separation and societal categorization are what breeds hate of an-Other. Hate arises from fear of the unknown. The intentionality, empathy, and self-awareness required to break from those thinking patterns are rarely met because the system of America continues to further the division.

We've seen as much in the twenty-first century.

As I watched the increased attack on Black history with countless book bans, reminiscent of those that powered the HBCU protests of yesteryear, in states such as Florida, Missouri, Texas, and South Carolina, I wondered why. Why would anyone attack such a fundamental pillar of their own country, gravely impact their young, if not for an intentional attempt to suppress what American democracy purports to uphold: liberty, justice, and freedom?

Then, in Mississippi, a bill was approved to create a new district in Jackson—a city with over 80 percent African American residents. The new gerrymandered district would cluster white neighborhoods together and establish a separate, white-controlled criminal justice system. This move chillingly mirrors the segregationist tactics of the Jim Crow era, reminding us of the sacrifices made by the likes of Barbara Johns, who fought for equal treatment under the law.

Legislators who have taken to actively disparaging Black Americans and Black history reveal their awareness of the pervasive consequences of America's historical and ongoing racial injustices. Instead of addressing the root causes and interconnected issues, they choose to erase them altogether.

This suggests a deliberate attempt to maintain the status quo: They know the *how* and the *why* but rather invest in the preservation of *us*.

The *how* and *why* matters.

Ignoring this is an assault on the very essence of justice and progress. What this last century of Black resistance, helmed by the young, should teach us is the undeniable power of collective action, charged by resolute conviction and a clear-eyed understanding of history. It's the torch of freedom that demands not only a destination but a mindful journey. Each step forward, each barrier broken, each voice raised in righteous anger, each act of defiance, however seemingly small, builds upon the footprint of those who came before, paving the way for a more just tomorrow. To disregard this legacy is to rob the future of its compass, of a world where justice is not a faraway craving but a lived truth.

It is this resistance born out of exclusion that has perfected what we revel in today's democracy. It is what propelled my ability—the freedom of it all—to exist in this country.

The *how* and *why* matters.

The framework of *how* and *why* formed during one of my stops on my 2020 road trip.

It was day thirteen. September 14.

I was in Kenosha, Wisconsin. This was twenty-three days after Jacob Blake, a twenty-nine-year-old Black man, was shot in the back seven times by a white police officer and left paralyzed from the waist down.

This was also four months after George Floyd was killed.

I was on my documenter duties, roaming the streets, tracking down the location that had made headlines, where protesters had burned down a car lot on Sheridan between 58th and 59th Streets in protest of Jacob's shooting.

Once I arrived, I paused to take the dealership in, shocked to see more than thirty cars completely ashen. As I looked on, transfixed by what was before me, snapping with my Canon, writing in my notebook, an elderly couple pulled up in a white vintage car, top down, with burgundy-and-gold trim, maroon leather seats, and a license plate that read "Merry."

I remember them, still, so vividly.

They were white and in their seventies. As I stood in the middle of the car yard, trying to understand how this burned-down lot did anything for the plight of Black people, the woman got out of the passenger side and dashed over.

"It's so sad," she began. "So, so sad."

Their names, she told me, were Harry and Beverly. She wanted me to call her Bev.

"Wow, all the damage, so sad," she went on.

I nodded. Still frozen by the gravity before us.

I didn't understand that residents were so enraged by the endless killings and torment of Black bodies that they'd taken to the destruction of a small business. At another glance, I tried to process it from the perspective of unbridled trauma and grief: perhaps it was a stark and visceral response to the relentless injustice they could no longer tolerate.

Within seconds, Harry joined us.

We quickly formed a semicircle.

They had on bright tropical shirts, Bev with her shades on, Harry with his ball cap. We got to know each other a bit, and soon, they knew about my journey. They knew my *why*. I asked them about their thoughts on race relations as we've seen it, especially with the compounding events of 2020. About their experiences with Black America.

Harry began by telling me that though the Jacob shooting was tragic, we didn't know all the facts. He went on to say that he follows statistics on gun and police violence, and from his research, Black-on-Black crime is more common than police shootings, especially in poor areas. That, because of this, crime rates will always be high in such neighborhoods as people try to survive the conditions they're in because "you live in poverty, you grew up in poverty, and there's a lot of working families, and there's not a lot of people with higher incomes to afford things," he said. "I mean, I can look at Milwaukee, and I can look at the stats. And where all of the most killings occurred, is where there's heavily Black people. And that's kind of the way it is."

Bev clarified her husband's point: "A lot of the children are growing up in broken homes without fathers."

As a kid, Harry lived in an all-white suburban area. At one point, property developers built a housing project half a mile from where he lived. His mother hated that "these people, low-income people, Black and white, were going to be there. Because this is the suburbs!" He explained how he grew up with *those people*, went to school with them, and played basketball with them.

"I'll tell you this," he said, "I'm six-four, and some of the African American guys were maybe five-eight or something like that, and they could jump higher than me."

"Oh, you know that movie, *White Men Can't Jump*!" Bev said without missing a beat.

Bev and I laugh at this. Harry, not in the slightest.

"But they were my best friends," Harry continued unfazed.

He had gone through high school being close friends with his Black teammates, and "that really made me feel for the rest of my life that they're no different than anybody else. And I've always [held] that to be true. I don't mind walking into a, let's say, a bar, if it's an all-Black bar, I wouldn't really have a problem with that. It's that I have to judge people individually."

"Each generation is different," Bev added. "Our parents were very prejudiced—it's that generation. Our granddaughter is transgender. That was something to accept, you know. So each generation, it gets easier for each one. And you're taught prejudice, you're not born with that, we understand that."

We got back to talking about poverty-stricken neighborhoods in contemporary America.

I told them that their assertion that poverty, essentially, is a choice is not that black and white. It's nuanced. The idea that anyone can pull oneself up "by the bootstrap" is a fallacy. I explained that I don't believe there's anyone living in a dire situation who doesn't want a better outcome for themselves. Most have been led to believe that they *are* their circumstances. It's become part of their identity. Many don't have the tools or resources to know the how. Most just need someone to show them the roadmap.

I took them back to my upbringing. To the guidance counselors and teachers in my middle school who rallied around me to ensure I tested out of my zip code public school in the Bronx. I took them back to my science and math high school in Manhattan and the amount of extracurriculars and resources that helped me see *me* and my potential. All of which led me to the colleges I went to for my bachelor's and master's. All of which led me there, standing at that lot with them, traveling the country with funds I received from a school I would not have attended if someone hadn't seen me.

It took people ahead of me to get behind me to show me the way out of my circumstances. Only then did my hard work yield the kind of dividends that propelled my life forward.

I ended my spiel by saying that such generalizations about poor Black people are the kind that have limited our progress.

"It's like a perpetual, vicious cycle," I told them, "where the circumstances just keep repeating itself. So, how can that be broken?"

We stood in silence.

"I don't have an answer," Harry broke.

"Yeah. I'm still searching for that answer myself," I said.

After another beat, Harry explained that after some time, people can no longer blame their situation for their lack of progress—so, *yes*, to him, poverty is, in fact, a choice—and it begins with how Black people show up in the world.

That matters, too, he felt—if not most of all because that's what perpetuates the stereotype Black people are trying to fight. I reiterated the conundrum within that very stereotype. We can't fight that which confines us and our progress because of the burden of the typecasts we must battle daily.

Harry disagreed and decided to use me to explain his point.

When they saw me standing at the lot taking pictures and jotting down notes, he said they knew from how I presented that "I meant business."

"Why? How? What do you mean?" I asked, a bit thrown. Because their observation sounded like its own stereotype.

"By the way you are dressed," he said.

I looked down at my green polka-dot maxi dress and white sneakers, accented by my brown backpack. Canon strapped around my neck. My permed pixie cut slicked down.

"Different people dress that you either want to be near them," Bev explained, "or you don't, regardless of your skin."

Harry said Black people can choose to rise and get out of their circumstances like I did. I disagreed, restating my earlier point about guidance counselors and the rest.

He then pointed to another example of a historic kind.

"If you had said in 1960 that someday there'd be a Black president? Man, there's nobody in the world that would believe that."

Barack Obama, I said, is another anomaly. He had a support system that only some have, one that was also rooted in education.

Bev nodded. Her face had lit up at the mention of Barack Obama.

"It's his personality," she said. "I don't look at his color. I like him. I loved him. I loved him. He was one of my favorites."

Harry nodded. "That was a huge step."

Harry didn't say much about his politics and didn't answer when I asked him whether he had voted for Barack Obama or would be voting for Joe Biden or Donald Trump. Bev eagerly told me she had voted for Barack Obama and would be casting her vote for Joe Biden.

Our conversation that Monday, standing there on that lot, lasted about thirty minutes, and in that time, Harry and I disagreed more times than we agreed. Bev and I gelled like we'd known each other for a long time. They took to me like concerned grandparents, asking me about safety on my journey and how I was doing it all.

This exchange, out of the hundreds, stuck with me most because of that very thing: our disagreement never overshadowed our respect for each other, nor did it diminish our eagerness to engage in thoughtful conversation. It highlighted the richness of our perspectives and spurred us to explore the intricacies of our differing viewpoints. That only deepened our mutual understanding and allowed us the gift of bonding as just, well, humans. As people. Period.

You're taught prejudice. You're not born with that.

I was most struck by that one line and characterization from Bev. It spoke to her character and her acceptance of things she once did not understand. But mostly, her reconciliation with what I deduced was her former thinking pattern.

What's most interesting about Bev and Harry was that the confrontation of their ingrained biases, of their fixed thinking pattern toward all Others, cemented when someone they deeply loved—their granddaughter who identified as trans—belonged to a minority group. This, it seemed, gave them pause and forced them to reevaluate how they engaged with society—specifically, with those different from them.

Our conversation also helped me ruminate more on a long-held stereotype placed on white people: that they are *the* villains to racial progress. White people are not antagonists in the fight for parity. Classism, passiveness, privilege, and apathy toward Otherism are the true foes, rooted in a fear of: if I stand in solidarity with *them*, would I lose all this advantage and privilege I've come to relish?

I was left with one significant thought that Monday: unity is not about putting aside our differences or pretending they don't exist. If it were, there would be no need to be unified in the first place. My conversation with Bev and Harry taught me that unity is coming together *with* our differences and recognizing that our dissimilarities enriches our collective experience. It requires open communication and a willingness to actively listen to understand. That kind of unity becomes a testament to our shared humanity and our ability to transcend barriers to create a more harmonious world that American democracy, the Constitution, aspires to.

So each generation, it gets easier for each one.

It gets easier, as Bev said, because people are confronted with their biases, at times within their own homes, which pushes them to intentionality. A reexamination of their *why*s and *how*s. That's what insulation does. That's what my own insulation had done. It limits your capacity for knowledge. And the greatest gift of humanity is our untapped capacity to learn, to grow, to become better than our yesterdays.

And to move from the ways of old, change is required. And yes, change is slow, change is incremental. But if we remain steadfast, change is possible.

That's the ultimate takeaway the young ones showcased in this book—and the many who were not—have proven. In revisiting that exchange with Harry and Bev, I couldn't help but witness the seeds of progress sown by generations of young trailblazers fighting for that very realization.

While Harry and Bev held different views, their genuine engagement with me, a younger Black person with a contrasting perspective, was a testament to the groundwork laid by activists and thinkers before me, before them.

It was as if the whispers of countless marches and protest songs hummed beneath the surface of our conversation, urging us to find common ground despite our differences. Their willingness to listen, to confront their own biases, and to ultimately bridge the gap with understanding was a ripple effect of the relentless waves of awakening pushed forward by the efforts seen during the movement of the Jena Six, the Bates Seven, the Scottsboro Nine, the Wilmington Ten, and many more.

It exemplified the longing that "each generation, it gets easier."

The kind of hope fueled by the tireless efforts of those who came before. And perhaps, in that exchange, we became tiny ripples ourselves, carrying the torch of understanding onward, toward a future where diverse voices truly come together to stitch the disparate strings of American life into a more inclusive and vibrant whole.

Since becoming a storyteller, I've been drawn to the unsung. To the disenfranchised. To those often relegated to the shadows. *Resist* is not meant to be exhaustive. Still, it was more than enough to enrich my knowledge and gratitude for Black America, for the Black culture that made me who I am today.

What I most take away from this journey into history is that as imperfect as America's young democracy is, it afforded me a life I once thought would remain in my head.

This.

The words I write.

The dreams I dreamt.

They were provided a path to be seen.

That's why it was important for me to make history personal. Beyond its ability to build knowledge and discernment, that deepening depth of understanding builds compassion. It expands our revelation of what history was and how it applies to our lives, individually and collectively. It shifts from being a theory or an obscure text in a book to becoming real. The personal experience and connections we make with it make it part of us.

Dissecting the lives of these courageous young minds also taught me that history is *now*. It unfolds every day with everyday people. It's written by those who live in it, ready to speak on it. If the lessons aren't learned from classism, sectionalism, racism, bigotry, hatred, division, all of it continues. History is not repeating itself. It's simply not being called upon. The viciousness of this unique American life for the Othered continues until there's a decisive turning point where there's a communal perspective shift and intentionality to make history personal. To make right what has long been wrong for many. A personal connection with history is the antidote to ignorance and insulation.

I treasured the time spent with those we now call historical figures.

I imagined the Nine being my brothers who got on the wrong train on the wrong day in the wrong era. I saw Barbara Johns and Laila DeWeese and wished I could have been as dogged in my youth. I marveled at Charlie Cobb's concept to liberate the minds of the young through Freedom Schools. So too with the Seven who sacrificed so much in the name of allyship so a Black football player they did not know personally could be afforded the same rights they walked in.

They were just like me, just like you.

They were simply trying to make a life for themselves and stumbled into history by speaking up and taking action against what was wrong.

That's history. It's that personal.

It is the formerly enslaved grandfather leading by example so his grandbabies could have a life better than he ever imagined. Perhaps that grandbaby would become an iconic changemaker. Perhaps that grandbaby would become president. It is refusing to let your circumstances define your destiny, like Benjamin Chavis. It is preserving your character for your community, like Johnetta Elzie. It is the many young ones who have carried on the freedom fight, decade after decade, refusing to accept stagnation and disenfranchisement.

That's what I walk away with.

It's nostalgia now.

It's appreciation now.

I am who I am, now and always, because of them.

Most of all, excavating these decades and movements helped me revisit my family and my experience in America. Moments I had not reexamined since they happened. The added context provided the perspective of just how grave our racial experiences were, demonstrating the importance of looking through the lens of history to see the pertinence to our lives. I always felt I had no right to claim Blackness because I wasn't a direct descendant of African American slavery. What this journey distilled for me is that I am a direct beneficiary of African American slavery, of those who looked like me, who toiled for my freedom and the democracy I cherish even more deeply knowing the price paid for its attainment and continuation.

Crucially, the most illuminating insights from history were not solely defined by actions but by the fervent optimism of the young. There's a verse in the Bible that says, "Better a poor but wise youth than an old but foolish king who no longer knows how to heed a warning." While the scripture underscores the importance of wise counsel, it's often the young who become the living testament to its truth. Emboldened by their untarnished idealism, they are most willing to take up the mantle of righteousness, even if it means stepping into the fire. And perhaps that's what we need most now.

Young ones tired of wailing, "Enough is enough," to be the nation's new breed of leaders. Young ones who have intentionally learned from history, cautious of its perils, ready with their folded chairs at the table. Young ones who can seize the cloak of change with ironclad determination, understanding that the echoes of the past reverberate in the corridors of the present. They've stepped up, time and again, armed not only with aspirations but with knowledge, empathy, and an unyielding commitment to shaping a future that transcends the limitations of yesterday.

With each step, they chart a trajectory that amalgamates the wisdom of the past and the promise of tomorrow, breathing life into a tapestry of progress fused with fibers of resilience and unity. Driven by their convictions, these harbingers of hope must light the path forward for a nation desperate for transformation as profound as it is imperative.

ACKNOWLEDGMENTS

A book begins with an idea. That idea turns into a robust proposal. And if you're lucky enough, you'd have an agent who sees the vision. Jessica Spitz, your pointed clarity and devoted collaboration is what started the journey of this book. I'm grateful for your friendship and partnership.

Sylvie Rabineau and Bradley Singer, I appreciate your continued support. I am thankful for every call, email, and advice.

Hannah Philips, thank you for giving this book the best home and for being gracious and diligent. To the Macmillan and St. Martin's Press teams, thank you for stewarding it with such thoughtful consideration.

To my Columbia University family, thank you for seeing and mentoring me since I was a student in the J-school.

Thank you to the magazine and news editors who gave me a chance when I was fresh out of grad school and hungry to find my voice. Your championing of my words remains invaluable.

Thank you to my Father's Heart Ministries community in Manhattan's Lower East Side. A heartfelt shout-out to the women who have lifted and carried me, Pastors Carol Vedral and Marian Hutchins and Randa Jones, and to the late Pastor Chuck Vedral for his healing words that mended me back to *me*. What was meant to be a year of service through AmeriCorps transformed my life.

To Pastor Ben Idahor, thanks for all the many prayers and Proverbs 3:5–6-type conversations—it's been an anchor.

And forever and always, my infinite love to my family.

Mom, your brilliance lit my path. Thank you for the gift of America. It is because of you that America became a most treasured reality. I appreciate and honor your resilience and grit.

Manny, Danny, AO, and Lee, I am proud to be your sister. Through all we've overcome, I admire how you all continue to strive for the best. I am grateful to be surrounded by strong, caring, and brilliant men.

Finally, this book would not be if not for those who inspired its words: those who came before me and those who still fight for righteousness. I'm grateful to them and to the many who continue to work in the shadows. They have long been the backbone of our communities, lifting us up without the need to be named or publicly acknowledged. They give and serve because it is just and right.

NOTES

INTRODUCTION

vii *"To be African American"* Caleb Gayle, *We Refuse to Forget* (Penguin, 2023), 214.

xiv *"shithole countries"* Alan Fram and Jonathan Lemire, "Trump: Why Allow Immigrants from 'Shithole Countries'?," Associated Press, January 12, 2018, https://apnews.com/article -north-america-donald-trump-ap-top-news-international-news-fdda2ff0b 877416c8ae1c1a77a3cc425.

xiv *hate crimes increased by 20 percent* FBI National Press Office, "FBI Releases 2019 Hate Crime Statistics," FBI, November 16, 2020, https://www.fbi.gov/news/press-releases/fbi -releases-2019-hate-crime-statistics.

I. A REVOLUTION AWAKENS

5 *More than four years* (and general background) Smithsonian National Museum of African American History and Culture, *We Return Fighting, World War 1 and the Shaping of Modern Black Identity* (Smithsonian Books, 2019).

5 *progress in consumerism* Lizabeth Cohen, "A Consumer's Republic: The Politics of Mass Consumption in Postwar America," *Journal of Consumer Research* 31, no. 1, https://dash .harvard.edu/bitstream/handle/1/4699747/cohen_conrepublic.pdf.

5 *fueling the economy* (and general background) Adam Tooze, *The Deluge: The Great War, America and the Remaking of the Global Order, 1916–1931* (Penguin, 2015).

5 *the modern era* (and general background) Paul Fussell, *The Great War and Modern Memory* (Oxford University Press, 1975).

5 *capitalism* (and general background) David Reynolds, *The Long Shadow: The Legacies of the Great War in the Twentieth Century* (W.W. Norton & Company, 2015).

6 *Cool Summers* James W. Loewen, *Sundown Towns* (New Press, 2005), 1–18.

6 *a rise in membership* David Pietrusza, "The Ku Klux Klan in the 1920s," The Bill of Rights Institute, https://billofrightsinstitute.org/essays/the-ku-klux-klan-in-the-1920s.

7 *Asa Philip Randolph* Cecilia A. Conrad, James Stewart, John Whitehead, and Patrick L. Mason, *African Americans in the U.S. Economy* (Rowman & Littlefield Publishers, 2005), chapter 7.

7 *Tulsa Race Massacre* Yuliya Parshina-Kottas, Anjali Singhvi, Audra D.S. Burch, Troy Griggs, Mika Gröndahl, Lingdong Huang, Tim Wallace, Jeremy White, and Josh Williams, "What the Tulsa Race Massacre Destroyed," *The New York Times*, May 24, 2021, https://www .nytimes.com/interactive/2021/05/24/us/tulsa-race-massacre.html.

8 *Born on December 13* (and general detailing) Barbara Ransby, *Ella Baker and the Black Freedom Movement: A Radical Democratic Vision* (The University of North Carolina Press, 2003).

9 *"He established himself"* The Civil Rights Documentary Project, Oral History Interview with Miss Ella Baker, Staff-Member–Consultant with SCEF, Southern Conference Educational Fund, by John Britton, interviewer, Washington, D.C., June 19, 1968, https://www.crmvet.org/nars/baker68.htm.

9 *"Grandpa would hitch"* Sue Thrasher and Casey Hayden, Southern Oral History Program Collection (#4007), Interview G-0008, The University of North Carolina at Chapel Hill, https://docsouth.unc.edu/sohp/html_use/G-0008.html.

9 *"You'd start off"* Sue Thrasher and Casey Hayden, Southern Oral History Program Collection (#4007), Interview G-0008, The University of North Carolina at Chapel Hill, https://docsouth.unc.edu/sohp/html_use/G-0008.html.

9 *"This was the kind of"* The Civil Rights Documentary Project, Oral History Interview with Miss Ella Baker, Staff-Member–Consultant with SCEF, Southern Conference Educational Fund, by John Britton, interviewer, Washington, D.C., June 19, 1968, https://www.crmvet.org/nars/baker68.htm.

10 *"What do you hope"* Patricia Hruby Powell, *Lift as You Climb* (Simon and Schuster, 2020).

10 *"He always called me"* The Civil Rights Documentary Project, Oral History Interview with Miss Ella Baker, Staff-Member–Consultant with SCEF, Southern Conference Educational Fund, by John Britton, interviewer, Washington, D.C., June 19, 1968, https://www.crmvet.org/nars/baker68.htm.

11 *"so light"* Sue Thrasher and Casey Hayden, Southern Oral History Program Collection (#4007), Interview G-0008, The University of North Carolina at Chapel Hill, https://docsouth.unc.edu/sohp/html_use/G-0008.html.

11 *Early 1900s* Jerrold M. Packard, *American Nightmare: The History of Jim Crow* (St. Martin's Griffin, 2003), 65.

12 *"My mother had a feeling"* The Civil Rights Documentary Project, Oral History Interview with Miss Ella Baker, Staff-Member–Consultant with SCEF, Southern Conference Educational Fund, by John Britton, interviewer, Washington, D.C., June 19, 1968, https://www.crmvet.org/nars/baker68.htm.

12 *"I was accepted"* Sue Thrasher and Casey Hayden, Southern Oral History Program Collection (#4007), Interview G-0008, The University of North Carolina at Chapel Hill, https://docsouth.unc.edu/sohp/html_use/G-0008.html.

12 *W.E.B Du Bois* Clarence G. Contee, "Du Bois, the NAACP, and the Pan-African Congress of 1919," *The Journal of Negro History* 57, no. 1 (1972): 13–28, https://www-jstor-org.i.ezproxy.nypl.org/stable/2717070?seq=6.

13 *Leonidas Dyer* Library of Congress, "Federal Law Against Lynchings," https://www.loc.gov/exhibits/naacp/the-new-negro-movement.html.

13 *President Joe Biden would finally* The White House, "Remarks by President Biden at Signing of H.R. 55, the 'Emmett Till Antilynching Act,'" https://www.whitehouse.gov/briefing-room/speeches-remarks/2022/03/29/remarks-by-president-biden-at-signing-of-h-r-55-the-emmett-till-antilynching-act/.

13 *Eighty-seven HBCUs* HBCU First Resource, "A History of Historically Black Colleges and Universities," https://hbcufirst.com/resources/hbcu-history-timeline.

13 *Morrill Land Grant College Act* Senator Justin S. Morrill, "Morrill Land Grant College Act," https://www.senate.gov/artandhistory/history/common/civil_war/MorrillLandGrantCollegeAct_FeaturedDoc.htm.

14 *across several HBCUs* "The New Negro on Campus: Black College Rebellions of the 1920's,"

The Annals of Iowa 44 (1978): 496–498, https://pubs.lib.uiowa.edu/annals-of-iowa/article
/id/3952/.

14 *Fisk University in Nashville* The WNET Group Documentary, "The Rise and Fall of Jim
Crow: Students Strike at Fisk University," https://ny.pbslearningmedia.org/resource/bf10
.socst.us.indust.fiskstrike/students-strike-at-fisk-university/.

15 *implemented new restrictions* Kenneth W. Goings and Eugene O'Connor, "The Classical
Curriculum at Black Colleges and Universities and the Roles of the Various Missionary Aid
Societies," *Bulletin of the Institute of Classical Studies Supplement*, no. 128 (2015): 75–96.

16 *The Crisis* W.E.B Du Bois, "A Record of the Darker Races," https://naacp.org/find-resources
/history-explained/history-crisis.

16 *Fisk prided itself* Lester C. Lamon, "The Black Community in Nashville and the Fisk University Student Strike of 1924–1925," *The Journal of Southern History* 40, no. 2 (1974): 225–244,
https://www.jstor.org/stable/2206893.

16 *"Discipline is choking"* W.E.B Du Bois, *The Education of Black People: Ten Critiques, 1906–
1960* (Monthly Review Press, 2001), 66.

17 *students responded* Marcia Lynn Johnson, "Student Protest at Fisk University in the 1920's,"
Negro History Bulletin, 33, no. 6 (1970), https://www.proquest.com/docview/1296746325
?pq-origsite=gscholar&fromopenview=true&sourcetype=Scholarly%20Journals.

17 *February 4, 1925* David Lewis, *W.E.B. Du Bois: A Biography 1868–1963* (Henry Holt and
Company, 2009), 464.

17 *April 16, 1925* Lester C. Lamon, "The Black Community in Nashville and the Fisk University Student Strike of 1924–1925," *The Journal of Southern History* 40, no. 2 (1974),
225–244, https://www.jstor.org/stable/2206893.

18 *Hampton University* James E. Alford, Jr., "Training the Hands, the Head, and the Heart: Student Protest and Activism at Hampton Institute during the 1920s," *Issues in Race and Society: An Interdisciplinary Global Journal. The Complete 2019 Edition*, https://ucincinnatipress
.manifoldapp.org/system/actioncallout/1c94db82–0fd5–4eb8-b8e1–8edc494ce22d
/attachment/original-4520e76d4bb77e5bf041670673ac1588.pdf#page=120.

18 *"If the principal"* James E. Alford, Jr., "Training the Hands, the Head, and the Heart: Student Protest and Activism at Hampton Institute during the 1920s," *Issues in Race and Society: An Interdisciplinary Global Journal. The Complete 2019 Edition*, https://ucincinnatipress
.manifoldapp.org/system/actioncallout/1c94db82–0fd5–4eb8-b8e1–8edc494ce22d
/attachment/original-4520e76d4bb77e5bf041670673ac1588.pdf#page=120.

18 *James resigned* James E. Alford, Jr., "Training the Hands, the Head, and the Heart: Student
Protest and Activism at Hampton Institute during the 1920s," *Issues in Race and Society:
An Interdisciplinary Global Journal. The Complete 2019 Edition*, https://ucincinnatipress
.manifoldapp.org/system/actioncallout/1c94db82–0fd5–4eb8-b8e1–8edc494ce22d
/attachment/original-4520e76d4bb77e5bf041670673ac1588.pdf#page=120.

19 *silk stockings popular* Angela J. Latham, *Posing a Threat: Flappers, Chorus Girls, and Other
Brazen Performers of the American 1920s* (Wesleyan University Press, 2000), 7–62.

19 *"Flappers are we"* Arnold Shaw, *The Jazz Age: Popular Music in the 1920's* (Oxford University Press, 1989), 4.

20 *silk stocking ban* Barbara Ransby, *Ella Baker and the Black Freedom Movement: A Radical
Democratic Vision* (The University of North Carolina Press, 2003), 59–60.

20 *"Fancy, colored or silk hose"* Barbara Ransby, *Ella Baker and the Black Freedom Movement:
A Radical Democratic Vision* (The University of North Carolina Press, 2003), 59–60.

20 *"talker"* Sue Thrasher and Casey Hayden, Southern Oral History Program Collection (#4007), Interview G-0008, The University of North Carolina at Chapel Hill, https://docsouth.unc.edu/sohp/html_use/G-0008.html.

20 *"little things"* Sue Thrasher and Casey Hayden, Southern Oral History Program Collection (#4007), Interview G-0008, The University of North Carolina at Chapel Hill, https://docsouth.unc.edu/sohp/html_use/G-0008.html.

21 *"I didn't seem particularly penitent"* Barbara Ransby, *Ella Baker and the Black Freedom Movement: A Radical Democratic Vision* (The University of North Carolina Press, 2003), 59–60.

21 *"I didn't have any silk stockings"* Sue Thrasher and Casey Hayden, Southern Oral History Program Collection (#4007), Interview G-0008, The University of North Carolina at Chapel Hill, https://docsouth.unc.edu/sohp/html_use/G-0008.html.

22 *773,00 words* "How Many Words are There in the Bible?," *Waiapu Church Gazette* 36, no. 7 (1945), https://paperspast.natlib.govt.nz/periodicals/WCHG19451001.2.24#:~:text=For%20the%20whole%20Bible%20the,152%2C185%20words%20and%201%2C063%2C876%20letters.

22 *1,189 chapters* "Bible at a glance," https://home.snu.edu/~hculbert/chapters.htm.

23 *"T.J."* Roberts Barbara Ransby, *Ella Baker and the Black Freedom Movement: A Radical Democratic Vision* (The University of North Carolina Press, 2003), 101.

24 *"Don't ask too many personal questions"* Sue Thrasher and Casey Hayden, Southern Oral History Program Collection (#4007), Interview G-0008, The University of North Carolina at Chapel Hill, https://docsouth.unc.edu/sohp/html_use/G-0008.html.

24 *"I've never credited myself"* The Civil Rights Documentary Project, Oral History Interview with Miss Ella Baker, Staff-Member–Consultant with SCEF, Southern Conference Educational Fund, by John Britton, interviewer, Washington, D.C., June 19, 1968, https://www.crmvet.org/nars/baker68.htm.

2. A RESISTANCE RISES

29 *freight train headed West* Douglas Linder, "The Trials of the Scottsboro Boys," University of Missouri at Kansas City, School of Law, 2007, https://papers.ssrn.com/sol3/papers.cfm?abstract_id=1027991.

29 *Memphis-bound* David Cates, *Scottsboro Boys* (Abdo Publishing, 2012), 14–16.

29 *The oldest of the nine* (and general backstory) WGBH Educational Foundation, "Scottsboro: An American Tragedy," https://www.pbs.org/wgbh/americanexperience/films/scottsboro/.

29 *During this time* Robert S. McElvaine, *The Great Depression: America 1929–1941* (Crown, 1993).

29 *Black Thursday* Gary Richardson, Alejandro Komai, Michael Gou, and Daniel Park, "Stock Market Crash of 1929," October 1929, https://www.federalreservehistory.org/essays/stock-market-crash-of-1929.

29 *3 percent to 25 percent* p. 51, https://www.bls.gov/opub/mlr/1948/article/pdf/labor-force-employment-and-unemployment-1929–39-estimating-methods.pdf (accessed from the Bureau of Labor Statistics on March 8, 2023).

29 *about 31 million people* Calculated 25 percent estimation using "General U.S. population" figure from census: https://www.census.gov/data/tables/time-series/dec/popchange-data-text.html.

29 *30 percent more* https://www.loc.gov/classroom-materials/united-states-history-primary

-source-timeline/great-depression-and-world-war-ii-1929–1945/race-relations-in-1930s
-and-1940s/ (accessed from the Library of Congress on March 8, 2023).

29 *the general population* https://www.census.gov/history/www/through_the_decades/fast
_facts/1930_fast_facts.html (accessed from the U.S. Census Bureau on March 8, 2023).

30 *hostile conditions* Debra L. Newman, "Selected Documents Pertaining to Black Workers
Among the Records of the Department of Labor and Its Component Bureaus, 1902–1969,"
National Archives Special List No. 40 (1977), https://cdn.calisphere.org/data/28722/6w
/bk0003z7p6w/files/bk0003z7p6w-FID1.pdf.

30 *many rarely had enough* Benjamin Roth and Daniel B. Roth, *The Great Depression: A Diary*
(PublicAffairs, 2009).

30 *peak of the Depression* David M. Kennedy, *Freedom From Fear: The American People in
Depression and War, 1929–1945* (Oxford University Press, 1999).

30 *Scottsboro Nine* Gerald F. Uelmen, "2001: A Train Ride: A Guided Tour of the Sixth
Amendment Right to Counsel," Vol. 58, Issue 1/2 Law & Contemporary Problems 13-29
(1995), https://scholarship.law.duke.edu/cgi/viewcontent.cgi?article=4263&context=lcp.

30 *March, four of the Nine* (and general chronology and charges) James Goodman, *Stories of
Scottsboro* (Knopf Doubleday Publishing Group, 1995).

30 *boxcar* John Lennon, *Boxcar Politics: The Hobo in U.S. Culture and Literature, 1869–1956*
(University of Massachusetts Press, 2014), 131–156.

32 *They were* Alabama Department of Archives and History, https://digital.archives.alabama
.gov/digital/collection/photo/search/searchterm/scottsboro%20boys%20intake.

33 *Two Huntsville Mill Girls* Hollace Ransdell, "Two Huntsville Mill Girls Hobo to Chattanooga," American Civil Liberties Union: "Report on the Scottsboro, Ala, Case," May 27,
1931, https://www.aclu.org/publications/report-scottsboro-ala-case.

33 *5,000 Black men lynched* American Civil Liberties Union, "ACLU's 1931 'Black Justice'
Report," May 1931, https://www.aclu.org/publications/aclus-1931-black-justice-report.

34 *saga to rock* WGBH Educational Foundation, "The Scottsboro Trial: A Timeline," https://
www.pbs.org/wgbh/americanexperience/features/scottsboronine-black-youth-arrested-for
-assault/.

34 *"revolting crime"* WGBH Educational Foundation, "The Scottsboro Trial: A Timeline," https://
www.pbs.org/wgbh/americanexperience/features/scottsboronine-black-youth-arrested-for
-assault/.

34 *"beasts unfit"* *The Huntsville Times*, March 26, 1931, "Revolting in Last Degree Is Story of
Girls," https://www.newspapers.com/article/the-huntsville-times/34921430/.

35 *"I had not done"* Clarence Norris and Sybil D. Washington, *The Last of the Scottsboro Boys:
An Autobiography* (G.P. Putnam's Sons, 1979), 21-22.

35 *Nine's court-appointed* Powell v. Alabama, 287 Y.S. 45 (1932), https://supreme.justia.com
/cases/federal/us/287/45/.

36 *"There were six"* Dinitia Smith, "Scottsboro 70 Years Later, Still Notorious, Still Painful," *The
New York Times*, March 29, 2001, https://www.nytimes.com/2001/03/29/arts/scottsboro-70
-years-later-still-notorious-still-painful.html.

36 *"Six of them had"* David M. Oshinsky, "Only the Accused Were Innocent," *The New York
Times*, April 3, 1994, https://www.nytimes.com/1994/04/03/books/only-the-accused-were
-innocent.html.

36 *"Pour it to her"* WGBH Educational Foundation, "Scottsboro: An American Tragedy," https://

www.pbs.org/wgbh/americanexperience/films/scottsboro/#transcript (under "transcript" menu).

36 *"put off five white men"* Weems et al. *v. State* transcript, http://law2.umkc.edu/faculty /projects/FTrials/scottsboro/Weems1.htm.

36 *"Within two hours"* John F. Wukovits, *An Appeal for Justice: The Trials of the Scottsboro Nine* (Greenhaven Publishing LLC, 2011), 34.

38 *International Labor Defense* Ellis Cose, "The Saga Of The Scottsboro Boys," July 27, 2020, https://www.aclu.org/issues/racial-justice/saga-scottsboro-boys.

38 *Samuel Leibowitz* Walter White, *A Man Called White* (University of Georgia Press, 1995), 131–132.

38 *"basic rights of man"* WGBH Educational Foundation, "Scottsboro: An American Tragedy; The Scottsboro Defense Attorney" https://www.pbs.org/wgbh/americanexperience/features /scottsboro-defense-attorney-samuel-leibowitz/.

38 *NAACP* Hugh T. Murray, Jr., "The NAACP versus the Communist Party: The Scottsboro Rape Cases, 1931–1932," *Phylon* 28, no. 3 (1967), https://www-jstor-org.i.ezproxy.nypl.org /stable/273666.

38 *Walter White* Walter White, *A Man Called White* (University of Georgia Press, 1995).

39 *May 1932* Manning Marable and Leith Mullings, eds., *Let Nobody Turn Us Around: Voices of Resistance, Reform, and Renewal: An African American Anthology* (Rowman & Littlefield, 2000), 280–281.

41 *who they really were* WGBH Educational Foundation, "Scottsboro: An American Tragedy; Who Were the Scottsboro Boys?," https://www.pbs.org/wgbh/americanexperience/features /scottsboro-boys-who-were-the-boys/.

41 *know their stories* Kelly Kazek, "The Sad Ends of the Scottsboro Boys: Their Lives in Brief Biographies," AL.com, April 15, 2013.

41 *"While in my cell lonely"* James Goodman, *Stories of Scottsboro* (Knopf Doubleday Publishing Group, 1995), 91.

41 *"It seems"* University of Missouri–Kansas City, School of Law Project, "The Scottsboro Boys."

42 *"Getting out"* University of Missouri–Kansas City, School of Law Project, "The Scottsboro Boys."

42 *"I laid on the top bunk"* WGBH Educational Foundation, "Scottsboro: An American Tragedy," https://www.pbs.org/wgbh/americanexperience/films/scottsboro/#transcript (under "transcript" menu).

43 *"I'm just being held"* James Goodman, *Stories of Scottsboro* (Knopf Doubleday Publishing Group, 1995), 275.

43 *"I was on a moving"* WGBH Educational Foundation, "Scottsboro: An American Tragedy; Who Were the Scottsboro Boys?," https://www.pbs.org/wgbh/americanexperience/features /scottsboro-boys-who-were-the-boys/.

44 *"I done give up"* WGBH Educational Foundation, "Scottsboro: An American Tragedy; Who Were the Scottsboro Boys?," https://www.pbs.org/wgbh/americanexperience/features /scottsboro-boys-who-were-the-boys/.

44 *"If I don't get free"* University of Missouri–Kansas City, School of Law Project, "The Scottsboro Boys."

44 *pretty much unheard of* Trish Hall, "I.Q. Scores Are Up, and Psychologists Wonder Why,"

The New York Times, Feb. 24, 1998, https://www.nytimes.com/1998/02/24/science/iq-scores
-are-up-and-psychologists-wonder-why.html.

45 *"The lesson to Black people"* Thomas A. Johnson, "Last of Scottsboro 9 Is Pardoned; He
Draws a Lesson for Everybody," *The New York Times,* October 26, 1976, https://www
.nytimes.com/1976/10/26/archives/last-of-scottsboro-9-is-pardoned-he-draws-a-lesson-for
-everybody.html.

45 *"Please tell all"* WGBH Educational Foundation, "Scottsboro: An American Tragedy; Who
Were the Scottsboro Boys?," https://www.pbs.org/wgbh/americanexperience/features
/scottsboro-boys-who-were-the-boys/.

46 *"Black fiends"* Douglas O. Linder, "The Trials of 'The Scottsboro Boys,'" http://law2.umkc
.edu/faculty/projects/FTrials/scottsboro/SB_acct.html.

46 *"Negro brutes"* Ellis Cose, "The Saga Of The Scottsboro Boys," ACLU.org, July 27, 2020,
https://www.aclu.org/issues/racial-justice/saga-scottsboro-boys.

46 *James Horton, Jr.* The Scottsboro Case, Opinion of Judge James E. Horton, https://
archive.lib.msu.edu/DMC/AmRad/scottsborocase.pdf.

46 *"Did you tell a man"* WGBH Educational Foundation, "Scottsboro: An American Tragedy,"
https://www.pbs.org/wgbh/americanexperience/films/scottsboro/#transcript (under
"transcript" menu).

48 *"Jan 5 1932"* Douglas O. Linder, Letter from Ruby Bates to Earl Streetman [handwritten],
http://law2.umkc.edu/faculty/projects/FTrials/scottsboro/bates-streetman.html.

48 *"Dearest Earl"* William F. Pinar, "The Communist Party/N.A.A.C.P. Rivalry in the Trials of
the Scottsboro Nine," *Counterpoints* 163, https://www-jstor-org.i.ezproxy.nypl.org/stable
/42977762?seq=20.

49 *"you testified"* WGBH Educational Foundation, "Scottsboro: An American Tragedy," https://
www.pbs.org/wgbh/americanexperience/films/scottsboro/#transcript (under "transcript"
menu); William Kunstler, *Politics on Trial* (Ocean Press, 2003), 80–82.

49 *power of the pen* HBCU petition letters, "Letters from the Scottsboro Boys Trials," https://
scottsboroboysletters.as.ua.edu/items/show/608.

49 *the editor of the* Britt Haas, *Fighting Authoritarianism: American Youth in the 1930s* (Ford-
ham University Press, 2017), 61–62.

50 *On April 12* "Letters from the Scottsboro Boys Trials," Alabama Digital Humanities Center,
The University of Alabama, https://scottsboroboysletters.as.ua.edu/items/show/515.

50 *a petition with more* "Letters from the Scottsboro Boys Trials," Alabama Digital Humanities
Center, The University of Alabama, https://scottsboroboysletters.as.ua.edu/items/show
/608.

50 *another telegram* "Letters from the Scottsboro Boys Trials," Alabama Digital Humanities
Center, The University of Alabama, https://scottsboroboysletters.as.ua.edu/items/show/521.

50 *Statewide, Ruby* Britt Haas, *Fighting Authoritarianism: American Youth in the 1930s* (Ford-
ham University Press, 2017), 61–81.

52 *Robert Russa Moton* "Letters from the Scottsboro Boys Trials," Alabama Digital Humanities
Center, The University of Alabama, https://www.scottsboroboysletters.as.ua.edu/items
/show/470.

52 *on December 7, 1933* "Letters from the Scottsboro Boys Trials," Alabama Digital Humanities Center, The University of Alabama, https://scottsboroboysletters.as.ua.edu/items/show
/605.

52 *"Christmas is coming"* Jay Bellamy, "The Scottsboro Boys: Injustice in Alabama," *The Journal of the National Archives* 46 (2014), https://www.archives.gov/files/publications/prologue/2014/spring/scottsboro.pdf.

53 *Norris v. Alabama*, 294 U.S. 587 (1935), https://supreme.justia.com/cases/federal/us/294/587/.

55 *Clarence was paroled* Thomas A. Johnson, "Scottsboro Defendant Applies for a Pardon," *The New York Times*, October 9, 1976, https://www.nytimes.com/1976/10/09/archives/scottsboro-defendant-applies-for-a-pardon-scottsboro-defendant.html.

55 *officially free* John Edmond Mays and Richard S. Jaffe, "History Corrected: The Scottsboro Boys Are officially Innocent," National Association of Criminal Defense Lawyers, 2014, https://www.rjaffelaw.com/documents/Jaffe_History_Corrected_March_2014.pdf.

55 *Andy Wright died* https://findagrave.com/memorial/152204814/andrew-wright.

56 *Roberson died* https://www.findagrave.com/memorial/14586006/willie-roberson.

56 *Weems died* https://www.findagrave.com/memorial/14583963/charles-weems.

56 *Williams died* https://www.findagrave.com/memorial/14584082/eugene-williams.

56 *Patterson died* University of Missouri-Kansas City, School of Law Project, "The Scottsboro Boys."

56 *Montgomery died* https://www.findagrave.com/memorial/14584030/olen-montgomery.

56 *LeRoy Wright died* https://www.findagrave.com/memorial/127502358/leroy-r.-wright.

56 *Powell died* https://www.findagrave.com/memorial/14583788/ozie-powell.

56 *Norris died* Albin Krebs, "Clarence Norris, The Last Survivor of 'Scottsboro Boys,' Dies at 76," *The New York Times*, January 26, 1989, https://www.nytimes.com/1989/01/26/obituaries/clarence-norris-the-last-survivor-of-scottsboro-boys-dies-at-76.html.

57 *convicted rapist* Susan Saulny, "5 in Jogger Case Plan to Sue, Lawyers Say," *The New York Times*, March 15, 2003, https://www.nytimes.com/2003/03/15/nyregion/5-in-jogger-case-plan-to-sue-lawyers-say.html.

3. AN UPRISING COMES

58 *"I will not just shut up"* ESPN, "Lebron James has no plans to 'shut up and dribble,'" February 17, 2018, https://www.espn.com/nba/story/_/id/22481008/lebron-james-cleveland-cavaliers-doubles-will-continue-discuss-social-issues.

59 *In 1996, when NBA player* Jacob Uitti, "Mahmoud Abdul-Rauf: 'I lost millions because I couldn't keep my mouth shut,'" *The Guardian*, October 15, 2022, https://www.theguardian.com/sport/2022/oct/15/mahmoud-abdul-rauf-nba-protest-national-anthem.

60 *were blacklisted* Kevin Draper and Ken Belson, "Colin Kaepernick and the N.F.L. Settle Collusion Case," *The New York Times*, February 15, 2019, https://www.nytimes.com/2019/02/15/sports/nfl-colin-kaepernick.html.

60 *Second World War* David Vergun, "Significant Events of World War II," *U.S. Department of Defense News*, August 14, 2020, https://www.defense.gov/News/Feature-Stories/story/article/2293108/.

60 *about 25 percent* Iowa PBS Documentary, "Impact of World War II on the U.S. Economy and Workforce," https://www.iowapbs.org/iowapathways/artifact/1590/impact-world-war-ii-us-economy-and-workforce.

60 *over 33 million* Calculation based on 25 percent of the U.S. population at the time of

132,164,569 (132,164,569 x .25 = 33,041,142.2), https://www.census.gov/history/www /through_the_decades/fast_facts/1940_fast_facts.html.

60 *dropped to 10 percent* Iowa PBS Documentary, "Impact of World War II on the U.S. Economy and Workforce," https://www.iowapbs.org/iowapathways/artifact/1590/impact-world -war-ii-us-economy-and-workforce.

60 *immense inflation* Chair Cecilia Rouse, Jeffery Zhang, and Ernie Tedeschi, "Historical Parallels to Today's Inflationary Episode," *The White House Written Materials*, July 6, 2021, https://www.whitehouse.gov/cea/written-materials/2021/07/06/historical-parallels-to -todays-inflationary-episode/.

60 *deadliest wars in history* Caitlin McLean, "When Did World War II Start? The Deadliest International Conflict Explained," *USA Today*, September 16, 2022, https://www.usatoday .com/story/news/world/2022/09/16/when-was-world-war-2/8035788001/.

61 *more than 12 million* Jonathan E. Vespa, "Those Who Served: America's Veterans from World War II to the War on Terror," *American Community Survey Report*, U.S. Census Bureau, p. 3–4; before World War II less than 500k; this number jumped to 12.1 million during the war, peaking at 16.1 million.

61 *struggling economy* Alan S. Milward, *War, Economy and Society, 1939–1945* (Penguin, 1977), 105–109.

61 *formation of the United Nations* "History of the United Nations," https://www.un.org/en /about-us/history-of-the-un.

61 *discrimination and segregation* John W. Jeffries, William M. Tuttle, Jr., Nelson Lichtenstein, and Harvard Sitkoff, "World War II and the American Home Front," National Park Service, U.S. Department of the Interior, National Historic Landmarks Program 2007 study, https:// www.nps.gov/subjects/nationalhistoriclandmarks/upload/WWII_and_the_American _Home_Front-508.pdf.

61 *Segregation in sports* David K. Wiggins and Ryan Swanson, eds., *Separate Games: African American Sport behind the Walls of Segregation* (The University of Arkansas Press, 2016).

62 *40,000 mostly white* "History of NYU: Milestones from 1831 to the Present," https://www .nyu.edu/about/news-publications/history-of-nyu.html.

63 *October 4, 1940* Arthur J. Daley, "Coach Puzzled by N.Y.U. Failure to Make Its Aerial Attack Click," *The New York Times*, October 4, 1940, https://timesmachine.nytimes.com /timesmachine/1940/10/04/113107842.html?pageNumber=32.

64 *Washington Square College Bulletin* Emily Rose Clayton, "Archivist Angle: The 'Bates Seven' Stood Against Racial Discrimination in College Athletics," March 15, 2020, https://www .nyu.edu/alumni/news-publications/nyu-connect-newsletter/march-2020/archivist-bates -seven.html.

64 *accused the administration* Donald Spivey, "'End Jim Crow in Sports': The Protest at New York University, 1940–1941," *Journal of Sport History* 15, no. 3, 1988, https://www-jstor-org .i.ezproxy.nypl.org/stable/pdf/43609226.pdf?refreqid=excelsior%3Aa8605827ba300a47176 7305397256318&ab_segments=&origin=&initiator=&acceptTC=1.

64 *seven NYU students* Donald Spivey, *Racism, Activism, and Integrity in College Football: The Bates Must Play Movement* (Carolina Academic Press, 2021).

66 *Black-owned publications* Donald Spivey, "'End Jim Crow in Sports': The Protest at New York University, 1940–1941," *Journal of Sport History* 15, no. 3, https://www-jstor-org.i .ezproxy.nypl.org/stable/pdf/43609226.pdf?refreqid=excelsior%3Aa8605827ba300a471767 305397256318&ab_segments=&origin=&initiator=&acceptTC=1.

66 *Mal, the coach* Times Wide World, "Stevens Goes Rival One Better In Worry Over N.Y.U. Reserves," *The New York Times,* October 19, 1940, https://timesmachine.nytimes.com /timesmachine/1940/10/19/94006351.html?pageNumber=18.

71 *"We were not social friends"* From the documentary on Naomi Rothschild archives, https:// naomirothschild.com/activism/bates/index.html.

71 *"We just did it"* From the documentary on Naomi Rothschild archives, https:// naomirothschild.com/activism/bates/index.html.

71 *"For somebody"* (and all the Seven's profiles) From the documentary on Naomi Rothschild archives, https://naomirothschild.com/activism/bates/index.html.

72 *Azulay death* https://ancestors.familysearch.org/en/LRJ7-VW3/jean-azulay-1921–2008.

73 *Mervyn Jones* Geoffrey Goodman, "Mervyn Jones obituary," *The Guardian,* February 25, 2010, https://www.theguardian.com/books/2010/feb/25/mervyn-jones-obituary.

73 *never return* "Mervyn Jones," *The Telegraph,* February 24, 2010, https://www.telegraph.co .uk/news/obituaries/politics-obituaries/7309497/Mervyn-Jones.html.

74 *Argyle Stoute* Alan Feuer, "Harlem Journal; Honoring Dr. Argyle Stoute, 97, a Man of Many Honors," *The New York Times,* July 24, 2004, https://www.nytimes.com/2004/07/24 /nyregion/harlem-journal-honoring-dr-argyle-stoute-97-a-man-of-many-honors.html.

75 *Madison, he became Indianapolis Recorder* mention, October 20, 1945, https://newspapers .library.in.gov/cgi-bin/indiana?a=d&d=INR19451020–01&e=-------en-20--1--txt-txIN-------.

75 *Negro Culture Association* "Black History Month at UW-Madison: Argyle Stoute," posted by Jillian Slaight for UW-Madison Archives, https://www.tumblr.com/uwmadarchives /138731118853/black-history-month-at-uw-madison-argyle-stoute.

76 *career in genetics* Claudia Dreifus, "Evelyn Witkin and the Road to DNA Enlightenment," *The New York Times,* December 14, 2015, https://www.nytimes.com/2015/12/15/science /evelyn-witkin-and-the-road-to-dna-enlightenment.html.

77 *In 1953* New York University, "NYU Football, what happened?," April 9, 2013, https:// nyunews.com/2013/04/09/football-4/.

77 *"For the past two"* "N.Y.U. Drops Football," March 9, 1942, https://content.time.com/time /subscriber/article/0,33009,885939,00.html.

77 *May 4, 2001* Edward Wong, "College Football; N.Y.U. Honors Protesters It Punished in '41," *The New York Times,* May 4, 2001, https://www.nytimes.com/2001/05/04/sports /college-football-nyu-honors-protesters-it-punished-in-41.html.

4. THE CIVIL RIGHTS MOVEMENT

81 *"It was time that Negroes"* Jeanne Theoharis, *A More Beautiful and Terrible History* (Beacon Press, 2018), 143

81 *"There wasn't any fear"* Larry Bleiberg, "Barbara Johns: The US' forgotten civil rights hero," BBC, December 12, 2022, https://www.bbc.com/travel/article/20221211-barbara-johns-the -us-forgotten-civil-rights-hero.

83 *Post–World War II* Neil A. Wynn, "The 'Good War': The Second World War and Postwar American Society," *Journal of Contemporary History* 31, no 3, 1996, https://www-jstor-org.i .ezproxy.nypl.org/stable/261016.

83 *experiences of returning Black soldiers* James Baldwin, *The Fire Next Time* (Knopf, reissue, 1992), 20.

84 *Black middle class* Edwin Harwood, "Black Progress Is Happening, Too," *The Wall Street*

Journal, February 2, 1971, from: Congressional Record, Proceedings and Debates of the 92nd Congress, Vol. 117, Part 2, 1624–1625.

86 *Robert Russa Moton High* The WNET Group Documentary, "The Rise and Fall of Jim Crow: Barbara Johns of Farmville, Virginia," full transcript, https://ny.pbslearningmedia.org /resource/bf10.socst.us.global.farmville/barbara-johns-of-farmville-virginia/.

87 *Barbara Johns* (and general detailing) Teri Kanefield, *The Girl From the Tar Paper School: Barbara Rose Johns and the Advent of the Civil Rights Movement* (Abrams, 2014); Robert Collins Smith, *They Closed Their Schools: Prince Edward County, Virginia, 1951–1964* (Chapel Hill, University of North Carolina Press, 1965), 53.

95 *spread across Farmville* Katy June-Friesen, "Massive Resistance in a Small Town: Before and after *Brown* in Prince Edward County, Virginia," *Humanities* 34, no. 5 (2013), https://www .neh.gov/humanities/2013/septemberoctober/feature/massive-resistance-in-small-town.

95 *roughly 4,000* Teri Kanefield, *The Girl From the Tar Paper School: Barbara Rose Johns and the Advent of the Civil Rights Movement* (Abrams, 2014), 31.

99 *"The problem is that"* Teri Kanefield, *The Girl From the Tar Paper School: Barbara Rose Johns and the Advent of the Civil Rights Movement* (Abrams, 2014), 32.

100 *"Don't let Mr. Charlie"* Teri Kanefield, *The Girl From the Tar Paper School: Barbara Rose Johns and the Advent of the Civil Rights Movement* (Abrams, 2014), 34.

100 *"were at first"* Robert Collins Smith, *They Closed Their Schools: Prince Edward County, Virginia, 1951–1964* (Chapel Hill, University of North Carolina Press, 1965), 53.

101 *consolidated with the* "Timeline of Events Leading to the *Brown v. Board of Education Decision* of 1954," National Archives, https://www.archives.gov/education/lessons/brown-v -board/timeline.html.

103 *Across the South* "The Closing of Prince Edward County's Schools," Virginia Museum of History and Culture, https://virginiahistory.org/learn/civil-rights-movement-virginia /closing-prince-edward-countys-schools.

104 *segregation in Prince Edward County* University of Virginia, Virginia Center for Digital History, "Television News of the Civil Rights Era 1950–1970," http://www2.vcdh.virginia .edu/civilrightstv/wdbj/segments/WDBJ1_12.html.

104 *Robert Crawford* University of Virginia, Virginia Center for Digital History, "Television News of the Civil Rights Era 1950–1970," http://www2.vcdh.virginia.edu/civilrightstv /glossary/people-061.html.

104 *Defenders of State Sovereignty* University of Virginia, Virginia Center for Digital History, "Television News of the Civil Rights Era 1950–1970," http://www2.vcdh.virginia.edu /civilrightstv/wdbj/segments/WDBJ1_06.html.

105 *"We must achieve"* P. O'Connell Pearson, *We Are Your Children Too: Black Students, White Supremacists, and the Battle for America's Schools in Prince Edward County, Virginia* (Simon & Schuster, 2023), 130.

5. THE REVOLT CEMENTED

108 *"When you're in Mississippi"* The Civil Rights Movement Archive, A Project by Bay Area Veterans of the Civil Rights Movement, "Charlie Cobb," https://www.crmvet.org/vet/cobbc.html.

110 *At the break of dawn* C-Span archive video, "1963 March on Washington," https://www.c -span.org/video/?10928-1/1963-march-washington.

110 *250,000, to be exact* "Official Program for the March on Washington (1963)," National

Archives, https://www.archives.gov/milestone-documents/official-program-for-the-march
-on-washington.

110 *June 21, 1963* "Eyes on the Prize," interview with John Lewis, https://americanarchive.org
/catalog/cpb-aacip_151-8k74t6fv60.

110 *President John F. Kennedy* The JFK Library Archives, "Making the March on Washington, August 28, 1963," https://jfk.blogs.archives.gov/2020/08/27/making-the-march-on
-washington/.

110 *leaders of this march* David Matthews, "Kennedy White House Had Jitters Ahead of 1963
March on Washington," CNN, August 28, 2013, https://www.cnn.com/2013/08/28/politics
/march-on-washington-kennedy-jitters/index.html.

110 *James Farmer* JFK Library Archives, Oral History Interview, James Farmer, https://www
.jfklibrary.org/sites/default/files/archives/JFKOH/Farmer,%20James%20L/JFKOH-JLF-01
/JFKOH-JLF-01-TR.pdf.

110 *John Lewis of the Student* JFK Library Archives, Oral History Interview, John R. Lewis,
https://www.jfklibrary.org/asset-viewer/archives/jfkoh-jrl-01.

110 *at this point* William P. Jones, *The March on Washington: Jobs, Freedom, and the Forgotten
History of Civil Rights* (W.W. Norton & Company, 2013).

111 *Birmingham* Martin Luther King, Jr., "Letter to Local Clergy," The Martin Luther King, Jr.
Research and Education Institute Archives, Stanford University, https://okra.stanford.edu
/transcription/document_images/undecided/630416–019.pdf.

111 *young people* David Halberstam, *The Children* (Fawcett, 1998).

111 *Greensboro* The Civil Rights Movement Archive, A Project by Bay Area Veterans of the
Civil Rights Movement, "The Greensboro Sit-Ins," https://www.crmvet.org/tim/timhis60
.htm#1960greensboro.

112 *firebrand grassroots organizer* PBS LearningMedia, "Ella Baker and the SNCC," https://ny
.pbslearningmedia.org/resource/mr13.socst.us.ellabaker/ella-baker-and-the-sncc/.

112 *Operation Mississippi* "MFDP Lauderdale County—Voting Information-Mississippi,
1962–1966 (Mississippi Freedom Democratic Party. Lauderdale County [Miss.] records,
1964–1966; Historical Society Library Microforms Room, Micro 55, Reel 3, Segment
65)," Freedom Summer Digital Collection, Wisconsin Historical Society, https://content
.wisconsinhistory.org/digital/collection/p15932coll2/id/55713.

112 *efforts extended statewide* "Leaflet for Mississippi Freedom Summer," National Museum of
African American History and Culture, https://nmaahc.si.edu/object/nmaahc_2011.109.3
?destination=/explore/collection/search%3Fedan_fq%255B0%255D%3Dtopic%253A%252
2Civil%2520rights%2522%26edan_fq%255B1%255D%3Dtopic%253A%2522Mississippi%
2520Freedom%2520Summer%2522.

114 *ended with a meeting* White House History, "President Kennedy Meets Civil Rights Leaders," August 28, 1963, https://www.whitehousehistory.org/photos/president-kennedy-meets
-civil-rights-leaders.

114 *White House's Oval Office* Library of Congress, "Civil Rights Leaders Meet with President
John F. Kennedy in the Oval Office of the White House after the March on Washington,
D.C.," https://www.loc.gov/item/2013648833/.

114 *September 15, 1963* Federal Bureau of Investigation, "Baptist Street Church Bombing,"
https://www.fbi.gov/history/famous-cases/baptist-street-church-bombing.

114 *October 7, Alabama troopers* Equal Justice Initiative, "Alabama Troopers Attack Black
People Registering to Vote in Selma," https://calendar.eji.org/racial-injustice/oct/7.

114 *coalition of local and national* Council of Federated Organizations, "Mississippi Freedom Summer" leaflet, https://nmaahc.si.edu/object/nmaahc_2011.109.3?destination=/explore /collection/search%3Fedan_fq%255B0%255D%3Dtopic%253A%2522Civil%2520rights%2 522%26edan_fq%255B1%255D%3Dtopic%253A%2522Mississippi%2520Freedom%2520S ummer%2522.

114 *Freedom Summer American Experience: Freedom Summer,* directed by Stanley Nelson (2014, Firelight Films production for American Experience), https://www.pbs.org/wgbh /americanexperience/films/freedomsummer/; The Civil Rights Movement Archive, A Project by Bay Area Veterans of the Civil Rights Movement, "Mississippi Summer Project Brochure," https://www.crmvet.org/docs/fs64-1.pdf.

115 *create a learning environment* Jon N. Hale, *The Freedom Schools: Student Activists in the Mississippi Civil Rights Movement* (Columbia University Press, 2016).

115 *Charles* Louie Estrada, "Pastor, Activist Charles Cobb Dies," *The Washington Post,* January 1, 1999, https://www.washingtonpost.com/archive/local/1999/01/01/pastor-activist-charles -cobb-dies/fa47d4e1-ee76-4d28-8b7e-5be2f260dcc2/; Charles Earl Cobb, 82, Minister and Advocate for Civil Rights," *The New York Times,* January 4, 1999, https://www.nytimes.com /1999/01/04/nyregion/charles-earl-cobb-82-minister-and-advocate-for-civil-rights.html.

115 *Martha* The Civil Rights Movement Archive, A Project by Bay Area Veterans of the Civil Rights Movement, "Charlie Cobb: Impact of the Sit-Ins," https://www.crmvet.org/nars /cobb1.htm#cobbhoward.

116 *father's alma mater* William Minter, Gail Hovey, and Charles Cobb, eds., *No Easy Victories: African Liberation and American Activists Over a Half Century, 1950–2020* (Africa World Press, 2007), 100–102.

116 *the teen plunged deeper* The Civil Rights Movement Archive, A Project by Bay Area Veterans of the Civil Rights Movement, "Charlie Cobb," https://www.crmvet.org/vet/cobbc.htm.

117 *Lawrence Guyot* "Charlie Cobb," SNCC Digital Gateway, https://snccdigital.org/people /charlie-cobb/.

118 *"Leaving now"* The Civil Rights Movement Archive, A Project by Bay Area Veterans of the Civil Rights Movement, "Charlie Cobb," https://www.crmvet.org/vet/cobbc.htm.

118 *White Citizens' Councils* WGBH Educational Foundation, "American Experience: White Citizens' Councils," https://www.pbs.org/wgbh/americanexperience/features/emmett -citizens-council/.

118 *all-white, all-men* Mississippi Department of Archives & History "The Mississippi State Sovereignty Commission: An Agency History," https://mshistorynow.mdah.ms.gov/issue /mississippi-sovereignty-commission-an-agency-history.

119 *John Lewis's* John Lewis, "Speech at the March on Washington," Voices of Democracy, The U.S. Oratory Project, https://voicesofdemocracy.umd.edu/lewis-speech-at-the-march-on -washington-speech-text/.

119 *Mississippi Freedom Democratic Party* John Dittmer, *Local People: The Struggle for Civil Rights in Mississippi* (University of Illinois Press, 1994).

119 *Summer's ten-week* Charlie Cobb, *On the Road to Freedom: A Guided Tour of the Civil Rights Trail* (Algonquin, 2008).

119 *recruiting volunteers* Elizabeth Martinez, ed., *Letters from Mississippi: Reports from Civil Rights Volunteers and Poetry of the 1964 Freedom Summer* (Zephyr Press, 2007).

119 *young white students* Mary King, *Freedom Song: A Personal Story of the 1960s Civil Rights Movement* (William Morrow, 1987).

120 *Charlie began penning a proposal* Charlie Cobb, "Prospectus for a Summer Freedom School Program," Freedom Summer Digital Collection, Wisconsin Historical Society, https://content.wisconsinhistory.org/digital/collection/p15932coll2/id/30109.

123 *The total cost to execute* Using Cobb's proposals, here is the calculation: The total cost for two sessions of one day of school was $3,995 (that'd be around $39,570 using the U.S. Bureau of Labor Statistics inflation calculator, https://www.bls.gov/data/inflation_calculator.htm). So for twenty days, the total would be $79,900 (in today's economy, $791,300). The cost for the two residential schools was $34,200, or $338,747 today. So combined, the total cost to execute both the day and boarding programs was $3,995 + $79,900 + $34,200 = $118,095, or $1,169,716 today.

124 *three volunteers* John Dittmer, *Local People: The Struggle for Civil Rights in Mississippi* (University of Illinois Press, 1994), 246–283; 418–419.

124 *dozen KKK members* Bruce Watson, *Freedom Summer: The Savage Season That Made Mississippi Burn and Made America a Democracy* (Penguin, 2010).

124 *met with increased harassment* The Civil Rights Movement Archive, A Project by Bay Area Veterans of the Civil Rights Movement, Charlie Cobb, "Some Notes on Education," https://www.crmvet.org/info/cobb_education.pdf.

124 *Freedom Schools* Charles E. Cobb, Jr. and Bob Moses, *Radical Equations: Civil Rights from Mississippi to the Algebra Project* (Beacon Press, 2001).

125 *Jacqulyn Reed Cockfield* The Civil Rights Movement Archive, A Project by Bay Area Veterans of the Civil Rights Movement, "Jacqulyn Reed Cockfield," https://www.crmvet.org/vet/reedj.htm.

125 *Pam Parker* The Civil Rights Movement Archive, A Project by Bay Area Veterans of the Civil Rights Movement, "Chude Pam Parker Allen," https://www.crmvet.org/vet/chude.htm.

125 *one of the program's white teachers* The Civil Rights Movement Archive, A Project by Bay Area Veterans of the Civil Rights Movement, "Interview on Being a Freedom School Teacher," https://www.crmvet.org/vet/chude.htm.

127 *achieved one of its most* The Civil Rights Movement Archive, A Project by Bay Area Veterans of the Civil Rights Movement, "Freedom Summer: The Results," https://www.crmvet.org/tim/tim64b.htm#1964fsresults.

128 *Stokely Carmichael* Stokely Carmichael, *Ready for Revolution: The Life and Struggles of Stokely Carmichael* (Scribner, 2003).

128 *at an SNCC rally at Stone Street* Mark Whitaker, *Saying It Loud: 1966—The Year Black Power Challenged the Civil Rights Movement* (Simon & Schuster, 2023).

128 *Black Power for Black People* "Black Power," The National Archives, https://www.archives.gov/research/african-americans/black-power.

128 *"We have been saying 'Freedom Now'"* Mark Whitaker, *Saying It Loud: 1966—The Year Black Power Challenged the Civil Rights Movement* (Simon & Schuster, 2023), 152–153.

129 *the Black Power movement* Dan Berger, "The Black Power Movement Is a Love Story," *Time,* February 23, 2023, https://time.com/6257292/black-power-movement-love-story/.

129 *speech he gave at* Stokely Carmichael, "Black Power" transcript, Voices of Democracy, The U.S. Oratory Project, October 29, 1966, https://voicesofdemocracy.umd.edu/carmichael-black-power-speech-text/.

129 *"Every civil rights bill"* "Black Power" audio and text transcript, American Radio Works, October 29, 1966, https://americanradioworks.publicradio.org/features/blackspeech/scarmichael.html.

6. BLACK POWER RISES

133 *New Hanover High School* (and overall detailing of the Ten's ordeal) Kenneth Robert Janken, *The Wilmington Ten: Violence, Injustice, and the Rise of Black Politics in the 1970s* (The University of North Carolina Press, 2015).

134 *During this period* Kenneth Robert Janken, "Remembering the Wilmington Ten: African American Politics and Judicial Misconduct in the 1970s," *The North Carolina Historical Review* 92, no.1, https://www-jstor-org.i.ezproxy.nypl.org/stable/44113248.

136 *allyship to the cause* "New Information Offered in Wilmington 10 Case," *The New York Times*, February 13, 1977, https://timesmachine.nytimes.com/timesmachine/1977/02/13/113458875.html?pageNumber=26.

137 *Robert Teel* Timothy B. Tyson, *Blood Done Sign My Name: A True Story* (Crown, 2007), 233

137 *"Shoot the son of a bitch"* Timothy B. Tyson, *Blood Done Sign My Name: A True Story* (Crown, 2007), 233.

137 *organized a large boycott* "1970 Oxford Murder Sparked Violent Protests," North Carolina Department of Natural and Cultural Resources, May 11, 2016, https://www.dncr.nc.gov/blog/2016/05/11/1970-oxford-murder-sparked-violent-protests.

138 *Harvey Cumber* Scott Nunn, "Death Toll Reaches Two in Racial Unrest," *StarNews*, June 6, 2018, https://www.starnewsonline.com/story/special/special-sections/2018/06/06/back-then-feb-1971-2nd-death-in-wilmington-racial-unrest/12031455007/.

138 *About a century before that day* Adrienne LaFrance and Vann R. Newkirk II, "The Lost History of an American Coup D'État," *The Atlantic*, August 12, 2017, https://www.theatlantic.com/politics/archive/2017/08/wilmington-massacre/536457/.

138 *integrated port city Wilmington on Fire*, directed by Chris Everett (Speller Street Films, Double7 Images, Blackhouse Publishing, 2015).

138 *a diverse population* According to the 1890 U.S. census, the demographics of Wilmington, North Carolina's demographic was: total population: 25,748; White: 13,627 (53 percent); Black: 12,107 (47 percent); Other: 14, https://www2.census.gov/library/publications/decennial/1910/abstract/supplement-nc.pdf, first table on page 32.

140 *In West Oakland* (and general detailing) Joshua Bloom and Waldo E. Martin, *Black Against Empire: The History and Politics of the Black Panther Party* (University of California Press, 2012).

141 *Bobby Seale* Bobby Seale, *A Lonely Rage* (Times Books, 1978).

142 *Then, on September 27* Gary Kamiya, "Officer's '66 killing of black teen sparked Hunters Point riots," *San Francisco Chronicle*, September 17, 2016, https://www.sfchronicle.com/bayarea/article/Officer-s-66-killing-of-black-teen-sparked-9228042.php.

143 *Artie McMillan* (and general detailing) Author conducted interviews with Artie McMillan over phone and in person between June 20, 2022, and October 6, 2023.

143 *We want freedom* Kathleen Cleaver and George Katsiaficas, *Liberation, Imagination and the Black Panther Party* (Taylor & Francis, 2001), "Appendices."

147 *community survival programs* "Community Survival Programs," PBS.org, https://www.pbs.org/hueypnewton/actions/actions_survival.html.

148 *anti-Apartheid student* Patricia Ward Biederman, "1980s Protesters Push Anti-Apartheid

Point Politely," *Los Angeles Times,* April 27, 1985, https://www.latimes.com/archives/la-xpm-1985-04-27-me-12676-story.html.

148 *student movement* Kathie Sheldon, "Anti-Apartheid Organizing on Campus," *The Radical Teacher,* no. 21, https://www-jstor-org.i.ezproxy.nypl.org/stable/20709346.

149 *Steve Biko* Lindy Wilson, *Steve Biko* (Ohio University Press, 2011).

149 *Barney Pityana* Steve Biko, *I Write What I Like: Selected Writings* (University of Chicago Press, 1978).

151 *In 1973, Steve was banned The Testimony of Steve Biko,* edited by Millard W. Arnold (Pan Macmillan South Africa, 1978).

153 *Hector Pieterson* Aryn Baker, "This Photo Galvanized the World Against Apartheid. Here's the Story Behind It," Time.com, https://time.com/4365138/soweto-anniversary-photograph/.

155 *Free South Africa Movement* Krissah Thompson, "On Mandela Day, D.C. Founders of Free South Africa Movement Look Back," *The Washington Post,* July 17, 2013, https://www.washingtonpost.com/lifestyle/style/on-mandela-day-dc-founders-of-free-south-africa-movement-look-back/2013/07/17/61db5a5e-eee1-11e2-a1f9-ea873b7e0424_story.html.

155 *HBCU students also formed* Amanda Joyce Hall, "Black Students and the U.S. Anti-Apartheid Movements on Campus, 1976–1985," *The Journal of Critical Global South Studies* 6–1, https://international.vlex.com/vid/black-students-and-the-924380954.

155 *Other campuses* "African Activist Archives," Michigan State University, https://africanactivist.msu.edu/browse/us-organizations/.

156 *They faced a daunting* Tom Wicker, "The Wind in the Pines," *The New York Times,* December 26, 1975, https://timesmachine.nytimes.com/timesmachine/1975/12/26/80107985.html?pageNumber=31.

156 *HBCUs like Howard* Jason Jett, "Wilmington Ten Supporters Call for Federal Intervention," Howard University's *The Hilltop,* February 10, 1978, https://dh.howard.edu/cgi/viewcontent.cgi?referer=&httpsredir=1&article=1203&context=hilltop_197080.

156 *The New York Times* Wayne King, "The Case Against The Wilmington Ten," *The New York Times,* December 3, 1978, https://timesmachine.nytimes.com/timesmachine/1978/12/03/112818892.html?pageNumber=499.

158 *the conviction* Craig M. Stinson, "Wilmington Ten," NCPedia.org, https://www.ncpedia.org/wilmington-ten.

158 *Sentenced to thirty-four years* "Benjamin Chavis, Jr.," The National Registry of Exonerations, https://www.law.umich.edu/special/exoneration/pages/casedetail.aspx?caseid=5021.

159 *"And so then"* Michael Myerson, *Nothing Could Be Fine* (International Publishers, 1978), afterword, https://archive.org/stream/nothingcouldbefi00myer_0/nothingcouldbefi00myer_0_djvu.txt; Tom Wicker, "So Many Quirks and Turns in It," *The New York Times,* March 18, 1977, https://timesmachine.nytimes.com/timesmachine/1977/03/18/75052458.html?pageNumber=20.

160 *"as much a victim"* Warren Brown, "U.S. Probe of Case of 'Wilmington 10' Gives Activist Hope," *The Washington Post,* February 14, 1977, https://www.washingtonpost.com/archive/politics/1977/02/14/us-probe-of-case-of-wilmington-10-gives-activist-hope/58fcc877-74a3-49c6-a581-1e396a8c6ae9/.

160 *Winston-Salem, home to the* Philip S. Foner, *The Black Panthers Speak* (Lippincott, 2002).

161 *On January 23, 1978* Wayne King, "Carolina Governor Shortens Terms for Wilmington 10 in Firebombing," *The New York Times*, January 24, 1978, https://timesmachine.nytimes.com/timesmachine/1978/01/24/110778731.html.

162 *"We want their feet"* Patricia Camp, "Black Panther Cofounder Addresses 200 at Rally Backing Wilmington 10," *The Washington Post*, February 5, 1978, https://www.washingtonpost.com/archive/local/1978/02/05/black-panther-cofounder-addresses-200-at-rally-backing-wilmington-10/141f310f-b9e1-4ebf-930c-5fdccb3b7bb8/.

163 *Barack Obama* Margot Mifflin, "Obama at Occidental," *The New Yorker*, October 3, 2012, https://www.newyorker.com/news/news-desk/obama-at-occidental.

163 *after the rally* Barack Obama, *Dreams from My Father: A Story of Race and Inheritance* (Crown, 2004), 105.

163 *students kept on* The South Africa Catalyst Project, "Anti-Apartheid Organizing on Campus . . . and Beyond," 1978, https://projects.kora.matrix.msu.edu/files/210-808-8293/aaorgandbeyond1978.pdf; "How American Students Affected the Anti-Apartheid Movement," *BET News*, https://www.bet.com/photo-gallery/ksyhc8/how-american-students-affected-the-anti-apartheid-movement/.

164 *pressured* Stephen Kaufman, "Pressure to End Apartheid Began at Grass Roots in U.S.," *U.S. Mission to International Organizations in Geneva*, December 16, 2013, https://geneva.usmission.gov/2013/12/17/pressure-to-end-apartheid-began-at-grass-roots-in-u-s/.

164 *Comprehensive Anti-Apartheid Act* House Resolution 4868, https://www.congress.gov/bill/99th-congress/house-bill/4868.

165 *collapse of the Soviet Union* Vladimir Gennad'evich Shubin, *ANC: A View from Moscow* (Jacana Media, 2008), 301.

165 *"it gave me a sense of"* Ari Shapiro, "Obama: Time for a Mutually Beneficial Alliance With Africa," NPR, June 28, 2013.

166 *with drug dealer Tyrone Robinson* "Arrest in Murder of Huey Newton," *The New York Times*, August 26, 1989, https://timesmachine.nytimes.com/timesmachine/1989/08/26/633389.html?pageNumber=7.

7. TOUGHER ON BLACKS

171 *"We have predators"* Senator Joe Biden, Crime Bill Speech November 18, 1993, https://www.youtube.com/watch?v=3HY45DY2B8w.

173 *three nooses* "Race, Violence . . . Justice? Looking Back at Jena 6," NPR, August 30, 2011, https://www.npr.org/2011/08/30/140058680/race-violence-justice-looking-back-at-jena-6.

173 *a privilege* Amy Goodman, "Tipping the Scales of Justice in Jena," *Common Dreams*, September 19, 2007, https://www.commondreams.org/views/2007/09/19/tipping-scales-justice-jena.

173 *Only white students* Amy Waldman, "The Truth About Jena," *The Atlantic*, January/February 2008, https://www.theatlantic.com/magazine/archive/2008/01/the-truth-about-jena/306580/.

174 *"Y'all want to go stand"* Amy Goodman, "It's Still About Race in Jena, La.," *Seattle Post-Intelligencer*, July 18, 2007, https://www.seattlepi.com/local/opinion/article/it-s-still-about-race-in-jena-la-1244014.php.

174 *"They said, 'If you go,'"* Amy Goodman, "It's Still About Race in Jena, La.," *Seattle*

Post-Intelligencer, July 18, 2007, https://www.seattlepi.com/local/opinion/article/it-s-still
-about-race-in-jena-la-1244014.php.

175 *student body of 521* Lesli A. Maxwell, "'Jena Six': Case Study in Racial Tensions," *Ed Week*,
September 28, 2007, https://www.edweek.org/leadership/jena-six-case-study-in-racial
-tensions/2007/09.

175 *Billy Wayne Fowler* Amy Goodman, "Tipping the Scales of Justice in Jena," *Common
Dreams*, September 19, 2007, https://www.commondreams.org/views/2007/09/19/tipping
-scales-justice-jena.

176 *early morning of November 30* Gil Kaufman, "Jena Six: What Sparked Protesters to Descend
on Small Town in Louisiana?," MTV News, September 19, 2007, https://www.mtv.com/news
/psk44a/jena-six-what-sparked-protesters-to-descend-on-small-town-in-louisiana.

176 *Gotta-Go Grocery store* "'A Modern-Day Lynching'–Parents of Jena Six Speak of Injustice, Racism in Sons' Prosecution," *Democracy Now*, September 21, 2007, https://www
.democracynow.org/2007/7/10/a_modern_day_lynching_parents_of.

176 *"I know they were in fear"* "'A Modern-Day Lynching'–Parents of Jena Six Speak of
Injustice, Racism in Sons' Prosecution," *Democracy Now*, September 21, 2007, https://www
.democracynow.org/2007/7/10/a_modern_day_lynching_parents_of.

177 *"If any fight would"* John Barr and Nicole Noren, "'Jena Six' Controversy Swirls Around
Football Star," ESPNews, September 21, 2007, https://www.espn.com/espn/news/story?id
=3030458.

178 *up to one hundred years* "Racial Discrimination and the Legal System: The Recent Lessons
of Louisiana," *Democracy Now*, July 10, 2007, https://www.democracynow.org/2007/7/10
/the_case_of_the_jena_six.

178 *Their bail* Bill Quigley, "Racial Discrimination and the Legal System: The Recent Lessons
of Louisiana," United Nations, *UN Chronicle*, https://www.un.org/en/chronicle/article
/racial-discrimination-and-legal-system-recent-lessons-louisiana.

179 *his all-star status* Amy Waldman, "The Truth About Jena," *The Atlantic*, January/Febru-
ary 2008, https://www.theatlantic.com/magazine/archive/2008/01/the-truth-about-jena
/306580/.

179 *"The DA is a racist"* "The Case of the Jena Six: Black High School Students Charged with
Attempted Murder for Schoolyard Fight After Nooses Are Hung from Tree," *Democracy
Now*, July 10, 2007, https://www.democracynow.org/2007/7/10/the_case_of_the_jena_six.

179 *"They want to take"* "Live from Jena: Two Mothers of the Jena Six React to Outpour of
Support for their Sons," *Democracy Now*, September 21, 2007, https://www.democracynow
.org/2007/9/21/live_from_jena_two_mothers_of.

179 *"I ain't got no"* "The Case of the Jena Six: Black High School Students Charged with Attempted Murder for Schoolyard Fight After Nooses Are Hung from Tree," *Democracy Now*,
July 10, 2007, https://www.democracynow.org/2007/7/10/the_case_of_the_jena_six.

180 *"You can just say, 'Forever'"* "The Case of the Jena Six: Black High School Students Charged
with Attempted Murder for Schoolyard Fight After Nooses Are Hung from Tree," *Democracy
Now*, July 10, 2007, https://www.democracynow.org/2007/7/10/the_case_of_the_jena_six.

181 *Violent Crime Control and Law Enforcement Act* U.S. Department of Justice Fact Sheet,
"Violent Crime Control and Law Enforcement Act of 1994," https://www.ncjrs.gov/txtfiles
/billfs.txt; Sheryl Gay Stolberg and Astead W. Herndon, "'Lock the S.O.B.s Up': Joe Biden
and the Era of Mass Incarceration," *The New York Times*, June 25, 2019, https://www
.nytimes.com/2019/06/25/us/joe-biden-crime-laws.html.

182 *the youngest senator* Jim Newell, "When Joe Biden Was the Candidate of the Young," *Slate,* June 11, 2019, https://slate.com/news-and-politics/2019/06/joe-biden-1972-race-senate .html.

182 Joe *Biden came up* Adam Entous, "The Untold History of the Biden Family," *The New Yorker,* August 15, 2022, https://www.newyorker.com/magazine/2022/08/22/the-untold -history-of-the-biden-family; John M. Broder, "Father's Tough Life an Inspiration for Biden," *The New York Times,* October 23, 2008, https://www.nytimes.com/2008/10/24/us /politics/24biden.html.

182 *"Joe Biden: He understands"* Edward-Isaac Dovere, "The Gray Race for the White House," *The Atlantic,* April 27, 2019, https://www.theatlantic.com/politics/archive/2019/04/biden -sanders-trump-2020/588211/.

182 *out of touch* Bo Erickson, "When a Young Joe Biden Used His Opponent's Age Against Him," CBS News, June 4, 2019, https://www.cbsnews.com/news/when-a-young-joe-biden -used-his-opponents-age-against-him/.

182 *"I knew blacks"* Joe Biden, *Promises to Keep: On Life and Politics* (Random House, 2007), 43.

182 *"the first sort of mainstream"* Mike Memoli, "Political Partners, Personal Friends: Inside the Obama-Biden bond," review of *Barack and Joe: The Making of an Extraordinary Partnership,* by Steven Levingston, *The Washington Post,* October 4, 2019, https://www .washingtonpost.com/outlook/political-partners-personal-friends-inside-the-obama-biden -bond/2019/10/03/e9088cba-e52d-11e9-b403-f738899982d2_story.html.

183 *In response to* the president's Senator Joe Biden, Democratic Response to Drug Policy Address, September 5, 1989, https://www.c-span.org/video/?8997-1/democratic-response -drug-policy-address.

183 *drug policy address* President George Bush Drug Policy Address, September 5, 1989, https:// www.c-span.org/video/?8921-1/presidential-address-national-drug-policy; text: https:// www.presidency.ucsb.edu/documents/address-the-nation-the-national-drug-control -strategy.

183 *"predators"* Senator Joe Biden, Crime Bill Speech, November 18, 1993, https://www .youtube.com/watch?v=3HY45DY2B8w.

183 *a year of its rollout* The Sentencing Project, "The Color of Justice: Racial and Ethnic Disparity in State Prisons," 13, https://www.sentencingproject.org/app/uploads/2022/08 /The-Color-of-Justice-Racial-and-Ethnic-Disparity-in-State-Prisons.pdf; The Sentencing Project, "Counting Down: Paths to a 20-year Maximum Prison Sentence," https://www .sentencingproject.org/app/uploads/2023/02/Counting-Down-Paths-to-20-Year-Maximum -Prison-Sentence.pdf; executive summary: https://www.sentencingproject.org/reports /counting-down-paths-to-a-20-year-maximum-prison-sentence/.

183 *five times higher* The Sentencing Project, "The Color of Justice: Racial and Ethnic Dispar-ity in State Prisons," https://www.sentencingproject.org/reports/the-color-of-justice-racial -and-ethnic-disparity-in-state-prisons-the-sentencing-project/.

183 *quarter of states* The Sentencing Project, "The Color of Justice: Racial and Ethnic Disparity in State Prisons," 12 states mentioned, https://www.sentencingproject.org/reports/the-color -of-justice-racial-and-ethnic-disparity-in-state-prisons-the-sentencing-project/.

183 *the rise of mass incarceration* Lauren-Brooke Eisen, "The 1994 Crime Bill and Beyond: How Federal Funding Shapes the Criminal Justice System," Brennan Center for Justice, September 9, 2019, https://www.brennancenter.org/our-work/analysis-opinion/1994-crime -bill-and-beyond-how-federal-funding-shapes-criminal-justice.

183 *In 1997* U.S. Department of Justice, Office of Justice Programs, "Prevalence of Imprisonment in the U.S. Population, 1974–2001," https://bjs.ojp.gov/content/pub/pdf/piusp01.pdf.

184 *the prison population* U.S. Department of Justice, Office of Justice Programs, "Prevalence of Imprisonment in the U.S. Population, 1974–2001," https://bjs.ojp.gov/content/pub/pdf /piusp01.pdf.

184 *Amadou Diallo* Jane Fritsch, "The Diallo Verdict: The Overview; 4 Officers in Diallo Shooting Are Acquitted of All Charges," *The New York Times,* February 26, 2000, https:// timesmachine.nytimes.com/timesmachine/2000/02/26/009040.html.

184 *The same was true in Louisiana* The White House Archive, President Clinton and Vice President Gore's Accomplishments: Louisiana, https://clintonwhitehouse4.archives.gov /WH/Accomplishments/states/Louisiana.html.

184 *the Community Oriented* U.S. Department of Justice, *Community Policing Defined,* https:// portal.cops.usdoj.gov/resourcecenter/RIC/Publications/cops-p157-pub.pdf.

184 *the Jena Six* Joseph E. Kennedy, "The Jena Six, Mass Incarceration, and the Remoralization of Civil Rights," *Harvard Civil Rights-Civil Liberties Law Review,* 2009, https://core.ac .uk/download/pdf/151520509.pdf.

184 *studies show that Jena had* "'Jena Six' Case: Hate Crimes And Race-Related Violence In Public Schools," October 16, 2007, https://www.c-span.org/video/?201553–1/jena-case#.

187 *man was on his way* Matt Flegenheimer and Al Baker, "Officer in Bell Killing Is Fired; 3 Others to Be Forced Out," *The New York Times,* March 23, 2012, https://www.nytimes.com /2012/03/24/nyregion/in-sean-bell-killing-4-officers-to-be-forced-out.html.

187 *The Jena Six's separate* Anthony V. Alfieri, "Prosecuting the Jena Six," *Cornell Law Review* 93, no. 6 (2008), https://scholarship.law.cornell.edu/cgi/viewcontent.cgi?referer =&httpsredir=1&article=3110&context=clr.

188 *that Mychal's sneakers* "Racial Tensions Rip Apart Tiny Jena, La." *Newsweek,* August 15, 2007, https://www.newsweek.com/racial-tensions-rip-apart-tiny-jena-la-99225.

189 *threw out Mychal's* "Charges Dropped for One of 'Jena Six'," ABC News, January 8, 2009, https://abcnews.go.com/GMA/story?id=3607084&page=1.

190 *Students empowered by* Richard G. Jones, "Thousands Protest Arrests of 6 Blacks in Jena, La.," *The New York Times,* September 21, 2007, https://www.nytimes.com/2007/09/21/us /21cnd-jena.html; Jenny Jarvie and Richard Fausset, "Protesters March to Support 'Jena Six'," *Los Angeles Times,* September 21, 2007, https://www.latimes.com/archives/la-xpm -2007-sep-21-na-jena21-story.html.

190 *Jasmyne Cannick* Jenny Jarvie and Richard Fausset, "Protesters March to Support 'Jena Six'," *Los Angeles Times,* September 21, 2007, https://www.latimes.com/archives/la-xpm -2007-sep-21-na-jena21-story.html.

190 *"racism still alive and kickin'"* Jenny Jarvie and Richard Fausset, "Protesters March to Support 'Jena Six'," *Los Angeles Times,* September 21, 2007, https://www.latimes.com/archives /la-xpm-2007-sep-21-na-jena21-story.html.

190 *Morehouse College* "Students from HBCUs, Other Schools Gear up for March in Support of Jena Six," Associated Press, September 18, 2007, https://www.diverseeducation.com /institutions/hbcus/article/15085422/students-from-hbcus-other-schools-gear-up-for -march-in-support-of-jena-six.

190 *They stomped for* "Ga. Students Who Support 'Jena 6,' Will Join Others in Louisiana," Associated Press, September 18, 2007, https://accesswdun.com/article/2007/9/90423.

191 *cultural pillar figures* John Barr and Nicole Noren, "'Jena Six' Controversy Swirls Around

Football Star," ESPN News, September 21, 2007, https://www.espn.com/espn/news/story?id=3030458.

192 *who said of the ongoing* Audie Cornish, "'Jena Six' Case Prompts Mass Demonstrations," *All Things Considered*, September 20, 2007, https://www.npr.org/2007/09/20/14574972/jena-six-case-prompts-mass-demonstrations.

193 *"No justice!"* Audie Cornish, "'Jena Six' Case Prompts Mass Demonstrations," *All Things Considered*, September 20, 2007, https://www.npr.org/2007/09/20/14574972/jena-six-case-prompts-mass-demonstrations.

193 "Free the Jena Six" "Protesters March in Support of Jena Six," NPR, September 20, 2007, https://www.npr.org/2007/09/20/14556993/protesters-march-in-support-of-jena-six.

194 *On October 16, witnesses presented* "'Jena Six' Case: Hate Crimes and Race-Related Violence in Public Schools," October 16, 2007, https://www.c-span.org/video/?201553-1/jena-case#.

194 *he presented data* "'Jena Six' Case: Hate Crimes and Race-Related Violence in Public Schools" October 16, 2007, https://www.c-span.org/video/?201553-1/jena-case#.

195 *each received* "Jena 6 Case Wrapped Up with Plea Bargain," *The Guardian,* June 26, 2009, https://www.theguardian.com/world/2009/jun/26/jena-6-louisiana-plea-bargain.

195 *$500 fine and seven* "Plea Agreement Reached in Jena Six Case," *The Southern Poverty Law Center,* June 26, 2009, https://www.splcenter.org/news/2009/06/26/plea-agreement-reached-jena-six-case.

195 *the Jena Six kept a* Mary Foster, "5 years later, Jena 6 move on," NBC News, August 25, 2011, https://www.nbcnews.com/id/wbna44275022.

195 *Some went on to college* Alan Bean, "Jena 6 Defendants Make the Most of a Second Chance," https://friendsofjustice.blog/2014/05/12/jena-6-defendants-make-the-most-of-a-second-chance/; Alan Bean, "Jena 6 Students Get Some Positive Publicity," https://friendsofjustice.blog/2009/08/25/1789/.

195 *"When people ask me where I'm from"* Alan Bean, "Jena 6 Students Get Some Positive Publicity," https://friendsofjustice.blog/2009/08/25/1789/.

195 *"Carry yourself in the right manner"* Abby Cruz and Kiara Alfonseca, "Member of 'Jena Six' Speaks Out on Race and the Justice System 15 Years Later," ABC News, December 4, 2021, https://abcnews.go.com/US/member-jena-speaks-race-justice-system-15-years/story?id=81490112.

195 *reportedly tried to end* "'Jena 6' Teen Attempts Suicide," NPR, January 5, 2009, https://www.npr.org/2009/01/05/99010714/roundtable-jena-6-teen-attempts-suicide.

196 *While incarcerated, Theo* Terry Carter, "Once Facing a 50-Year Sentence, a Jena 6 Member Now Looks to His Future: Law School," *ABA Journal,* April 14, 2015, https://abajournal.com/news/article/once_facing_a_50_year_sentence_a_jena_6_member_now_looks_to_the_future_law.

196 *"I was forced to be hopeful"* Terry Carter, "Once Facing a 50-Year Sentence, a Jena 6 Member Now Looks to His Future: Law School," *ABA Journal,* April 14, 2015, https://abajournal.com/news/article/once_facing_a_50_year_sentence_a_jena_6_member_now_looks_to_the_future_law.

196 *a criminal statute* "RS 14:40.5 Public display of a noose on property of another or public place; intent to intimidate," https://law.justia.com/codes/louisiana/2009/rs/title14/rs14-40.5.html.

196 *the lasting effect of the crime bill* Lauren Gambino, "'Things Have Changed': Can Biden Overcome the Racist Legacy of the Crime Bill He Backed?," *The Guardian,* October 17,

2020, https://www.theguardian.com/us-news/2020/oct/17/joe-biden-race-crime-bill-1994
-policing.

8. A RESURRECTION OF BLACK LIBERATION

198 *saw young voters turn out* Tom Rosentiel, "Young Voters in the 2008 Election," Pew Research Center, November 13, 2008, https://www.pewresearch.org/2008/11/13/young-voters
-in-the-2008-election/.

199 *"young and old"* "Transcript of Barack Obama's Victory Speech," NPR, November 5, 2008, https://www.npr.org/2008/11/05/96624326/transcript-of-barack-obamas-victory-speech.

200 *Between 1999 and 2019* Using https://fatalencounters.org/ database, the calculation is as follows: (1) Filter by RACE (column E), select all but WHITE. (2) Filter by DATE (column I), select only 1999 to 2019 dates.

200 *in this period* Using https://fatalencounters.org/ database, the calculation is as follows: (1) Filter by RACE (column E), select all. (2) Filter by DATE (column I), select only 1999 to 2019 dates.

200 *Around 6 p.m.* (and general detailing) CNN Editorial Research, "Trayvon Martin Shooting Fast Facts," CNN, February 15, 2023, https://www.cnn.com/2013/06/05/us/trayvon-martin
-shooting-fast-facts/index.html.

200 *his father's girlfriend* (and general detailing) Sybrina Fulton and Tracy Martin, *Rest in Power: The Enduring Life of Trayvon Martin* (Random House, 2017).

201 *With a population of* Sanford, Florida, demographics data, https://sanfordfl.gov
/government/economic-development/demographics/; Population census data, https://www
.census.gov/quickfacts/sanfordcityflorida.

201 *fourteen-year-old son* Dan Barry, Serge F. Kovaleski, Campbell Robertson, and Lizette Alvarez, "Race, Tragedy and Outrage Collide After a Shot in Florida," *The New York Times*, April 1, 2012, https://www.nytimes.com/2012/04/02/us/trayvon-martin-shooting-prompts
-a-review-of-ideals.html.

202 *It was a pleasant* Weather on February 26, 2012, https://www.wunderground.com/history
/daily/KSFB/date/2012–2-26.

202 *Chad had asked* Dan Barry, Serge F. Kovaleski, Campbell Robertson, and Lizette Alvarez, "Race, Tragedy and Outrage Collide After a Shot in Florida," *The New York Times*, April 1, 2012, https://www.nytimes.com/2012/04/02/us/trayvon-martin-shooting-prompts-a
-review-of-ideals.html.

202 *Rachel Jeantel* Jelani Cobb, "Rachel Jeantel on Trial," *The New Yorker*, June 27, 2013, https://
www.newyorker.com/news/news-desk/rachel-jeantel-on-trial.

202 *Sean Noffke* "George Zimmerman Trial: Witness Sean Noffke," Local 10 News, June 26, 2013, https://www.local10.com/news/2013/06/26/george-zimmerman-trial-witness-sean
-noffke/.

202 *"Sanford Police Department"* "Transcript of George Zimmerman's Call to the Police," City of Sanford, Florida, https://archive.org/details/326700-full-transcript-zimmerman
/mode/2up; searchable text available at http://law2.umkc.edu/faculty/projects/ftrials
/zimmerman1/zimcalls.html.

202 *"This is Sean"* "President Obama: Trayvon Martin Made America Confront Its Original Sin," *The New York Times*, February 26, 2022, https://www.youtube.com/watch?v
=C1kTEit6-qw.

204 *Trayvon was like any* (and general detailing) Sybrina Fulton and Tracy Martin, *Rest in Power: The Enduring Life of Trayvon Martin* (Random House, 2017).

204 *His friends and football coach* Kim Segal, "Protesters Declare 'I am Trayvon Martin,' But Who Was He?," CNN, https://www.cnn.com/2012/03/30/us/trayvon-martin-profile/index .html.

205 *"Are you following"* "Transcript of George Zimmerman's Call to the Police," City of Sanford, Florida, https://archive.org/details/326700-full-transcript-zimmerman/mode/2up; searchable text available at http://law2.umkc.edu/faculty/projects/ftrials/zimmerman1 /zimcalls.html.

207 *Rachel said she told* "Lawyer: Girl on Phone with Trayvon Martin Cuts Shooter's Self-Defense Claim," CNN, March 20, 2012, https://www.cnn.com/2012/03/20/justice/florida -teen-shooting.

207 *"And what, if, if anything"* "The George Zimmerman Files: Critical Phone Calls," http://law2 .umkc.edu/faculty/projects/ftrials/zimmerman1/zimcalls.html.

208 *9-1-1* Police transcript, https://famous-trials.com/images/ftrials/zimmerman/documents /Zimmerman_Document_E.pdf.

209 *laid out on the grass* "Jury Sees Images of Trayvon Martin's Body," YouTube video, 1:01, https://www.youtube.com/watch?v=wguTBaFUg1c.

210 *"Trayvon Martin looked like I did"* President Barack Obama, "President Obama: Trayvon Martin Made America Confront Its Original Sin," *The New York Times,* February 26, 2022, https://www.youtube.com/watch?v=C1kTEit6-qw.

210 *the teen's hoodie became a symbol* Manuel Roig-Franzia, "What Became of Trayvon Martin's Hoodie?," *The Washington Post,* March 17, 2022, https://www.washingtonpost.com /lifestyle/2022/03/17/trayvon-hoodie-in-smithsonian/.

210 *Lebron even took* Alex Rodriguez, "Trayvon Martin: Miami Heat Pose in Hoodies," *Miami New Times,* March 23, 2012, https://www.miaminewtimes.com/news/trayvon-martin -miami-heat-pose-in-hoodies-6528715.

211 *South African American* "Daniel Maree: A Civil Rights Leader for the 21st Century," *The Denver Post,* September 6, 2013, https://www.denverpost.com/2013/09/06/daniel-maree-a -civil-rights-leader-for-the-21st-century/.

211 *Daniel Maree* "The Million Hoodies Movement for Justice," https://olbios.org/the-million -hoodies-movement-for-justice/.

212 *more than a thousand* Ryan Devereaux, "Trayvon Martin's Parents Speak at New York March: 'Our Son Is Your Son,'" *The Guardian,* March 22, 2012, https://www.theguardian .com/world/2012/mar/22/trayvon-martin-million-hoodie-march-new-york.

212 *the event's Facebooking the ral page* "A Million Hoodies March for Trayvon Martin—NYC," Facebook event invitation, https://www.facebook.com/events/347784265268106/.

212 *During the rally* Margot Adler, "Crowds Join Slain Youth's Parents in 'Hoodie March,'" NPR, March 22, 2012, https://www.npr.org/2012/03/22/149126029/crowds-join-slain -youths-parents-in-hoodie-march.

212 *"My heart is in pain"* Jennifer Preston and Colin Moynihan, "Death of Florida Teen Spurs Outcry and Action," *The New York Times,* March 21, 2012, https://archive.nytimes.com /thelede.blogs.nytimes.com/2012/03/21/death-of-florida-teen-spurs-national-outrage-and -action/.

212 *"We need this kind of"* Margot Adler, "Crowds Join Slain Youth's Parents in 'Hoodie March,'" NPR, March 22, 2012, https://www.npr.org/2012/03/22/149126029/crowds-join -slain-youths-parents-in-hoodie-march.

213 *"This is a tragedy"* President Barack Obama, "Obama Answers Question on Trayvon

Martin 3/23/2012," https://www.c-span.org/video/?c5059011/user-clip-obama-answers -question-trayvon-martin-3232012.

213 *"With every time"* Philip Agnew remarks, "Dream Defenders—Beyond the Soundbites," YouTube video, 9:04, https://www.youtube.com/watch?v=Xx5tCP1yEIE.

214 *three Black women organizers* "Alicia Garza, Patrisse Cullors, Opal Tometi: Activists; The Three-Word Civil Rights Movement," *Politico Magazine* (2015), https://www.politico.com /magazine/politico50/2015/alicia-garza-patrisse-cullors-opal-tometi/.

214 *Those three words* Sam Sanders, Andrea Gutierrez, Anjuli Sastry Krbechek, Liam McBain, Jinae West, Aja Drain, and Jordana Hochman, "Trayvon, Ten Years Later," NPR, February 25, 2022, https://www.npr.org/2022/02/24/1082855107/trayvon-martin-ten-years -later.

215 *John Crawford III* Mark Berman, "No indictments after police shoot and kill man at an Ohio Wal-Mart; Justice Dept. launches investigation," *The Washington Post*, September 24, 2014, https://www.washingtonpost.com/news/post-nation/wp/2014/09/24/no-indictments -after-police-shoot-and-kill-man-at-an-ohio-wal-mart-justice-dept-launches-investigation/.

215 *Johnetta Elzie* (and general detailing) Author conducted interviews with Johnetta Elzie on July 28, 2023, and August 8, 2023.

215 *Young Pharaoh* Frances Robles and Julie Bosman, "Autopsy Shows Michael Brown Was Struck at Least 6 Times," *The New York Times,* August 17, 2014, https://www.nytimes.com /2014/08/18/us/michael-brown-autopsy-shows-he-was-shot-at-least-6-times.html.

215 *"Im about to"* @emantreeman, "Im about to hyperventilate," Twitter, August 24, 2019, 9:03 a.m., https://twitter.com/emantreeman/status/498152622012907520.

216 *Darren received a dispatch* (and general detailing) Jake Halpern, "The Cop," *The New Yorker,* August 3, 2015, https://www.newyorker.com/magazine/2015/08/10/the-cop.

217 *the Department of Justice report* Memorandum: Department of Justice Report Regarding the Criminal Investigation Into the Shooting Death of Michael Brown by Ferguson, Missouri Police Officer Darren Wilson, March 4, 2015, https://www.justice.gov/sites /default/files/opa/press-releases/attachments/2015/03/04/doj_report_on_shooting_of _michael_brown_1.pdf.

217 *his six years on the force* German Lopez, "Who Is Darren Wilson, the Officer Who Shot Michael Brown?," *Vox*, January 27, 2016, https://www.vox.com/2015/5/31/17937866/darren -wilson-ferguson-police-officer-michael-brown.

220 *her best friend* Ray Downs, "Still No Answers Seven Months After Police Shoot and Kill Stephon Averyhart," *Riverfront Times*, September 15, 2014, https://www.riverfronttimes .com/news/still-no-answers-seven-months-after-police-shoot-and-kill-stephon-averyhart -2603992.

220 *Howell School District* Trymaine Lee, "Missouri School Busing Causes 'Crippling' Fallout," MSNBC, December 8, 2013, https://www.msnbc.com/msnbc/heres-how-not-deal-failing -schools-msna226786.

222 *a video on YouTube* Frances Robles and Julie Bosman, "Autopsy Shows Michael Brown Was Struck at Least 6 Times," *The New York Times,* August 17, 2014, https://www.nytimes .com/2014/08/18/us/michael-brown-autopsy-shows-he-was-shot-at-least-6-times.html.

222 *It was around this time* (and general detailing) Author conducted interviews with Johnetta Elzie on July 28, 2023, and August 8, 2023.

222 *"immediately after that"* (and general detailing) Author conducted interviews with Johnetta Elzie on July 28, 2023, and August 8, 2023.

222 *"It's still blood on the ground"* Johnetta Elzie (@Nettaaaaaaaa), "It's still blood on the ground where Mike Brown Jr was murdered. A cone in place where his body laid for hours today," August 9, 2014, 7:00 p.m., https://twitter.com/Nettaaaaaaaa/status /498302845196574721.

223 *At a candlelight vigil* Associated Press, "Timeline of Events in Shooting of Michael Brown in Ferguson," August 8, 2019, https://apnews.com/article/shootings-police-us-news-st -louis-michael-brown-9aa32033692547699a3b61da8fd1fc62; Johnetta Elzie, "Ferguson Forward: 'When I Close My Eyes At Night, I See People Running From Tear Gas,'" *Ebony,* September 8, 2014, https://www.ebony.com/ferguson-forward-when-i-close-my-eyes-at -night-i-see-people-running-from-tear-ga/.

224 *DeRay Mckesson* Jay Caspian Kang, "'Our Demand Is Simple: Stop Killing Us,'" *The New York Times,* May 4, 2015, https://www.nytimes.com/2015/05/10/magazine/our-demand-is -simple-stop-killing-us.html.

225 *This Is the Movement* Molly Sims, "Fighting Chance: How Johnetta Elzie Became a Civil Rights Crusader," *Oprah.com,* https://www.oprah.com/omagazine/johnetta-elzie-this-is-the -movement.

225 *Samuel Sinyangwe* Elizabeth Day, "#BlackLivesMatter: The Birth of a New Civil Rights Movement," *The Guardian,* July 19, 2015, https://www.theguardian.com/world/2015/jul/19 /blacklivesmatter-birth-civil-rights-movement.

225 *Mapping Police Violence* "Mapping Police Violence," https://mappingpoliceviolence .org/.

225 *in 1994, Congress had mandated* "What Is Police Brutality? Depends on Where You Live," NBC News, January 13, 2014, https://www.nbcnews.com/news/us-news/what-police -brutality-depends-where-you-live-n8816.

226 *The Washington Post* "Pulitzer Prize-Winning Fatal Force Database Updated with Federal Ids of Police Departments Involved in Fatal Shootings," *The Washington Post,* December 6, 2022, https://www.washingtonpost.com/pr/2022/12/06/pulitzer-prize -winning-fatal-force-database-updated-with-federal-ids-police-departments-involved -fatal-shootings/.

226 *Fatal Force Database The Washington Post,* https://www.washingtonpost.com/graphics /investigations/police-shootings-database/.

226 *Police Scorecard* "Police Scorecard Project Methodology," https://policescorecard.org /about.

227 *270 Black people* Using https://fatalencounters.org/ database, the calculation is as follows: (1) Filter by RACE (column E), AFRICAN AMERICAN. (2) Filter by DATE (column I): August 2014-March 2015. (3) Total count is 271.

227 *They were released* Doug Porter, "Ferguson Report: Black Lives, Still Trying to Matter," *San Diego Free Press,* August 11, 2015, https://sandiegofreepress.org/2015/08/ferguson-report -black-lives-still-trying-to-matter/.

228 *"I think it's wonderful"* Sandhya Somashekhar, "Protesters Slam Oprah Over Comments That They Lack 'Leadership,'" *The Washington Post,* January 2, 2015, https://www.washingtonpost.com/news/post-nation/wp/2015/01/02/protesters-slam-oprah -over-comments-that-they-lack-leadership/.

228 *Similarly, Hillary Clinton* Barrett Holmes Pitner, "How Hillary Let Down #BlackLives-Matter," *The Daily Beast,* August 18, 2015, https://www.thedailybeast.com/how-hillary-let -down-blacklivesmatter.

228 *"The next question by"* GOOD *Magazine*, "Hillary Clinton Talks With BlackLivesMatter | EXCLUSIVE | Part 1," YouTube video, 7:52, August 18, 2015, https://www.youtube.com /watch?v=1eCraUvIq-s&list=PLUgRTD1mpwSV7arDsfvTHRta0lM0hs8nX; Andrew Prokop, "Hillary Clinton's Brutal Frankness to Black Lives Matter Reveals Her Approach to Politics," *Vox*, August 19, 2015, https://www.vox.com/2015/8/19/9174077/hillary-clinton -black-lives-matter.

228 *Longtime activist* Jason Rosenbaum, "Johnson, Sharpton Lead Electrifying Rally for Michael Brown," St. Louis Public Radio, NPR, August 17, 2014, https://www.stlpr.org /government-politics-issues/2014–08–17/johnson-sharpton-lead-electrifying-rally-for -michael-brown.

228 *"there's a difference"* Yamiche Alcindor and Brandie Piper, "Clashes on Second Night of Ferguson Curfew," *USA Today*, August 17, 2014, https://www.usatoday.com/story/news /nation/2014/08/17/missouri-brown-curfew-protests/14207423/.

228 *Sharpton's National Action Network* Darryl Fears, "Thousands Join Al Sharpton in 'Justice for All' March in D.C.," *The Washington Post*, December 13, 2014, https://www .washingtonpost.com/national/health-science/sharpton-to-lead-justice-for-all-march-in -dc/2014/12/13/36ce8a68–824f-11e4–9f38–95a187e4c1f7_story.html.

229 *"We started this"* Elizabeth Day, "#BlackLivesMatter: The Birth of a New Civil Rights Movement," *The Guardian*, July 19, 2015, https://www.theguardian.com/world/2015/jul/19 /blacklivesmatter-birth-civil-rights-movement.

229 *"We, the youth"* Elizabeth Day, "#BlackLivesMatter: The Birth of a New Civil Rights Movement," *The Guardian*, July 19, 2015, https://www.theguardian.com/world/2015/jul/19 /blacklivesmatter-birth-civil-rights-movement.

232 *Trayvon was buried* (and general detailing) Sybrina Fulton and Tracy Martin, *Rest in Power: The Enduring Life of Trayvon Martin* (Random House, 2017).

232 *"Home Going Celebration"* Edecio Martinez, "Fla. Teen Trayvon Martin Killed by Neighborhood Watch Volunteer," CBS News, March 19, 2012, https://www.cbsnews.com/pictures /fla-teen-trayvon-martin-killed-by-neighborhood-watch-volunteer/. Photo caption: "Here is the program to the funeral service for Trayvon Martin, which was held on March 3, 2012."

232 *My Brother's Keeper* The White House, "Remarks by the President on 'My Brother's Keeper' Initiative," February 27, 2014, https://obamawhitehouse.archives.gov/the-press -office/2014/02/27/remarks-president-my-brothers-keeper-initiative.

233 *his mom used to call him* (and general detailing) Author has spoken with Lezley McSpadden-Head on several occasions including via phone and text messaging, inclusive of formal interviews such as the one conducted on May 19, 2021, for *The Washington Post*: https://www.washingtonpost.com/nation/2021/05/21/what-would-have-been-his-25th -birthday-michael-browns-mother-reflects-life-cut-short-ongoing-fight-justice/.

233 *was buried on August 25, 2014* "'Crying for Justice': Thousands Mourn Michael Brown at Funeral," NBC News, August 25, 2014, https://www.nbcnews.com/storyline/michael -brown-shooting/crying-justice-thousands-mourn-michael-brown-funeral-n188346; "Funeral Held for Michael Brown," photo slideshow, *Los Angeles Times*, https:// www.latimes.com/nation/nationnow/la-na-michael-brown-funeral-ferguson-pictures -photogallery.html; "Michael Brown Funeral: St Louis Mourns Ferguson Teenager," BBC News, August 25, 2014, https://www.bbc.com/news/world-us-canada-28924099.

234 *St. Peter's Cemetery* https://www.findagrave.com/memorial/134186325/michael-orlandus _darrion-brown.

235 *Advancing Effective, Accountable Policing* "Advancing Effective, Accountable Policing and Criminal Justice Practices to Enhance Public Trust and Public Safety," Presidential Document by the Executive Office of the President, May 31, 2022, https://www.federalregister .gov/documents/2022/05/31/2022-11810/advancing-effective-accountable-policing-and -criminal-justice-practices-to-enhance-public-trust-and.

235 *Wanda Johnson* Rita Omokha, "They Were Sons," *Vanity Fair*, https://www.vanityfair.com /news/2021/05/they-were-sons-mothers-of-black-men-killed-by-police-remember-their-losses.

9. THE MATTER OF GEORGE FLOYD

238 *"I just cried so much"* (and general detailing) Author conducted interviews with Laila DeWeese on September 30, 2020, and March 24, 2021.

238 *Laila DeWeese* (and general detailing) Author conducted interviews with Laila DeWeese on September 30, 2020, and March 24, 2021.

240 *Samir Abumayyaleh* Aymann Ismail, "The Store That Called the Cops on George Floyd," *Slate*, October 6, 2020, https://slate.com/human-interest/2020/10/cup-foods-george-floyd -store-911-history.html.

240 *The Black man staggered* Eric Levenson, "Here's What Happened to George Floyd From Every Perspective and Angle," CNN, April 5, 2021, https://www.cnn.com/2021/04/05/us /george-floyd-video-angle/index.html; Nicholas Bogel-Burroughs, "Prosecutors Show Surveillance Footage of George Floyd in Cup Foods for the First Time," *The New York Times*, March 31, 2021, https://www.nytimes.com/2021/03/31/us/christopher-martin-cup -foods.html.

240 *He swayed intermittently* MSNBC, "Prosecution Shows Video of George Floyd Inside Store Where He Allegedly Used Counterfeit $20 Bill," YouTube video, 5:42, March 31, 2021, https://www.youtube.com/watch?v=D4LmDdC-elQ.

241 *Christopher Martin* Nicholas Bogel-Burroughs, "Prosecutors Show Surveillance Footage of George Floyd in Cup Foods for the First Time," *The New York Times*, March 31, 2021, https://www.nytimes.com/2021/03/31/us/christopher-martin-cup-foods.html.

241 *The soaring man* ABC News, "Surveillance Cameras Show George Floyd Moments Before His Encounter With Police," YouTube video, 14:15, March 31, 2021, https://www.youtube .com/watch?v=lLuFY6dQmpA.

241 *"took him a little"* Nicholas Bogel-Burroughs, "Prosecutors Show Surveillance Footage of George Floyd in Cup Foods for the First Time," *The New York Times*, March 31, 2021, https:// www.nytimes.com/2021/03/31/us/christopher-martin-cup-foods.html.

241 *Christopher raised the bill* NBC News, "Chauvin Trial: Surveillance Video Shows Inside Convenience Store," YouTube video, 3:35, March 31, 2021, https://www.youtube.com/watch ?v=ifAGCaPk6uQ.

241 *the bill to be counterfeit* Nicholas Bogel-Burroughs and Will Wright, "Little Has Been Said About the $20 Bill That Brought Officers to the Scene," *The New York Times*, April 19, 2021, https://www.nytimes.com/2021/04/19/us/george-floyd-bill-counterfeit.html.

242 *911, what's the address* "Transcript of 911 Call on George Floyd Released," KARE 11, NBC affiliate, May 28, 2020, https://www.kare11.com/article/news/local/george-floyd/transcript -of-911-call-on-george-floyd-is-released/89-34f18837-3b09-421b-b3db-e2c0f5dfa6fa.

244 *NCIC Plate Check* Trail Exhibit 151, "MN v. Derek Michael Chauvin Trial-JENA SCUR-RY-911 DISPATCHER—DIRECT," https://www.gettyimages.co.uk/detail/video/back-to -exhibit-151-you-will-see-a-line-8-08-thats-your-news-footage/1472308232.

244 *"Hey, man. I'm sorry!"* Arrest transcripts, 27-CR-20–12951, filed in District Court, State of Minnesota, https://www.mncourts.gov/mncourtsgov/media/High-Profile-Cases/27-CR -20–12951-TKL/Exhibit207072020.pdf, https://www.mncourts.gov/mncourtsgov/media /High-Profile-Cases/27-CR-20–12951-TKL/Exhibit407072020.pdf (accessed June 4, 2023).

244 *"Hey, man. I'm sorry!"* Arrest transcripts, 27-CR-20–12951, filed in District Court, State of Minnesota, searchable full text, https://archive.org/stream/george-floyd-arrest-transcript /George%20Floyd%20arrest%20transcript_djvu.txt (accessed June 4, 2023).

245 *Dragon Wok* Eric Levenson, "Here's What Happened to George Floyd From Every Perspective and Angle," CNN, April 5, 2021, https://www.cnn.com/2021/04/05/us/george -floyd-video-angle/index.html.

245 *805 East 38th Street* https://www.google.com/maps/@44.9341044,-93.2625725,3a,75y,98. 96h,89.18t/data=!3m6!1e1!3m4!1sUhSMTsOFr3f2hCY8fNGccA!2e0!7i16384!8i8192?en- try=ttu. This was the corner George Floyd was first told to sit next to; in the frame taken on a cell phone by Christopher Belfrey, here, https://www.cnn.com/us/live-news/derek -chauvin-trial-03-31–21/h_ea0bb7d0382f6c2cefc2bcaa7dda25d7, you can see the "805" on the wall. And compared to the map view above, it's the same location.

245 *"Stand up"* Arrest transcripts, 27-CR-20–12951, filed in District Court, State of Minne- sota, https://mncourts.gov/mncourtsgov/media/High-Profile-Cases/27-CR-20-12951-TKL /Exhibit207072020.pdf (accessed February 3, 2023). Arrest transcripts, 27-CR-20–12951, filed in District Court, State of Minnesota, https://mncourts.gov/mncourtsgov/media/High -Profile-Cases/27-CR-20-12951-TKL/Exhibit407072020.pdf (accessed February 3, 2023); searchable full text available at https://archive.org/stream/george-floyd-arrest-transcript /George%20Floyd%20arrest%20transcript_djvu.txt (accessed February 3, 2023).

247 *Judeah Reynolds* (and general detailing) Judeah Reynolds and Lily Coyle, *A Walk to the Store* (Beaver's Pond Press, 2022).

247 *three dollars* Steve Jefferson, "Young Witness Recounts Testimony During Derek Chauvin Trial," 13 WTHR, NBC affiliate, April 21, 2021, https://www.wthr.com/article/news/local /george-floyd/young-witness-judeah-reynolds-testimony-george-floyd-derek-chauvin-trial /531–42dfe061-aa86–4848–828d-dc658f857e02.

247 *day off from working* Wade Hudson and Cheryl Willis Hudson, eds., *Recognize! An An- thology Honoring and Amplifying Black Life* (Random House, 2021), 86.

247 *multi-athlete* "Pen America to Honor Darnella Frazier, Young Woman Who Documented George Floyd's Murder," PEN/Benenson Courage Award, PEN America, December 8, 2020, https://pen.org/press-release/pen-america-to-honor-darnella-frazier-young-woman-who -documented-george-floyds-murder/.

247 *Roosevelt High School* Josh Marcus, "Darnella Frazier, Teen Who Filmed George Floyd's Murder, Awarded Pulitzer Prize," *Independent*, June 11, 2021, https://www.independent.co .uk/news/world/americas/darnella-frazier-george-floyd-pulitzer-b1864411.html; Janelle Griffith, "A High School 2 Miles From Where George Floyd Died Plays Outsize Role in Chauvin Trial," NBC News, April 24, 2021, https://www.nbcnews.com/news/us-news/teen -who-filmed-george-floyd-s-arrest-minneapolis-police-chief-n1265006.

247 *while the Minneapolis native* Josh Marcus, "Darnella Frazier, Teen Who Filmed George Floyd's Murder, Awarded Pulitzer Prize," *Independent*, June 11, 2021, https://www.independent .co.uk/news/world/americas/darnella-frazier-george-floyd-pulitzer-b1864411.html.

249 *"If I had not taken"* Jemima McEvoy, "Derek Chauvin Trial Sees Witnesses, Juror Struggle Emotionally With Recounting George Floyd's Death," *Forbes*, March 31, 2021, https://www .forbes.com/sites/jemimamcevoy/2021/03/31/derek-chauvin-trial-sees-witnesses-juror -struggle-emotionally-with-recounting-george-floyds-death/?sh=48e2d0815e89.

250 *"It wasn't right"* Melissa Macaya, Mike Hayes, Meg Wagner, Melissa Mahtani, and Veronica Rocha, "Derek Chauvin Is on Trial for George Floyd's Death," CNN, March 30, 2021, https://edition.cnn.com/us/live-news/derek-chauvin-trial-day-two-testimony/h_dcf4cbebb42c0456f7cd2501d8de102a.

250 *"He was terrified"* Yamiche Alcindor and Sam Lane, "'He was terrified': Witnesses Offer Emotional Testimony About Floyd Death in Chauvin Case," full transcript, *PBS News Hour*, March 30, 2021, https://www.pbs.org/newshour/show/he-was-terrified-witnesses -offer-emotional-testimony-about-floyd-death-in-chauvin-case.

250 *kneeled harder* Bill Chappell, "'It Wasn't Right,' Young Woman Who Recorded Chauvin and Floyd on Video Tells Court," NPR, March 30, 2021, https://www.npr.org/sections/trial -over-killing-of-george-floyd/2021/03/30/982729306/it-wasnt-right-young-woman-who -recorded-chauvin-and-floyd-on-video-tells-court.

250 *the officers "put their"* Melissa Macaya, Mike Hayes, Meg Wagner, Melissa Mahtani, and Veronica Rocha, "Derek Chauvin Is on Trial for George Floyd's Death," CNN, March 30, 2021, https://edition.cnn.com/us/live-news/derek-chauvin-trial-day-two-testimony/h_dcf4cbebb42c0456f7cd2501d8de102a.

250 *Charles McMillian* Josh Marcus and Graeme Massie, "Charles McMillian: Witness Who Knew Derek Chauvin Breaks Down as He Watches Video of George Floyd Arrest," *Independent*, March 31, 2021, https://www.independent.co.uk/news/world/americas/charles -mccmillian-george-floyd-video-b1825207.html.

251 *Donald Williams* Katrina Pross, "'I called the police on the police,' Says Witness of George Floyd's Arrest," *Twin Cities,* March 30, 2021, https://www.twincities.com/2021/03/30/derek -chauvin-george-floyd-trial-witness-testimony-cell-phone-video/.

251 *Genevieve Hansen* Ray Sanchez, "The Witnesses in Derek Chauvin's Trial Describe Their Guilt and Sadness After George Floyd's Death," CNN, April 1, 2021, https://www.cnn.com /2021/03/31/us/derek-chauvin-trial-witnesses-guilt-helplessness/index.html.

252 *At 9:25 p.m.* FOX9 KMSP *Local News*, "The Death of George Floyd: A Timeline of a Chaotic, Emotional Week in Minneapolis," June 1, 2020, https://www.fox9.com/news/the-death -of-george-floyd-a-timeline-of-a-chaotic-emotional-week-in-minneapolis.

252 *put out a statement* "Investigative Update on Critical Incident," May 26, 2020, https://web .archive.org/web/20200526183652/https://www.insidempd.com/2020/05/26/man-dies -after-medical-incident-during-police-interaction/.

253 *"They killed him"* Brian Dakss, "Video Shows Minneapolis Cop With Knee on Neck of Motionless, Moaning Man Who Later Died," CBS News, May 27, 2020, https://www .cbsnews.com/news/minneapolis-police-george-floyd-died-officer-kneeling-neck-arrest/.

254 *no "medical incident"* Elisha Fieldstadt, "'I can't breathe': Man Dies After Pleading With Officer Attempting to Detain Him in Minneapolis," NBC News, May 26, 2020, https://www .nbcnews.com/news/us-news/man-dies-after-pleading-i-can-t-breathe-during-arrest -n1214586.

255 *Crump's statement* Ben Crump (@AttorneyCrump), "MEDIA ALERT: I have been retained to represent the family of George Floyd, the man killed by Minneapolis Police on May 25. #JusticeForFloyd #ICantBreath," Twitter, May 26, 2020, 7:27 a.m., https://twitter .com/AttorneyCrump/status/1265303494086582272.

255 *"Nobody deserves to die"* Darnella Frazier, Facebook, March 11, 2021, https://www .facebook.com/darnellareallprettymarie/posts/1670313089836457.

256 *One of those marches* Eder Campuzano, "Portland Climate Strike: Students Ditch Class, Fill Downtown Streets, Hawthorne Bridge as Part of Global Protest," *The Oregonian,*

September 20, 2019, https://www.oregonlive.com/news/2019/09/oregon-students-are-ditching-class-to-push-for-a-green-new-deal-today-heres-what-to-expect.html.

257 *autopsy revealed* Hennepin County Medical Examiner's Office, Autopsy Report, https://www.hennepin.us/-/media/hennepinus/residents/public-safety/medical-examiner/floyd-autopsy-6-3-20.pdf (accessed February 7, 2023).

258 *"That's really just fancy"* Fred de Sam Lazaro and Alison Thoet, "Medical Examiner Doubles Down on Original Autopsy Finding, Labels Floyd's Death a Homicide," *PBS News Hour,* April 9, 2021, https://www.pbs.org/newshour/show/medical-examiner-doubles-down-on-original-autopsy-finding-labels-floyds-death-a-homicide.

258 *the names of the four officers* "Minneapolis Releases Identities of 4 Officers Involved in George Floyd's Arrest," CBS, May 27, 2020, https://www.cbsnews.com/minnesota/news/minneapolis-releases-identities-of-4-officers-involved-in-george-floyds-fatal-arrest/.

258 *ongoing street demonstrations* Derrick Bryson Tyler, "George Floyd Protests: A Timeline," *The New York Times,* November 5, 2021, https://www.nytimes.com/article/george-floyd-protests-timeline.html; Beth Dalbey, "Voices From the George Floyd Protests: 'Please Stop Killing Us,'" *Patch,* June 3, 2020, https://patch.com/us/across-america/voices-george-floyd-protests-please-stop-killing-us.

259 *"We are disrupting"* Instagram, May 27,2020, https://www.instagram.com/p/CAtfn8pp0kh.

259 *Meanwhile, as the teens* Samantha Fischer, "3 Years Later: Where Are the Ex-MPD Officers Convicted in George Floyd's 2020 Murder?," KARE 11, NBC affiliate, May 24, 2023, https://www.kare11.com/article/news/local/george-floyd/former-minneapolis-police-department-officers-convicted-in-george-floyds-murder-where-are-they-now/.

259 *Xavier and Akil successfully* Darwin Bond Graham, "How 2 Oakland Students Got 15,000 People to March Against Police Violence on Monday," *Berkeleyside,* June 2, 2020, https://www.berkeleyside.org/2020/06/02/how-oakland-students-got-15000-people-to-march-against-police-violence-on-monday; Sydney Johnson, "Oakland Students Organize Protest of George Floyd Death, Pleading to Be Heard," *EdSource,* June 1, 2020, https://edsource.org/2020/oakland-students-organize-protest-of-george-floyd-murder-pleading-to-be-heard/632891.

259 *in Nashville, Tennessee* Jessica Bennett, "These Teen Girls Are Fighting for a More Just Future," *The New York Times,* July 3, 2020, https://www.nytimes.com/2020/06/26/style/teen-girls-black-lives-matter-activism.html.

259 *The interracial group* Brinley Hineman and Kerri Bartlett, "'Do not be silent': Meet Nashville Teens Who Launched a Movement for Social Change," *The Tennessean,* July 2, 2020, https://www.tennessean.com/story/news/local/williamson/franklin/2020/07/02/meet-nashville-teens-who-launched-movement-social-change/5349352002/; Catherine Park, "'If we can do it, so can you': Nashville Teens Lead 10,000 in Peaceful Protest," Fox 35, June 7, 2020, https://www.fox35orlando.com/news/if-we-can-do-it-so-can-you-nashville-teens-lead-10000-in-peaceful-protest.

260 *more than 10,000* Margaret Renkl, "These Kids Are Done Waiting for Change," *The New York Times,* June 15, 2020, https://www.nytimes.com/2020/06/15/opinion/nashville-teens-protests.html; Alejandro Ramirez, "Teens Lead Thousands in Peaceful March Through Nashville," *Nashville Scene,* June 5, 2020, https://www.nashvillescene.com/news/pithinthewind/teens-lead-thousands-in-peaceful-march-through-nashville/article_783748c4–0bc8–518c-a8d8–19ddcecabb56.html.

260 *"We didn't have a podium"* Jessica Bennett, "These Teen Girls Are Fighting for a More Just

Future," *The New York Times,* July 3, 2020, https://www.nytimes.com/2020/06/26/style/teen
-girls-black-lives-matter-activism.html.

260 *In Washington, D.C.* "Young Activists Find Their Voice Organizing Protests for Racial
Justice in D.C.," NPR, June 7, 2020, https://www.npr.org/2020/06/07/871600315/young
-activists-find-their-voice-organizing-protests-for-racial-justice-in-d-c.

260 *"We spotted each other"* Katanga Johnson, "Floyd's Death Spurs 'Gen Z' Activists to Set
Up New DC Rights Group," Reuters, June 8, 2020, https://www.reuters.com/article/us
-minneapolis-police-protests-day/floyds-death-spurs-gen-z-activists-to-set-up-new-dc
-rights-group-idUSKBN23E0UM/.

261 *Angus King* Katherine Tully-McManus, "Protesters Flood Capitol Hill and Across Washington, Lawmakers Among Them," *Roll Call,* June 7, 2020, https://rollcall.com/2020/06/07
/protesters-flood-capitol-hill-and-across-washington-lawmakers-among-them/.

262 *continued to march on* Marie Fazio, "Minnesota Students Walk Out of Schools in Solidarity With the Racial Justice Movement," *The New York Times,* April 19, 2021, https://www
.nytimes.com/2021/04/19/us/minnesota-school-walkout-chauvin-trial.html.

262 *to fixing racial inequities* Hannah Leone, "Teen Activism in Chicago Spurred by Police Killing of George Floyd: 'We are fed up and this is the last straw,'" *Chicago Tribune,* June 9, 2020,
https://www.nytimes.com/2020/06/26/style/teen-girls-black-lives-matter-activism.html.

262 *Brianna Chandler* Jessica Bennett, "These Teen Girls Are Fighting for a More Just Future,"
The New York Times, July 3, 2020, https://www.nytimes.com/2020/06/26/style/teen-girls
-black-lives-matter-activism.html.

262 *borders—from Europe* Javier C. Hernández and Benjamin Mueller, "Global Anger Grows
Over George Floyd Death, and Becomes an Anti-Trump Cudgel," *The New York Times,* June
1, 2020, https://www.nytimes.com/2020/06/01/world/asia/george-floyd-protest-global.html.

262 *Across London* Mark Brown, "Thousands Gather In Britain to Support US George Floyd
Protests," *The Guardian,* May 31, 2020, https://www.theguardian.com/us-news/2020/may
/31/crowds-gather-in-britain-to-support-us-george-floyd-protests.

262 *deep-rooted legacy* Alana Samuels, "The Racist History of Portland, the Whitest City in
America," *The Atlantic,* July 22, 2016, https://www.theatlantic.com/business/archive/2016
/07/racist-history-portland/492035/.

262 *graduation rates* Susan Anglada Bartley, "The Utopian Dream of Portland Is Lit by Flames
of Racist Hatred: Educating the Next Generation Is Our Only Hope for Change," *Hampton
Think,* June 29, 2017, https://www.hamptonthink.org/read/the-utopian-dream-of-portland-is
-lit-by-flames-of-racist-hatred-educating-the-next-generation-is-our-only-hope-for-change.

263 *one hundred consecutive days* Eder Campuzano, Brooke Herbert, Beth Nakamura, Dave
Killen, and Mark Graves, "100 Days of Protests in Portland," *The Oregonian,* September 5,
2020, https://www.oregonlive.com/portland/2020/09/100-days-of-protests-in-portland.html.

263 *On September 30* Author was in attendance, Portland, Oregon.

263 *the killing of twenty-seven-year-old Patrick Kimmons* Ericka Cruz Guevarra, "2 Portland
Officers Cleared in Fatal Shooting of Patrick Kimmons," Oregon Public Broadcasting,
October 31, 2018, https://www.opb.org/news/article/patrick-kimmons-officers-cleared
-portland-grand-jury/.

265 *prominent perpetrator* State of Minnesota, County of Hennepin, Derek Chauvin Criminal
Complaint, https://mncourts.gov/mncourtsgov/media/High-Profile-Cases/27-CR-20–
12646/AmendedComplaint06032020.pdf.

265 *Derek Chauvin's forty-three-day trial* Melissa Macaya, Mike Hayes, Meg Wagner, Melissa

Mahtani, and Veronica Rocha, "Derek Chauvin Is on Trial for George Floyd's Death," CNN, March 30, 2021, https://edition.cnn.com/us/live-news/derek-chauvin-trial-day-two -testimony/h_dcf4cbebb42c0456f7cd2501d8de102a; Democracy NOW!, "'Check His Pulse': In Derek Chauvin Trial, Outraged Bystanders Describe Witnessing George Floyd Death," April 1, 2021, https://www.democracynow.org/2021/4/1/derek_chauvin_trial_day_3.

265 *had been a repeat offender* http://complaints.cuapb.org/police_archive/officer/2377/; Stephen Montemayor, Jennifer Bjorhus, and Matt McKinney, "Even to Friends, Former Officer Derek Chauvin Was an Enigma," *Star Tribune,* August 8, 2020, https://www .startribune.com/those-who-know-derek-chauvin-say-they-would-not-have-predicted -his-killing-of-george-floyd/572054552/; Abbie Vansickle and Jamiles Lartey, "'That Could Have Been Me': The People Derek Chauvin Choked Before George Floyd," *The Marshall Project,* February 2, 2021, https://www.themarshallproject.org/2021/02/02/that-could-have -been-me-the-people-derek-chauvin-choked-before-george-floyd; in partnership with *The New York Times,* https://www.nytimes.com/2021/02/02/us/derek-chauvin-george-floyd -past-cases.html.

266 *Latrell Toles* Pilar Melendez, "Minneapolis Man: Cop Who Kneeled on George Floyd 'Tried to Kill Me' in 2008," *The Daily Beast,* May 28, 2020, https://www.thedailybeast.com /minneapolis-man-alleges-derek-chauvin-tried-to-kill-him-before-he-kneeled-on-george -floyd.

266 *LaSean Braddock* Janelle Griffith, "'He choked me out': Others Detail Allegations of Abuse by Officer Who Knelt on George Floyd," NBC News, March 3, 2021, https://www.nbcnews .com/news/us-news/he-choked-me-out-others-detail-allegations-abuse-officer-who -n1259207.

266 *Zoya Code* "Top Lieutenant Calls Derek Chauvin's Actions 'Totally Unnecessary,'" *The New York Times,* April 2, 2021, https://www.nytimes.com/live/2021/04/02/us/derek-chauvin-trial.

266 *millions in settlements* Dana Thiede, "Minneapolis Approves Multi-Million Dollar Settlements for Two Derek Chauvin Victims," KARE 11, NBC affiliate, April 13, 2023, https://www.kare11.com/article/news/local/minneapolis-approves-multi-million-dollar -settlements-for-derek-chauvin-victims/89–3f37e485-d5bd-4fb5-a3b7–78d675390383.

266 *As the trial* Nicholas Bogel-Burroughs and Tim Arango, "Darnella Frazier, the Teen-ager Who Filmed George Floyd's Arrest, Testifies at the Trial," *The New York Times,* March 30, 2021, https://www.nytimes.com/2021/03/30/us/darnella-frazier-video-george -floyd.html; Nicholas Bogel-Burroughs and Marie Fazio, "Darnella Frazier Captured George Floyd's Death on Her Cellphone. The Teenager's Video Shaped the Chauvin Trial," *The New York Times,* April 20, 2021, https://www.nytimes.com/2021/04/20/us/darnella -frazier-video.html.

266 *"When I look at George Floyd"* Yamiche Alcindor and Sam Lane, "'He was terrified': Witnesses Offer Emotional Testimony About Floyd Death in Chauvin Case," full transcript, *PBS News Hour,* March 30, 2021, https://www.pbs.org/newshour/show/he-was-terrified -witnesses-offer-emotional-testimony-about-floyd-death-in-chauvin-case.

266 *in Houston's Third Ward* Julian Gill, "Before Dying in Minneapolis Police Custody, George Floyd Grew Up in Houston's Third Ward," *Houston Chronicle,* May 27, 2020, https://www.chron .com/news/houston-texas/houston/article/George-Floyd-police-brutality-minneapolis -dead-vid-15296192.php; Michael Hall, "The Houston Years of George Floyd," *Texas Monthly,* May 30, 2020, https://www.texasmonthly.com/news-politics/houston-years -george-floyd-dj-screw/.

266 *one of seven* Gabrielle Canon, "'My brother got justice': George Floyd's Family Praises Guilty Verdict," *The Guardian,* April 20, 2021, https://www.theguardian.com/us-news/2021 /apr/20/george-floyd-family-reaction-guilty-verdict.

266 *James D. Ryan Middle School* Manny Fernandez and Audra D. S. Burch, "George Floyd, From 'I Want to Touch the World' to 'I Can't Breathe,'" *The New York Times,* April 20, 2021, https://www.nytimes.com/article/george-floyd-who-is.html.

267 *"On the grind"* DJ Screw featuring AD, Chris Ward, and Big Floyd, "Sittin' on Top of the World Freestyle" lyrics, track 15 on *Chapter 324—Dusk 2 Dawn* album, https://genius.com /Dj-screw-sittin-on-top-of-the-world-freestyle-lyrics.

267 *for a fresh start* Maya Rao, "At George Floyd's Treatment Center, Recovering Clients See Racism in Addiction Assumptions," *Frontline PBS* in partnership with *Star Tribune,* April 11, 2021, https://www.pbs.org/wgbh/frontline/article/at-george-floyds-treatment-center -recovering-clients-see-racism-in-addiction-assumptions/.

268 *who died on May 30, 2018* https://transcripts.cnn.com/show/cnr/date/2021–04–12 /segment/10.

268 *"He had a good attitude"* Joanna Walters, "An Athlete, a Father, a 'beautiful spirit': George Floyd in His Friends' Words," *The Guardian,* May 29, 2020, https://www.theguardian.com /us-news/2020/may/29/george-floyd-who-was-he-his-friends-words.

268 *Christopher Harris* Joanna Walters, "An Athlete, a Father, a 'Beautiful Spirit': George Floyd in His Friends' Words," *The Guardian,* May 29, 2020, https://www.theguardian.com/us -news/2020/may/29/george-floyd-who-was-he-his-friends-words.

268 *five children* "George Floyd's Son Joins Texas Protesters in Peaceful Demonstration," ABC, June 1, 2020, https://web.archive.org/web/20200604094727/https://abc7.com /george-floyd-son-bryan-back-lives-matter-black-protest-minneapolis/6224513/; Nicquel Terry Ellis and Tyler J. Davis, "'He'll Never See Her Grow Up': George Floyd Mourned by Children, Family, Friends and Strangers," *Milwaukee Journal Sentinel, USA Today,* May 28, 2020, https://www.jsonline.com/story/news/2020/05/28/george-floyd -remembered-gentle-giant-family-calls-death-murder/5265668002/; Jorge L. Ortiz, Nora G. Hertel, and Mark Emmert, "'He Was Like the General': Mourners Grieve George Floyd at Minneapolis Memorial Service," *USA Today,* June 4, 2020, https://www.usatoday .com/story/news/nation/2020/06/04/george-floyd-memorial-service-thousands-flock -minneapolis/3142320001/; Gabrielle Canon, "'My Brother Got Justice': George Floyd's Family Praises Guilty Verdict," *The Guardian,* April 20, 2021, https://www.theguardian .com/us-news/2021/apr/20/george-floyd-family-reaction-guilty-verdict.

268 *On June 9, 2020,* Arelis R. Hernández, Brittney Martin, Marisa Iati, and Lateshia Bea-chum, "'Fight for My Brother.' As George Floyd Is Laid to Rest, His Family Implores the Nation to Continue Quest for Justice," *The Washington Post,* June 9, 2020, https:// www.washingtonpost.com/national/george-floyd-funeral/2020/06/09/52774b02 -aa70–11ea-a9d9-a81c1a491c52_story.html.

269 *Derek Chauvin was found guilty* Eric Levenson, "Derek Chauvin Found Guilty of All Three Charges for Killing George Floyd," CNN, April 21, 2021, https://www.cnn.com/2021 /04/20/us/derek-chauvin-trial-george-floyd-deliberations/index.html.

269 *of all charges* State of Minnesota, County of Hennepin, Derek Chauvin Sentencing Order, https://mncourts.gov/mncourtsgov/media/High-Profile-Cases/27-CR-20–12646/MCRO _27-CR-20–12646_Sentencing-Order_2021–06–25_20210625145755.pdf.

269 *22.5 years* "Video: Derek Chauvin Sentenced to 22.5 Years for Murdering George Floyd," *Wall Street Journal,* June 25, 2021, https://www.wsj.com/video/video-derek-chauvin -sentenced-to-225-years-for-murdering-george-floyd/F82D2F26-E44A-437C-A5AC -396BC06C31E5.

269 *first white police officer* NPR, "Live Updates: Trial Over George Floyd's Killing," https://www .npr.org/sections/trial-over-killing-of-george-floyd/; Associated Press, "Minnesota Officer

Says He Fatally Shot Unarmed Woman to Save Partner's Life," April 26, 2019, https://www
.nbcnews.com/news/us-news/minnesota-officer-says-he-fatally-shot-unarmed-woman
-save-partner-n998786; Phil Helsel and David K. Li, "Ex-Minneapolis Officer Who Killed
Justine Damond Sentenced to 12.5 Years," NBC News, June 8, 2019, https://www.nbcnews
.com/news/us-news/ex-minneapolis-officer-who-killed-justine-damond-sentenced-12–5
-n1013926.

269 "*A year ago*" Darnella Frazier, Instagram and Facebook, May 25, 2021, https://www
.instagram.com/p/CPT5_oIBlie/; https://www.facebook.com/darnellareallprettymarie
/posts/1727632277437871.

270 *Seth Corbin CBS Mornings*, "Darnella Frazier's Attorney Discusses Teen and the Impact
of Her Recording of George Floyd's Death," YouTube video, 5:54, June 15, 2020, https://www
.youtube.com/watch?v=eoJQ5p9M1CQ.

270 "*just a seventeen-year-old high school*" Paul Walsh, "Teen Who Recorded George Floyd
Video Wasn't Looking to Be a Hero, Her Lawyer Says," *Star Tribune,* June 11, 2020, https://
www.startribune.com/teen-who-shot-video-of-george-floyd-wasn-t-looking-to-be-a-hero
-her-lawyer-says/571192352/.

270 *two miles* Janelle Griffith, "A High School 2 Miles From Where George Floyd Died
Plays Outsize Role in Chauvin Trial," NBC News, April 24, 2021, https://www.nbcnews
.com/news/us-news/teen-who-filmed-george-floyd-s-arrest-minneapolis-police-chief
-n1265006.

270 "*She set the stage*" Janelle Griffith, "A High School 2 Miles From Where George Floyd
Died Plays Outsize Role in Chauvin Trial," NBC News, April 24, 2021, https://www
.nbcnews.com/news/us-news/teen-who-filmed-george-floyd-s-arrest-minneapolis-police
-chief-n1265006.

270 *Her legal team* Author conducted phone and Zoom calls and email exchanges with Darnella
Frazier's legal representation at Stinson LLP between January 19, 2023, through August 11,
2023.

270 *Pulitzer Prize* "Darnella Frazier," 2021 Special Citations and Awards, https://www.pulitzer
.org/winners/darnella-frazier.

270 *PEN America* "Pen America to Honor Darnella Frazier, Young Woman Who Documented
George Floyd's Murder," PEN/Benenson Courage Award, PEN America, December 8, 2020,
https://pen.org/press-release/pen-america-to-honor-darnella-frazier-young-woman-who
-documented-george-floyds-murder/; https://pen.org/user/darnella-frazier/.

270 *The then third grader* Ko Bragg, "Four Girls Testified in the Derek Chauvin Trial. Here's
What They Told the Jury," *The 19th News,* March 31, 2021, https://19thnews.org/2021/03
/four-school-aged-girls-derek-chauvin-trial-heres-what-they-told-the-jury/.

271 *returned to CUP* Oliver Laughland and Amudalat Ajasa, "'I allowed myself to feel
guilty for a very long time': The Teenage Cashier Who Took George Floyd's $20 Bill," *The
Guardian,* May 23, 2021, https://www.theguardian.com/us-news/2021/may/23/christopher
-martin-george-floyd-minneapolis-cup-foods.

INDEX

Abdul-Rauf, Mahmoud, 59
Abumayyaleh, Samir, 240
ACLU. *See* American Civil Liberties Union
Affirmative Action decision, 166–67
Affordable Care Act, 210
African Americans. *See* Black Americans
Agnew, Phillip, 213
akata (Black Americans), 171
Alexander, Michelle, 173
Allen, Edwilda, 92
Almond, James Lindsay, 103
American Civil Liberties Union (ACLU), 53
American Communist party, 37–39
American exceptionalism, 174–75, 197
American Freedmen's Aid Commission
    (union), 13–14
American Recovery and Reinvestment Act,
    210
Amnesty International, 161
anti-Apartheid activities, 150, 152, 154–56,
    163
anti-lynching law, 12–13
Apartheid, 151–53
Appleby, Anita Krieger, 64, 69–72
Arbery, Ahmaud, 255–56
Arradondo, Medaria, 254, 257
Ashe, Arthur, 163
attempted murder charges, 178
Auden, Wystan Hugh, 73
autopsy, of Floyd, G., 257–58
Averyhart, Stephon, 220, 222
Azulay, Jean Bornstein, 64, 69–70, 72–73

Bailey, Caseptla, 176, 179, 189
Bailey, Robert, 174, 176–78, 189, 195
Baisden, Michael, 192
Baker, Andrew, 258

Baker, Blake, 11
Baker, Ella Josephine, 23–24, 126
    in civil rights movement, 4–5,
        71
    father's conversations with, 9
    as grassroots organizer, 111–12
    lived experiences of, 25
    resistance instilled in, 10–11
    at Shaw Academy, 12
    silk stocking ban fight of, 19–22
    slavery and, 7–8
    SNCC formed by, 112
    social activism of, 18–19
Banks, Lester, 98
Bantu Education, 152–53
Barker, Justin, 177, 188, 195
Bates, Leonard, 59, 61–68,
        76–77
Bates, Ruby, 32–36, 46–50
"Bates Must Play" (slogan), 64–68, 78
Bates Seven, 59
    cafeteria petition by, 68–69
    empathy lesson from, 78
    mass demonstrations by, 66
    NYU suspensions of, 69–70
    participants as, 64
BCM. *See* Black Consciousness
        Movement
Beard, Ray, 178
Belafonte, Harry, 156
Bell, Melissa, 188
Bell, Mychal, 177–78, 188–90, 193–95
Bell, Sean, 187
Belton (Bulah) v. Gebhart, 101
Benefield, Trent, 187
Berry, Mary Frances, 155
Beverly (citizen), 277–82

Biden, Joe, 171, 183, 196, 235, 271
  anti-lynching law passed by, 13
  Beverly voting for, 281
  crime bill sponsored by, 181–82
  Promise to Keep by, 182
  violent crime admonished by, 180
Biko, Alice Nokuzola, 149
Biko, Mzingayi Mathew, 149
Biko, Steve, 149, 151–52, 154
Birth of a Nation (film), 6
Black Americans
  akata as, 171
  as athletes, 60, 70
  civil rights movement of, 109–11
  crime bill causing deaths to, 200
  culture of, 283–84
  education for, 144
  employment for, 143
  as farmers, 120
  men, 28, 33–34
  in Mississippi, 125–26
  mistreatment of, 115–16
  New Negro Movement for, 7
  in Northern states, 6
  racial experience of, 82
  racial integration and, 5–6
  racial pride of, 133
  racism against, 56–57
  register to vote by, 127
  separation of, 99
  sheriff hunting for, 31–32
  social activism and, 3–4
  as soldiers, 83–84
  subservience, 89–90
  unemployment rates and, 29–30
  unequal education for, 119–20
  voting power nullified for, 139–40
  white vitriol toward, 99, 221–22
  women, 4
  as workers, 7
Black colleges, 14
Black communities, 101, 144, 146, 172
Black Consciousness Movement (BCM),
    149–50, 151
The Black Panther (newspaper), 161
Black Panther Party, 131, 140–41
  activism by, 165
  anti-Apartheid movement by, 152
  disbanding of, 166
  equality jargon by, 148
  neighborhood defense by, 146
  principles of, 142
  Ten Point Program of, 142–45, 150
  in Winston-Salem NC, 160–61

Black people, 227
  hatred of, 259
  players on Southern fields, 64, 68
  poverty and, 280
  resistance by, 276–77
  white men killing, 139–40
Black Power Movement, 133, 140, 147–48,
    154–55
Black Power speech, 166
Black South Africans, 152–53, 155–56
Black students
  injustice to, 134
  school board expelling, 137
  school board refusal toward, 87
  shipped to white high schools, 135
  white people teaching, 122–23
Black youth, 51, 61–62, 211, 229
#BlackLivesMatter (BLM), 214–15, 223–24,
    257, 263–64
Blackness, understanding, 82
Black-on-Black crime, 278
Blair, Ezell, Jr., 111
Blake, Jacob, 277
Blalock, Edgar, 44
Bland, Sandra, 227
BLM. *See* #BlackLivesMatter
blood as symbol, 223–25, 237
Bloody Sunday, 127
Blumkin, Pearl, 52
Board of Athletic Control, 70
Boggs, Caleb, 182
Bolling v. Sharpe, 101
Bowser, Muriel, 261
boycott, at New Hanover High School,
    134
Braddock, LaSean, 266
Brady, Tom P., 118
breadlines, 30
Breithaupt, Roy, 174
Bridge, Edmund Pettus, 127
Bridges, R. R., 33, 36
Briggs v. Elliott, 101
Brown, Devin, 186
Brown, Linda, 85
Brown, Michael, 214–27
Brown, Oliver, 85
Brown, Xavier, 258–59
Brown v. Board of Education, 85, 102
Brown v. Topeka Board of Education, 101
Burke, Arthur, 75
bus service, Russa Moton High without,
    98
Bush, George H. W., 183
Bush, George W., 76, 193

cafeteria petition, 68–69
Caldwell, Charley, 192
Campaign Zero, 229–31
Cannick, Jasmyne, 190–91
capitalism, 5, 29
car lot, burned down, 277
Carmichael, Stokely, 128–29, 141, 166
Carter, Lester, 46–47
Carter, Melvin, 254
caste system, 99
Castile, Philando, 60
Central Park Five, 57
Chances (Jones, M.), 73
Chandler, Brianna, 262
Chaney, James, 124–25
Chase, Harry Woodburn, 68, 72, 77
Chauvin, Derek
    arrest of, 259
    cold heartless look of, 250
    Floyd, G., killed by, 246–52
    Frazier testifying against, 265–66
    guilty verdict of, 269
Chavis, Benjamin Franklin, Jr., 136–37, 284
    conviction of, 158
    interview of, 160
    as NAACP director, 162
    as one of Wilmington Ten, 140
Chavis, John, 136
Chicago Unbeatable Prices (CUP) Foods,
    240–42
chicken coop classrooms, 86
children, 120–21, 235–36
Children's Crusade, 111
Civil Rights Act, 114, 134
civil rights movement, 57
    Baker, E., in, 4–5, 71
    of Black Americans, 109–11
    Brown, M., and violations of, 226–27
    defending, 9
civility, 23
The Clansman (Dixon), 6
Clinton, Bill, 181
Clinton, Hillary, 228
Cobb, Adrienne, 114
Cobb, Ann, 114
Cobb, Charlie, 109, 126
    background of, 115–16
    Dorrough pointing gun at, 117
    Freedom Schools proposal by, 121
    SNCC advance of, 117
    volunteer recruitment by, 119
Cobb, Martha, 115
Cockfield, Jacqulyn Reed, 125
Cohen, J. Richard, 194

cold heartless look, 250
college students, segregation and, 113
Collins, Nya, 259
Community Oriented Policing Services
    (COPS) program,
    184
Comprehensive Anti-Apartheid Act, 164–65
Congress, 54, 164–65
Congress of Racial Equality, 113
consensual sex, 46–47
COPS. *See* Community Oriented Policing
    Services program
Corbett, Gibb Stevens, 138
Corbin, Seth, 270
Corey, Angela, 207
counterfeit money, 241–44
coup d'état, by white supremacy, 139
Coward, Jim, 67
Crawford, John, Jr., 214–15
Crawford, Robert, 104, 118
crime bill, 196
    Biden sponsoring, 181–82
    Black communities targeted by, 172
    Black deaths from, 200
    the Jena Six influenced by, 184–85
    law enforcement funds from, 184–85
crime rates, 278–79
The Crisis (NAACP), 16
Croner, Mary, 88
Crump, Benjamin, 255, 257
Cullors, Patrisse, 214
culture, 11–12, 151–52, 283–84
Cumber, Harvey, 138
Cunningham, Brittany Packnett, 224
CUP. *See* Chicago Unbeatable Prices Foods

Davenport, Inez, 87
Davis, Ossie, 156
Day, Tiana, 262
death penalty, 49, 52, 54
death threats, 101
Declaration of Independence, 106, 145–46
defiance, willful, 25
democracy, 24, 199–200
demographic shift, 19–20
demonstrations, 18, 66
Department of Justice, 160, 212–13, 226
Depradine, Eric, 192
Depression Era, 29
desegregation, 85, 98, 104–5, 134–35
DeWeese, Laila, 238, 255–57, 262–65, 273
Diallo, Amadou, 28, 184
dilapidated sheds, 86–87
discrimination, 30, 70, 83–86, 141

Diuturni Silenti (address), 16
Dixon, Thomas, Jr., 6
Dobbins, Ory, 36
Dobzhansky, Theodosius, 75
Don't Shoot Coalition, 225
*Dorothy Davis et al. v. County School
     Board of Prince Edward County*
     lawsuit, 101
Dorrough, Charlie, 117
Du Bois, W. E. B., 12, 14, 16
Du Bois, Yolande, 16
Dyer, Leonidas, 13

economic sanctions, 164
Edmund Pettus Bridge, 127
education
   Bantu schools inferior, 152–53
   for Black Americans, 144
   Black American's unequal, 119–20
   Black colleges for, 14
   Georgianna providing cultural knowl-
       edge and, 11–12
   investment lacking in, 172
   quality of, 107
   as weapon, 167–68
Elams, William, 10
Ellison, Keith, 259
Elzie, Johnetta, 222, 227–32, 284
   blood as symbol to, 223–25, 237
   Brown, M., shooting personal to, 215
   societal inequities faced by, 220–21
Emancipation Proclamation, 7, 113
empathy, lessons in, 78
employment, for Black Americans, 143
Epps, Reginald, 140, 158
equality, 106, 148
Evans v. Buchanan case, 182
Evers, Medgar, 113

Facebook posts, 191, 253, 255, 269
Fair Housing Act, 129
Fanon, Frantz, 147
farming, 9, 120
Fatal Force Database, 235
FBI code name (Mississippi Burning), 124
feminism, 19
Ferguson, James, 157
First Amendment rights, 261
First World War, end of, 5–24
Fisk University, 14–15, 17–18
flappers, 19–23
Floyd, George
   autopsy of, 257–58
   background of, 266–68

burial of, 268
Chauvin, D., killing, 246–52
in CUP Foods, 240–42
death aftermath of, 256–62
Frazier filming killing of, 247–52
911 call concerning, 242–47
police brutality killing, 238–39
pronounced dead, 252
remembrance of, 270–71
Floyd, Gianna, 268
Floyd, Larcenia Jones, 268
Floyd, Quincy Mason, 268
FOIA. *See* Freedom of Information Act
Foster, Duane, 218
Fourteenth Amendment rights, 39, 53, 102,
     145
Fowler, Billy Wayne, 175
Fowler, Mack, 178
Francis Howell School District, 220–22
Frawley, Benjamin, 21–22
Frazier, Darnella, 238
   Chauvin, D., testimony by, 265–66
   Facebook post of, 255, 269
   Floyd, G., killing filmed by, 247–52
   footage posted by, 253–54
   viral video of, 261
Free the Jena Six, 191, 193
freedom, from slavery, 10
Freedom of Information Act (FOIA),
     229–230
freedom of speech, 60
Freedom Rides, 113
Freedom Schools, 120–21, 123–26, 284
Freeman, Mike, 258
Freud, Sigmund, 73
Frey, Jacob, 254
Fuller, Jade, 259
Fulton, Sybrina, 200, 205, 212

Garvey, Marcus, 146
Garza, Alicia, 214
generational divide, 228–229
Gentlemen's Agreement
   Bates, L., free from, 65
   Jim Crow laws and, 62, 68
   NYU students opposing, 64–65
   racism in, 59
   universities abandoning, 76
Georgianna (Ella's mother), 11–12
Giuliani, Rudolph, 184
global rallies, 50–51
"God Bless America" (song), 100
Goode, Eslanda, 72
Goodman, Andrew, 124–25

Gotta-Go Grocery store, 176
government, racism in, 144
graduation, of Johns, B., 101–2
grassroots organizer, 111–12
Gray, Freddie, 60, 234, 258
Great Depression, 61–62
Green, Brandy, 200–201
Green, Chad, 201
Green, Kennedy, 259
Gregg, James, 18
Gregory Congregational Church, 135
Griffin, L. Francis, 95, 100–101
guilty verdict
    of Bell, M., 188–90
    of Chauvin, 269
    of Patterson, 49–50
    of Scottsboro Nine, 37, 49–50, 52, 54
    Scottsboro Nine with dismissed, 51
    of Wilmington Ten, 158
Guyot, Lawrence, 117
Guzman, Joseph, 187

Hall, Allen, 157–60
Hammerstein, Oscar, II, 273
Hampton, Fred, 148, 162
Hampton University, shutting down, 18
Hansen, Genevieve, 250–52
Hansford, Justin, 224
Harlem Hellfighters, 75
Harlem Renaissance, 6, 19
Harris, Christopher, 268
Harry (citizen), 277–82
Hawkins, Alfred E., 35
HBCUs. See Historically Black Colleges and
    Universities
Hendricks, Audrey Faye, 111
Hill, Oliver, 95, 97–100
Historically Black Colleges and Universities
    (HBCUs), 13
    anti-Apartheid activism from, 154–55
    flappers influence on, 20
    Jim Crow laws adaptation by, 15
    NAACP presence at, 54
    student activism at, 162–63
    wealth distribution and, 51
homeless transients, 30
Hood, Koree, 191
Horton, James, Jr., 46
Horton, Jerome, 204
"Hot Time in the Old Town Tonight"
    (song), 37
Houston, Charles Hamilton, 84
Howard University, 18, 50, 116
Hunt, James B., 161

"I Have a Dream" speech, 109, 114, 166,
    261
identity, factors in, 132
ILD. See International Labor Defense
Immigration and Nationality Act (1965),
    130
immigration reform, 130
inequity, 29
inflation, unemployment rates and, 60–61
Ingraham, Laura, 77
injustice, 41–46, 134, 213, 236–37, 257
integration, at New Hanover High School,
    133–34
international crisis, of racism, 55
International Labor Defense (ILD), 38–39
investments, education lacking, 172

Jackson, Jesse, 228
Jackson, Juanita, 54–55, 84
Jackson County jail, 31–32
Jacobs, Jerry, 140, 158
James, Judge, 47, 50–51
James, LeBron, 58, 77, 210
Jeantel, Rachel, 202, 205
Jena High School, 173–76
the Jena Six, 197
    attempted murder charges of, 178
    crime bill influence on, 184–85
    Free the Jena Six, 191, 193
    plea deals of, 195
    racial brawl and, 176–80
    sit-in demonstration of, 173–76
    support of, 190–94
    trials of, 187–90
Jim Crow laws, 5, 11, 173
    Communist party arguments against, 39
    discrimination from, 30
    Gentlemen's Agreement and, 62, 68
    HBCUs to adapt to, 15
    in Southern states, 83–84
Johns, Barbara, 81–83, 276
    background of, 88–89
    boldness of, 107
    crowd quieted by, 100
Johns, Barbara (continued)
    family home burned down of, 102
    graduation of, 101–2
    NAACP letter from, 95–96
    Powell, W., marrying, 105–6
    "Strike the School" chant by, 94–95
    student representation by, 91–92
    teacher hearing concerns of, 87–88
    teachers to leave assembly by, 93–94
    white power fears of, 90–91

Johns, Robert, 88–89
Johns, Sallie, 89
Johns, Vernon, 88–89
Johns, Violet, 88–89
Johnson, Dorian, 216–17
Johnson, James Weldon, 72
Johnson, Lyndon, 114, 127–28
Johnson, Matthew, 142
Johnson, Mordecai, 18
Jones, April, 192
Jones, Boyd, 92–93, 96
Jones, Carwin, 178, 189, 195
Jones, Ernest, 73
Jones, Marcus, 179, 188
Jones, Mary, 73
Jones, Mervyn, 64, 73
Jones, Tishaura, 231
Judson Hall Disciplinary Committee, 69
Junius, Eric, 158
jury, Scottsboro Nine, 53–54
jury of peers, in trials, 145
justice system, 28–29, 56

Kaepernick, Colin, 59–60
Kellum, Laura, 54
Kennedy, John F., 110, 113–14
Kennedy, Robert F., 105
Kilby Prison, 37, 39, 55
Kimmons, Patrick, 263–64
King, Angus, 261
King, Martin Luther, Jr., 127–29, 182
    Black Power Movement and, 147
    "I Have a Dream" speech of, 109, 114,
        166, 261
    SCLC working with, 136
    Southern Christian Leadership Confer-
        ence of, 24
KKK. See Ku Klux Klan
Klobuchar, Amy, 254
Ku Klux Klan (KKK), 6, 124,
    166
Kueng, J. Alexander, 244–49

LaBayne, Jacqueline, 260–61
land grant college system, 13–14
Lane, Thomas, 244–52
Laney, Emsley, 134
Lasker Award, 76
law enforcement, 181, 184–85
Lawrence, Eloise H., 50
leadership, of young people, 126–27
Legal Defense Fund, 161
Leibowitz, Samuel, 38, 46–48, 52–53
letter, Bates, R., writing, 48

letter-writing campaign, 54
Lewis, John, 110, 119, 123, 127–28
Liberation Day, 134–35
Lincoln, Abraham, 7, 13, 113
lived experiences, 25
Lookout Mountain, Tennessee, 30–31
Louisville Police Department (LPD), 56
Lowndes County Freedom Organization,
    128
LPD. See Louisville Police Department
Lynch, Marvin, 33
lynchings, 34–35, 90

Makhubo, Mbuyisa, 153
Malcolm X, 141
mandatory religion exam, 22
Mandela, Nelson, 150–51, 163, 165
Mapping Police Violence, 225–27, 235
Maree, Daniel, 211–12
marginalization, 172
Marrow, Henry, 137
Marshall, Thurgood, 84, 102
Martin, Christopher, 241
Martin, Tracy, 200–201, 212
Martin, Trayvon, 200
    airplanes loved by, 204
    Black youth activism from, 211
    burial of, 232
    Obama influenced by death of, 209–10
    Sanford Police phone call about, 202–8
    Zimmerman shooting, 208–9
massacre, violent, 139
Maurer, George, 38
McCain, Franklin, 111
McCain, John, 198–99
McIlwaine, Thomas, 96
McKenzie, Fayette, 15–18
Mckesson, DeRay, 224–25, 227
McKinley, Reginald, 191
McKoy, James, 140, 158
McMillan, Artie, 142–43
McMillian, Charles, 250
McNeil, Joseph, 111
McSpadden-Head, Lezley, 218
Meredith, James, 113, 128, 134
"Meredith March Against Fear" (speech),
    128–29
Miller, Benjamin Meek ("B. M."), 35, 38,
    50, 52
Miller, Tyisha, 185
Million Hoodies Movement for Justice, 211
Million Youth March, 185
Minneapolis Police Department statement,
    252–53

Minnesota Bureau of Criminal
    Apprehension, 253
Mississippi Burning (FBI code name), 124
Mitchell, Jerome, 158
Mitchell, Tiffany, 217
Montgomery, Alabama, 127
Montgomery, Olen, 32, 35, 43–44, 55–56
Montgomery, Viola, 43
Montgomery bus boycott, 89
Moody, Miles Addison ("Milo"), 35
Moore, Wayne, 140, 158
Morehouse Anti-Apartheid Rally, 164
Morrill, Justin, 13
Morrill Act, 14
Morrill Land Grant College Act (1862), 13
Morris, Luther, 36
Morris Isaacson High School,
    153
Moses, Bob, 108, 119, 122–23
Moton, Robert Russa, 52
My Brother's Keeper Task Force, 232
"My Country 'Tis of Thee" (song), 99
Myers, Dave, 63

NAACP. See National Association for the
    Advancement of Colored People
NAG. See Nonviolent Action Group
Nash, Diane, 115
National Action Network, 228–29
national anthem, protest of, 59–60
National Association for the Advancement
    of Colored People (NAACP)
    anti-lynching law pushed by, 12–13
    Chavis, B., as director of, 162
    The Crisis from, 16
    HBCU presence of, 54
    Johns, B., letter to, 95–96
    Marshall as director of, 84
    school board suit filed by, 100–101
    school desegregation focus of, 85
    Scottsboro Nine not defended by, 38–39
    white communities opposition to, 84–85
National Guard, 140
National Party, 151
National Student League City College, 52
nationalism, 147
NBA All-Star Game, 202
Negro Culture Association, 75
Negro Leagues, 61
neighborhood crime, 173
neighborhood defense, 146
New Hanover High School, 133–34
New Negro Movement, 7
New York Knicks, 58

New York Police Department, 28
New York University (NYU)
    Bates, L., ineligible to play for, 67–68
    Bates, L., joining, 62–63
    Bates Seven suspensions at,
        69–70
    football program shut down of, 77
    Gentlemen's Agreement opposed at,
        64–65
    Missouri Tigers playing, 67
    student petition to, 70
newspapers, 156–57
Newton, Armelia Johnson, 141
Newton, Huey, 141–42, 146, 149, 166
Newton, Walter, 141
911 call, concerning Floyd, G., 242–47
Nineteenth Amendment, 19
no justice, no peace (slogan), 189, 262
Noffke, Sean, 202
Nonviolent Action Group (NAG), 116
Norris, Clarence, 32, 35, 45,
        54–55
Norris v. Alabama case, 53
Northern states, Black Americans in, 6
NYU. See New York University

Obama, Barack, 131, 182, 281
    anti-Apartheid speech by, 163
    democracy optimism by, 199–200
    Martin, Trayvon, death influencing,
        209–10
    McCain defeated by, 198–99
    My Brother's Keeper Task Force from,
        232
    systemic injustices end from,
        213
O'Neal, Paul, 234
Operation Mississippi, 113–15
oppression, 101, 139, 154
overcriminalization, of Black men, 28
oyinbo (white American), 171

Paint Rock, Alabama, 31–32
pardons, official, 166
parents, petition signed by, 99–100
Parker, Pam, 125–26
Parks, Rosa, 103
Patrick, Marvin, 137, 140, 158
Patterson, Haywood
    brash demeanor of, 42–43
    guilty verdict of, 49–50
    in prison, 55–56
    trial of, 35, 46, 52
    white teen stepping on, 30–32

Paultre, Nicole, 187
PDX Black Youth Movement, 238, 257, 262–64, 273
Perdue, Beverly, 166
Pervall, Joseph, 100
Peterson, Russell, 182
petition, parents signing, 99–100
Phenix, George, 18
Pieterson, Hector, 153–54
Pityana, Barney, 149
plea deals, for the Jena Six, 195
Plessy v. Ferguson case, 84, 102
police brutality, 146, 227
    Brown, M., shot in, 214–20
    end of, 144, 262
    Floyd, G., killed by, 238–39
    Floyd, G., killing video showing, 247–52
    Kimmons killed by, 263–64
    mother's losing children to, 235–36
    nationwide, 225
    racially biased, 261
police officers, 17
The Police Scorecard database, 226
political activism, 272
political campaigning, 198–99
political prisoner, 162
Pope, John, 266
poverty, 28
    Black people and, 280
    crime rates related to, 278–79
    discrimination and, 141
    violent crime related to, 180–81
Powell, Ozie, 32, 35, 39, 44
Powell, William, 105–6
Powell v. Alabama case, 39
prejudice, 103, 197, 279
Price, Cecil, 124
Price, Victoria, 32–36, 46–48
Prince Edward County, Virginia, 85–86, 104–5
progressive movements, 4
Promise to Keep (Biden), 182
prostitution, 32
protesting, of national anthem, 59–60
public schools, 104, 194
Purvis, Bryant, 178, 195
Purvis, Kenneth, 173–74, 177

race
    Black American's experience and, 82
    Black American's integration and, 5–6
    Black American's pride of, 133
    equality and, 71

fight against prejudice, 100
profiling by, 210, 217
quotas by, 130
Scottsboro Nine injustice by, 41–46
South Africa oppression by, 154
sports inequities by, 77–78
racism
    against Black Americans, 56–57
    against Black soldiers, 83–84
    fighting against, 124–25
    in Gentlemen's Agreement, 59
    in government, 144
    international crisis of, 55
    nothing has changed with, 109–10
    police brutality based on, 261
    reckless eyeballing laws as, 33
    systemic, 211
A Raisin in the Sun (play), 218
Randolph, Asa Philip, 7, 104
rape charges, Scottsboro Nine with, 32–34
reckless eyeballing laws, 33
Reeves, Jeremiah, 103
Reno, Janet Wood, 225
resistance, 10–11
retrials, of Scottsboro Nine, 39, 46–49
Reynolds, Judeah, 247, 270–71
Richmond, David, 111
Rights of White People, 137
Riley, Akil, 258
Roaring Twenties, 19–20
Robert Russa Moton High
    bus service ended to, 98
    chicken coop classrooms of, 86
    Johns, B., bringing concerns to teacher of, 87–88
    new building plan for, 92
    school disrepair of, 86–87
    students striking at, 95–96
Roberts, Thomas ("T. J."), 23–24
Robertson, Willie, 32, 35, 44–45, 55–56
Robeson, Paul, 72
Robinson, Jackie, 76
Robinson, Randall, 155
Robinson, Spottswood, 97–100
Robinson, Tyrone, 166
Roddy, Stephen Robert, 35
Rodgers, Richard, 273
Roosevelt, Eleanor, 69
Roosevelt, Franklin, 52, 61
Ross, Josephine Elizabeth, 8–11
Ross, Mitchell, 8–11
Rothschild, Naomi Bloom, 64, 69, 73–74
Rustin, Bayard, 104

SAEP. *See* South African Education Program
Sandlin, J. Street, 44
Sanford, FL, 200–203
Sanford Police, phone call to, 202–8
SASO. *See* Southern African Students'
  Organization
Schoenfeld, Robert, 64, 69, 74
school board
  Black students and refusal of, 87
  Black students expelled by, 137
  NAACP filing suit against, 100–101
  public schools shut down by, 104
  Williston shut down by, 134–35
schools, student's disconnect with, 15
Schwerner, Michael, 124–25
SCLC. *See* Southern Christian Leadership
  Conference
Scottsboro Defense Committee, 53
Scottsboro Nine
  appeal letter from, 39–40
  assault and attempted murder charges
    against, 32
  backgrounds of, 41–46
  Bates testimony against, 48–49
  Black youth represented by, 51
  during Depression Era, 29
  four separate trials for, 35
  freed but not free, 55–56
  global rallies supporting, 50–51
  guilty verdict dismissed of, 51
  guilty verdict of, 37, 49–50, 52, 54
  Howard University signing petition for,
    50
  ILD defending, 38–39
  in Jackson County jail, 31–32
  jury screening for, 53–54
  to Kilby Prison, 37
  lynch mobs gathering for, 34–35
  NAACP not defending, 38–39
  Price testimony against, 46–47
  racial injustice against, 41–46
  rape charges included against, 32–34
  retrials of, 39, 46–49
  Roosevelt not intervening in, 52
  student letter-writing campaign for,
    51–52
  student-led pushback for, 28–29
  train with homeless drifters and, 30–31
  trial testimony of, 35–37
  white teens ruckus with, 31
Seale, Bobby, 141–42, 146, 149, 161–62,
  166
Seale, Thelma, 141
sectionalism, 28

segregation, 113, 138–39, 150, 275
self-defense, 146
Selma, Alabama, 127
Selma-to-Montgomery march, 127–28
sentences reduced, 161
separate but equal, 102, 150–51
Serino, Chris, 212
sexism, 22
sexual assaults, 7
Sharpton, Al, 193–94, 228–29
Shaw, George Bernard, 74
Shaw, Theo, 178, 189, 195–96
Shaw Academy, 12
Shaw High School, 20–23
Sheiebler, George, 66
Shepard, Ann, 140, 158
sheriffs, Black Americans hunted by, 31–32
shooting
  of Arbery, 255–56
  of Averyhart, 220
  of Brown, M., 214–20
  of Crawford, J., 214–15
  of Martin, Trayvon, 208–9
  of Powell, O., 44
shut up and dribble, 77
silk stocking ban, 19–22
Sinyangwe, Samuel, 225–26
Sithole, Antoinette, 153
sit-in demonstration, 173–76
slavery, 7–8, 10–11, 90, 120–21
Sloan, Justin, 176
Smith, Emma Rose, 259
Smith, Mary Louise, 103
Smith, Mikayla, 259
SNCC. *See* Student Nonviolent
  Coordinating Committee
social activism, 3–4, 12–13, 18–19, 24–25
social media, 186–87, 229,
  260–61
  Frazier footage posted on, 253–54
  political campaigning on, 198–99
societal inequities, 220–21
South Africa, 154, 156, 164
South African Education Program (SAEP),
  162
South Bronx, 27
Southern African Students' Organization
  (SASO), 149
Southern Christian Leadership Conference
  (SCLC), 24, 136, 191
Southern fields, 64, 68
Southern states, 83–84
Soweto Uprising, 153
sports, racial inequities in, 77–78

stabbing, of Patterson, 43
Stand Up For Trayvon rally, 213
Stand Your Ground law, 214
Sterling, Alton, 60
Stevens, Mal, 62
Stokes, Carrie, 91, 95
Stokes, John, 91
Stoute, Argyle, 64, 74–75
Streetman, Earl, 48
"Strike the School" chant, 94–95
Strode, Woody, 76
Stroud, Jay, 157
student activism, at HBCUs, 162–63
Student Coalition Against Apartheid and
    Racism, 164
student demonstrations, 18
Student Nonviolent Coordinating
    Committee (SNCC), 24
  Baker, E., forming, 112
  Cobb, C., advancing within, 117
  Operation Mississippi by,
    114–15
  white opposition faced by, 123–24
student representation, 91–92
Student Review (publication), 49–50
students
  in dilapidated sheds, 86–87
  Gentlemen's Agreement opposed by,
    64–65
  HBCUs activism by, 162–63
  Johns, B., representation of, 91–92
  legal desegregation and, 98
  letter-writing campaign by, 51–52
  NYU getting petition from, 70
  Russa Moton High strike by, 95–96
  school's board of trustees disconnect
    with, 15
  Scottsboro Nine pushback led by, 28–29
  segregation and, 113
sundown towns, 6, 30
Supreme Court, 104
  Affirmative Action decision by, 166–67
  Almond against decision of, 103
  Brown v. Board of Education by, 102
  Leibowitz taking case to, 53
  Norris v. Alabama case from, 53
  Powell v. Alabama from, 39
  Prince Edward County integration by,
    105
suspensions, of Bates Seven, 69–70
Swain, Barbara, 133
systemic injustices, 213
systemic racism, 211
systemic segregation, 150

Taggart, E. W., 54
target demographic, 122
Taylor, Breonna, 56, 255
teachers, 87–88, 93–94
Teel, Robert, 137
Teens 4 Equality, 259–60
Templeton, Eugene, 135–36
Ten Point Program, 142–45, 150
terrorism, white supremacy is, 264
Terry, Charles, 182
testimony, Allen recanting, 158–60
Thao, Tou, 246, 248–50
Thomas, Timothy, 185
Thomas, Zee, 259–60
Thunberg, Greta, 257
Till, Emmett, 102–3, 111–12
Timbers, Tammy, 191
Tindall, Connie, 134, 158
Toles, Latrell, 266
Tometi, Opal, 214
Travers, Mary, 163
trials, 35–39, 46–49, 52, 145
  of the Jena Six, 187–90
  of Wilmington Ten, 157–58
Trump, Donald, 234, 256
Tulsa Race Massacre, 7
Tunstrom, Jovanni, 268
Turner, Shayla, 262
Tutu, Desmond, 156
Tyus, Markeanna, 270

unconscious biases, 275
unemployment rates, 29–30, 60–61
universities, Gentlemen's Agreement
    abandoned by, 76
University of Missouri, 63–64, 67

Vereen, Willie, 140, 158
Violence Against Women Act, 181
violent crime, 180–81
Violent Crime Control and Law
    Enforcement Act. *See* crime bill
viral video, 261
Virginia Supreme Court, 104
vocational training, 16
volunteer, 119
voting, 127, 139–40
Voting Rights Act (1965), 128, 130

Wade, Dwayne, 210
Walden, Bill, 159
Wall, Joseph Barrye, 99
Wallace, George, 127
Walters, Reed, 174–78, 188, 194

Walz, Tim, 254
Warren, Earl, 102
Washington, D. C., 110–29
Washington, Kenny, 76
Watson, John, 91
"We Want Black Power" (chant), 129
wealth distribution, 51
weapons, Scottsboro Nine and, 36
Weems, Charles, 32, 35, 45–46, 55–56
"Where is our party" (speech),
    119
White, Walter, 38
White Citizen's Councils, 118
white people, 171
    Black Americans getting vitriol from, 99,
        221–22
    Black people killed by, 139–40
    Black students shipped to high schools
        of, 135
    Black students taught by, 122–23
    communities of, 84–85
    culture of, 151–52
    jury of all, 53–54
    Patterson stepped on by, 30–32
    Scottsboro Nine ruckus with, 31
    SNCC facing opposition by, 123–24
    women, 33–34, 57
white power, 18, 90–91
white supremacy, 56
    Black subservience to, 89–90
    coup d'état by, 139
    is terrorism, 264
    by National Party, 151
whiteness, 28–29, 33
William, Judge, 52–53
Williams, Donald, 251
Williams, Eugene, 32, 35, 42, 55–56

Williams, Gerhard Mennen, 55
Williams, Kerrigan, 260
Williston Industrial High School, 134–35
Wilmington, NC, 134–35, 138–40
Wilmington Ten, 139–41
    guilty verdict of, 158
    legal challenge of, 156
    newspaper coverage of, 156–57
    official pardons for, 166
    sentences reduced for, 161
    trial of, 157–58
Wilson, Darren, 216–19, 225–26
Windham, Matthew, 176
Windham, Scott, 174
Winfrey, Oprah, 227–228
Witkin, Evelyn Maisel, 64, 69, 75–76
women, sexual assaults of, 7
Wonder, Stevie, 163
work ethic, 25
Worthington, Melvin, 175
Wright, Ada, 41, 50
Wright, Andrew ("Andy"), 32, 41–42,
    55–56
Wright, LeRoy ("Roy"), 32, 35, 41,
    55–56
Wright, William, Jr., 140, 158

Young, Whitney, Jr., 110
young people, 26, 126–27, 272, 285–86

Zimmerman, George, 211–12
    arrest and acquittal of, 213–14
    Martin, Trayvon, shot by,
        208–9
    Sanford Police phone call with, 202–8
Zoila, Mimi, 262
Zuckerberg, Mark, 186